Twenty Years of Stanford Short Stories

Twenty Years of Stanford Short Stories

Edited by
Wallace Stegner and Richard Scowcroft
with Nancy Packer

Stanford University Press
Stanford, California, 1966

Stanford University Press
Stanford, California

© 1966 by the Board of Trustees of the
Leland Stanford Junior University

Printed in the United States of America

L.C. 66-25958

This volume is affectionately dedicated to the memory of
RICHARD FOSTER JONES
whose interest made the Stanford Writing Program possible
and whose wisdom strengthened and enlarged
all those who participated in it

Contents

Wallace Stegner

Introduction

Temptations attend the publication of such a volume as this. College writing programs are so often treated with condescension that one's impulse is to anticipate tabloid sneer with tabloid defensiveness. We might have put this book out challengingly. Here, we might have said, are twenty-nine stories written in creative writing classes in a single university between 1946 and 1964. They have been selected, not easily, from one hundred seventy-five stories published over those years in fifteen volumes of *Stanford Short Stories*. It is a fair question whether a collection as large, as various, and as distinguished could be assembled out of all the nonacademic short story writers in the San Francisco Bay Area during the same years. Furthermore (we might have said), while Stanford students were writing and publishing these one hundred and seventy-five stories they were also producing a five-foot shelf of novels, all of them respectable and some of them brilliant, and many many poems.

But instead of attacking stereotypes that will rise up again as soon as they are knocked down, I should prefer to make this anniversary—the Stanford writing program is twenty years old in 1966—the occasion for as honest a review as I can make. I have worked in the system, believed in it, defended it, but I have never been out of whispering range of doubt. Now I find myself possessed of evidence such as no commentator on creative writing ever had before. Here is the early work of more than a hundred young writers. The later careers of a great many are known to me. I can examine talent in the light of what talent has come to, and that examination may possibly tell us something about changing forms and styles in American writing, and about the economics of the writing profession in America, as well as about the success of the university's attempt to sponsor creativity in literature.

I am not interested in defending all writing classes; many of them, I am sure, are dull or insipid. I am not interested in defending the Stanford program itself if the facts suggest flaws or failures. The circumstances, moreover, are propitious to an impartial examination. The usual reason for a summary of accomplishments is either the hope of attracting financial support or the need of justifying someone's life. But the Stanford program, thanks to the generosity of the Jones family, is not in any particular need of money; and I feel more need to examine my life than to justify it. Twenty years of it, and nearly twenty years of the lives of Richard Scowcroft and other colleagues, are invested in this program. If we have been pounding sand down a rathole all these years, it is time we knew. We have never pretended that we taught young writers much of anything—in fact, we have drawn back from the danger of being *too* influential—but it has been our faith that we helped create an environment in which they could learn and grow. It would be interesting to know whether or not we succeeded in providing such an environment, or whether they would have been better off keeping a diary in the Peace Corps, or working in a steel mill, or writing for a newspaper. Were these writers, I wonder, warmed and brightened by any promethean fire they found at Stanford, or did they merely strain their eyes trying to learn?

The answers, obviously, may be various and contradictory. Moreover, what is before me is the record of one program, one university, and conclusions should not extend beyond that one. Geography, regional culture, personality, chance, and much else have undoubtedly made this program different from those elsewhere. Nevertheless, the Stanford experience may be as representative as any. California contains something of everything, frequently before it becomes visible in other places. During the past twenty years Stanford writing students have come from all over the United States, from every sort of geographical, ethnic, and educational background; and as a leaven there has always been a sprinkling of gifted people from England, Australia, Canada, India, South Africa, Greece, Iran, the Philippines. Sometimes the teacher of such a group has the sense that he is reading the next decade's fiction before it is quite written. Does the same teacher, looking back, discover a capsule history of literary and cultural change?

And how good does it seem, years later? Have the stories kept their power to evoke and move, or do they now seem only superior classroom exercises embalmed in volumes that when opened give off a ghostly exhalation of chalk dust? Do we find here any support for the common assumption that the colleges stultify real creativeness, and promote in its place the careful, dutiful, expected, and correct?

It is worth a look to see, a look which is made both pleasanter and more poignant by the fact that it involves the remembering of many people. A few of them I do not remember gladly, and the feeling is undoubtedly mutual. But the great majority of these young men and women, desperate with the gift of words and nailed to the cross of a literary ambition, have been not only my students but my friends, and not only my friends but my fellows. There is an inescapable classroom inequality between teacher and students, but here we were not quite teachers, they were not quite students. At our best we communicated nearly as equals, for it is very hard to sustain a position of superiority when any of a half-dozen people in the class may at any time produce something that you wish you had written yourself.

II

First, a few paragraphs of history.

Some sort of Stanford writing program was made inevitable when I walked into my first writing class at Stanford in 1945 and found myself facing a dozen students, GI and otherwise, of whom at least five were more talented or more finished, or both, than anyone I had ever seen in a classroom. The first story submitted to me was Eugene Burdick's "Rest Camp on Maui." It is in this book, not necessarily because it is the best that Burdick ever wrote, but because it was the beginning of everything. It was published in *Harper's Magazine,* won second prize in the O. Henry volume for 1946, and started Bud Burdick on his brief, hot career: Houghton Mifflin Fellowship, Rhodes Scholarship, *The Ninth Wave, The Ugly American, Fail-Safe*—money, international notoriety, enormous and controversial public influence, early death.

But it started something else, too, in the people around him: an excitement, a challenge, a feeling that anything was possible, now that the abruptly-ended war had freed talent and energy for the things that had been suppressed for four or five years. Besides Bud Burdick there were four people in that group who clearly had possibilities of a literary career. All did something, several a good deal. One is now the wife of a publisher, another the wife of a professor. One is an editor of *The Reporter.* One has drifted out of sight. Of their later careers, more later. For the moment they are five students, the five whose stories made up the first volume of *Stanford Short Stories,* and they are demonstrating within a classroom a talent, maturity, and technical skill that are a continuous excitement to me, to themselves, and to the less talented and less advanced students around them. They showed me instantly one thing: a few good ones in a group make the whole group better.

It was too good to let dwindle away as the GI students graduated and left. It must be perpetuated, if perpetuation was possible. I drew up a proposal, which I myself thought rather grandiose, that involved five $2,000 fellowships in fiction, poetry, and playwriting, together with some scholarship and prize money and some aids to publication. This, before I showed it to anyone else, I took to the head of my department, the late R. F. Jones. Professor Jones showed it to his brother, Dr. E. H. Jones, who was visiting him. Dr. Jones, it turned out, had Texas oil lands and a love for literature. Before I had had the chance to show the proposal to anyone else, he had agreed to fund it for five years as an experiment. Five years later he renewed his support, and after another two years he began the permanent endowment which has been virtually completed since his death by other members of the Jones family.

Over the years the original outline has changed somewhat. The five fellowships are now six, the stipend has risen to $3,500.

The prizes are gone—they bred a good deal of rather hostile competitiveness, and it was very hard to enlist panels of judges. There are now no fellowships in playwriting, partly because it proved hard to administer from one department fellowships which must be supervised in another, partly because good young playwrights turned up scarce: in our fellowship competitions, the applicants in drama were consistently inferior to those in fiction and poetry. For the past ten years or so the normal distribution of fellowships has been two in poetry, four in fiction. There is in addition always one Australian in residence, working under a two-year fellowship administered by the University of Melbourne.

Throughout its existence, the Stanford writing program has been two things. It has been a laboratory for undergraduates, beginners, amateurs, many of whom have no expectation of becoming writers, but who take writing courses as an exercise in synthesis, part of a liberal education. In that aspect it is closely related to all college composition courses, but more particularly it derives from the "daily theme" classes of Dean Briggs at Harvard around the turn of the century. On top of these courses, in which students are demonstrably *taught* to write, there are mounted small seminars or workshops in fiction and poetry, composed of people so bent upon becoming literary artists that they will kick anything in the face, including a liberal education, in order to do so; and in these, people are not so much taught to write as encouraged to. The advanced seminars of graduate and special students, with a sprinkling of the most gifted undergraduates, have a clear resemblance to the summer writing sessions that began with the Breadloaf Writers Conference in 1925. They are different in that the term is longer—for most students the full school year—and in that creation takes place in the constant company of criticism, not in advance of it.

Any university writing program which awards fellowships and prizes, gives degrees, helps with publication through magazines or books, and encourages a professional attitude toward writing challenges both bohemia and Grub Street. Like them, it acts as a lure and a coagulant; it represents one form of opportunity and one kind of apprenticeship. Underlying the proliferation of university writing courses is the perception that in a country without a real literary capital, a country moreover of great distances and great diversity, the primary cultural centers, apart from a handful of cities, are university and college communities. If bohemia has in the last generation moved onto the campus—and it has—that is a pretty good sign that it has found the campus tolerant of its eccentricities. Except in the summer conferences, there has been little intrusion by Grub Street; whatever else university writing classes are, they are not ordinarily commercial.

Looking back over it, as it was and as it now is, I cannot think of serious changes that I would make. Financial aid, the creation of an environment in which good writing is valued with a passion, a permanent staff of writers who are also effective critics and teachers, a little aid to publication, a little sweetening of the mixture with distinguished literary visitors—those are indispensable parts of the program. If this approach does not work, I can think of none that will.

And how *has* it worked? The question brings us back to the writers themselves, and what they have written: in this case, to the short stories.

III

Do they hold up to a critical later scrutiny? I began reading through the fifteen volumes of them with uneasiness and doubt; I continued with growing confidence; I finished with exhilaration. Unless my taste is incorrigibly affected by the fact that these are stories by my friends and former students, and that I *want* them to be good, the level in these volumes is extraordinarily high, and the peaks are truly distinguished. Before they ever got into their individual annual volume, I had probably read each of them, in one version or another, a half-dozen times. But they come off the page at me now with vigor and freshness; they stand the hard test of multiple rereadings; and they are as various as the people who wrote them.

In spite of a certain roughness—it reads as if it had been hewed out with an axe—"Rest Camp on Maui" still rumbles with power like the tank which dominates one of its central episodes. I am touched by the generous sympathy for the defeated in "A Stranger's Funeral," and by the humanity that moves under an armor of resolution in "The Lady Walks." The lonely prep world where Teetee Wood lies cold and dead chills me; I get gooseflesh at Miriam Merritt's game that is definitely not for children. I am filled with renewed admiration for the control in "The Boats" and for the subtlety of perception and feeling in "The Wounded." "The Grapefruit Thinker" amuses me as much as it did when I read it aloud to the group eighteen years ago. I am shattered and shaken all anew by "Our Felix" and "Hey Sailor, What Ship?" There is not a story among the twenty-nine selected for this volume that I could not defend strongly on artistic grounds, and for every story that made the anniversary volume there were at least two fine stories reluctantly omitted.

It would have been relatively easy to make a selective anthology entirely from the work of people whose names would be recognized. It would have been equally easy to make it out of two representative stories from each volume of *Stanford Short Stories*. Instead of doing either, we chose to make it out of those stories that seemed the very best. As a result, there are whole volumes unrepresented, there are some well-known names that are not here, and there are some stories ("The Hero's Children," for one) that were written by undergraduates who never afterward to our knowledge published a line.

On the basis of the record, I have to conclude that the writers represented in this book found the university a good environment for creation. Perhaps, in a way, too good, for some of them seem to have written better at Stanford than they have since leaving there. Something—perhaps guidance and criticism, perhaps the absence of editorial or commercial pressure, perhaps the atmosphere of completely free inquiry which a university and especially a writing program may provide, perhaps the stimulation of talented companions—something or a combination of somethings released their gifts as their later environments do not seem to have done.

Are their stories "correct," academic in the bad sense? It is a question for any reader to answer for himself. Personally I do not think so in the least. Undoubtedly there is a certain formal similarity among them, for they are all true short stories, and how is a short story distinguished except by its form? They share a singleness, a concentration, a limitation of scope and a sharpness of focus, that any story worth the name should possess. But how different in tone and handling is the psychic disintegration in

"City of the Angels" from that in "Back Again"! What various
children are those in "The Death of Pierce," "Undertow," "The
Boats," and "Our Felix"! How different is the family in "Night
Guard" from that in "Night on Octavia Street," and how different
from both is that in "We Know That Your Hearts Are Heavy"!
How multiple is the vision of war that we get from reading in con-
junction "Rest Camp on Maui," "A Camp in the Meadow," "A
Stranger's Funeral," and "Down the Road a Piece"! How pri-
vate and personal, each in its own way, is the malaise of "That
Time of Year" and that of "Geraldine"!

Is there a curve, a detectable progression or change in the
stories across twenty years? An examination of the subject matter indicates, as one would have expected, that the war, which
provided more than half the stories in the first two volumes, falls
quickly away and disappears in later ones. But the examination
reveals no clear pattern of substitution. There has been no overwhelming common experience since to compare with the war, and
those causes and agitations which stir the campuses now—inte-
gration, Viet Nam, the amorphous "freedom" movement that
may refer to anything from civil rights to intellectual anarchy,
and from psychedelic drugs to sex, do not seem to be effectively
represented. It is a good question why. Perhaps because as
causes they provide only black-and-white characters, them and us,
the bad ones and the good ones. Perhaps because they are only,
for most writers, beliefs and causes, not experience, and hence
do not readily get themselves incorporated into fable and character and event.

Except that the war has disappeared as the universal and uni-
versally respected experience, a story does not seem to be much
different now from what it was twenty years ago. It is franker in
its language, but not otherwise different. Injustice and poverty,
regional and ethnic local color, family relations, *rites du passage*,
psychological revelations and the psychic states on the fringes of
sanity—these are still the basic stock in trade. And though one
of the editors of this book facetiously suggested that we call it
From War to Pot, we couldn't have found a pot story if we had
wanted one.

And is this not odd? By all the evidence, we are undergoing
a profound, swift change from an essentially rational (however

mad) society built on Greece and Rome and a body of traditional thought painstakingly assembled, to a society which asserts itself more and more as mystical, irrational, and terpsichorean. In our "advanced" echelons we are already more African than Greek; what jazz may have heralded, drugs and sexual emancipation continue and perfect. Traditions, including traditional forms in art, go down: the youth who trusts no one over thirty is no devotee of the Great Books. His aim—call it rather a drive—seems to be not to keep his head, but to lose it; he wants not clarity but ecstasy, not understanding but hallucination. According to the apocalypts, orgasm cures wounds, and pot should be sold for balsams, and the academic corollary of this is the "free" university, sans administration, sans buildings, sans fees, sans degrees, sans faculty, sans grades, sans books, sans everything, an assemblage of free souls throbbing together.

It is all over every campus, but it does not show here. Or rather, it shows in many of the novels, and in many of the less successful stories, but not in the stories that make their way into this book. The university is after all the Establishment, and it may be awkward to blow an anti-wind-instrument tune on a borrowed French horn. More likely, it is simply difficult to combine anti-traditional thinking and the inescapable demands of the short story form. The habit of anarchy implies a corresponding habit of incessant improvisation and a repudiation of all formal restrictions. But you do not improvise a good short story. When the apocalyptic writer writes what he calls a short story, he more often than not produces something authentically short, but not authentically story: an open-ended sketch, a whirling gust of images, an impression, a howl, a freehand map of the author's mind. It could be that the revolt against all sorts of authority means the swift extinction of the short story as we know it, but being over thirty I will confidently predict that just as swiftly new forms will have to be devised to replace it. Anarchy is the law of nature, Henry Adams said, and order is the dream of man. And even young anarchs are men. Dreaming.

Quite apart from any effect the "freedom" revolution may have had on the products of Stanford writing classes, it is very clear that in recent years the short stories have declined both in volume and in the general level of their quality. This is not to say that there have been no good recent writers of stories. Nancy Packer, Merrill Joan Gerber, Robert Stone, and others are as good as the best, and are·here *with* the best. But in 1946 there were many more magazines publishing stories than there are in 1966. The audience is now smaller, the possible rewards fewer; and the decline that I just half-facetiously attributed to an impatience with form is accentuated by a skimpy market. The smaller the demand, the smaller the supply; the fewer stories we write, the less we know how to write them. At Stanford, where there were for many years enough good stories annually to make a solid volume, we have recently been able to make up a volume only every other year. That at the same time the novelists have become more active seems to demonstrate that the decline in short stories is principally a feeling on the part of writers that however useful stories may be as apprentice pieces, they are not the stuff on which to build a career.

How one *does* build a career is a troubling problem. For it almost seems that we have been training people for a profession that does not exist, or at least does not very often exist in the terms that passionate young talent hopes for. One of the saddening observations that I made during my review of the first twenty years is that talents are as numerous as salmon eggs, and for the same reason: those that can survive to maturity will be few.

Of the hundred and twelve authors represented in the first fifteen volumes of *Stanford Short Stories*, who are themselves a selection from hundreds of students, I have entirely lost touch with too many—thirty-seven. Of the seventy-five whose present activities and whereabouts I know, many are still writing, but only thirteen could certify on their income tax forms that they are full-time "writers," and some of these are writers in a sense they did not anticipate, train for, or elect. Only the merest handful support themselves by writing independently things that they originate and that seem to them important. Of the others, one writes movies in Hollywood, one is CBS correspondent in Moscow, one is a newspaperman, two or three are free-lancers, the rest supplement their writing by a little lecturing, editing, or teaching on the side.

And the remaining sixty-two, many of whom, as students, seemed at least as talented and dedicated as the thirteen? They have found the jobs that a gift of words fits them for: twenty-five are teachers, seven are editors, two make documentary movies, three are in the federal service, one is a San Francisco supervisor, one is a city planner, five are in business, five are in advertising or public relations. Eleven are housewives, that position of security and authority that may be the luckiest place of all. And two, Bud Burdick and Perrin Lowrey, are dead. Alive, they both combined writing with teaching.

Some of the gainfully employed people find time and energy to write; a few of them, especially the housewives (who may be counted as gainfully employed), write a good deal. But by and large the high talent, the high hope, the passion and the dedication and the anger, whatever was there crying for expression, have come to approximately the same result as the efforts of the casual undergraduate who plays at the writing game as one aspect of a liberal education. Literature in America turns out to be an art that can be practiced fully only by people with an independent income, by a very few who hit the jackpot and keep on hitting it, and by housewives. As a *profession*, on the other hand, writing may be practiced by a limited number of well-trained craftsmen able to provide what the market wants and can use. The rest of all the potential writers either give up slowly and reluctantly, scattering a thin production across years devoted mainly to other work, or end up in one of writing's sibling professions such as teaching or publishing.

These findings, though not surprising, are distressing when they are drawn from the lives of men and women one has watched through the ripening period when talent and experience and training began to come together to make little miracles. The first time a young writer achieves print, it seems to him that anything is possible. I have watched it scores of times, and it is not good for the souls of elderly writing teachers to look back on all those people whom he and everyone else knew to be extremely promising, and to contemplate what their promise has come to. I have not been one of those who hold America to be a great neon wilderness that kills its artists: the artist who is a real artist and who will not be destroyed can make it in this country as in any other. But the casualties are miserably high, the destruction of hope brutally common, the waste of high talent and high energy appalling. It paralyzes the mind as if it had been touched with liquid nitrogen, to think of the vast indifference that a young writer must launch himself into. If astronauts had as little chance of hitting the moon, NASA would disband tomorrow.

Should we then call it futile, an attempt to sponsor within the protected and "artificial" climate of a university an art that the society itself will not support? Certainly the Stanford writing program cannot turn out literary artists, or even professional writers, the way a chemistry department can turn out chemists. And yet there are these stories, those novels, those poems—real achievements, provocative insights, expressions of human solidarity, modulations of the composite human voice. I suspect that to the people who wrote them, including those whom economics or other cause forced away from literature, they are profoundly important: the first and only time they got the chance to speak heart to heart with the world. They may be important to the world too. I do not subscribe to the notion that universities are isolated monasteries; but if I did I would have to add that the monasteries preserved learning and the arts through centuries of darkness. From the relative sanctuary of a university it is possible to guess that the revolutionary aspects of what passes for the literary life—chaos made manifest, innovation made God, showmanship preferred before eloquence—are ephemeral and brief, and at the same time quaintly repetitive. As Robert Frost remarked, there are no news ways to be new.

But there are old ways to be wise, and old ways to reach a reader's heart and mind. Ultimately, art is traditional; it learns more from the art that precedes it than it learns from nature. If chaos is indeed the law of nature, then order *must* be the dream of man, and the best of all orders is art. The university can frankly sponsor it, and afford to assist the people who aspire to it, and if it never receives any other reward for its efforts than the twenty-nine stories in this volume, it should express itself satisfied.

Twenty Years of Stanford Short Stories

Donald A. Allan

A Stranger's Funeral

The valley of the Bavarian town of Beilngries is an emerald
trough, walled by limestone cliffs buttressed by soft green slopes
of pasture land. Water seeps underground through porous limestone passageways and feeds a bright stream that glitters along
the valley floor, and running through the town, turns the wheel
of the mill and twists away toward the Danube at Regensburg.
At one end of the valley the stream cuts across a dusty road
which a short distance beyond is dignified as the main street
of Beilngries. Binding the intersection of the two winding rib-
bons there used to be an arched stone bridge, carefully con-
structed by subjects of King Ludwig. On a clear, still, April
morning, just before the end of the war, the bridge was ripped
apart by an explosion that blasted its granite blocks high into
the air in a cloud of dust and smoke.

A mile from the bridge, just off the road that climbs the
valley wall, a barn-like building clings to the hillside. The
building is a brewery, although it still looks more like the
monastery for which it was originally designed. It is built
right into the steep hillside, so that from each of its three
stories one can walk out onto the ground. The middle floor
has been converted into a beer hall, and around this central
hall is a trellised veranda which offers a beautiful view of the
grassy slope and the valley below. On the morning of the explosion Sam stood alone on this veranda, sunning himself.

For a quarter of an hour the tiny green-uniformed figures

had been working at the bridge; now they were scurrying down
the road into the town. Sam watched them run, and saw the
cloud of smoke and stone erupt above the treetops, seconds before the sound of the explosion made him duck. He had been
expecting the explosion since early that morning when the
Hauptmann had come into the one-room army hospital and
ordered all patients removed to the old brewery above the town.
Still, after a year as a prisoner of war, he could not prevent this
reflex ducking, nor control the stab of familiar fear at the
sound of the blast.

The blowing of the bridge had been long awaited by Sam.
It culminated his year of hunger, of frustration, of boredom and
yearning in the crowded prison-camp barracks, and of misery
on the nightmare march from Poland. It climaxed his weeks of
sweating out the news and waiting in the German army hospital
where he had faked illness to prevent being sent farther south
to the new camp. The demolition of the bridge symbolized the
tearing down of the barbed wire, the removal of the last barrier
between him and the American tanks even now approaching
somewhere back along the dusty road that led out of sight over
the hills.

Sam boosted himself onto the veranda railing and sagged
against a pillar. He told himself to relax, to let the sunshine
melt the frozen filaments of his nerves, and for a while he concentrated on making every muscle go limp. Nothing can go
wrong now, he assured himself. Even if they don't come today,
they'll get here tomorrow or the day after. What's a day? Or
a week? It's in the bag. A noise from the road startled him,
and he realized that he had never relaxed. He sat up again and
rolled a cigarette with a square of newspaper and some ersatz
tobacco scavengings he kept in a tin box. The noise from the
road had been made by a long line of villagers struggling up
the hill to the brewery. They were pulling carts and carrying
boxes and sacks full of household treasures, and some were
driving animals. The procession led up the road and through
a great doorway beneath the veranda to a series of caverns and
tunnels in the limestone, once used as crypts for the monks,
later as a storehouse for the beer, and now as a refuge for the
frightened people of the town.

If the explosion had heralded freedom for Sam, for the

Germans it represented the raising of a drawbridge at an entrance to their fast shrinking *Festung*. In the big hall behind him the wounded from the hospital lay on stretchers or sat huddled against the walls. When the dynamite went off several of the patients cried out. The others exchanged glances and simply said: "There goes the bridge." "They must be getting close now." And "Yes, it won't be long now."

Sam looked up the road where the white powdered limestone radiated the morning heat. Not a person, not even a cow or a dog was in sight. He strained his ears for some sound that would announce the approach of the tanks, but the air was as still as the road was empty. He stretched and tensed his muscles as hard as he could, so that when he released them they would relax completely, and all the time excitement and anticipation grew inside him in a quivering core. It was the same sort of feeling he had had before his first mission. It was similar to the tension he used to feel just before a race, in the long second between the starter's "Get set!" and the sound of the gun. He was waiting now for the sound that would set him free; free to run wherever he wanted, to laugh, to eat, to shout away the restraints of the past year. Instead he heard the ringing of a bell.

It was a telephone. It shocked him because it was the first telephone bell he had heard in Germany. Sam looked into the hall and saw the Hauptmann talking on an army field phone. In a minute he hung up. The wounded raised themselves on their stretchers, and every man in the hall watched him, waiting for him to speak.

"That was the hospital at Plankstettin," said the Hauptmann. "They have reached Solngriesbach with a large force of tanks and armored cars."

"How far is Solngriesbach, sir?" someone asked.

"Twenty-five kilometers."

The men lay back on their stretchers with little comment. Again someone said, "It won't be long now." Sam turned back and looked up the road. Twenty-five kilometers, at say fifteen miles an hour. Back in the valley the little stream, gilded in the sunlight, frothed silver around the wreckage of the blasted bridge. The bridge already looked more like a crumbled relic of antiquity than a casualty of war. Everything seemed clean, the sky, the air, the green meadow, and the pink village were

as bright and fresh as the water running in the brook. God!
What a beautiful day, Sam thought. It was of mornings like
this that the fellows in the camp used to say, "It's a fine day for
the war to end!" Today the war *would* end, for him. His heart
swelled. Tonight! Ah, tonight! He would eat and smoke and
sleep. He would be able to talk again, to crawl out of his stoic
cyst. And soon there would be steaks and orange juice and
asparagus, and fresh milk, and shrimp, but absolutely no more
potatoes. There would be a plane or a boat that would take him
to America, and then he would find a phone booth and . . . .
He heard steps behind him and saw Willi, the ancient hospital
orderly, approaching with a bottle of beer.

"The Hauptmann had the beer brought up from the caves,"
he said. "Have one. It's beer saved from before the war. It
was saved for the victory."

Sam took the bottle and drank. It was very good. Even
though he hadn't tasted any since he left the States, he knew that
it was very good beer, and he smiled as he thought how appropriate it was that he should toast the victory in German beer.
Inside the hall some voices were singing "ein prosit" in four-
part harmony. The ambulatory cases were helping the ones on
the stretchers to drink.

Willi listened a minute, smiling. " *'Für Gemutlichkeit'* an-
statt des Sieges. Maybe it's better. Tonight you'll be drinking
whiskey, eh?"

"Maybe," Sam said. Even with gentle Willi, Sam couldn't
put aside his prisoner's restraint.

"What do you think they will do to us, Lieutenant? Will
we be sent to Russia? I'm an old man, Lieutenant. My sons
are dead and my wife is all alone in Barmstadt and I haven't
heard from her in months."

"I wouldn't worry, Willi," Sam said. "I know you will be
treated fairly. Probably they'll send you home."

"That's right, Lieutenant. The war is truly over, and we
should all go home. I'm an old man." He looked at an oversized gold pocket watch and went back inside to help with the
patients.

Inside the singing stopped. It was almost perfectly still
again, except for an occasional moan from the stretchers, and

a few frightened noises from the cattle inside the caves. A woman came to the doorway below and called frantically, "Anna, Anna." She saw Sam and a flash of fear crossed her face. A little spotted dog bounced around the corner of the building and she caught it to her bosom, smiled weakly at Sam and popped back inside. The Hauptmann came out of the door, and it was bolted behind him.

The Hauptmann climbed the steps to the veranda, his usually brisk steps lagging with fatigue. Sam looked at his Luger, and remembered the Hauptmann had a good camera too. He did not speak to Sam as Willi had, or smile at him as the old woman had, but stiffened his lean body and strode into the hall, without looking to either side. Sam didn't expect any overtures from this man. On the other hand, the Hauptmann never smiled at his own men. They called him "The Robot," but never in spite. His cold superiority annoyed Sam, and he decided to take the Luger when the tanks came.

Against his will the feeling of happiness blossomed within him. In the camp he had learned to suppress his hopes. After the optimism of the invasion days had come the Battle of the Bulge. And on the day when the big Red Cross trucks had parked outside the camp, and everyone had gone wild in anticipation of getting food parcels, only athletic equipment had been unloaded. But now he could no longer maintain his pessimism. The realization was beginning to come that he was nearly free. After all the doubts and fears of waiting, the day was really here. He wanted to shout and jump in the air, to do something violent to work out the pressure rising inside him. He slid off the railing and went into the hall to see if there was any beer left.

Just as he stepped through the doorway, the phone rang again. He stopped, as everyone in the room stopped. It rang a second and a third time before the Hauptmann reached the box. Almost as soon as he picked it up he put it down, only saying "Thank you" into the mouthpiece. He turned to the men, and looked at his watch before he spoke.

"Gentlemen," he began softly, "they have passed Plank-stettin and are on the road to Beilngries. They should arrive in five minutes." The eyes of the Hauptmann held the weight of these words as he looked for a moment into the eyes of each man in the room. The muscles of his jaw bulged and relaxed, and he continued. "You who have so bravely fought for Germany must call your courage to its greatest test. We meet the enemy defenseless, and we shall be taken." He pulled his Luger from its holster and threw it on the floor, where it slid close to Sam's feet.

"There is no disgrace in our surrender. Your flesh bears record of your service: you could not do more. As a soldier I praise you; as a German I give you my heartfelt thanks. Comrades, we part in sadness, but not in shame. Wherever you go, whatever may be said or done, keep up your courage and remember that it is in your own hearts and before God that judgment is made. God's will is ever done. As my last order as your Captain I ask you to pray for Germany."

The Hauptmann knelt and each man bowed his head. Sam saw tears, and a new and deeper pain showed in the eyes of the men on the stretchers. He hesitated in the doorway, feeling he should not be there, yet unwilling to move. He felt as though he had intruded at the funeral of a stranger, but one where the universality of the ceremony inevitably touched him. Unthinking, Sam too cast his eyes on the floor, where they rested on the Luger. In his mind no words formed, but as always, when the minister at home said, "Let us pray," an unformed longing choked in his throat. God, Oh God, make things . . . . better.

To his left he heard a gulping cough that accelerated and ran away into the sobs that come after shock has worn off and pain long endured bursts out uncontrolled. There was another sound, and in his distraction Sam listened to it for a minute before he recognized the growl of motors. The sound swelled up into a rattling racket of grinding steel, and the spell in the hall was broken.

Sam turned in the doorway and saw the first tank top the rise and rumble down the road above the brewery. He ran to the veranda railing and saw the bright red identification panels and the white star of the American tanks. They were really here. It was really over. He repeated the words in his mind almost as if he were trying to pump up his exuberance.

The first tank was almost abreast of the brewery now, and

Sam could read the name painted on its side, "Mary Alice." Sam picked up his box of belongings and went down the steps to the path. The spotted dog bounced ahead of him on the path, barking wildly at the tanks. Halfway to the road Sam stopped and looked back, remembering the Luger. The old woman stood in the doorway to the caves with her hands over her face. Above her, on the veranda, the Hauptmann stood, hands clasped behind his back, eyes focused on a point of infinity to the south. In the windows of the big hall some of the wounded were watching the column of tanks roll down the road into the valley.

Sam turned back down the path. A cloud of dust rose from the road and flattened out over the whole valley. As he reached the road the first tank came to the bridge, forded the stream, and crawled up the other side.

Eugene Burdick

Rest Camp on Maui

The rest camp was as ugly as a place can be in the Hawaiian Islands, which is saying that it was as ugly as slums in New York, mud flats in Georgia, or drought land in Arkansas. Bulldozers had scraped the foliage and trees off several hills and left them red and naked. The hills had been covered with tents and a few Quonset huts. The only tropical thing about the camp was the sun and the heavy, sweet sugar-cane odor which was laced with the sharper odor of flowers when the wind shifted away from the valley.

Lieutenant Terry walked down a row of tents with the correspondent at his side. He stopped in front of a tent and pulled the flap aside to let the correspondent in. Three Marines stood up. A fourth Marine standing in front of a mirror was rubbing Aqua Velva on his face. He rubbed it with short, smooth strokes along his chin and then up his cheeks, splitting his fingers apart to pass on either side of his ears. Terry watched the Marine rub the liquid on his face and said nothing. Then the Marine turned around and clicking his heels together, said, "Lieutenant Terry." He said it in a mocking, affected way that meant he liked Terry and felt at ease with him.

Terry started to speak rapidly: "Men, this gentleman here is a correspondent who wants to talk to you for a while. Give him whatever information he wants and we'll check it later for security. Mr. Black, this is Sergeant Fellows, Corporal Young, Private Selfensky, and Private Shannon."

By the end of the introduction the Marines all seemed re-

With permission of the New American Library, which will publish in September 1966 a collection of Mr. Burdick's stories, entitled *A Role in Manila*. Copyright 1946 by Harper's Magazine, Inc.

laxed and their faces went a little blank. They shook hands
with the correspondent, squinting over his shoulder as they
grasped his hand.

Fellows was round and red like a beery friar.

"Glad to meet you, Mr. Black. Glad to help you anyway
we can," he said.

His voice was so flat that the cordiality of the words seemed
to be squeezed thin and reluctant. He went back to the mirror
and sprinkled some more Aqua Velva in his hands and started
to rub his face.

The correspondent picked up his knapsack and opening it
slipped out a bottle of whisky and put it on the table, saying,
"Something to help pass the afternoon."

The four Marines all heard the bottle come down on the
table and turned to stare hard at it. The bottle looked big and
new and shiny. Their faces were eager and individual now.
Their eyes glistened and Fellows licked a corner of his mouth
several times quickly, without looking away from the bottle.
They turned and looked at Terry. It was against regulations to
drink in camp and they watched to see what Terry would say.
Terry looked at Fellows and winked and said, "I'll be back
for you in two hours, Mr. Black." He turned and walked out
the flap.

Fellows laid out four heavy, metal mess cups and a chipped
glass. He picked up the bottle, ripped the cellophane cover off
the top, and unscrewed it. He poured out the whisky until the
whole bottle was neatly divided into five equal parts.

"I'm not drinking today. Go ahead and use mine," the correspondent said.

Fellows looked up from the bottle and smiled at the correspondent. He picked up the chipped glass and split the whisky
in it equally among the four metal cups. The whisky had a
heady, rich odor that quickly filled the tent. Selfensky laughed
and picking up a cup said, "Skol." They rinsed their mouths
with the liquor and the heavy fumes flooded up their noses and
tickled beautifully. The strength of the whisky brought tears
to their eyes and they swallowed it quickly. They all smiled at
the correspondent and when he started to talk again the conversation was more relaxed.

The correspondent took off his cap and laid it on the table.

It was crumpled like the caps that Army pilots wear. It was cleverly bent and the wire stretcher had been removed from it.

"Men, I'm trying to get the personal angle on some of these shows you've been in," he said.

They felt good now and they grinned when he said "show." Correspondents always said "show," "bloody do," or "rat race," especially in the books they wrote.

"I want to get your attitude on politics and women and how you feel about things back in the States. There weren't any women on Tarawa or Iwo, but how about the women in Sydney and the Hawaiian girls?"

Fellows started to talk loudly about the Australian chicks. The correspondent kept grinning and saying he couldn't print that, but you could see he wanted to hear more of it. Fellows talked about the Sydney girls out at King's Cross and down at Woolamooloo Dock and how at first they would always shack up with a girl apiece, but later when they got broke, a half dozen of them would all shack up with one girl to save money. The Marines hardly listened to Fellows' talk. They sipped at the whisky and smoked cigarettes.

Lord, Young thought, it's wonderful how good cigarettes taste when you suck in the smoke through the whisky breath of your throat.

Usually Young liked to listen to the older fellows talk about women. He was only nineteen, the youngest man in his platoon. He'd joined the Corps when he was seventeen and never had a chance to hang around girls much. He had never had a girl, but he picked up the salty talk quickly and felt pretty sure that he sounded like any other Marine talking about women. Today he felt good and mellow and leaning back in his chair he thought about the time on Okinawa.

He and Fellows had been on a patrol on the northern end of the island and they had come to another one of those little villages that were almost deserted. As they walked past the little houses they saw a few stunted people disappearing around corners or sitting in front of the tiny houses. Even the dogs looked runty and little. In front of one house a woman and her husband were seated on the ground. The husband was puffing on a small clay pipe and looking straight ahead. He looked as if he had been carved and lacquered and he had a smooth, oily little potbelly that gleamed out of a hole in his shirt. The woman was seated with her back to the wall and she had dark, long hair. It was so black that it looked steelblue. She must have been forty years old and her skin had an exquisite pattern of wrinkles over it, but somehow it looked soft and well-cared for. Perhaps she had powder on her skin. It looked as if it might have a nice odor to it.

Fellows laughed and said, "Look," as he tossed her a small, wax-covered package of K-ration. It landed on her lap and she picked it up and examined it slowly and then looked up at the sergeant. A gift from a man in uniform could mean only one thing to her. She slid down until her shoulders were on the ground, but her head was still angled up against the house. She unfolded her kimona and drew it carefully back from her body until she was naked from the waist down. Young looked at her husband and he was still puffing his pipe slowly and looking straight ahead. The woman looked at the sergeant again and turned her head until the side of her face was flat against the rough material of the house. She closed her eyes. Young thought for a moment it was an odd movement of coquetry, but knew instantly it wasn't. It was artless and completely uninspired, the movement of a tired animal. Lying in the sun on her kimona in the peculiar posture she should have seemed disgusting, but to Young she seemed very lascivious, although she made not the slightest movement and lay inert on the ground.

Young said hoarsely, "Come on, Sarg, let's get going."

"Yeah, yeah," said Fellows, looking at the woman. "She's probably got a lot of screwy Jap diseases we never heard of."

Fellows was no longer smiling and as they went on through the village he said, "You know kid, they always lay still like that. They're screwy people. I had Asiatic duty once. I know the screwy bastards."

Young stopped in the middle of the street and suddenly vomited. He felt greatly relieved and laughed loudly as Fellows hit him on the shoulder and said, "Take it easy, kid, take it easy."

Later Young had thought of the woman when they'd start to talk about their girls and wives and what they'd do when they got back to the States.

Fellows was still talking about the Aussie women and the

correspondent was writing occasionally in a black notebook.
Young moved behind him and read what he had written: "Marines like Aussie girls, but first love still clean-cut American
girls."

The correspondent's pen moved across the notebook again:
"Jews in the Corps. Personal, human angle?" He looked up
inquiringly.

"How have the Jews in the Corps made out? I'd like to
give them a good write-up in my book," he said.

Fellows nodded at Selfensky and said, "Ask Selfensky, he's
a Jew."

Selfensky looked straight at the correspondent for a moment
and the Marines knew he wanted to talk about Lieutenant Cohen.
Usually Selfensky clammed up when someone made a mistake
and talked about Jews in front of him, but today he felt loose
and oily inside and talking seemed easy. He chewed at his lip,
trying to form words, and then the correspondent said, "Yeah,
Selfensky, you probably know more about this than anyone here.
You know, some of my best friends are Jews. Damn fine fellows, I really like them."

Selfensky's face went a little hard and he stopped chewing
his lip and said, "Ask Fellows. I don't know hardly anyone
outside my company."

"Yeah, yeah, I know just about everyone in this damn divi-
sion," Fellows said. He started telling the correspondent about
Horowitz, a Pfc in the quartermaster, who organized an all-
Marine show.

Selfensky took a sip of the whisky and he felt a little tight
and beautifully lightheaded. He hadn't thought about Lieutenant Cohen for a long time. Selfensky remembered how proud
he had felt when he got the word that his company was getting
a Jewish officer for a platoon leader replacement. There were
only a few Jewish enlisted men and no Jewish officers in his
company. He had been disappointed when he first saw Cohen.
He was of medium height and had dark eyes and long and very
white graceful hands. Selfensky had hoped he would be a big
rugged Jewish football player like Sid Luckman or a huge, fast,
powerful boxer. Cohen was very quiet and kept to himself, but
he was marvelous on weapons. Instead of fieldstripping his

platoon's weapons on a clean, canvas-covered table he made them take them out in the sand in a fox-hole. They had to strip them with their eyes bandaged and put the parts in their pockets to keep them from getting sandy or losing them. Cohen could beat anyone by a minute or so. He was always asking questions about new gear and equipment and remembered most of it. Once he took a two-day pass and went to visit a tank outfit. When he came back he could drive a tank. The men started to like him.

One day a big Polack had called Cohen a kike. Loud and clear so that Cohen could hear it, and then looked at Cohen so that he couldn't ignore it. Cohen told him to report to the back of the rifle range and about twenty men drifted along to see what would happen.

Cohen took his shirt off and said, "Corporal, take off your shirt."

The Pole was a little nervous, but he laughed when he saw that Cohen was actually going to fight him with no rank or rate showing. He outweighed Cohen by forty pounds.

Cohen stood very straight and white and said, "Corporal, I can't possibly beat you in an ordinary fist fight. This is going to be a no-holds-barred fight. Do you agree?"

"Yeah, Jew-boy, that's okay with me," the Pole said.

Selfensky felt sick and wondered if he should try to stop the fight, but the Pole had already started after Cohen. The Pole hit Cohen twice—hard blows on the chest. Then Cohen seemed to be all over the Pole, like a mongoose after a dog. He kicked the Pole hard in the shins and as the Pole straightened up Cohen had his finger inside the Pole's lip and ripped it back from the corner of his mouth. The Pole kept hitting Cohen hard, but he was a little scared now. Cohen went after his hands next and when they separated he had broken the little finger of the Pole's right hand. It hung back from his hand at such an impossible angle that it hurt you to look at it.

Cohen drove his knee into the Pole's groin a couple of times and Selfensky could see panic in the Pole's eyes. The Pole tried to kick and knee too and that ended it quickly. Cohen stood back and smashed him time after time in the face. The Pole got weaker and soon his knees buckled and he put his face in his hands and sank to the ground. The broken little finger stuck straight out from the other fingers curled around his face.

The Pole turned into sick bay and said he'd been in a fight with some civilians. Cohen visited him in the hospital and when the Pole got out he transferred to Cohen's platoon. Cohen still worked his men hard and by the time they were ready to stage for Iwo his platoon was the toughest in the company. The men were lean and hard and they all looked tougher than Cohen, whose hands were still white and graceful-looking.

Their company went into Iwo on D plus 2. Selfensky remembered how much like practice it all had seemed as they went down the nets into the LCVP's and circled around waiting for the rest of their wave. They joked and kidded a bit and a BAR man pretended he was seasick over the side. It didn't seem too bad even when they got up close to the beach and could hear the mortars crumping and could see the F6F's suddenly leave their 500-pound bombs hanging still in the air and then the bombs would start to speed up and go so fast you could hardly see them as they hit into the big mounds of sand and soon exploded blackly.

As soon as the platoon hit the beach, however, and started to march through the black volcanic sand, things didn't look so good. The first thing they saw was an aid station that had been hit. There were broken plasma bottles hanging from rifles and a long stream of bandage unrolled neat and white across the black sand. Cots and crates and blankets were all smashed together and big, tarry clots of blood and flesh were plastered over everything. The corpsmen had already set up a few yards down the beach, but you could tell that they didn't expect to stay there long. Funny how corpsmen always looked like kids. Even the middle-aged men looked like kids when they wore the big helmets with red crosses on them and brassards on their arms. Like kids playing soldier.

They moved off the beach fast and alongside the air strip, avoiding the little flags that indicated mines. The mortar fire started to pick up. They hit the line very soon and found the outfit they were supposed to flank. There were a lot of dead Marines around, but no one was bothering about them and Selfensky wondered where the Japs were. He hadn't seen a Jap body or a Jap position yet, although the machine-gun fire was heavy now and then and occasionally there was some artillery fire. Then a company runner arrived and gave Cohen a field dispatch and he moved the platoon to the right and into a big shell hole.

"We're going to clean out that pillbox on the hill," he said. "We'll have tank support and everyone except the BAR men keep close to the tank. BAR men keep the pillbox under fire all the time. A couple of grenades ought to do it, but don't pitch one until you're sure you can hit the slit."

Selfensky looked up the low hill and finally saw the long, camouflaged slit. It looked like a crevice between two rocks, but occasionally there would be a stream of smoke-puff from it.

They had to wait a half-hour for the tank so they broke open their K-rations. Selfensky didn't like the candy in the ration and traded it to another man for the little can of cheese.

The tank came early, lumbering down the side of the air strip, with dust thick and black all over it. Wherever there was grease on the tank the dust bulged out in huge mounds, like soft, black cancers growing out of the steel. The tank didn't stop when it came to their shell hole, but the turret swung toward them as if in question and turned back toward the pillbox. The gun barrel pointed at the pillbox like a long, commanding finger. They threw the paper and tins into the bottom of the hole and started out behind the tank. At once the fire started to increase and mortar shells began to plop around the tank. The pillbox was firing fast now and the smoke puffed steadily out of it. The BAR men lagged a little behind and suddenly they started to fire into the pillbox. You could see the hot, angry tracers powdering the stone around the pillbox and smoke stopped coming out of it.

They were only a hundred yards from the pillbox when they all heard the first screaming ricochet of an anti-tank shell. Mortar projectiles don't ricochet, they just plop into the ground and explode, but high velocity anti-tank projectiles will ricochet off almost anything. The turret of the tank spun around frantically trying to locate the anti-tank gun. All you could see was dust and mortar shells exploding and ugly little hills held to-

gether by dust and great chunks of concrete that you couldn't
see. There were two more snarling ricochets and then the fourth
round shattered into the tank. It made a terrible ringing sound
and Selfensky's ears stopped hearing for a minute and he felt
a sharp, cold pain at the base of each tooth. The hatch and tank
captain turned slowly over in the air, the tank captain's clothing
shredding away from him in the air. When he hit the ground he
lay there white and broken and naked.

The tank was smoking, but the motor was running smoothly.
The dust had been shaken from the tank and the green and
brown camouflage paint looked smooth and new. Selfensky felt
fear grip his stomach and suddenly felt very exposed against
the sand. He wished he had had a bowel movement back in the
shell hole. He heard his name called and looking up saw Cohen
lowering himself into the hatch of the tank and motioning to
him to follow.

Inside the tank was hot and dusty and the sweat started to
stand out on Selfensky's face. He felt secure inside the thick
steel walls despite the hole in the side of the tank and the two
men who had died looking over their shoulders into the turret.
Cohen boosted the gunner up to him and Selfensky pushed him
out the hatch and let him slide to the ground. The driver was
harder to get out and Selfensky was sweating hard. He was
feeling better all the time, however, and he was amazed at how
safe and snug a tank was. He looked at the hole in the side of
the tank and saw that the steel was several fingers thick. Damn
it, this was all right! Cohen looked up from the driver's seat
and said, "Tell the Pole to take over the platoon and we'll try
to get up to the pillbox."

The tank started slowly up the slope and through the peri-
scope the pillbox slit got larger and suddenly smoke started to
puff out of it again. Selfensky could feel the bullets hitting the
side and bouncing off and he grinned down at Cohen.

Cohen's greens were dark with sweat now and his large
white hands were moving over the controls rapidly. They were
about fifty feet from the pillbox when a scrawny little Jap started
to slide sideways out of the slit and Selfensky saw he had a
satchel charge in his right hand. The Jap came hopping bowlegged down the hill, his face all contorted and probably yell-

ing. He covered about half the distance to the tank when he started to stagger. It looked as if someone were hitting him with an invisible sledge hammer. His forehead dissolved in a red splash and his legs snapped back under him as the BAR slugs tore into them. Sudden, red decorations started to spread over his shirt. He smacked backward into the ground and the satchel charge slipped from his hand. Cohen stopped the tank and crawled over into the gunner's position. He didn't know how to work the sight, but at this range he could fire by eye and not miss. He fired five rounds into the slit and when the pillbox looked like a smoking black eye in the hill he stopped.

Cohen grinned up at Selfensky and started the tank back down the hill. They were about halfway down when they hit one of the 500-pound aerial bombs the Japs had mined the island with. Later they told Selfensky that the tank flopped over on its back and lay there like a great, helpless turtle. Selfensky only remembered coming to and knowing he didn't hurt anywhere and almost immediately he knew where he was. Cohen was hanging face down from the driver's compartment and the explosion had clamped the compartment around his legs. He hung from his knees down into the turret. Selfensky was puzzled at Cohen's position for a few minutes and then he started to crawl towards him. At once he heard a rasping sound and a great pain itched up his leg. The bone was sticking almost straight out from his leg and when he moved he had pulled it across the rough surface of the tank. He looked again at Cohen and hoped he was dead because he was sure to lose both his legs.

Cohen's voice sounded low and clear in the hot turret, "Take it easy, Selfensky. Stay where you are and they'll get you out of here."

Cohen's eyes looked big and soft and Selfensky felt embarrassed looking at them upside down. He tried to turn his head so he could see straight into Cohen's face, but Cohen said, "No, no, Ski. Take it easy, boy." Selfensky's whole body ached to have Cohen die or faint before he looked up and saw his legs.

"Two little Jew-boys gone astray, eh Lieutenant," Selfensky said and wondered if it sounded funny.

Cohen closed his eyes as blood started to bubble out of his nose down into them and Selfensky reached over and wiped them out. The eyes opened and were big and soft again.

Cohen started to sing and Selfensky couldn't place the words for awhile. Then he remembered the song. He'd learned it long ago at the synagogue and forgotten it. He started to sing softly with Cohen. Cohen sang beautifully, like a cantor. The words sounded big and glorious in the tank. It sounded like many voices singing. Selfensky felt that his voice was huge and powerful and a queer exultation seized him. He didn't know how long they sang, but gradually Cohen's voice became softer and then it stopped. Selfensky hated to look up because he knew that if Cohen's eyes were open and big and soft he'd go crazy. Finally he looked up and Cohen's eyelids were closed and there was a stream of blood from each nostril that ran out of his nose, across the eyelids, and into the dark hair. Selfensky reached out and took Cohen's cold hand and started to say the old Jewish prayer for death: ". . . . O, may death be an atonement for all the sins, iniquities, and transgressions of which I have been guilty before thee . . . ."

He was holding Cohen's hand and sitting in the same position when they came and cut the tank open with a welder's torch.

Fellows had just finished telling the correspondent about the show Horowitz had put on. How he'd dressed up a bunch of big Marines like women and brought them out as a chorus line.

"It was really a laugh," Fellows said. "Horowitz had cut coconuts in two and they wore them under brassieres. They did an awful dance and one big gook fell on his butt twice. Then one of them dropped a coconut out of his brassiere and it bounced on the deck and that really brought down the house. So they all started dropping them out on purpose and pretty soon the whole deck was covered with them. Horowitz was mad about that, but it sure made a good laugh."

Fellows was red-faced now; sweating a little. He had just enough whisky left in his cup to twirl around and he was waiting before he drank that. He kept thinking he wouldn't see any more for a long time. Fellows wished suddenly that he had a whole quart to start in on. He could drink forever and not get sick or sleepy; he'd just keep feeling better and better. The correspondent had an indifferent look on his face and they all knew this wasn't the kind of stuff he wanted to hear, but they didn't care.

The correspondent started to write in his note book again and Fellows could see the words: "Jewish boys in the Marines, famed for their entertainment on Broadway and in Hollywood, arrange musicals, shows, and other laugh-fests to keep America's finest fighting men relaxed between battles."

"Where does this Horowitz come from in the States?" the correspondent asked. "People like to read about where the boys come from."

"Oh, he came from Nebraska. His old man had a peanut farm or something out there," Selfensky answered.

"Not so good, Ski." The correspondent winked at Selfensky. "Jewish boys should come from Brooklyn or Chicago. Gives them more human interest."

The correspondent looked at the empty bottle and Selfensky could see that he was measuring the dope he had got against the whisky and feeling cheated.

"Any of you boys pick up any medals in these shows?" the correspondent asked, changing the subject rapidly. The Marines looked at one another for a second and then because they were feeling good they all started to laugh.

"Sure, we all got the Purple Heart," Fellows said.

The correspondent shook his head patiently. "No good, people expect Marines to have Purple Hearts. Any other medals aside from that?" His voice hung somewhere between irritation and patience.

"Yeah, Shannon there has a Silver Star and a Navy Cross. He's got so many medals that they had him go on a bond tour back in the States."

Shannon held back the good, loose feeling in his head and chest and grinned at the correspondent.

"That must have been a pretty fast life after being out here for a couple years. I'll bet you were anxious to get back to your outfit after all those cocktail parties and speeches by politicians," the correspondent said.

"No, I liked it. They sent me back right after Iwo and it

was swell. Lots of good food; I gained twenty pounds the first
month back. They always fixed me up with a date and I hadn't
been out with a girl for three years. Some of the girls still write
me. It was a hell of a lot of fun. Everyone was swell to me and
the workers at the plants would come up and ask questions about
their kids in the Corps and take me out to their homes for dinner.
I hated like hell to come back out." Shannon's grin had faded
to a serious smile and the other Marines were looking at him
oddly.

"I don't know, Shannon," the correspondent said. "What
would you say if I wrote you up as being more scared by the
speeches and the good-looking girls than you ever were on Iwo?
I'll put your name in it and it ought to make a good story.
People like that human-interest angle. What do you say?"

The correspondent was mildly excited about the new angle.
He didn't notice that the Marines were all quiet and they were
watching Shannon.

Shannon was not smiling now and he was trying to understand what the correspondent meant. His mind telescoped the
long hot months of training; the nights in combat he had urinated into his pants rather than look for the pit; the grease-
packed K-rations; the sleep that was not sleep, but unconscious-
ness; the Pfc who threw himself on a grenade that had been
dropped by accident and whose body jumped two feet into the
air and fell back a crumpled sack of khaki; the warm canteen
water that turned the dust in his throat into mud. All these his
mind telescoped into one experience. He laid it next to the
memories of the laughing girls and iced lemonade and the keen
exhilaration of three beers and the fragrant pork roasts and blue
water in country streams and the yellowing corn.

Shannon smiled uncertainly over his shoulder at Fellows.
He felt a sudden relief, for he could tell that Fellows knew what
the correspondent meant.

Fellows finished off his whisky and looked in the bottom of
the cup and put it on the table. He stood up and walked over in
front of the correspondent.

"Get out of here, you son-of-a-bitch," he said.

His voice sounded a little tired, but the words came like

cold drops of metal out of his mouth. The correspondent looked up startled and started to say something.

"Get out, you lousy bastard," Fellows said again.

His face wasn't red any more and there was even a little white around the nose. He wasn't the slightest bit drunk.

"Look old man, you don't understand . . . ." the correspondent started to say.

"Come on, bum, move on," Fellows said, and walked back to his chair.

Five minutes later the correspondent went into Lieutenant Terry's tent and said he was ready to go back to town. Terry looked at the correspondent and started to whistle.

"How did you make out?" he asked.

"So-so, they didn't have a hell of a lot to say. A little too prima-donnaish," the correspondent answered.

They went back down the road that overlooks the beautiful valley of Maui. As the sea came into view, sparkling and blue, Terry started to sing:

> There'll be no promotions,
> This side of the ocean,
> So cheer up my lads,
> Bless 'em all,
> Bless 'em all, bless 'em all,
> The long and the short and the tall. . . .

Maxwell Arnold

The Grapefruit Thinker

A ray from the sun that belongs to Los Angeles broke through the Sunday morning fog and bounced off a badminton court into the bedroom of a slick new bungalow in Beverlywood. It finished Jimmy's father with any extra sleep he had coming that morning, flashing an obbligato to a Fats Waller reveille.

There was a time the Waller racket might have been prevented. It had been a mistake all right to give Jimmy his own radio-phonograph, and a new Philco table model at that. All Jimmy had to do was lay a record in the turntable drawer and shove in the drawer to make the record play. Perhaps it was only in Los Angeles, where infancy is royal, that a four-year-old could have his own radio-phono to listen to Gene Kelly narrating *The Little Red Hen* or, if his childish taste ran precociously, to a dead Fats Waller playing *Your Feets Too Big*. In fact, Jimmy could play anything he wanted as long as he didn't monkey with the big console in the living room—which was the best idea about the Philco, because it kept Jimmy in his own room. Everyone had his own room: Jimmy, Jimmy's father, Jane; the console and the baby grand had the living room; Old Grandad and White Horse took the den, where a guest had a never-changing choice of them at an occasional cocktail party or a game of charades, and then Jane would also serve potato chips which she would tell a guest should be dipped in the cream cheese dish in the center of the tray. And a grand baroque toilet; an atomic blue kitchen; and a badminton court in the back of the house, exclusively operated by Jane and four or five of her old Tri Delt sisters from UCLA. Never could get Jimmy's father in a game because he preferred squash, which he hadn't played since he'd left Harvard. All this in Beverlywood, and all on pressure cookers. Jimmy's father was doing well with pressure cookers.

Jimmy's father sat up in bed and shivered through a simulated yawn, which he dropped when he heard Jane clatter on her beach clogs through the kitchen into Jimmy's room. He heard them talking loudly above Fats Waller, and he was pleased to hear her say that Jimmy would have to stop playing records because it was time to go to Sunday nursery.

"Please, Jane," he heard Jimmy say, and he still winced whenever he heard his son's fashionable use of his wife's name. Jimmy pleaded, "One more Fatsie."

"No more, Jimmy; we have to go now." This sounded final to Jimmy's father, but then he heard another record start and Fatsie began to holler that the joint was jumping, with a siren screaming when Fatsie hit the second verse.

The record stopped with a loud scratch and Jimmy's father heard Jane say, "That's all, now. Your father's trying to sleep." Jimmy's father thought she had been a little late with that advice, and now he heard them go through the living room to the front door.

"Jane!" he called.

The answer came sharply back to the bedroom. "What is it?"

"When are you coming back?"

"Right away."

"How about my breakfast?"

"I left some coffee on the stove and there's a grapefruit in the Kelvinator."

"Grapefruit?"

"Yes, a half a grapefruit. I couldn't get any oranges yesterday. Goodbye, dear."

"Goodbye, Daddy," Jimmy shouted, and the front door banged. Jimmy didn't call his father by his first name, since that really didn't seem just right, and Jane always said Dear, so Jimmy's father actually didn't have any name at home at all.

Jimmy's father got out of bed and dressed in some old

clothes in the bathroom, where it was warmer. He believed he
had never been so cold in a house in the East as he had been in
California, where they pretend it isn't cold by heating their
homes with nothing more than a gentle gas system.

He didn't care very much for grapefruit, either, and that
made him sore. He had lived in Los Angeles five years, ever
since he'd married Jane, and he'd been betrayed with more
canned orange juice and orangeade than he'd ever seen in all
his life in Rhode Island, and now here it was you couldn't even
buy an orange any more right where they grew them.

Besides, he didn't like losing out on his Sunday sleep, particularly since Jane had taken some more of it by talking late
in bed the night before. She'd even got around to God and,
what was worse, space, and she'd wondered if space was infinite.
Jimmy's father had said he thought it was in a way, but that
it was really spherical. "What do you mean, dear?" Jane had
asked. "Well, look at it this way. Suppose I gave you a tele-
scope which could see to the end of space and you looked through
it. What you'd see would be the back of your head." Jane had
thought that one over for a minute and then she'd said, "Isn't
that Einstein?" "Einstein?" "Sure," she'd said, "that sounds
like him. I remember him from college." He hadn't liked that,
because he hadn't known about Einstein at all. He'd thought it
out for himself, and now it was Einstein all the time who had
the idea. When he'd told her this she had said, "I always told
you you should have majored in philosophy." "That's physics."
"All right, physics. Well, goodnight, dear." "Okay, goodnight,"
he'd said, and had gone back to his own room at last.

He took the grapefruit from the Kelvinator and sat down at
the kitchen table to eat it. Jane said in California you don't
ever hear of anybody putting sugar on it, but he sprinkled it
heavily and scooped out a section. It wasn't too bad for a change.

He frowned and took another bite. Funny, the taste that it
had. There was none of the bitterness that always came, even
through the sugar. It had a soft, rich flavor, a kind of heavy,
exotic roundness. He stopped eating and suddenly, in a nostalgic
slide, he had the experience of smelling and tasting the past, of
feeling a rush of air of another time, the weather of a past place
and day. In a moment he knew it was Harvard, somewhere—
the Yard, playing touch football by the Charles, working at

poker in his rooms until early morning, Harvard Square, that last paper on Cardinal Wolsey, old Merriman, the ivy at Radcliffe and the lawns at Wellesley, the University Theater, a record booth in Briggs and Briggs, the marble at Widener, Huyler's—all in a sweep of memory, but still the smell and taste unrecaptured until he remembered the linen-covered tables in the dining room at Eliot House, and here he knew he had it exactly.

It was like Proust, but Proust had known the taste in his cake and had located it, and he couldn't. It was possible that the gastric juices and memory kept the same time on Cartesian clocks, but he didn't know what had started the works ticking. It was just a grapefruit, and there wasn't anything remarkable about that, except it had a different taste. He went on taking slow, careful mouthfuls, knowing there was something in the grapefruit that was different, but he couldn't find it. It wasn't *any* grapefruit; somehow it had got a taste of Harvard in it.

He went to the Kelvinator and took out another grapefruit and cut it. He dug out a spoonful, but this time it was only grapefruit. He wet his finger for a taste from the sugar bowl, but it was just sugar. He found nothing by sprinkling sugar on the new grapefruit; it was just sugar and grapefruit, and the other had been sugar and grapefruit and something else—a good taste, heavy and golden, something that belonged outside of a Beverlywood kitchen.

He inspected the rind of the grapefruit he had first eaten and the one he had just taken from the Kelvinator. Both Sunkist. Perhaps the half grapefruit lying in the Kelvinator had picked up a taste from something else in the box. He checked everything: beef, tomatoes, lettuce, celery, milk, cream, jello, carrots, a piece of Milky Way. It couldn't have been any of these and it was foolishness to try, but he took a taste of each, even scraping off some raw beef. It wasn't any of them. Yet he made certain and filled his mouth with grapefruit and sugar and added tastes of all the food. It didn't work; he hadn't found it.

He had a new idea and rushed back to the bathroom to squeeze a spot of toothpaste on his tongue, returning to the kitchen to swallow it with grapefruit. Squibbs and Sunkist: nothing.

He had exhausted the first run of experiments, and now he

believed he would have to sit down and think it out. It was unlikely that he could find a solution in taste combinations, and he sat at the kitchen table drinking his coffee, trying to resolve the problem mentally. Grapefruit plus sugar plus X equaled the Eliot House dining room. If the equation could not be filled with carrots, lettuce, jello or Squibbs, then perhaps the unknown quantity was environmental. But nothing worked there: there was nothing of Harvard in the kitchen, on the table, in the bed he had just left, in the bathroom where he'd dressed, in the old clothes he was wearing—none of these had been touched with a Harvard remembrance. Time wasn't X: not the hour, day, month, week; it wasn't weather—California's cold was nothing like Cambridge winter, or the colder days of late New England autumn . . . . or winter slowly dying in April.

X couldn't have been a dream the night before. He had had an easy dream, about capital stock in pressure cookers splitting and climbing, subsplitting and soaring. He hadn't read anything in a book before bed, and he hadn't had time for a book in months, anyway. It was in the grapefruit, the grapefruit, what the hell was there in that grapefruit?

X was in the grapefruit. He picked up the husk and squeezed a teaspoonful of juice from it. The same taste all over again, a flavor that belonged in a dining room six years ago.

He heard the Mercury roll into the driveway, and in another minute Jane, blond and pigtailed, clattered through the kitchen door.

"Poor darling," she said. "I'll fix you a nice breakfast now."

"Okay."

"What do you want? Bacon and eggs?"

"I guess so."

"Do you want a waffle too?"

He was poking a spoon into the grapefruit and didn't answer. He picked up the shell and squeezed juice into his spoon until the shell was torn.

"I asked you, dear, if you wanted a waffle too," Jane said.

"I don't think I want anything."

"You don't want anything? Do you feel all right, dear?"

"I'm okay." He licked the spoon for another taste of the grapefruit, but now there was only the taste of stainless steel.

"You must have liked that grapefruit," Jane said.

"It was good."

"I put some honey on it before I left."

He was tapping the spoon on his mouth, and it was a moment before he stopped and said, "You what?"

"I said I put some honey on it for you. You used to tell me they always gave you honey for your grapefruit at that place you ate in Harvard."

"For Christ's sake."

Jane watched him closely as he picked up the grapefruit and missed a toss to the garbage pail. "I guess the honey soaked in and you didn't see it," she said. "You'd better pick up that grapefruit before the ants get at it."

"Okay."

"And what are you doing with that other grapefruit? Why didn't you finish it?"

"For God's sake, let me alone a minute," he said. He put his head in his hands and scowled at the table.

"You don't have to be so nasty," Jane said.

"Maybe I do to get through that suntan of yours sometimes."

"What are you talking about?"

"Christ, let me alone, will you? Go call a Tri Delt and have a badminton party."

"What's the matter with you?"

"Nothing," he said. "I'm just thinking." He went to the cupboard and began to take out bottles and canned goods.

"Now wait a minute. Don't go messing up my kitchen." He was taking the caps off the bottles and sniffing catsup, mayonnaise, vinegar, and salad oil. "Please tell me what's going on," she said. "I never saw you act so crazy."

"That's right. If I told you, you'd say I was nuts, so forget it."

"Honestly, if you don't tell me what you're looking for . . . ."

"All right, but don't ask me anything more. I'm looking for the taste in the grapefruit."

"The what?"

"The grapefruit made me think of Harvard. It had a funny taste to it and I'm trying to find out what it was."

"But I told you about the honey. It was the honey."

"I know," he said, starting in with a can opener on some diced pineapple. "But that doesn't count. I'm forgetting about that."

"What do you mean it doesn't count? The honey, dear, the honey."

He set down the can of pineapple after taking a quick taste. "Look," he said, "you spoiled it. I had a nice problem I was working on and you spoiled it by telling me about the honey. Well, I'm not paying any attention to that because I can figure out the problem myself without any help from you. I'll get the same answer by working it out alone."

Jane took the grapefruit shell from the floor and dropped it in the garbage pail. His eyes followed her across the kitchen, and he said, "It's the scientific method. You never heard of that at UCLA, did you?"

"I never heard of what you're doing *any*where."

"Sure you never. All they taught you was badminton."

"And at Harvard you get the scientific method."

He didn't answer, and Jane turned around to watch him open a can of Del Monte peaches. When he put a slice in his mouth, adding grapefruit and sugar from another spoon, she said, "A Harvard man." He looked at her, his mouth full of peaches, grapefruit and sugar, and Jane said, "Of all the men in this town and I had to marry a Harvard man."

He got his mouthful down in two swallows. "*Town* is right," he said.

Richard K. Arnold

A Problem in Creation

Red was lying on the bed, fair-skinned and calm, unaware
of everything in the small room except the book she was reading.
Young decided he'd better do some concentrating himself. He
shuffled through the papers on the card table and pulled out
part of a story he was trying to rewrite. It was about a friend
who had met an accidental death in the Pacific, a thousand miles
from the nearest battle. This friend had been uneducated, and
yet had a fine, inquisitive mind. The problem was to get him
down in all his beauty. Yes, it was beauty, all right, because
there is usually something beautiful about the fated, and Earl
had certainly been fated. A biological sport, that's what he had
been. A freak of nature.

The way Earl had died was a mistake; it was a cheat. There
were too many unfair ways to die: live wires that waited for an
innocent touch; automobile steering wheels, just a fraction of
an inch wrong; boulders that crashed down onto mountain high-
ways from steep slopes; the suicide who hit you before he struck
the pavement; the ice in the driveway, the careless foot in the
bathtub, the bullet meant for someone else, the line drive into
the grandstand; the hair, the thread, the nail in the machinery—
all the erroneous deaths away from battlefields and contagious
hospitals; the ends joining, the jaws snapping ruthlessly shut in
the areas of peace and health, the areas of life, in the land of the
living. The petty deaths. You really had to be extremely careful with your life, but sometimes even the sharpest watchfulness
couldn't help, wouldn't make a single bit of difference.

With permission from *The Pacific Spectator*, Vol. I, No. 3, Autumn 1947. Copyright 1947 by
The Pacific Coast Committee for the Humanities of the American Council of Learned Societies.

So you were so beautiful but you had to die someday. Young tried to say the hell with it. Death was a subject you buried somewhere in the back of your mind, a thing you tucked away in a far corner of your subconscious and maybe just took out once in a while with morbid curiosity, the way a wounded man will sneak a look at a wide and deep gash in his leg even when he knows the sight will shock and horrify him.

Well, he really did have to think about death if he was going to write about it. His fingers did a nervous kind of tap dance on the typewriter keys without kicking the letters home. He paused to light a cigarette and smiled when he caught his wife's eye. Red smiled back.

"My Grand Baroque baby," Young said, as the memory of their argument drifted lightly back into his mind.

Red's hands made a gesture of tolerant impatience. "Oh, let's forget the silver. Give me a cigarette, will you, darling?"

Young tossed the pack and matches over onto the bed and felt a little irritated because, after all, Red had started that argument about the silver pattern, and Young thought that, since he was so blameless, he really had the right to remind her of it. But the irritation dissolved inside him. Red's hair had a nice soft shine under the bed lamp. Her eyes were warm and friendly as she smiled at him again.

"It's awfully quiet tonight, isn't it?" he said. Usually there was an unsteady hum this time of evening. The house was on a main street, their room faced the main street, and, then, too, their landlady's fourteen-year-old granddaughter invariably pounded the piano for a couple of hours. But tonight their room, the house, the neighborhood were hushed and still. It was so quiet that sometimes you could hear cigarette paper burning as you smoked.

"I guess Mrs. Bell and Jean went to a movie," Red said. She blew out cigarette smoke almost daintily.

"That's where we should have gone," Young said.

"What's the matter, baby? No luck on the story?"

"Oh, you know how Earl was. I can talk about him, but he's hard to get on paper. Like the tone of his voice." The way Earl had talked, and later the way Earl had slipped and fallen off the gangway right smack into the motor whaleboat became vivid to Young again. Death had come so fast, such a surprise. Just thinking about this filled Young with an anxious concern.

"Red, you're always careful, aren't you?"

Red looked puzzled. "How do you mean?"

"I mean, about crossing streets and when you drive the car and plug in the heater and things like that. All the things you do when I'm not around to watch you."

"You shouldn't worry about me, Young." Red's face was childlike and serene. Her voice seemed to try to be reassuring: "I can take good care of myself."

"No, you can't. I've seen you sometimes, seen you freeze right in the middle of traffic, and if I hadn't been there to yank you out of the way, you'd have been run over or something."

"You shouldn't worry like that," Red said, and half-smiled.

"Ah, Red, I just don't want to lose you, that's all. We've got to be careful about our lives."

"Well, I'm careful, silly." She got up from the bed and Young liked her long-legged walk over to him. She kissed him and said, "You shouldn't worry about things like that." Her tone was that of a gentle mother soothing a problematic but favorite child.

"I guess I've got death on the brain tonight," Young said. His fingers aimlessly tapped at the typewriter.

Red's eyes were warm as she put her cheek down against his. "I know. Sometimes I worry about you, too. But I don't want you to worry about me."

Young heard the front door of the house rattle, and then Mrs. Bell's voice, thin and old. Mrs. Bell never bothered them, and their room was pretty nice. The only trouble was sharing the bathroom, and even there it wouldn't have been so bad if the old lady didn't always forget to unlatch the door on their side when she was through.

Young patted his wife on the back of her legs and shuffled through the papers again. Red went back to the bed and lay down with her book. There was something young and touching about Red's legs. They were beautifully shaped, but they looked a little fragile and unsturdy, like a colt's legs. Her mouth fell open a little, and Young could see that she was back in the world of her book.

Young moved slowly back into the world of his story. The Bells had finished with the toilet and washbasin. He heard the latch unclick, and he could imagine the old woman crawling into bed with her granddaughter, and the granddaughter as far over on her side of the bed as she could manage, so that the old, dry flesh wouldn't touch her.

The boxed-in and fidgety feeling that Young had most of the time in small rooms gradually slipped away, and he felt as if he were back on a ship lying at anchorage in the Western Caro-lines. The smell of sweat drifted up onto deck from the troop compartments like the smell of spoiled food. A Pacific squall whipped across the sky dark and heavy and destructive-looking as a raid of locusts, and the sharp, transient rain drummed on the steel plating of the transport. The ship's radio oozed a female vocal of a Gershwin song, lazy and provocative, and from within his own quarters he could hear dice clacking on the surface of an acey-deucey board. Far off to starboard lay the humid, fertile, uninviting island—a green desert. And standing next to him at the rail on the sheltered outboard passageway was Earl, his face sad and resigned, his attitude humble, his eyes shy and true and perplexed, his mind searching and sensitive.

There he was, with that soft voice and that bright, unex-pected smile that transformed his features into the mold of a cocksure but benevolent conqueror.

There he was, and Young's fingers re-created him furiously. As Young wrote, he had the same feeling of the whole relation-ship as when he had lived it: Earl just had to die. It was in the cards, the stars; the soft voice and the sad face. Earl was the freak, the pawn, and he just had to die the kind of death that was insignificant in wartime. Earl had the qualities of a hero, but not on this planet. No, here and now, then on that summer day on the tail end of that civilized war, he had to be a fall guy. Raw of mind and big of heart and razor-edged of feeling, three thousand miles away from a woman he loved but didn't trust, Earl just had to go. Young had felt it then. He had seen it then and he was writing it now.

Young heard his wife's voice and stopped typing. He felt a little woozy and sick, as if he'd gone through a heavy physical workout.

"I'm going to bed," Red was saying. There were faint shadows under her eyes and she rubbed her hand against the back of her neck as she did when she was very tired. Her lips showed a touch of erotic pleasure. Young smiled at that look of the mouth and felt tender for all the nights it reminded him of.

"I'm going to stay up a little longer," he said, and his fingers lightly played an arpeggio on the Underwood.

Young was a little distracted as he went to work on another page. Red undressed over by the closet, and he looked up surreptitiously from time to time. He felt a tinge of paternalism at her slight, vulnerable shoulders; her lovely, tilted breasts—well, no paternalism there; the rib bones stuck out a bit, and he was protective again. Everything was slim, well-fashioned, but just a little bit fragile looking. Young felt touched and loving, and thought, Red, Red, please be careful when you cross a street. In her white cotton nightgown—prim and old-fashioned but warm and comfortable, he guessed—she was a child of twelve getting ready for bed in a Southern frame house.

"It's so quiet, isn't it?" Red said as she came by the card table and opened the bathroom door. In her slender hands she held soap, toothbrush and paste, brush and comb.

"Yes, it's quiet, all right. Unreal," Young said, and watched Red slip into the bathroom and close the door.

He thought of her standing in there, alone in that small, square space, that cubicle that was so tiny compared to the rest of the world. Such an insignificant amount of space and yet containing something tremendously important to him.

The water running in the bathroom pointed up and set off the silence in the room. It was like being in a grave near a waterfall. No, that was silly. What made him think of graves? And besides, it was the bathroom that was the grave. Bathrooms were places of dead things. They were where you rubbed dirt off your skin, lifeless, dead matter from living pores. Bathrooms were where you brushed old food from between your teeth, and killed living hair with the stroke of a razor. Life, decay; destruction, death. You urinated and excreted in bathrooms and flushed the death away. There were even things for paralyzing, drowning, and, finally, washing away, sperm; and those things were used in bathrooms, too. All you had to do was run the water in the basin, yank out the plug in the bathtub, and the death was disposed of. Yes, and rinse the toothbrush, scour the razor blade, launder the towels, sterilize the syringe. Bathrooms were efficient, well-equipped, compact mortuaries. In the bathroom there were few reminders of life. Maybe a strand or two on the hairbrush; maybe a fingerprint on a toothbrush; or the delicate mist of somebody's breath on the mirror.

Pretty thoughts. He felt a slight shiver inside himself, and got up from his chair and crossed the room to the bed. He smoked a cigarette and looked back at the table. The only light in the room spread over the card table from the floor lamp. The sheets of paper lay scattered and dimly shining around the typewriter. From where he sat, the paper looked blank. He shivered again when he looked at the chair he'd been sitting in, empty now. The glass dish on the arm of the chair was a sea of dull, gray ashes.

Young sat, almost transfixed. That night he had created a life of words on paper, but now as he looked at the patches of whiteness on the checkerboard surface, it was as if everything in the world were empty and dead.

He strained his eyes, but his eyes could see no words, no life. The scene was pitiless in its implications, for it seemed to say: Look at this. Here is your creation, here is a part of your existence, your brain, your guts; here is a section of you lying here like coffee stains on a tablecloth, an end product of living. And, look, no one walking through here, coming near here, would stop and examine the paper; no one would suspect that a life was lying on this table. No one could see that here—pressed and flat and cold—was a part of a human being.

Young knew that life stood out on those sheets of paper like a black rabbit in the snow. If you looked at the snow. If you put on your boots and walked in the snow.

The faucet squeaked in the bathroom, the latch clicked on the door. His wife tiptoed into the room.

"What's the matter, Young?" Red's eyes were disturbed as she looked at him.

"Come over here," Young said, softly.

She moved over to him and stood by the bed with her hand on his shoulder. The silence became a faint drone in Young's ears. The room seemed doomed and forsaken. Outside there was not a hint of busses or streetcars, trains or automobiles, of feet or paws.

"I was just imagining I was dead and looking at those papers over there," he said. "I don't know if I can tell you the way it felt."

Red's eyes were half-closed and her head was cocked as she stared at the table. Each sound of her breathing was like the passing of an hour, as if time itself were dying.

"Yes," she finally said, and her voice was very soft, "it *is* like death." Young watched her face. Her features looked drawn and rather old and Young could tell from her voice and the pale tightness of her cheeks that she had felt death, too.

His eyes slid back to the table.

"You know," he said, "from here it's almost as though the paper were blank. And as if there were nothing of me over there at all."

Red sat down on the bed next to him. She propped her elbow on one knee and cocked her head on her hand.

It was strange; it was overwhelming. Red was born and raised in the country, the Southern country with its slow, ebbing life, its black beans and cotton, its Christ. Young belonged to the Eastern and Northern city, with its quick lunches and its slash of movement, its high blood pressure and its pot of gold. They had different stock, different schools in their pasts, and not a friend in common. Their homes, their people, their cultures weren't at all alike. And yet he and Red had stumbled onto each other out of pure chance and then held on out of longing and need. And here in the same room they could both feel the same thing.

Red stirred, and Young saw tears in her eyes. The tears did not roll down her cheeks but swam massed and cloudy in her eyes.

She put her arms around Young, and he closed into them and held her very tight. Young knew that Red got the same feeling and emotion in this room as he had, the feeling of something he would never be able to tell anyone else. The fascination of the table scene fell from him. The sadness grew and lingered, intense and merciless.

"Young," she said, and he felt the moistness of her eyes

against his cheek, "I wish we could die at the same time. Sometimes I'm terribly afraid of dying, but if I knew you'd be with me, I don't think I would be."

"Aw, baby," he said and stroked her back gently. "Don't think about that. About you and me, I mean. Not that way."

"I can't help it." Red looked up at Young, her face lovely, fated, frightened. "Looking over at that table I could see how both of us would have to die, and I'm afraid."

"No, no. Don't be afraid."

He held her very close and felt her trembling. This was Red, and she was twenty-three and her growing had ended and now everything went down toward the grave, toward the anonymity, the nothing, from here on. He felt the sadness stick to his throat and in his stomach, and he knew the beauty of this girl that wasn't physical beauty at all, but the beauty of fatedness, realization, and need. Someone not wanting to be alone with death and decay, puzzled, frightened, crying.

He looked over her shoulder at the card table and thought how difficult it was to get even a fragment of such beauty onto the white blankness, to make the words stand out poised to live like a black rabbit in the snow. Young knew that mostly he could only hold the beauty and aliveness in his arms, and that in quiet rooms where you can hear the faintest quiver of your own nostrils, the paper will lie white and cold and pitiless.

Boris Ilyin

Down the Road a Piece

Where the Up-country begins in South Carolina there are rolling hills from which the gray topsoil has been eroded, leaving brick-red clay. In winter the clay shows starkly through the pale grass. There are not many houses. There are patches of woods—gray ghost woods. There are clay roads which in places have sunk below the level of the slopes over which they lead. The roads lead sometimes past small cotton patches with small, withered stalks from last year; lead past an occasional Negro cabin; past a winter-flooded creek which appears for a moment among the bare-branched underbrush of the draws. They lead over the slopes, cross other roads, dwindle into trails. The winter air is moist and cold, and the sun is distant.

During the war there were always troops in the area, on maneuvers. Long files of infantry, heads bent forward, moved along the roads; long convoys of heavy trucks, blunt-nosed and determined, ground between the files. In the intervals between their two-week problems the troops camped in the ghost woods, spilled over onto the bare hills. Their shelter tents were hung with drying laundry; their portable road signs were at every intersection, pointing; the smoke from their fires hung blue and moist, a few feet above the ground.

Toward evening, one day, a little boy came riding along one of the red clay roads, kicking continually with his heels at the ribs of his mule. He had on faded overalls with new blue patches at the knees, and a sweater under the overalls, and a knitted blue

With permission from *The Pacific Spectator*, Vol. IV, No. 1, Winter 1948. Copyright 1948 by The Pacific Coast Committee for the Humanities of the American Council of Learned Societies.

toboggan on his head, against the cold. He was playing a game, leaning over to one side and then to the other, slashing with a stick at the grass which grew out from the banks of the road. Now and then he held the stick like a gun, firing at pursuers. He was careful, though, not to slip off, and not to let the bulging gunnysack in front of him fall to the ground. His legs were not very long, and he was riding bareback. The mule clumped along without paying any attention to the boy's game, her neck bobbing up and down energetically on the upward slopes, her whole attitude businesslike and grown-up. She was going home; what went on on her back was of little importance.

At one of the bends in the road the boy came in sight of a soldier, who was walking in the same direction, hands in pockets. The soldier was long and thin, and his field jacket hung loose on him. He wore a helmet liner, but no pack and no rifle. He was walking slowly, staring at the ground, but after a while he turned, hearing the mule behind him, and stood still, head to one side, waiting for the mule to come up.

The boy held the stick over the withers, not like a gun, but like a whip now. He stared intently at the soldier as he rode up, and said "Howdy" faintly.

"Hello, kiddo," said the soldier.

The boy looked away a little, straightening the filled gunny-sack and frowning.

"Whoa!" he shouted to the mule sternly, tugging at the rope bridle. The mule threw its head up, showing pink eyeballs, but clumped slower, and the soldier began to walk alongside, tall and angular, taking loose-kneed strides.

"You got a fine animal there," said the soldier.

" 'Tis a mule," said the boy. "Whoa!" He glanced at the soldier timidly.

"You live around here, kiddo?"

"Down yonder," said the boy, pointing ahead.

"You like it down here?"

"I reckon."

The soldier walked along, hands in pockets, stooping a little, but looking up at the boy. His face under the round helmet liner looked very long and thin, and his eyes were light blue and whimsical, as if everything he said was teasing, and yet as if he were sad about something.

"Your old man a farmer?"

"Yeah. Yessir."

"What you got there in the sack?"

"Lightard."

"What?"

"It's lightard." The boy thought a moment. "For burnin' on the fire," he added, looking sideways at the soldier. The other nodded, not smiling.

"Are you in the infantry?" the boy asked.

"That's right. I guess you're in the cavalry, ain't you?"

The boy looked to see if the soldier were joking. "I'm aimin' to be in the parachutes when I get big," he said.

The man nodded, but he was looking down at the road now as he walked, pinching thoughtfully at the loose skin above his Adam's apple.

"Are you campin' out here someplace?" asked the boy.

"Yeah," said the soldier, looking down still. "What's your name, kiddo?"

"Jacks'n Cole."

"I got a kid back home about your age. How old are you, kiddo?"

"Nine goin' on ten."

"My kid is ten," said the soldier, pinching at his throat with long, rough-nailed fingers.

"I got a brother twelve," said Jackson. "How come you ain't totin' a rifle?"

The soldier looked up, grinning. "A what?" he said, "A raffle?"

Jackson dropped his eyes to the gunny sack, not replying. The soldier stopped grinning, except with his eyes.

"You mean a rifle. We got it nontactical for awhile. I'm off duty. I'm just taking a walk."

"You a machine gunner, maybe?" asked Jackson, fingering his stick. The soldier began to smile again. "I aim to be a machine gunner in the parachutes," said Jackson, forgetting the stranger and aiming with his stick into the distance.

They went up a short slope, and when they reached the crest the boy pointed to some scattered shelter tents which they could see in the valley to their left.

"Is that your camp there?"

"That's right," said the soldier, his eyes narrowing as he stared at the tents, lines forming around his eyes. The smoke from the campfires lay in streaks over the shallow, barren valley. The little figures of soldiers moved here and there.

"I guess you're goin' overseas soon, huh?"

"Maybe," said the soldier. "I guess so."

"I never seed a machine gun up close."

"Ride over with me and I'll show you one."

Jackson hesitated, then shook his head. "My pap won't let me go nigh the camps."

"Why's that?"

The boy shrugged his thin shoulders quickly. "He don' like to have no truck with soldiers," he replied. "Pap says stay away from the camps."

"Well, you do like your pap says, then."

They went on in silence for several minutes. The sun had just set, and a cold, wet breeze began to stir the faded grass. The smoke-pall in the valley began to change shape slowly.

"Yeah," said the soldier at last. "I got a kid just your age. I haven't seen him or his mother for over a year, now."

"Has he got a rifle? My brother got a rifle. I get to shoot it."

"No, he ain't got any rifle," said the soldier. "He lives in a city, in Pittsburgh."

"I been to Columbia oncet," said Jackson, lifting his head high and looking down the road. "There's my house yonder, in those trees."

The house was a white blur in the gray ghost-trees. Around the grove ran the bleak terraces of a cotton field, but the windows of the house were yellow with light. It was turning dusk, and the breeze was colder.

"It looks like a nice house," said the soldier.

"You could come and see us," said Jackson hesitantly.

"No thanks, kiddo. They don't let us go into the houses around here."

"Sure 'nuff? Why?"

"Just orders, kiddo. I'd like to come. I'd like to be inside a house."

"Maybe if you come my pap will let me go see the machine guns later."

But the soldier stopped and raised his hand a little. "I've got to be getting back. So long, kiddo."

Jackson turned and waved too, as the mule clumped on. The soldier looked again toward the lighted windows and buttoned the top button of his field jacket. The lights of the distant camp-fires were visible—tiny dilating dots. The breeze was a gusty wind, now, and the smoke-pall was gone from the valley.

Rhoda LeCocq

Behold a Pale Horse

They did not speak often during the ten-mile drive from
Gold City's courthouse to the ranch. The girl and her younger
brother sat in the back and their parents in front and they all
bounced up and down on the springs when the car hit a rut. The
boy bounced as if he enjoyed it, letting his fifteen-year-old body
go, muscles lax. The girl braced herself, shifting after each
bump to a tensely upright position.

She had prominent cheekbones and sun had tinged her skin
copper-tan. At eighteen her figure was almost as compact and
full as her mother's, but the blue eyes held an expression of
childlike trouble, confused and pleading. She stared out the
window at New Mexico's blue and amber spaces and twisted a
turquoise bracelet on one wrist until, beneath the bracelet, flesh
reddened with friction.

Her mouth quivered. "Mother," she said, "it's all my fault,
isn't it? I did everything wrong."

The woman turned. Deep quiet lay in her. "No, Evvy," she
answered in quick comfort. "You swore to tell the truth. You
couldn't say you saw his gun when you didn't."

"Gawddammit!" the man at the wheel mumbled. "They all
know Ray Poole packs a gun. Stupid sheepherders on that jury
don't know justice from a—from a sink hole. It wouldn't surprise me any if half of them didn't sneak into the mine right
after Poole. They sure sided with him every . . . ." Words
muttered off in his throat, an impotent personal thunder.

Dorothy Jeffers faced her husband. "Ralph," she began, "what does it mean exactly—'out on peace bond'?"

"It means he's free," he answered in a tone of pained derision. "For a month, they'll suspect him first if—if anything happens to us. After that—"

"Oh, Ralph!" she said, and the words came out on a weary sigh.

Again, they rode silently. The man drove fast, squinting at the sunlit road flecked with shiny mica. Dust swirled behind the wheels, hung in the hot dry air before it sifted down. When the road turned to the right and narrowed along the side of a gulch, Evelyn rolled down a window and now there was the smell of pine and juniper and piñon. She gazed up at a cloud drifting over the tip of the Sangre de Cristo range.

Ahead, the steep sides of the gulch bent outward to a valley. It was a wide oval valley like a copper coin grasped in the fist of the mountains—the tan rolling land and the green and tan wrinkled hills all around. The car stopped at a gate; the man leaned forward over the wheel so Brad could push past the seat, get out, and open the gate. A shaggy collie trotted across the yard, barking a welcome.

Brad said: "Hi, Ranger, hi," and jumped with a swagger on the running board. The collie ran alongside as the car rolled up before a low adobe house. The main section of the house had been built on a straight line, a creek flowing behind and a scattering of cottonwoods on each side of the creek; but one wing, of lighter adobe with large modern plate-glass windows, jutted out in an L, facing the highest mountain peaks.

"Go on in," the man said. "Your mother and I want to talk a minute."

In her own room, Evelyn removed a sport dress and hung it in the closet, and took down a pair of blue jeans from a hook. She tucked a white blouse inside the jeans, clipped a silver conch belt around her waist and then, seated on a footstool before the window, she pulled on Navajo moccasins. Her fingers quivered as they pushed at large beaten-silver buttons.

All the time she changed clothes, she could hear Brad's whistle in the kitchen, the tinny sound of the cookie jar cover

when he dropped it on the floor and the smaller clatter of replacement. The familiar sounds seemed to divide her mind:
one half, calm, usual—home, cookies, Brad's whistling; the
other half, the remembered strangeness of the courtroom.

She relived the scene. The walk to the witness stand; the
jury, men who usually doffed their hats on a Saturday morning
shopping expedition to Gold City, now seated, solemn and stolid,
in a double line; the judge behind the high bench. She sat, facing the courtroom's crowded rows. The faces were curious,
vaguely hostile, as if she, not Poole, were on trial. Poole, himself, was slouched in a chair at the foot of the witness box, flat
blue eyes intent in a red-veined face. His stubby legs were
spread wide, elbows propped on chair arms, hands gripped
together over his stomach where it pouched below the belt.
Evelyn stared at his hands.

Was it only a week before that those blunt fingers had reached
through their car window to grab keys from the ignition? She
could still see the keys, flashing around and around in a circle,
as Poole twirled them on a forefinger.

"Will you tell the jury the defendant's exact words when
he stopped your car?"

"Well, he said: 'I'm going to shoot the lousy lot of you'—
and then he swore. He acted insane."

"You'd done nothing to provoke this attack?"

"Nothing, nothing at all. Mother and Brad and I were just
driving up to the mine to bring dad's lunch pail. You see, that
morning, he forgot . . . . And then, when we came opposite
Mr. Poole's shack, he ran out in the road so we couldn't pass and
started yelling about dad ordering him off the property the day
before. And dad certainly had a right to order him away when
he hung around the mine and robbed—"

Another man was on his feet, crying: "Objection. The suspicions of the witness are irrelevant." Poole stared up at her.
His dull hateful gaze contained a threat.

"You will please restrict testimony to those facts seen and
heard by yourself, Miss Jeffers. Continue. Mr. Poole ran out
in the road, you say?"

"Yes, and he'd have shot us too, if mother hadn't shamed

him. Mother's so wonderful. She told him right out he was a coward, picking on two women and a boy. Brad didn't even have a gun."

"But Mr. Poole had one? He pulled a gun on you?"

"Well, he started to— He reached—"

"But you didn't actually see a gun?"

The jury leaning forward at her useless protest: "No, but his pocket bulged—"; the pleased sidewise grin on Poole's face, his slight nod of triumph. Again, she felt helpless, afraid, unable to believe that her testimony was not enough to convict.

In the kitchen, Brad's whistle broke off and she heard the whistle, softened, begin once more. She raised the window sash and leaned out. Her brother stood near the cottonwoods, back to the house, head turned toward a point across the valley.

She, too, watched a tongue of smoke rise in the luminous air. The smoke hung over the outer edge of western foothills, spread out, wisps scattering in the wind. Another puff from that chimney two miles away—and now the smoke seemed a pall, covering the brightness of descending sun with horror.

Evelyn climbed over the sill and ran to join Brad. "The smoke, Brad. The smoke! It's from Poole's cabin, isn't it? He's back, living there."

"Where'd you think he'd go?" Brad went on whistling, tunelessly.

How could Brad? she wondered. "But don't you remember?" she asked. "He said he'd get us all, later. He won't forget."

Brad nodded.

The quivering under her ribs began again, as it had when she first met Poole, and on the road a week past, and in the courtroom. "I hate the way he looks at me," she said.

Last week, she thought, there had been the sure expectation of relief. This time Thursday, this time day after tomorrow, Poole will be in jail for good. Now, when would it end? Would it always be like this? Over and over. Locking doors that had never been locked before. And the thick reminding smoke, dark across the valley . . . .

Sun glazed the mountain peaks and, disappearing, left a hot

scarlet streak in the sky threaded by vicious orange. Always
before, Evelyn had welcomed the cool arrival of night in the
valley. But now, dark seemed more terrifying than light. The
valley was a vast shelterless bowl in which she cringed while
night inserted a deadening thumb, pressing her to earth. She
could no longer see the smoke in the twilight. And this, oddly,
was more frightful. "Let's go in," she said.

At dinner, she began: "Dad. About Poole . . . ."
Her father laid down his fork with an air of studied patience.
"Evelyn! Once and for all, we'll not spend our lives rehashing
this episode. Poole'd like nothing better than our acting like
timid sheep. So, we go on as before, see? Nothing's changed.
The man's free. We can't do a thing about it."
"But Dad, I'm sure he'll try. He wants us out of here, and
he's not a man who forgets. Haven't you heard what he did to
Juan—?"
"More potatoes, Sis?" Brad thrust a gold-rimmed dish in
her hand. His eyes warned that she should know better than to
argue with dad in this mood. "Take it easy," Brad whispered.
"Can't believe everything the Mex say." Evelyn didn't answer.
Silently, she finished the meal.
Dinner over, her father and mother went into the side wing
living room and she and Brad cleaned up. Evelyn stacked the
dishes: glasses first, then silver, plates next. There was a window
over the sink and, hands busy in the dishpan, she peered out
past her own reflection in the glass. The cottonwoods were a
lighter blur against the night sky—and perhaps . . . . There!
Across the creek! Was someone standing there quietly, watching?
I'm a perfect target here in the light, she thought, and
could see a round hole in the smashed pane, the bullet coming
at her. She dropped a cup with a splash, reached for the shade
and yanked it to the sill. Her hand left a wet patch on the shade's
fawn-colored material.
"What'd you do that for?"
"I just wanted it down."
Brad tossed the dishtowel over one arm as he walked to
the back door. When his eyes had adjusted to darkness, he
reported: "There's no one in the yard, Evvy."

"Did I say there was?" She flung a handful of silver into the rack with an angry clatter.

Brad strolled to the cupboard and began stacking dry dishes on the shelves. "I don't get it," he remarked. "Your being this scared . . . ."

Moistness flushed under her lids. She bent her head over the pan. The water, grease-topped, undulated from the cup's splash, the silver's removal.

The water in the creek that day had flowed in smooth ripples between her fingers. She was Brad's age then, and they had recently moved here. A hot day, and it seemed the natural thing: to walk up the creek and strip off her clothes for a swim.

Until she glanced up from the shiny water and saw him standing on the far bank. His pudgy body leaned against a cottonwood trunk and the red-veined face looked swollen by an emotion she could not completely understand. The flat eyes inspected her nakedness, and she ran for a sheltering thicket, ran without quite knowing why panic reached so deep—and the water clung to her flesh with an oily caress.

Poole's eyes never lost their secret knowledge. She had glimpsed it again today. "Did you tell?" Hatred, and then triumph: "No, you'll not tell. You're afraid. But, if you speak . . . ."

"He'll kill me first," she said to Brad.

"Why?"

But how could she explain her fear? Now, as then, words refused to form. "Oh shut up, shut up, shut up!" she cried instead. "You're all so brave, you and Mother and Dad. I'm the only coward in the family, I guess."

Brad's arm came around her shoulder. "Lordy, sis, I didn't say that. Why, when we ran into the rattler last summer, you never turned a hair. Couldn't have shot straighter myself." He patted her shoulder. "That's what I don't get. Your being so rabbity about Poole."

"It's different," Evelyn said.

Daytimes, she found easier. In daylight, she could pretend no threat lay beneath the ordinary routine. Each morning, she dressed before the window, eyes trained to catch the first billow of smoke from Poole's cabin. Then, reassured, she said to herself: "He is there, so he cannot be here." She imagined his body, bent before the stove, lengths of wood in his hands to feed the flame.

She helped her mother with household chores: sweeping and dusting, the new curtains to be made for the living room. The sewing machine buzzed pleasantly through green material, and tiny ravelings of thread lay sprinkled on black and mustard colored Navajo rugs. Sun beat through wide windows but behind the three-foot adobe walls, she remained cool, secure, and quiet.

"Here, Evvy, my dear. Another curtain to hem. Shall I hang one and see how they'll look?"

"Yes, Mother. Yes, do."

Oh, the normality of it! Curtains and the smell of cake baking in the kitchen oven and her father and Brad clumping in on high-heeled boots of an evening . . . .

Her father would sit in the big leather chair near the stove, reading *Engineering Forum* or *Miner's Review*, while Brad squatted crosslegged before the gun rack busy with a rifle to be cleaned. In the lamplight, the beamed ceiling was a shadow-study in geometry which Evelyn, lying on the window seat, traced with her eyes. Or she would move lazily to the bookshelves near the windows to read a page here and there. But, always, evening passed and she must go, alone, to her room.

The night belonged to Poole.

He was an immense, squatting, evil presence outside dark windows. He was a peering toad with gimlet eyes that saw through the night. He was remembered whispers in a schoolyard: "They say— They say— A Mexican sheepherder named Juan used to work for Poole. He tried to quit and that year he didn't return from the mountains. He never came back at all. Ashes and bones, that's all they found. Poole said: an accident, the stove . . . ."

"But how do you know he lied?"

"The padlock. Ssh—the padlock. Who placed the padlock on the *outside* of the door?"

And now she swam, creek water cool against naked flesh.

And she looked up and the water turned to hard green scum, stinking under the sun. And running, running, she reached— not the shore but the cabin. And the door was locked from the outside while flames rose all around and Poole grinned through a window, full lips back from rotting teeth.

Awake, nightgown damp with sweat, she crouched beneath the blankets, arguing with herself: Father says it is all right, that Poole was frightened off by being hailed into court. Father knows, doesn't he? It is only rumor that Poole killed Juan; with us, he would not dare. Wouldn't he? How do you know he is not outside now, right now?

Sometimes her mother entered the room, her mother so calm and unafraid.

"Evvy, darling, your window. You forgot to open it."

When her mother left, she would run, barefooted, to lower the bedroom window again and push the blind more securely against the glass.

In spite of herself, she asked once: "Dad, does adobe burn?"

"No, why?

Catching the glance between her father and mother, she knew additional shame that they might guess her terror. "Oh, I only wondered."

Her cheekbones became more distinct; the oval of her face narrowed; beneath blue eyes, dim grey circles appeared in paling flesh. She was dismayed when her mother noticed.

"You're not in the sun enough, lately. We've worked too hard on the curtains. Why don't you go for a ride, Evvy? The mare needs exercise."

"No, Mother, really I'd rather not. I love helping." And, evasively, "Besides, next week I'll be out all the time. Dad's ready to dynamite the land."

Every fall, before she and Brad returned to school, they shared the rite of loosening the earth with dynamite so the fields became a rich welcoming cradle for the seeds. This autumn, more than any preceding, Evelyn enjoyed the shared labor.

From a tiny shed near the barn, they carried yellow-jacket dynamite; and her father cut carefully through greasy yellow

paper, sawing each explosive candle in half before she and
Brad attached caps, fuse lengths, and buried the sticks in the
hard-packed earth.

They worked cautiously, as taught, until, behind the house,
a wide swath of newly turned ground stretched dark under the
sun. The acrid odor of dynamite tickled Evelyn's nose. As they
finished placing a stick near the fence, her father lit the fuse
and they all ran to stand behind the barn while it exploded.

Evelyn peeked around the corner. The kitchen door bounced
open suddenly and Ranger dashed down the steps and across
the yard.

"Ranger!" Brad yelled and started away from the barn's
shelter.

"Get back!" her father ordered. He hauled Brad behind
the barn again.

"But you know Ranger's crazy about dynamite . . . ."
Brad began excitedly. Then, he began to whistle and call to
the dog.

Evelyn felt screams rise in her throat as the dog ignored Brad
and reached the earth where the fuse burned lower. He scratched
at the round pit in which the half-stick of dynamite lay.

On a muffled "pfum," the charge went off. Dirt sprayed
upward, the dog's body flung twenty feet in the air with the dirt,
and Evelyn's screams followed Ranger's slow rise. All the
smothered screams of the night poured out now, as if she greeted
her own death.

The dog fell, feet downward; and, when he landed, his paws
tore again at the earth as if they had never parted from it. Evelyn continued to scream.

"It's all right, Evvy, all right," her father soothed. "Ranger's
okay. That dirt's hard as adobe, protected him from the blast.
Evvy! Stop now. Quit that!"

At last, she grew calm again. Strangely, calmer than before.
She could laugh at Ranger's mishap with the rest of the family;
and for many days, the dog's miraculous escape furnished
dinner-table conversation.

More than a month had passed now, and sometimes Evelyn
neglected the morning ritual of dressing before the window,

watching for the first smoke to the west. Gradually, her dreams occurred with less frequency. She told herself fear would disappear entirely. Poole's image had haunted her before and vanished. Now, it would fade again. Nothing could happen now. Nothing had happened. None of the family had glimpsed Poole in this month. He was keeping out of their way.

Then, one night, Ranger began to bark. The four of them sat in the living room, listening. Ranger's husky-throated chase went from back porch to creek and beyond. Evelyn's book dropped in her lap; her mother's knitting needles poised in the air. Over the rim of study table, Brad and her father watched each other.

"Want me to take a look, Dad?"

Her father nodded.

Evelyn jumped to her feet and reached the rifle rack before Brad. "Let me go." Her mother leaned forward in her chair. No, don't stop me, Evelyn protested silently, and loaded the gun.

"All right." Her father spoke in a tone of gentle approval. "Go ahead, Evvy."

Rifle cradled against hip, she stepped out on the porch. But, the door shut behind her, courage evaporated. She had been wrong. Poole was not gone. He lurked in the darkness, a ghost-ugly shape, hovered around the corner of the house, in the deeper night cast by the barn's roof. She fled over the open stretch between house and creek. The moon, in its last quarter, shed cold light over the land, trickled in pale flecks of shadow through the cottonwood branches. Behind the cover of a tree trunk, she paused, gasping.

Now she was alone. Alone, against Poole. She had been a fool to be lulled by a false sense of security. He had only waited to strike. She could sense his eyes on her, searching, sneering. He knew. He gloated over her fear. Her heart beat in staggered tempo like a worn-out metronome, and Poole played the tune as he pleased, directing the time.

Beyond the fence, she could make out Ranger's blond hide glimmering light against newly dynamited earth. His voice a combination of frenzied barks and worried growls, he pointed

his muzzle to a mesquite thicket. So, Poole? Is that where
you hide?

She raised the rifle and sighted down the barrel. Her arm
and hand ached with the gun's weight. A slow uncontrollable
tremor traveled up her muscles and she rested the gun on a
fence post.

Now! Now he must reveal himself. He'll walk from the
thicket. He'll stare into the moonlight. His nasty dull eyes will
look straight at me—

And I will be unable to shoot!

Her body sagged against rough split wood. The rifle slid
along the fence until the stock hit the ground and the barrel
pointed in a crooked, powerless slant toward the sky. She
waited without pretense. It was all inevitable. Poole would
shoot. She could not. For Poole had won, long ago, when the
threat in his eyes had silenced her tongue.

How much did it hurt—to die?

Ranger raced from the thicket and she clutched a fence post
in both hands. The dog barked wildly, zigzagged over the field
after a small leaping animal. For a moment, she disbelieved.
That she was alive. That Poole did not stand there in the
menacing moonlight.

Then, she wept. She did not think. There seemed nothing
left to think. Exhausted, she rested there, sobbing. Finally,
she wiped her face on an edge of blouse and picked up the gun.
She walked back toward the house, moving as if leg tendons
were sore and stiff. As she passed the back porch, the kitchen
door closed softly. Her father? Brad? One of them had
watched, then, realizing better than she that she could not be
trusted to face danger.

"Well?" her father asked from the kitchen doorway, when
she entered by the front.

"A rabbit." Unable to endure further pretense, she excused
herself and went to bed. There, ashamed, hating herself for this
final defeat, she huddled under the blankets. Window and blind
were tight closed again.

On the following morning, Ranger disappeared. All day,
intermittently, they searched the ranch. Her mother suggested

the dog had chased the rabbit into the hills. "Never fear, he'll show up when he's hungry."

But, in late afternoon, when the dog still failed to appear, Brad saddled up and galloped across the valley for a last hunt. Long red shadows warmed the mountain peaks before he returned, Ranger's body over the saddle.

"What got him?" Her father's voice sounded strained.

Brad shook his head, unable to speak. His face was frankly tear-stained. He lowered the dog to the ground. The collie's eyes were rolled back, whites empty of veins; his tongue hung out. An ashen froth caked on his muzzle. "Found him—west of the valley," Brad said finally.

"Poole!" Evelyn said and stepped nearer her mother.

"Couldn't it be the dynamite the other day?" her mother insisted. "An internal injury, perhaps, that affected him later."

"Or poison," her father muttered. "We'll drive to town tomorrow—see about a new dog."

When they reached the general store the next morning, Poole's pickup truck was parked in front. Her mother glanced at it and then at her father.

"We have to meet sometime," her father said.

When they walked in, Poole stood at the counter. One wooden carton was already stacked high with provisions; the clerk staggered from the storeroom carrying an armload of red-jacket dynamite.

"Sure you want this, not yellow-jacket?" the clerk asked Poole. "Red-jacket's mighty powerful."

"Only thing'll dent that clay around my shack," Poole said. "Pack it up, while I dump this stuff in the car." He picked up the heavy wooden carton. Then, as he turned, his hands slipped from the corners. The carton smashed to the floor. Her father jumped aside before it hit his feet.

Poole looked up as if seeing them for the first time.

"What do you think you're doing?" her father said. His face tightened as he stared at Poole.

Poole grinned. "Now, look, Jeffers," he said. "An accident's an accident. I don't bear no grudge."

"No?"

Poole packed spilled groceries back into the carton and set
it carefully back on the counter. He handed the clerk a dripping sack. "Best git me 'nother dozen eggs," he ordered and,
turning to her father: "Stand to reason, Jeffers, I'll break eggs
just to step on your toes?" He shifted the rim of his hat in his
hands. "Look," he went on. "What say we call it quits? Country's too big—not enough neighbors hereabouts—for bad blood,
huh?"

"Well—" Her father's tone was noncommittal.

"Now, that's real big of Ray," the clerk put in. "Plenty of
folks hereabouts figure you weren't neighborly, orderin' him off
your property, Jeffers. Ray had cause for anger, and he ain't
usually a man to forget. Don't seem right, you goin' around
lookin' for injury, Jeffers."

Her father glanced toward her mother.

"Sorry we had that set-to, ma'am," Poole added hastily.
"Wasn't thinkin' straight that day, looks like."

"All right," her mother agreed, "I accept your apology."

No, no, don't believe him, Evelyn thought. Poole's gratified
smile increased her terror, the thick lips parted over decay-
browned teeth. What is he planning now? Why does he shake
my father's hand as if he is our friend?

"And the little lady—all forgiven?" Evelyn realized he
spoke to her. She stared into his eyes, looked away, shuddering.
Her mother's expression urged her to answer. Somehow, she
nodded. As they left the store, her body burned as if coated by
creek scum hardened in the sun.

"Dad, Dad, I hate him so," she whispered and began to cry.

Her father's face looked tired. He backed the car into the
road, scraping gears as he shifted. When he spoke, he spoke to
her mother and his voice held a helpless note: "What can a man
do?"

"Don't, Ralph," her mother said. "We're not complaining.
You've done all any man could." She glanced sharply at Evelyn.
"Pull yourself together," she instructed. "None of us trust
Poole, but maybe he was sincere today. In any case, the town's
with him, and we must try not to antagonize the man further."

Evelyn tried to obey, but even by dusk she could not settle

down. She moved restlessly from pot-bellied stove to book-shelves, from chair to window seat, as night closed in. Brad seemed uneasy, too. His jaw set mournfully and he turned his head now and then, as if listening for the pad-pad of a dog's feet or the scratch of claws on a door.

"How long before we get a new pup, Dad?"

"Maybe a week."

Brad settled down, finally, to greasing a pair of boots.

The night seemed so silent. Only the sighing of wind around house corners, the rustle of her father's newspaper, the click of knitting needles.

"I'll tell you what," her mother said in forced brightness. "Let's play hearts, the four of us." She took a card deck from a table drawer and began pushing extra chairs into a neat square around the table. Brad bestowed a final stroke on the toe of the boots and sat down. Evelyn closed her book and strolled from window seat to table, sat facing the long row of windows.

"Deal," her father said. "I'll be with you, soon as I put another chunk of wood on the fire." He bent over the wood basket behind the stove.

From across the room, there was a small scuffling sound, as if something, or someone, scraped against the adobe wall outside. Her mother came around the table, body between Evelyn and Brad and the windows. "What was that?"

Her father stood up. "Where?" Evelyn heard him say.

And then there was nothing—nothing but the echo of the word, blazing in pinwheels. "Where? Where?" The word called and she followed, swimming down a river in space. The rush of air against her face—the river, billowing. It swept her onward and she traveled with the current to catch the word—"Where? Where?" This must be death: the single echo of a word in the silence, the bright warm river . . . . And herself, floating clean and light upon its surface. It pressed against her chest, the silence, and the word skimmed down the river and speared her heart. She tore at it, and now there was pain and she was surprised. Pain? When she was a dead star of silence sinking to quiet depths that muffled fear . . . .

Evelyn opened her eyes, stared up at the stars where the

roof gaped open like a torn tin can. The weight still lay on her chest but pain moved to her hands. She held them up and saw they were real and that a tiny dribble of blood ran down the palms. The skin shone ruddily and she moved her head to the right.

Hot coals burned sluggishly into splintered floorboards where the pot-bellied stove was overturned. The windowed wall was gone and the window seat where she had lain, reading, a short time ago. The thick adobe wall had blasted inward, a mass of bricks and powdered dust, and shattered glass stuck in overturned furniture like sharp bright daggers. A familiar acrid odor stung her nose. Dynamite.

A face was bending over her. With difficulty, Evelyn recognized her father beneath the black soot coating his skin. He struggled with the weight on her chest, a fragment of ceiling plaster, and then she could breathe again. She lifted herself on an elbow.

The porch door was open and Brad was seated in the same chair that had been at the table. He sat there, head in his hands; and, all at once it seemed so odd, she must laugh. A door in one wall and no other whole walls or roof, and Brad, blasted chair and all onto the porch. She knew she laughed because the laughter hurt her chest, but there was no sound. No sound at all— except a strange deaf ringing in the ears like a bell tolling far away, clapper muffled in cheesecloth.

Her father tugged at her arm, pointed toward the porch. She staggered outside, gulping air; and then she saw her mother at the foot of the stairs. The scream ripped in her throat, but she could not tell when it came out. She stooped down and her mother's eyes rolled weakly upward. Tears coursed in white channels through the soot on her cheeks.

She is alive, Evelyn thought, and the thought was a miracle. Glass stuck in sharp reddening spears along her mother's arms and legs, in her throat and face—tiny needles of glass in a human pincushion. She plucked at a sliver with her fingernails. Her mother's head shook once, slowly, and Evelyn realized the glass must remain or the skin, like a sieve, would release the life's blood.

Brad and her father arrived, carrying a rug. They laid it beside her mother and began moving her, gently, into its folds. Her mother's eyes focused on Evelyn, a question in them.

"I'm all right." Evelyn formed the words with her lips. And, as she spoke into the smoke-filled night, she knew she had spoken the truth. Silent, quiet strength poured into her. On steady feet, she ran to the kitchen, found a pan and filled it with water. Back and forth she went, from kitchen faucet to hot coals eating the floor, until the fire was drenched.

Still moving in new assurance, she rushed to the porch. Her father and Brad had started across the yard, but she had time. Behind her strength, now, inspiring it, she felt anger such as she had never known before. Hard anger, with a knot in it. She longed for Poole to walk from the shadows. She could move toward him, unafraid. Kill him with her own hands, smother the life from his pudgy body and feel no emotion at all.

She ran to the back of the house. Yes, here at the foundations he had placed the dynamite. A piece of scorched paper blew across the yard and she caught it. Red, shiny red in the moonlight. The store clerk would remember selling red-jacket dynamite to Poole. But was that enough? When she re-entered the courtroom, no doubt must remain. Evidence must convict Poole.

Headlights cut around in a wide swath. The beam lit a shape near the fence and Evelyn caught her breath, then stumbled across soft earth. Poole, head twisted to the side, lay where he had fallen. Around a fence bar, broken reins hung in a loop, witness to Poole's miscalculation: a dynamite charge and a skittish horse.

She watched him uncertainly. His chest heaved on a breath but he did not rouse. So easy, get his gun, shoot. But, there on the ground, unconscious, Poole was only a fat little man whom she neither feared nor hated. Insane violence had brought him here at last, at her feet, dependent upon her mercy.

The headlights swerved again. She could not remain, wondering what to do. She took a hesitant step away and her feet sank into loose earth. She glanced about. Poole, too, must have left a trail. Stooping, she began to untie the laces of one shoe.

The laces tangled but then she had them free, his shoe pulled off. He stirred. Evelyn raced for the car, shoe clasped to her chest.

They had laid her mother in the back seat and Evelyn huddled on the floor beside her. She felt quiet and triumphant. Somehow, she knew her mother would live and Poole would be punished for this suffering. He could not escape; the shoe promised retribution. Even if he regained consciousness before the sheriff arrived, he must flee like a hobbled horse across the plain. Wherever he sought sanctuary, fear would hover outside dark windows.

Her mother's lips moved in the starlight and Evelyn leaned down. "Everything's fine," she whispered, although no one could hear. But a faint smile came upon her mother's lips, a trusting smile. And Evelyn held the body of her mother in her arms; and all the way to the hospital, when they hit the ruts, she guarded her mother's body against the pain.

John A. Lynch

The Fields of Wheat

Riding up through Michigan one day, a man said to Eddie,
"Why, they're like a symbol, you know. The fields of wheat.
Like peace on earth, I guess."

Eddie looked out the window of the truck and saw the fields
stretching away at either side of the road. Along a path a child
and a dog romped, in the direction of a clapboard house, and
farther away a reaper moved through the wheat, cutting it, for
the harvest.

There were ditches along the road, and in the ditches dust-
choked weeds grew. There were fences beyond the ditches, wire
fences, held up at intervals by gnawed and weather-lined posts.
And beyond the fences he saw the fields stretching away.

He had come up from a dry river bottom once into a field
such as these were. There had been no fence, though, only a low,
cracked perimeter of plowed-up soil, and it had been in a far away
place, and, it seemed, a long time ago. They had been hungry
then, tired, and thirsty. As soon as the first men had edged into
the field, following a deep-worn path that seemed to know no
direction, but wandered at its own ease through the wheat, the
men had begun to reach out and strip the still-unripe grain from
the stalks. They rubbed the loose bits of wheat between their
palms then, breaking off the husks. They blew the chaff away,
holding their cupped palms upward, and they ate the grains of
wheat.

They drank from their canteens, the last bit of water there

With permission from *The University of Kansas City Review*, Vol. 16, No. 3, 1950. Copyright
1950 by the University of Kansas City.

was, and they lay down beside the path and stretched out in the
hot sun to rest. There was no shade in the wheat, only the sun,
and after a while they began to crawl on their bellies through the
grain and they began to dig with their shovels and picks and
knives into the soil that was hard but still a little cool. They dug
in the soil slowly, stopping now and then to bend down the stalks
of wheat and strip the grains into their palms and eat them, tasting
the mealiness of the wheat.

They lay there an hour and the sun moved very little. From
time to time one would say, "Why can't we get on?" but there was
no answer. Only that they were there and they would remain
there until told to move forward. A man came back from a patrol,
walking upright through the wheat, to say that there was a woods
ahead a half-mile, but it was across a road and on the road he had
seen the bodies of men, and they couldn't get beyond for some
time. We are waiting for rations, he said, and for water, and for
the sun to go down.

The men crawled farther through the field of grain and lay
in the hot sun and waited. All over the field could be heard the
rasp and crunch of shovels digging in the hard earth, the clunk
of picks. Then a man came crawling up from the rear and said
there was a man there who could not stand it much longer. Well,
tell him, the sergeant said, tell him, for God's sake, to lie on his
stomach, and keep his helmet on. Don't let him take his helmet
off, whatever he does. And stay with him, keep an eye on him.

A man came by on his hands and knees and said, "Why don't
they shoot? They know we are here, what are they waiting for?"
"Yes," someone said, "why don't they shoot?"

They lay there another hour and watched the sun. It had
moved a little farther across the sky, going down now, but beneath it the heat mounted and increased, and there was no water
to relieve it. "Well, I'm going to sleep," a man said. "I don't
care what you guys do. I'm going to sleep and you can wake me
when they make up their minds." He had dug a shallow hole in
the earth, half as long as his body, and he rolled into this on his
back, stretching out, so that his legs lay on the ground above. He
pulled his helmet down over his eyes, the steel edge of it resting
on the bridge of his nose, and he pretended to sleep. The others
watched him, and they knew that he only pretended. But they said
that they would wake him, they gave him that satisfaction.

It was much quieter than it had been, the men were settling down, and no longer could there be heard the shovels and the picks digging at the earth, for the men had all found in one way or another that they had dug deep enough. They lay in the sun, first on their stomachs, then on their backs, then curled up on their sides. They uncapped their empty canteens and felt that the metal lips of them were hot from the sun. They stripped the heads from the wheat and ate the grains, rolling them in their palms and blowing the chaff away with a little puff. A man began to clean his rifle.

The sun moved farther down the sky, but its work was done, and it didn't seem to make any difference one way or another now. A stretcher came by, a man at either end struggling to hold it up. There were no sounds from the man they carried, and his face was gray, as if they had waited too long. "Don't ask me, ask him," the man in the lead said, looking at the ashen face rolled to its side on the canvas. "We're taking him to the river," the other said. "I think he's done." They picked the stretcher up, heaving it forward, and a man behind got to his knees and said, "I want to go, too." He was red-faced and he got to his feet heavily, dragging himself, leaving his shovel and his rifle behind.

The others lay in the field, and far off to the left they heard the first sharp chatter of a machine gun. It came suddenly, a flash of sound, but they heard it as if they had been waiting for it for a long time. A man let his breath out audibly. "Theirs," someone said. Nearer, another gun answered, a little slower, and an echo came back from the woods ahead, very light, but distinct, the four quick beats. A man whose rifle was apart began quickly to assemble it. The guns sounded once more, the ripping one, the slower one. Then they did not sound again. The men settled back on the ground, in their holes and beside them, and waited.

Shortly after dusk the first shells began, and the men got up and moved out of the field, and went on.

He remembered a time two years later, in the East, when it was over and they had got together, several of them, and begun to recount the impetuous things, the odd, the mock-heroic, and something of the terror and the fright. They had last met in the South, when their training cycle broke and they had gone separate ways, promising to keep in touch, and some day, God willing, to meet again. They had said it gravely then, shaking hands several times before they would let up. And then, more lightly, with a laugh: "Keep your head down. See you!"

They met at the house of one of them, and talked of the days they had been apart, where each of them had been, the things that they had seen. They laughed a little, talked easily, and now and then they spoke a name and someone said, "No, I hear he's dead."

They had been to foreign lands and spoke of them, the cities, towns, the rivers, remembered for the hundred different things that happened there. They told of a harbor at night, the stillness, and the slide of ships through black water. They told of beaches, and the men moving up like ants across impassable sand, but passing. The times, the places, remembered for what happened, and, too, for what did not. They told of a road into a forest, a canopy of trees, and of a shelling suffered there. One spoke of a time in a shattered, homeless village, and another said, finally, "There was this wheat field . . . ."

"I think I could have helped a man," he said, "but he was way in deep, and it was night. Then I got cut off and I lay there in a ditch, beside the field, and they passed so close to me I could have touched them. It was like being hunted.

"They knew that we were there and they were looking for us. I lay there a long time, and when they finally went away I heard him call. It was so dark you couldn't see anything, and when I went out I couldn't find him. I walked a long time, hearing him, but I couldn't find him."

They could all remember it, for they had known it in degree, the time, the night, the fear, the sense of bewilderment and being lost. The man who could not run and fell behind, the man who hugged the earth and crawled a thousand yards, finding his way out. The field where bullets clipped the wheat and sought the men, back and forth, methodically, from unseen guns, until the gunners tired and turned to somewhere else. The voices heard in darkness, calling out of a depth of wheat, but giving up no sign, no indication of direction, and the final abandonment to night: remembered for a hundred things.

"There was this wheat field . . . ."

He knew a time when they had tasted abjectness, when they had been gathered into a wide valley to wait for the day that they should be sent to the front. They came in at night, driving in trucks through the rain, climbing down in a field where they could not see thirty feet, and hearing orders shouted from one place to another but not seeing the men who gave them. Now and then a light flashed and someone swore to put it out, and the light went out and there was only the blackness and the constant shuffling and slopping of feet in the rain, and then they had huddled in some sort of formation and started to march. They went for a while on a hard, paved road and the men stamped the mud from their shoes as they walked, and then they entered the mud again.

By dawn they had come into the center of the valley, where the listing, the classifying, and the herding of ten thousand men went on, and here they were swallowed up. They drew rations the first day and exchanged their clothes and drew their rifles and went to their tents to clean them. From then on they gathered in long lines to eat, in long lines to be inspected. They slept ten in each tent, but on the road they were thousands. They were within thirty miles of the front, and every day a few were siphoned off and sent away in trucks, and every night a few more came in to replace them, to fill their positions in the long lines and in the tents.

They were sent on marches, and when they came back they gathered in long lines to take a shower, and at night went out again to march. They dug defense positions along a river, and when they had finished, they went somewhere else and dug again. They sat in a field and listened to the sound of captured guns, the crack of bullets six feet overhead. And once in a while a man was killed, and everywhere a lecture on security went out.

In the lowest part of the valley the fields were a foot deep with clover, and the men worked at tactics here. If there was a house, they scouted it, approached it, surrounded it, and demolished it with dummy rounds. If it were a road, they flanked it, cut it, saved its bridges, and possessed it.

They went into higher ground and there worked among the orchards and the fields of wheat, taking cover, seeking positions of offense, attacking in formation, creeping down the paths.

They attacked a farmer's house one day, and through his

fields they left circuitous trails of broken wheat. The men came six at a time, crouching, running, stopping, attacking, sometimes taking the trails already made, sometimes striking out new ones. The farmer stood by and watched and could do nothing. Behind the men, orders were shouted, directing them how to run, how to fall, how to set up their guns.

When they were finished, they gathered on a knoll above the fields, and they looked back on the damage they had done. "That's war," one said, laughing, and lying back to smoke a cigarette. But many of the others felt badly, and they watched as the farmer went out and walked along the paths and tried to make the broken wheat stand up again.

Beyond the field they could see the green clover, the roads, the tents, and far beyond them the other side of the valley. And everywhere they looked they could see the men like themselves who had come in at night and who would go out by day, a little at a time, the replacements.

They marched on the roads in solid, square-cut formations; they exercised in the fields in wide-armed precision; they sat in groups and listened; they stood in long, identical lines to receive identical items of issue. One group of men looked just like another, and when they had moved about and interchanged positions, they seemed not to have moved at all.

"If you stood us all in rows, we'd look just like the wheat," a man said. Some of them laughed, and others kept silent. They watched the farmer in his trampled fields, and, beyond, the men who marched and moved from one end of the valley to the other, all of a purpose.

There were the dusty weeds, the fences held up by weathered posts, and the fields stretching away, the child and the dog, and the reaper moving near them.

"They're like a symbol," the man said, away with his own thoughts, riding up through Michigan, looking out at the fields of wheat.

Jean Powell

The Lady Walks

It was early afternoon. The last hovering wisps of brown fog
had scattered and dissolved, and as the two heavy glass doors of
the clinic swung out and back they glittered, riddled with sunlight. Ravita gazed at them with a feeling which was almost
exultation. She would pass through those doors once more and,
after today, Time with the empty eyes would no longer stand still.
Already he had begun to move swiftly past her. The eyes in the
hollow sockets were fixed on her; the voice said, "A little while,
now; a little while." And, because it was Ravita's nature to be
proud and self-confident, she did not feel afraid or surprised, but
only relieved, loosened, her own eyes already turned to the wind-
filled space behind his head.

Walter, tall, fair-haired, with bluff features, got out of the car
and stood beside her. "What are you staring at?" he asked. No
you don't, thought Ravita. You don't guess my secret yet. Presently she would have to tell him, but not yet. Until confirmation
came today from the doctor, she would guard her knowledge, like
an encased jewel, for her own solitary glory.

"I'm not staring at anything," she said. "I'm only looking at
the building."

"Davis Tumor Clinic," Walter said ironically, reading. "A
nice building, too." It was, of course. Chiefly it was decorous.
It was low and modernistic in design, sheathed in golden-gray
stones, and skillfully blurred with variegated vines, small palms,
and scarlet-starred poinsettias.

"Yes, very nice," she said.

Walter turned suddenly, his moccasins making a scrubbing
sound on the black asphalt of the parking lot. "Why are you so
stubborn?" he asked. "Why is it you haven't ever let me go in
there with you?"

Because I am alone, she answered without moving her lips.
I have always been and now have most need to be and I am proud
of that very need, do you understand? "It would be stupid," she
said aloud, not looking at him. "It would only take your time.
If you came in with me now, you'd miss your class."

"The students would rejoice," Walter said, undeflected. "I've
never even seen your doctor."

"Why should you? I'm the patient, after all."

"It seems other people don't agree with you. I notice most of
them come here in twos and threes."

"Well, of course you're right," said Ravita. She was annoyed,
partly because he was forcing her to protect him, but chiefly because he did not understand her will to be alone and was by his
persistence reducing them to an ordinary marital level. "Look,
Walter. Day after day I've watched husbands bring their wives
to this fantastic place, and wives bring their husbands too, for
that matter. I've seen brothers and sisters tagging after other
grown siblings, and aging children escorting their parents, and
friends coming all the way from Bakersfield or Diego—for what?
To sit around and make everybody nervous, including themselves.
Well, it's stupid."

She paused, and then added obliquely, "I had not guessed,
until this winter, how adolescent Americans are."

Walter nodded. A sharp, curious expression came into his
face. "Who said that in Utopia people will still go to cafés, and
the band will still play in the square, but there will be no families?" he asked.

"Silone."

"Yes." Walter, the schoolteacher, commended her memory
with a glance. "He is an Italian," he reminded her.

"All right. Human beings, then, are adolescent."

Walter's face became expressionless. "I give up," he said
pleasantly. "Good-bye, Suffragette. I'll see you at the tea at
four." He turned and walked back toward the car, his briefcase
shoulder, the left, drooping slightly.

Ravita smiled. Her annoyance vanished and she felt affection for Walter because he had let her win their argument. Ravita's dominance over her husband was a delicate, thin-stalked thing, and had grown because his original feeling for her had been larger than hers for him. Therefore she valued it highly and was inclined to be gentler with him than she might otherwise have been. Too much love, she well knew, lowered the bars around the spirit and left every wild thing free to enter and prey upon it and subdue it.

Of her own spirit Ravita had always been a jealous guardian, and never so much as in these past months, when for the second time in her life it had been challenged and attacked. Each time, she remarked to herself now in surprise, as she began to cross the parking lot toward the clinic with long slow steps, it had been attacked through the flesh; and this time, as before, her surrender had been sudden and distasteful and she had been compelled to double her guard elsewhere. Of her flesh, too, she had always been proud; that was what made it difficult.

The first onslaught had been through love, and thinking of it Ravita stopped by the edge of the walk and touched a flaming poinsettia. How harsh the blossom was, she mused; its petals were not the petals of flowers but were leaflike and strong; there was no scent, only that shrieking color.

She had been an only child, reared with adoration, and conscious of her beauty from an early age. For more than four years once, with all her pride, she had been reduced to the common flesh, as abjectly and despairingly, confidently and stupidly loving as a chargirl. Looking back, it seemed like madness. She had wanted marriage, which the man had refused to give; had tried like any craven trollop to trick him by having a child. When that failed, she had seen a doctor and learned that the physical fault was hers. Dismayed, she told the man, who became scrupulous with disapproval; he reversed his theories, clambered into a fine rejection, and left her. Ravita was twenty-five. She suffered horribly and denounced humanity. She resolved that never again would she strip herself naked for either wretchedness or joy; she concentrated upon the restoration and reassertion of her earlier proud spirit. She began deliberately to make a life of the in-between, of the complacent middle range, reserving the high and low registers for memory and for art. If she had believed in an afterlife, she would have saved them for that, too.

Gradually she achieved a complete averment of her spirit's entity. Virginal, that reaffirmation had been, with the fine-cut arrogance of her youth; solitary, not fierce, but stony to the destroying touch. She succeeded also in her attempt to look back upon that unhappy period as a time of illness, if not of a delicate insanity, and began to deprecate the pangs it had caused her and to stress her capacities as a self-healer.

When she met Walter Anderson, Ravita was thus in one sense beyond the need of another human being. Nevertheless she was acutely aware of social stringencies. She was thirty. She wanted the fact and aura of marriage, and Walter was so dissimilar to her lover that it was easy to trust him. During the eight years she had been married, Time had placidly stood still, and not until this winter had she been reduced again to the terms of her own flesh.

She reached the clinic and went inside, the shining doors falling shut behind her. She saw that, although it was not two o'clock, the reception room was cluttered with patients. The room was extremely large and beautiful, touched caressingly by hidden light, furnished with chairs and couches of bright cheerful rose and green and blue. A huge mirror at one end reflected massed greenery at the other: stone pools, ferns, cacti, tiny palms.

Often the patients waited here for two or three hours, for there were many of them, and the four specialists were rushed. They sat with nervous pinching fingers and stiffened faces, the men who spoke through an aperture in the throat, the women whose eyes slid dark and quick with worry. The nurses came out and called them back one by one and then the long half-hours converged acutely, drawn to meet this moment: their modesty laid bare, their fear unhooded. The doctors were truth wrapped close in gentleness, but somewhere behind the doctors—where exactly, in the next examining room, behind the X-ray machine, in the pathology lab?—truth, keeping its more ancient guise, shone like a noncorruptible sword, and smote with a clear loud ring.

But Ravita, having already heard that sound, was here only for confirmation. She did not, she discovered, want to sit today on one of these raucous luxury couches. At the front desk she gave her name to a girl with red braids marching across the top of her round head and a constant personal-yet-generalized smile; like the doctors', that smile, a trick of environment, no doubt.

She went toward the back of the building, past the examining rooms and dressing booths, until she reached the X-ray department, with its straight, severe chairs along the walls and the swinging dark doors cut by peering squares of glass. She seated herself erectly on one of the straight chairs.

Across the hall and staring at Ravita with lonely eyes was, once more, the child with the distended belly. She was about seven and slight, with long straggly hair. Her pointed face was thinner than ever today and the tumor pushing against her woolen jumper gave her the look of a five-month pregnancy. Her staring dark eyes were lusterless; she rested her head tiredly against her mother's shoulder.

The girl's mother, a chattery, loosely pretty brunette, met Ravita's gaze with recognition. She would begin to talk, Ravita knew, and wished to prevent it, but could not. "She has to be tapped again," the mother said, sighing.

She should not speak in front of the child, thought Ravita. She replied stiffly, "How unfortunate."

"And how she hates it!" the mother went on. "I had to drag her out of the house. To look at her so quiet now, you'd never think how she was screaming a half-hour ago." Almost proudly she glanced down at the girl, whose face held no expression at all.

"Well, it's no fun, is it, Pat?" asked a woman with a pinched gray face, who was sitting near by in a wheel chair.

The child shook her head slightly in reply.

"It's less than two weeks since she was tapped the last time," continued the mother, tossing her hair to indicate amazement. "How that stuff collects so fast beats me. Three hundred c.c.'s they took out of her, can you imagine?"

"It feels better after it's out, doesn't it, Pat?" the woman in the wheel chair said sympathetically.

The child's eyes rolled toward her in terror, but she said nothing.

"Sometimes we have to have a lot of things done to us before we can get better," the woman explained in a gentle lying voice. "Look at my leg, now," and she held it out, great and swollen. "I can't even walk, Pat; think how that would be!"

"My soul," the child's mother said, "that leg certainly is something. Does it give you a lot of pain?"

"Some," replied the woman, "but most of it is here." She touched her abdomen. "What the connection is I haven't figured out."

"It certainly is something," the mother said again.

Ravita turned her head away from them. She could not be drawn now into this taking and giving of sympathy. Let the child die, she thought dispassionately, taking with her, her early and last full womb. There are enough still upon this earth; and not they even, not the healthy and well, can touch me now one-half as deep and sure as the machine beyond the door. Yet the machine, too, had failed. I have not been touched, she thought.

After a few minutes, two men came in from the back entrance. One was middle-aged, and had grown a goatee to hide his scarred and twisted chin. The second was the little Chinese whom Ravita had seen the morning he first came to the clinic. It had been difficult to tell by the face that day if he were man or woman. His scanty hair had fallen long; the right cheek and eye were wrinkled and puckered into the nothingness of extreme old age; the left cheek was greedily gnawed by the living cancer.

The girl behind the front desk, the one with the red braids, had come back to ask the old man some questions. Ravita, gripped with nausea and disgust twelve feet away, had observed how the girl's blue eyes had not once slipped down to the terrible cheek but had clung smiling to the old man's own eyes, as if she were determinedly reminding herself that there only was the part of him that mattered, the part which said that he, too, had a soul. The doctor, when he came, had no such scruples; he had looked eagerly at everything, even as he beckoned the old man into the examining room; and the nurse, who after the examination had been called in to do the dressing—Ravita did not know how she felt, but she had walked fast.

Today the old man was neatly bandaged; his puckered slanted eyes darted brightly from side to side as he made his way up to the front.

What was this, thought Ravita, a procession of the lame, the halt, and the blind? The unfit, whom we would forget, whom deep in our hearts we still carry to the bony mountaintops and leave there to die? And she, Ravita, would turn away, leaving them, but for this chain which dragged now bitterly deriding against her proud will: was she not, too, in that sad parade, a makeshift thing like the others, since she sat here shorn of her right breast, a sponge rubber facsimile in its place? Radical mastectomy, the doctors called it, hiding under words the fact: one part of her womanness stripped away, her perfection lost.

"But, darling, if it's to save your life, it's such a little thing," Walter had said, bungling with his devotion. "Thousands of women have it done. It makes no difference. Surely you don't think it makes a difference to me?"

She had turned away despairing. Thousands of women—but she was not one of thousands. She was herself, Ravita, whose beauty had been authentic and irrefutable since childhood. As to the question of his loving her, she had not even thought to be concerned about that, they were not children discovering one another in a haymow; she understood love well enough to know that a defect in her would but increase Walter's tenderness.

No, it was ignominy that Ravita was fighting. It was that she had felt, for the first time, last September. Pain in her perfect breast; then, curiously, a swelling in the armpit. The doctor's hands had caressed her; his godlike, impersonal touch reminded her of her earliest ventures into petting twenty-odd years ago, when only a naïve, genuine desire to learn had prompted the touch and the allowing of the touch. So she had thought, sitting erect and amused in the small examining room that first day, the white clinic gown pushed back from her bare shoulders. She had been so amused that she smiled at the doctor, her charming, gay, social smile; the doctor's eyes lifted and met hers; they looked at her with profound gentleness; she was dimly shocked. This was something she had not known before.

Under the doctor's eyes, she had felt disgraced and reduced and she was filled with anger; the anger passed as she realized that here, for the second time in her life, was a challenge. It was in this manner that Ravita had gone on to meet the blood tests, the X-ray films, the biopsy, the surgery, the dressings, the X-ray treatments, and, two days ago, again the X-ray films; the whole endless ritual and she the least of the acolytes, and yet at the same time she higher than any of it, above and apart from it and never in any degree converted or persuaded. Nor would she be today, though it was for her final confirmation that she had come, and she waited only for the doctor to move his hand in the shaping of a scrofulous cross, murmuring, "You, too, my daughter."

The child Pat and the woman in the wheel chair had been taken some time ago. Now a nurse Ravita had not seen today came swiftly down the hall, her brown curls jumping under the starched cap. She began to smile and talk when she was still several feet away.

"Hello, Mrs. Anderson," she said. "Want to get ready for your examination?"

"Thank you, yes," Ravita said quietly, waiting.

"After you're ready, you can go into room six." The nurse's light-colored smile began to slide on to the next patient.

"I know where it is," Ravita said. She rose quickly and went back into one of the little dressing cubicles. She took off her coat and her shirred peach-toned blouse and hung them on a hanger; she stripped to her waist and put on one of the white cotton gowns which lay folded on a shelf. The gown was knee length and it fastened by strings down the front. Before she left, she looked at herself in the mirror. Even in this hideous gown, she thought coolly, she was the most beautiful in the clinic. She would keep her beauty, moreover, until the end. The creamy skin and straight body might alter, as indeed the body already had; but the clear features, the dark eyes and hair, the glance of self-possession, would remain. She picked up her purse and walked rapidly and proudly down the hall to examining room six and went in.

There were two white metal chairs in the examining room; Ravita seated herself on one of them. After a moment the doctor came in and closed the door. Today it was not the clinic founder but the head of the radiology department, which was to be expected, since he dictated the film reports. He was tall, with the thin unexpected neck of an adolescent and mild greenish-colored eyes; and, perhaps because he was younger than the other three specialists, his manner was less suave and more diffident than theirs.

"Good afternoon, Mrs. Anderson," he said quite formally. Then for a few minutes he said nothing more. He drew the second metal chair over to Ravita, lifted her gown aside and examined her, his eyes and fingers moving swiftly and perceptively. When he had finished, he pushed his chair back. "Well, your wound

certainly healed well," he said, as if the healing had been a special
assignment.

Ravita ignored the remark. She hoped that she would not
have to pull words out of him; she did not want to waste time.
"What did the chest X-rays show?" she asked directly.

The doctor hesitated, fumbling with her chart, a bulky manila
folder with her name on a green paper tab along the edge. He
turned to the progress notes and read the last paragraph, as if
he himself had not dictated it. "Well," he said, "I'd rather like
to speak to your husband about them."

So that was it, Ravita thought in anger. They used the relatives as dummy shields to receive the bullets.

"Whatever you have to say to him, you can tell me," she said
coldly.

"Yes, of course," the doctor said, and cleared his throat.
Again his eyes moved to the last page of typing in her chart.
"There seem to be one or two little indications of something here,
Mrs. Anderson, and we are going to start you on a new series of
treatments right away. Tomorrow morning, perhaps, if that is
convenient with you."

Ravita leaned forward. "What do you mean, 'one or two
little indications'?" she demanded, forcing his eyes to meet hers.
"The cancer has gone to my lungs, isn't that what you mean?"

He blinked, and put her folder down on the white sheet of the
examining table. "As far as we can tell, yes," he said hesitantly.
"But there is no cause for any alarm. As I said, we will start
treatment tomorrow."

"Why don't you tell me it is hopeless?" Ravita asked. Her
voice was still cold. "I know about the treatments and the new
drugs, Dr. Harris; they may retard but they do not cure. There
is no cure, is there?"

"If the disease is caught in time and the primary source completely taken care of," he began, using the words of his bible
rhetoric.

"In my case," she cut in. "In *my* case."

He turned his eyes once more upon her folder. "At present,
no cure, no."

"There!" said Ravita, and a thrill went through her.

But he had been too well taught how to gloss; he could not

stop. "No reason for despair," he said quickly. "The treatments and drugs you mentioned are often very efficacious indeed, and new and better ones may be perfected any day. If you come regularly . . . ."

The wretched creature with his mumbling words. "My God," Ravita said contemptuously, "do you think I am afraid to die?"

"No, of course not," he said. He fell silent. He made a small pleat in the cuff of his white coat.

"Please read me the film report in the chart," said Ravita.

Nervously the doctor's long fingers picked up the folder; he glanced once more over the last page. "This is irregular," he said, "and I doubt if you will understand the terms."

"So it won't matter if it is irregular. Read it to me, please." She spoke commandingly. It was for this, after all, that she had come. She leaned forward tensely, not to miss a word.

" 'January 18, 1949. Both leaves of the diaphragm clear,' " he began. " 'Numerous diffuse, hazy infiltrations in both lung fields. Largest area measures about two centimeters in diameter. There is possible mediastinal involvement.' " He stopped, cleared his throat, and his greenish eyes looked almost timidly at Ravita. Her glance did not waver and he returned to the page. " 'Impression: extensive bilateral pulmonary metastases from carcinoma of the right breast.' "

A succession of thrills ran through Ravita. There was her accolade; there was nothing more to wait for. She had memorized the last sentence as he read and she repeated it slowly to herself and the sound of "carcinoma" and of some of the other words was beautiful. If the devil wrote poetry, she thought, he would use such words.

She rose, pulling the white gown together over her breast. "A couple of months?" she asked.

He looked at her and then looked away. "Perhaps more."

"Thank you," said Ravita. She held her head high as she left the room. When she reached the cubicle she dressed with care, for she had waited less than an hour and a half today for the doctor and thus had ample time to get to the tea. Now, she thought, half in anger, she could tell Walter; there was no longer any reason to keep it from him.

Ravita walked along the street searching for the right house number. 102, 104, she read. The tea this afternoon was one in an endless series, given by a committee of students and amenable faculty wives. One or two professors were invited each week; staff members and friends of the college volunteered their homes. All the students were free to attend, but the teas were an old story and frequently there were no more than six or eight present.

This was Walter's week, and as usual he wanted Ravita there with him. She did not mind teas; she always rather liked to attend college functions and be pointed out for her beauty. *So young, so fair* . . . . But thirty-eight was not young. She had got over being young a long time ago. For more than ten years she had had nothing to do with age at all, she had been herself, Ravita, standing still with Time. *Did you know that Mrs. Walter Anderson* . . . . She would not have it. No clucking tongues or pitying eyes. Not for her. 112. Here was the house. She walked up the path and pushed the bell.

The door opened and a young man stood there: one of Walter's students, no doubt. Why did young men so love to open the doors of other people's houses? The young man was tall, with curly hair and reddish skin and a smiling face.

"Come in, come in!" said the young man exuberantly. "I'm John Emery!" And he looked at her with the smiling face.

Yes, I'm sure you are, Ravita thought. But, recognizing his appreciative glance, she allowed the obedient social expression to order her features. "How do you do, John?" she said. "I'm Mrs. Anderson."

"Oh, Mrs. Anderson!" he cried, letting her see that in his opinion Mr. Anderson had chosen well. "Come in, come in! The party is gathering."

Ravita walked past him into the hall. There was a narrow table with a silver dish on it and a mirror above the table. A Japanese girl in a white apron slid up to her and said, "I'll take your coat." The coat fell from Ravita's shoulders; she thanked the girl. Another student, or a full-time maid? Probably a student, for the girl was not obsequious.

"The food is in here," said John Emery, hovering. He pointed to the dining room on the left. Five or six people, mostly young, stood round the table. Two graying faculty wives, priestesses of coffee and tea, sat at either end. The right hands of the young people reached down to the white tablecloth and back: the hands picked up small frill-edged paper napkins, spoons, minuscule round and square sandwiches with no tops, cupcakes with green frosting, salted nuts. The old familiar, the rarely considered, scene; and Ravita felt today as if she had never observed it before.

"Thank you," she said to John Emery. "I don't care for anything." Did that sound discourteous? "I'll wait for Mr. Anderson," she added.

She left John Emery and went down two steps into the living room. Again, as when she had looked at the dining room, she felt as if her vision were sharpened, and she gazed with the greatest clarity and a certain strangeness at a room which, though large, and, she supposed, gracious, was no more so than a hundred other rooms she had entered. There were brocaded love seats, cream-colored chairs and couches, bookcases, a grand piano, a fireplace with a fire burning in it brightly, Dresden figurines on the mantel.

In the room were half a dozen people, all young; their youth gave the room a hectic yellow glow. There was no stability in them; they were all, figuratively, Ravita felt, on the edge of their chairs. They laughed, talked, and balanced their teacups on their knees. Ravita had never minded young people; they were too amorphous to envy; but today she did not want them to cluster around her and be polite. She nodded stiffly to the group, fending their approach before it was made. Plateless and cupless, she sat down on one of the love seats by the fire and folded her hands in her lap. After a moment the talk of the students, which had fallen to a simmer at her entrance—shouldn't they greet her, who was she, now?—started to bubble again and had soon climbed to its steady, eager, senseless roll.

"No, I always meant to take him, but here I am a first-semester senior with fifteen units of required staring me in the face. Oh tragic fate!"

"I've heard he's getting reactionary, is that true?"

"Tim Duggan is going to run for senior class president next fall."

"Cripes, he'll get it, too."

"He won't. Who'd vote for him?"

"All the women." Laughter.

"He's going to let her direct the symphony. Isn't that amazing?"

Ravita's hands, loosely folded in her lap, did not move. The young and healthy, putting food into themselves, could send it out in gesture and remark. But the food she ate no longer went straight to the benevolent tissue; the evil was drawing it now, slipping it into her lungs, transforming it into useless and breath-cutting fluid. The more she swallowed the thinner would she become, the shorter would grow her breath.

It was interesting to think of this. She looked down at her postured hands, still, for a time to come, soft and shapely; soon gaunt and clawlike. No longer would eighty-five-cent nail polish matter, or the pink and scented lotion smoothed each day upon the lying skin. For the cell, which we think so obedient, is lawless and feckless, and, disciplined for generations, may suddenly run amuck. For the flesh is truant, the pathologist squints through the lens and, like a judge determining moral intent rather than deed accomplished, pronounces malignant or benign.

She glanced about restlessly and, startled, she saw on the out-thrust of the grand piano a bronze head of Nefertite. Her glance stopped there. How sensitive and clear the features were. Ravita was always moved by the Egyptian's lonely gravity, her aspect of serene, self-acknowledged beauty. Years ago, in a class of ancient history, she had discovered and become akin to Nefertite. It was strange to find her in this room, an emblem surely of second-rate culture; yet she could never look at her too much. And gazing at that golden, eternally ageless profile, she felt as though she were piercing through the skin to the flesh beneath. Flesh, Neferite, made of cells? Dichotomized also by flesh and spirit? You, too, lonely and proud one? Ravita was touched by an impersonal sadness. She turned her head to shake it off; and returned, against her desire, to the room and the chattering students.

Two girls sat near her on low hassocks, their bright plaid skirts flowing onto the floor around them. Ravita had been distantly conscious of their babbling voices. Now a boy in a dark suit came up to one of the girls and looked piercingly down at her. He had a bullet-shaped head covered with kinky black hair, long thick brows which nearly met, and glowing, round brown eyes.

"I am sorry you did not think it necessary to come last night," he said. He spoke with a German accent and an intense formal air. "We discussed the causes of fascism, as you may know."

The girl had a lively manner and was wearing glasses with red rims. "Well, I'm sorry, too, Rudolph. I'll bet it was a good meeting," she said. "But I just couldn't make it."

"So I observed. I said to myself that of course it is foolish to expect a busy and popular young lady like Betty to keep all her engagements." His posture was bad, Ravita saw. His bulletlike head jutted out from hunched shoulders.

"Oh, honestly, Rudolph!" the girl exclaimed. "I only said I'd come if I could, and then I found I could go somewhere else easier because somebody else had a car." She looked up and laughed merrily, obviously hoping that the boy would laugh, too. Instead, he grew rigid.

"Now I see how you choose your friends," he said rapidly and intensely. "It is very nice to know that you choose them by whether they have cars. Thank you for explaining." He whirled around and returned to the center of the room.

Betty stared after him, poking at the bridge of her red glasses. "It's so funny," she said to the girl beside her. "I started going with Rudolph because he seemed so different and I wanted to prove he was just like anyone else. His father was killed in a gas chamber and Rudolph and his mother escaped to Holland. Well, I sure have proved it. He gets jealous like any fellow and makes me just as mad as any of them do."

The other girl laughed. "He's got a lot of brains, though," she said.

"I know it," Betty said, "but he still makes me mad."

What extreme banality, thought Ravita; and she could no longer concentrate on the students. At the same time, she was having difficulty in directing her own thoughts and could not help wondering if there were not something off-center about them. Then of course the question, what was center? What precisely should she be thinking about right now? The death of people she had known, of friends and relatives, did not tell her. For the most part they had died suddenly, in accident or war, or privately, beyond her knowledge. On the few occasions when she had been present, they had seemed to ignore the entire situation until the last moment and had then either passed into a coma or become maudlin. Her father, she remembered, had insisted that she pick out a good husband, and in his right mind he would not have given marriage that much importance.

No, the only people whose deaths had touched her profoundly were those whose final thoughts she had known; and these were not people at all, properly speaking, but characters in literature. Only in art, perhaps, was it easy to die well. But even they, whose reputed thoughts she could recapture, were valueless to her now; for if a dramatic purpose had not been served by their taking off, most of them had at least regretted death and wished to live longer. As for herself, she continued to feel that although it was strange that she was going to die, she was not sorry; that just as she could continue to live tranquilly for fifty years, she could also live not at all. It is only the young who think they will live forever. With each year the acceptance of death increases, and she was thirty-eight.

At the same time, she wished to die well. That was not, she believed, a prevalent desire. Since she had been going to the clinic, she had seen many people, each absorbed in his own individual process of dying, and she had observed that they died as commonly as they lived. To do either wih distinction was beyond their capacity. It was not beyond hers. She would hold to this present and make it proud. She would not, she promised herself (sitting here in the midst of youth with the fire dancing and Nefertite sure beyond any belief in the swelling outthrust of the grand piano), in her last extremity, turn usual, mouthing the large, shiftless, secondhand terms which despair makes ready in the lips of the custom-taught, the cloudy mediocre. When everything else had gone she would yet hold fast to discrimination and thus, as she had ever bridged it, to distinction.

Yet there were other problems too. There was Walter, who had given her always only kindness. What can you do with people like that, she thought with exasperation, when in the end you must hurt them? Leave them groveling, to stand erect again holding that kindness—diminished, spilled, a little of it?—for someone

else to warm his hands in. But could you ever be sure of that?
Not ever, she answered herself. That was the bitter, untried olive
of the questioner.

"What you want, Ravita."

"Oh, don't be silly. What *you* want."

"But that's it."

"You talk such bosh; be an individual."

Looking at her, smiling, no fear in his face. "I can leave that
to you." And then she, with all her egotism, mysteriously
strengthened and warmed and, thus confident, often she changed
what she wanted to what she thought he did, and he saw through
it all . . . . and that was their marriage.

She started. He was coming. She heard his voice in the hall
and would not turn to see. Then it was lower and she knew that
he had gone into the dining room, wishing to gratify anyone who
might possibly have made the tea, frosted the cakes, or poured
nuts from a white paper bag into the crystal dish. But he would
not stay long. She felt herself drawing him on a thin skein and
half-turned her head to break it off, to let him stay as long as he
wished.

As she turned she saw him coming across the hall and down
the two wide polished steps, balancing the tea things in one hand,
nearly striking the door molding with his tall blond head. He
looked toward her, his face expressionless as he had long ago
taught it to be. He was not good-looking, she thought. Other
people sometimes said he was but she had never seen it. At first
he had been only different from the other one and then he had
become Walter and then it had not particularly mattered, as
nothing particularly mattered after the big things were over.

After that first expressionless, privately questioning glance,
Walter smiled quickly at her. Then he went on to the students,
made the complete round with greetings and remarks, even managing, somehow, to shake hands and to gesture with his free right
hand while balancing the plate and cup in his left. He was really
remarkably able in many ways, Ravita thought, watching him
and smiling; and then suddenly, oddly, even as she smiled, she
felt a slight, tentative tug at her heart. Again she wanted him not
to hurry; to take his time.

But when the round of badinage and inquiry was over, Walter
came to the love seat and sat beside her. He did not speak at once.

Instead, intensely large and integrated, he picked up a sandwich and took it in a bite; he flung a handful of nuts into his mouth; he gulped tea. He put the plate down and chewed vigorously. Ravita sat with her head uptilted, watching his face: the fair and well-known skin, the straight rough brows, the bluff features. She felt again that odd, tentative pull, and she could not bear it that he should be hurt. Yet, believing that his defenses would be stronger here than at home, she reached out and took his hand.

His fingers closed around hers, he looked at her quickly. "How was it?" he asked her.

"The same," Ravita said, watching the fire.

"I'm going to have a talk with him," Walter said in a hardened voice. "This nonsense has gone far enough."

"There's no need for that," Ravita said.

He was staring at her. "What do you mean?"

"I mean that I know." How the fire danced, she thought! The flames had blue hearts. She had not noticed them before.

"You know what?" demanded Walter, his voice coming rough.

"What there is to know."

"What's that?"

"I have a few months."

Walter said nothing and Ravita did not look at him. Although his fingers still clasped hers, there was no movement or pressure in them, they were like dead fingers. Be strong, she said to him in her mind. Be strong. Don't be hurt. And she thought that this had been the best place to tell it, here in locale, with the fire burning, tea being served, his students laughing and chattering, and the expanding, prismatic yellow of today touching book and figurine.

"We're going to see some other doctors," Walter said finally.

The protest period, she thought. "Why bother?" she asked quietly. "These four men are the best in Los Angeles, you know that. Perhaps they're the best in the country."

"There must be something," he began. "It seems impossible . . . ."

"Well, there isn't anything. They'll fiddle around and use me as a guinea pig for some of their new drug injections, but that will be that."

"Maybe they'll get something right away," he said, rubbing

her thumb quickly with his. "I was reading another article on it night before last."

Walter and Dr. Harris. "Cancer is as old as living matter," she said.

"They'll lick it someday." Walter sounded angry. "Why not now?"

At the word "someday," Ravita smiled. Were they indeed living on the precipice of tomorrow, she wondered idly, or was that an illusion like all others of its kind, apposite to every highly self-conscious age, and was this rather another stretch of yesterday's ancient road? She suspected the latter, but it did not make any difference to her one way or another.

"Will it be hard?" Walter asked slowly.

"Not for a while," she said. "Toward the end, I expect, when the morphine stops taking."

"God." His hand came to life. It gripped hers so tightly her rings cut.

"No histrionics," she said. "I've always considered it quite a fluke that anyone is alive."

"I know you have. But that, Ravita!"

"And I have always said that whatever anyone else has done, I can do too. If not better." She had hoped that out of his identification with her, he would derive a confidence from hers. She looked at him now but she could not tell what he was thinking. His jaw was set firmly; under the rough brows his blue eyes looked ahead straight and expressionless. She began for the first time to grow nervous, although whether for his sake or her own she did not know. It was a strange nervousness, like a tiny beat in the pit of her stomach. If he had no confidence, it could be that her own was not real. But that was nonsense.

"Don't you believe that I can?" she asked. (*I will, whatever comes, remain a person, she said firmly to herself. I will stay me.*)

"Of course I do, darling."

"Very well, then." Ravita sat up straight, folded her hands once more in her lap, and gave Walter a smile. "Now shall we return to the party?" she asked.

"All right." They drew slightly apart. Walter worked his shoulders once or twice. Their faces assumed new expressions, and they turned from the fire, toward the living room.

"But wherever fascism has grown it has been under the guise

of nationalism," Rudolph was saying. He had apparently been speaking for some time. He looked very intense; the brown eyes glowed; his head shot out reptilelike from the hunched shoulders. He had forgotten Betty, Ravita observed. He had moved from one emotion to a second, and like many youthful intellectuals he would give completely of himself to each.

"What did they cry in Spain," Rudolph continued, "but Spain? And in Italy, but Italy? Germany is not the only one. It is always thus. And so in America." He waved his hands. He looked bitter, disappointed, tragic; he indicated that to him, more than to any man, it was given to comprehend the worst.

"What about Spain?" Walter asked, in the tone he used to draw out his best students. "I thought the story there was a little different."

"I was of course generalizing," Rudolph replied quickly. "You are right, Professor. There it was modified by the aspect of Catholicism." He nodded his kinky bullet head. "You must understand too that reaction is identified with nationalism only in the countries of greatest advancement. In countries which have not yet attained their independence, it is the progressive element which is nationalistic."

"So why be pessimistic?" cried Betty. Then, like a child, she clapped a hand over her mouth. "I was trying to think it was right because it worked out that way," she said. "How dopey of me."

"It must be appalling," Walter remarked in a light guarded voice, "to be young in an age which doubts progress."

"Oh, Doctor Anderson, you're not that old!" one of the girls exclaimed. "Anyway, I sort of believe in progress. I think if you have had a happy childhood, you do."

"Spoken like a true psych major," John Emery said in a hearty voice.

There was a brief flash of laughter which faded rapidly. Rudolph, with his words, had become a center; and the others returned to him, stripped of their casual dogmatism, expressing only earnestness and curiosity.

"What do you think, Rudolph?" asked John Emery. "How does it look to you?"

Rudolph sighed, lifted his shoulders, and hunched them again. "Myself, I am pessimistic," he said. "I should like to think we are not too far on the wrong road; but the signs are bad."

Ravita, glancing about, saw that the faces of the listening students were grave. One or two looked actually frightened, as if Rudolph were not only a prophesier but an announcer of doom, speaking into the microphone as the pictures shattered and the walls crashed around him. The red-spectacled Betty had forgotten her annoyance. He was no longer the boy she had quarreled with, but a voice. "Oh no!" she cried in a heartbroken, pleading tone.

Rudolph's thoughtful dark gaze met hers. "Little Betty," he said, amused and caressing. "I hope not, of course."

It was so entirely imbecilic that Ravita could stand it no longer. She pierced her aloofness for the first time and spoke. "What difference does it make anyway?" she asked in a clear cold voice.

They all looked at her then. The hydra head swung round and gazed. Ravita looked back at them. All right, she thought. If it was such a horrible thing to say, laugh.

But no one laughed. "It makes all the difference," said Rudolph, still feeling the spokesman. "Else why is anything? Is it not, after all, our world?"

Betty poked at her glasses. "Most of the time we do forget about it," she said, courteously pretending to touch Ravita's side, "and just work or have fun or something. But underneath—or anyhow when we stop to think—why then it really seems to mean everything."

"Yes," Rudolph said tensely, nodding his head. "Many times I have thought of suicide. Oh yes. Society is so filled with stupidity. But always I say to myself, this is my only chance to watch how it goes."

"Or to give it a push," John Emery remarked, jovial again.

"Well, I see I spoke out of turn," Ravita said with her automatic social smile. The students laughed and by degrees returned to themselves; their conversation circled as before, but she no longer listened, nor could she have uttered another word. Rigid, stricken into silence, she stared at the fire. The burning wood crackled and sparks went up with a hiss.

Ravita sat stiff and alone and her aloneness filled her slowly with fear. Though Walter sat beside her, his hands were on his knees now and she no longer felt his nearness. The students spoke in low voices among themselves; she felt that they had closed themselves against her. She did not know why she cared about this, but for some reason it seemed to matter. They were so young and foolish, she would have said; they knew nothing of life because they had not begun to mold it individually; like adolescents they worked, conversed, struggled, and played in groups. Yet their words rose from the blue hearts of the fire; their syllables revolved in the sparkling blue and gold flames of the proper grate.

Why is anything, they had said; and nothing had ever been why. *It is our world*, and, surrounding her unclaimed, it had not been hers. Time had had empty eyes and she had stood still with him and the pulp had drained from her sockets too and she had not cared; and now that he was moving she could not bring him back, no never. But he moved not from her alone, he moved from everyone. The dyings she had scrutinized in the clinic were common because they *were* common and hers was; and distinctive because they belonged to each. *Watch how it goes* and she could not, never again to see, to witness the debacle or the creation, to guess at the level or the climbing of the road . . . . This was pain. It was pain she had never known. It seemed physical as a blow; it tore her with a juggler's cleaving knives. She sat alone in the room in a fog of agony and the words and gestures of the students, Walter beside her, Nefertite on the piano, the flames in the grate, twisted jerkily through the fog. She felt that she could not endure it; that she would have to bend double or cry out or fall to her knees.

She did not know what to do. Her aloneness in pain terrified her. She reached out and clutched Walter's hand. And this was not the end, she thought in horror, this was not the end but the beginning. The end could never be reached without help. "Distinction," oh mad word! What had she been prating about through this hollow afternoon? How could she say, what could she ever say to beg . . . .

"Be with me," she said in a low voice. She had intended to say "bear," but the "be" came out.

Walter's large warm hand pressed hers. His kind blue eyes looked deep into her frightened ones. "Of course," Walter said. He understood, he had been there before her. But she—she had only begun to walk.

Clay Putman

The Wounded

It was morning and Lieutenant Colum awoke feeling something as impertinent as an elbow digging into his side, and he hoped that this was not going to be another of *those* mornings. He wanted to turn over to an expanse of clean sheet and to rise leisurely and dress himself in a familiar room. In a moment he would have to go out and stand before a rectangle of men still staggering with sleep and proclaim in a brusque voice (but with a nice tone of camaraderie) that all were either present or accounted for. A rhythm fixed itself in his mind, metallic and compelling, and above the rhythm there rose a fearful, sleep-reviling sound, and he found that this was quite a different morning after all. The sound was the shriek of a train whistle, and the rudeness against his side was the girl, and the girl was speaking to him. "I am almost recovered. I am almost well. Only my stomach, and not inside but the way it looks, you know. Put your hand there and see: that is always the first thing and the most difficult to lose, no matter how well one eats afterward—look at the children's little bellies, how swollen they are. There, that is so much better!

"Once I had a lovely little stomach, that was a long time ago when I had a contract with the UFA people and Herr Kolb made a film about Fraulein Elsbeth and her broom—'The Heroine of the Broom' it was called—you know she was the Mannheimer who kept her virtue during a war with the French; I really cannot say which war, but a very important one I assure you, and Herr

Kolb gave me always the tightest dresses to wear. I played a convent girl who stabbed a French colonel of artillery during an orgy; I wore a hideous yellow thing, but it was only a very little part and the film was never finished, because the Italians capitulated and I was sent to work at an officers' laundry in Frankfurt. You are very strong and you have such nice wrists; I hate big wrists on a man, and big ankles. Yours are very nice; Herr Kolb had short legs which were pink and quite fat, like the balustrade around the opera house in Trenta. Pink marble, and there was a wonderful view of the river. He would come behind the girls and pinch our bottoms and throw back his head and laugh and his head jerked. And at the officers' laundry there were only bad things to eat and I pulled the wild onions that grew in the ditches, because I was hungry. Oh, my breath! It was like a goat's, you know. And my stomach began to stick out. So good. So nice. Put your arms around me. The belly grows as the flesh shrinks— does that not sound like a proverb? We Italians are said to be fond of proverbs, but I personally do not regard them.

"I think that we are an afflicted race. Proverbs and God; they are too much together, and all my life I have never been able to tell one from the other. Have you ever heard the tale of the man who carried his head between his legs? In my town they tell this. It is most tragic, having happened a long time ago: the man was born with his head between his legs, and he wore trousers, of course, to cover his nakedness. Everywhere he went he could not see, because his head was covered with his trousers, and there were a great many other complications which I cannot remember. But one day the priest stopped the man in his village—there was a festival, and jugglers, I believe—and the priest asked the man why he concealed his head. The man replied that it was for the sake of modesty. And the priest blessed the man and granted him permission to remove his trousers on holy days and on every third Sunday, for the things he concealed belonged to God . . . .

"I think that I would like to contain you wholly. We are like a poultice for each other and I can drain you as if you were a wound until I feel you motionless. You know when I sleep and dream we are doing this I am in a kind of rhythm which I can't explain, and I awake and try with my hands to find the same rhythm and it's like trying to remember a song you have heard a long time ago, in your youth. Is it strange to talk? There was an

air raid once in Frankfurt and it lasted for four days, almost
continually, and the people took their bedding down into the
shelters—only there weren't enough for all, and they slept in the
underground and in wine cellars, and I went and slept with an old
woman in an eider-down comforter which smelled of her. There
were babies there and old ones, and I began to think how curious
it is that they smell so much alike, the old and the young: as if of
a place which one has just left and the other is getting ready to
enter. And the old woman would move her body close to me for
the warmth, and she would lie there in the dark and talk. 'Only
let me speak,' she said. 'You do not need to listen,' and she would
press her old chin against my back and mumble and chatter.

"I am glad that things like that are done in the dark. I am
glad that I am going home. I am glad for you, and for so many
things. Oh, now! Now!"

"I love you."

"You don't have to say that."

"I love you now."

"Oh, yes! Yes, please!"

II

Lieutenant Colum heard the door of the compartment slide
open, and he identified the Satyr's complicated voice, saw the
little Italian's wattled face imposed against a flickering slice of
scrubbed sky and sprawling clouds. He yawned, and it was painful, with an inrush of cold oxygenless air. The open door of the
compartment framed a shifting landscape of barren hills under a
glistening coat of hoarfrost.

"Good morning," said the Satyr. "The Captain is preparing
coffee in his compartment."

And then the Captain's voice from the corridor: "Evander,
my dress trousers are gone—my best pinks! And this guinea
whoremaster says they can't have been stolen." The Captain stood
in the doorway, his face screwed up like a petulant child's, and
as he spoke he emitted one of his morning noises.

The Satyr blinked his lashless little eyes in the direction of
the Captain, crossed himself elaborately, and said, "Ah, the
matins have commenced: our day is begun. But what the Captain
says is impossible, excuse me. No one has entered."

"I packed them myself, Evander," the Captain said, forlornly.

Lieutenant Colum dressed rapidly and brought the girl a cup of coffee which the Captain had prepared upon his spirit stove. The train had begun to climb during the night, he realized, and by late that evening they would have topped the pass that led down into Italy.

"What *am* I to do?"

"About what, Captain?"

"My trousers, Evander. I had so looked forward to appearing, this once, really well turned out. God damn them to hell, my boy—they go too far!"

Evander Colum breathed deeply of the raw air. The scene from the windows of the train was as pure and serene as one of those old lithographs which had used to hang in his father's room; everything too perfect, as if suspended against a luminous sky behind thick glass, pressed inward by gilt and heavy wood. Across the glazed fields and bending trees ran gleaming hills, clusters of roofs, and frozen outcropping shadows, and beyond these ran sky and clouds, clean and cold. The whistle shrieked as if it were already weary of the ascent, and the engine blew back cottony balls of pungent smoke.

He felt as if his night's passage over the mountains had erased something, as if in his sleep he had been carried far away and set in a new place. It was as if he had gathered some of the cleanness from the things around him. This was the third day of the journey of repatriation for the two hundred Italian "Co-operators" (and for the girl also, whom Evander had met, pitied, fed, made love to, perhaps loved, and at any rate was now taking home). It had not been necessary for the Captain to make the journey at all, he reflected, but the old gentleman had declared himself in need of a slight change of scene; his sciatica had lately begun to take a fresh course, and he looked forward as much as Evander to seeing —as he preferred to call it—"The Source." In Rome the Captain planned to engage himself upon some very exacting research for the completion of his study of the Carlogenezzi family, a tribe of warriors, bankers, cretins, and high-placed martyrs of the six-teenth century. Evander tolerated the old Captain because he was gentle and undemanding and generous to a fault, although somewhat given to an unfortunate vulgarity in moments of strain. The Captain had been, for twenty-seven years before his call to active duty (which had come rather late in the course of the war), an instructor of tactics and Romanic languages at a small mili-

tary academy in Duluth. And it was there, he supposed, that the
Captain had perfected that studied wantonness of speech, so pre-
pubertal in its inflection, so roguishly infantile, as to cause Evander to blush with an almost parental horror whenever the Captain
was distressed.

When the train stopped at Patsch to take on a supply of water,
Evander climbed down to the station platform in order to stretch
his legs. The station stood at one end of the village square, mid-
way on the route that climbed to the Brenner Pass. One hundred
yards or so from the station the tracks were swallowed by a tunnel
and emerged again directly opposite from the village across a
wide gorge.

The Satyr was directed to tell the Italian troops that they
might walk the distance of the platform as long as the train remained in the station.

It had begun to snow, and cats and dogs and children wandered up and down in the same aimless fashion, peering into the
open boxcars; and the Italian soldiers were sending the village
urchins scurrying to the wine shops, and some of the little soldiers
in their hand-me-down uniforms stood beating their arms in an
agony of cold and strangeness.

"Are you happy?" Evander asked the girl.

"No, not happy," she said. "But I am going to be. Soon, and
then I shall be happy. When I see my sister, and when you come
and let me tell her about you."

The Satyr approached, touched his ebony walking stick to his
forehead, and engaged Lieutenant Colum in conversation. "Sir,
I have taken the liberty of forbidding the *soldati* to trade their
rations for wine. I regret that they have already disposed of a
number of cases. Observe, sir, the remarkable stature of those
young women. Have you a cigarette? Excuse me, in my joyous
youth I came many times to these mountain villages, and nowhere—" He paused, and his pale little eyes swam in their sallow
pouches of flesh—"and nowhere have I found their equal for
producing such *fermezza!*"

What liberties he takes, Evander thought, smiling as he
watched the Satyr delicately balancing on his heels, his tortured
face thrust upwards, splotched and cracked like the face on some
wooden saint in a German cathedral.

"Where is your home, Satyr? You've never spoken of it."

"In Verona. A city of lovers, Tenente."

"I believe you. What will you do?"

"I think I shall retire to the mountains and wait for the good times to come back—the prodigal times. To sit in the Dolomites and drink good wine and wait is what I want. I am an old man. It seemed that the wine in all the other places was of an inferior vintage, or else my palate had come to lack a certain fine appreciation. With age, with age. I grew bored with the war and arranged with a firm in Rome to send me each month a number of books. I was a sergeant-major in Africa, but Tunis, in addition to its excessive smell of goats, had beds which stood five feet above the floor and made everything utterly ridiculous. Ah, it is the saddest time of a man's life, I think: to look around him and see nothing but the years, and so few. I was with an Arab woman in my tent one day when a man came up and screamed that the Americans had landed. The times, sir, we are poisoned with the times. But what will you do, now that the war is over? I can believe it now . . . ."

"I don't know, Satyr."

"I suppose you are still too well blooded to sit in the mountains—which is an old man's pastime. You have a life, and I am an old man."

The train gave a lurch preparatory to starting, and the Italians began to clamber back into the cars, exchanging farewells with the villagers. Evander stood on the iron bar below the door opening in order to see that everyone had boarded the train; and the Captain, flushed with wine, climbed heavily into the car and clumped the Satyr on his back. They had begun to move when Evander saw a man running across the cobbled square, swinging in each hand a green bottle. The man dashed alongside the train, now gathering speed, and threw the bottles into the hands of his friends. Evander realized that the train was already rolling too rapidly for the man to climb aboard, and the Satyr, standing above him in the doorway, began to shout in rapid Italian. "Tell the sonovabitch to wait for the last car," the Captain roared to the Satyr. Evander felt himself overcome with laughter; it was like some absurd nightmare; he saw the man's face uplifted guiltily, apologetically, and he had a momentary vision of a debauched and hideously angry little boy in rompers scolding a playmate. His throat ached with the hard laughter, and he thought that something very silly was going to happen. Tears stung his eyes as he watched the man leap and grapple for a moment with the hands of his companions; he heard the man's scream and saw him jerked under the wheels; and the Captain still swore, and Evander found that he could not breathe. Everything was very black, and he saw patterns of light and darkness flick past his eyes. He could get no air into his lungs, his mouth tasted acrid and foul, and then he realized that they had entered the tunnel and were burrowing under the mountain. The sound of the whistle was all around him, in his ears and in his throat; then steam and vapor brushed his face, and the train rushed into the light.

They did not succeed in signaling the brakeman to halt the train until several miles had been traveled, and the engineer was very surly about the whole thing, saying that he could not answer for the consequences in reversing the train on such a grade. But finally they inched back to the station, the wheels complaining upon the tracks, and found that all the village had turned out. The chaplain, a swarthy little Sicilian with ludicrously bowed legs (he walked *that* way, according to the Satyr, from a groinal necessity), placed the body in a sleeping bag, zipped it up tightly, and told two men to polish their boots and go to sit with poor Ghiobbe in the rear car. He asked permission to purchase candles and said that everything would be all right on account of the cold, don't worry, and at Verona, or perhaps in Milano, the body could be handed over to the authorities who were in these cases very understanding. It was the times, of course, and did the Tenente not realize that it was actually a very stupid, regrettable thing to have happened?

To Evander the man's death seemed, like the Captain's swearing, needlessly vulgar. The man had died prankishly, and with a kind of undergraduate violence. The Captain swore steadily for most of the morning and refused to eat anything at midday, and he complained of his sciatica, which he was now sure had grown much worse with the change in altitude. In the afternoon he took to his bed, saying he feared that he had received a chill; and when Evander brought him a cup of broth the old man's teeth rattled and he said, "I can't understand it, my boy. I honestly cannot fathom it. Surely . . . . surely one of us might have done something!"

"It wasn't our fault, Captain."

"One has to use care in handling these things," said the Satyr. "Sometimes, very often, what you touch makes you dirty."

The girl shivered, and Evander brought his jacket from their compartment and put it about her shoulders, and when he asked her what she was thinking about and if it was good to be going home, she said that she thought of the old woman in the eiderdown comforter and it was good to be going home. That night it snowed for quite a while.

III

On the morning following the incident at Patsch, Evander discovered that the Italians, having disposed of the bulk of their rations in exchange for wine, were now hungry. At their morning halt the chaplain ventured into his compartment, bleary-eyed, suffering from an immense hangover, and announced that his *soldati* were without bread, without oil, and what could the Tenente do? The Captain, from whom nothing was expected, commiserated with the chaplain, saying that it was indeed very sad, but they—clearly, you understand—had brought the thing upon themselves. What, really, could they expect of a sick man?—and finally he ordered the Satyr to divide their own rations with the two hundred Italians, and the Satyr waxed sarcastic, saying that perhaps the chaplain might arrange a small miracle of the loaves and fishes. "But I felt I had to make at least a gesture," said the Captain to Evander. "You don't understand these people as I do, my boy."

They had arrived at the pass during the preceding evening, had crossed the valleys of the Schmirn and the Vals, had now begun to descend the mountains through looping, spiderlike bridges. As they entered into a great gorge split by a river and surrounded by gray and startlingly white cliffs, the Captain began to expound upon its many connections with medieval warfare. His metier, of course, was the Macedonian phalanx, but he had always, since his earliest youth, contemplated a revision of Ferrara which would embrace the peasant wars of the early sixteenth century, giving at least a portion of long-overdue attention to the family of the Carlogenezzi.

He became quite carried away at finding himself in this storied region. He rearranged the bunks in the car to represent

the three strategic villages concerned in the battle of Guido and
Legendre. This was Domegliara, this Pescantina, and that one,
do leave the blanket rumpled in just that fashion, my boy, Parona.

So the hours passed. Evander gave up trying to read, the girl
had retired to their compartment, and the Satyr sat menaced by the
advancing tides of Church and State. The Crusade of the Inno-
cents had been laid out, Padua demolished, and Dante pursued to
Luzanna, when the Satyr at last requested the Captain to with-
draw his forces for he wished to go to the door in order to relieve
himself.

Everything was very sad. The day slowly contracted to twilight, and it became cold. Evander sat muffled in his overcoat by
the open door, staring out into the advancing night, thinking. He
thought about the Captain, about the girl, and about poor Ghiobbe.
He felt himself more than ever estranged from the others; a fear
of all familiar places moved in him. There was the matter of
Ghiobbe's death—senseless and vulgar—how could you lament
the death of a pastry cook who died with a green bottle of bad
wine in each hand? It was a kind of miniature calamity: a tiny
war in itself and a silly little aftermath which you could only
regret with any sincerity as a lapse in taste. He found himself
trying to reconstruct Ghiobbe's life, and he could only summon
up a picture of a swarthy, pock-marked little man rolling strips
of dough in a desert bivouac and singing an air from *Aida*.

He lay that night a long time without sleeping, and the girl
turned over and over in her sleep, and once she pressed her chin
against his spine and groaned. He woke her and drew her to
him, but her body remained slack and she did not answer his
whispers. There was no warmth beneath the blankets. He felt
as if the cold had penetrated his body and was clotted there in a
fortress of ice beneath his skin. He awoke from a sleep with the
dream images clinging to his eyelids and found himself shivering;
and he rose and lit a match to identify the place in which he
found himself. He went to the door and slid it a little open, listening to the relentless click of the wheels, coming muffled and dense.
The stars looked hammered and polished and immensely near:
gleaming as he had seen ice gleam on cold, oiled armor.

He was the first to rise in the morning and he found that the
train now moved through fertile valleys and that there were vine-

yards and chestnut trees on low, scalloping hills. The Captain
and the Satyr were sitting on their bunks sipping coffee and gnawing on the dry biscuits which were the remains of their rations,
when the train began to slide to a halt. Evander looked at the
Captain. Shouts came from the other cars, excited and distressed;
and Evander saw, down the incline of the tracks, rapidly walking
down a graveled road between two rows of poplars, the four members of the train crew. The Bavarian engineer walked angrily,
whipping up a flurry of dust, and he seemed to be nodding his
head righteously. He turned once and shook his fist.

This was the last that they saw of the train crew, and in the
Satyr's opinion the mutiny was owing to the engineer's vile Bavarian temper. One had to accept these things uncomplainingly:
non è mia colpa, clearly. He was an old man.

And the Captain was a sick man, and plainly distressed. He
had never heard of such an outrage, the whole thing was unpar-
donable, and the only course to be taken was for Evander, or
somebody, to go on foot to Ala and contact the authorities. As
for himself, he intended to remain in his bed, for he had known
ever since the regrettable incident at Patsch that he was quite,
quite ill . . . .

Evander and the girl, who would interpret for him, set out
along the road in the opposite direction from that taken by the
mutinous Bavarians. They passed through a small village, found
that there was no telephone but that they were welcome to ride
with Ciriaco as far as Ala, thirty miles distant. Yes, there were
Americans in Ala. Where, indeed, were they not?

Ciriaco, it appeared, was a journeyman embalmer, and they
would ride in his master's coach. They drove behind an aged
white horse hideously caparisoned, in a black landau hooded in
the rear with heavy velvet draperies and topped with a red canopy
from which fell black tassels. There were plumes on the horse's
bridle, and bells which jingled like the bells of a mass, and the
peasants along the road uncovered their heads and stood silent
with averted eyes as the coach passed. On the door of the vehicle
was a brightly painted mourning madonna who wept pearls down
her pink cheeks; and Evander sat grossly uncomfortable and
Ciriaco regarded them smirkingly as he flicked the whip over the
old horse.

Once they passed a woman on the road who cried out with alarm upon seeing the coach.

"What did she say?" Evander asked the girl.

"She asked who has died, and she says that we do not need to fear dead serpents—it is a proverb. This fool of a driver has drawn the curtains on purpose because he wants to look important."

The woman on the road had a sad, gothic face and blotched skin, and she shook her head and made a motion in the air with her hands.

"No one has died!" the girl shouted. She half raised herself on the seat and shouted again. "No one has died!"

And then she was crying. Evander put his arm around her, and she said: "I was thinking about what the Satyr said. Excuse me. I was thinking about what he said about Ghiobbe . . . . you get dirty."

They found an American transportation battalion in the town, and Evander was permitted to sign a tally-out for an engineer, two brakemen, and a fireman, all natives of Ala who assured him that they excelled in the matter of locomotion. The American colonel further assigned them a car and a driver to carry them back to their train.

Evander was thankful for the noise as they drove back along the rutted road, and because of the noise he did not have to listen to the talk of the others. He wished that this ride did not have to end, fearing the moment when they should come upon the stricken train. At last he fell asleep, with his head jolting against the forked bars at the side of the jeep, and in his shallow sleep he could feel his fingers doubling and unfolding; and he remembered what the girl had said about the rhythm she had tried to find with her hands. When he awoke sharply at intervals, as his head fell from the space between the bars, he was startled to see the other crouching figures around him. The girl sat between him and the driver, her head bent forward, and he saw that she was not asleep but he could find no words to speak to her. He felt constricted, pressed down, as in the tunnel at Patsch; but he slept again and his head sought the comfort between the forked bars. . . . . Poor Ghiobbe. Ghiobbe the anticlimax. The war is over and you don't have to be afraid of dead serpents. The dirt rubs off, but some day they'll invent a new kind of war in which you don't have to die, get dirty, or have remorseful thoughts next morning. Let's have a *nice* war next time . . . . and his fingers clutched and expanded, performing silent, meaningless gestures.

IV

It was dark again and the train shone with fires that had been kindled up and down its curving length as it lay coiled around a hillside. There was the sound of music, of guitars and accordions, and much laughter. Evander rubbed his eyes as he climbed out of the jeep and stood staring for a long time before he moved. Hoarse shouts rose from the direction of the fires, and someone was shrilly singing.

They were dancing in the light of the fires, men and women forming grotesque patterns of swaying bodies and tightly laced arms, and a ring of children circled insanely, like trolls on some midnight orgy, around a bed of coals. The chaplain thrust himself through the dancers and came staggering toward Evander with a bottle of wine held above his head. "Drink, Tenente—everyone is very gay. They have come to say a *requiescat* for poor Ghiobbe."

Evander made his way through the dancers in search of the Captain; the women turned to stare at him, first coldly and then calmly and finally with warmth; and Evander, beneath his anger, felt numbly afraid and he could not yet find his voice. They were in the cars and out of the cars and under them; they had brought wine and music and love, and he was met everywhere with offers of these things. The men whooped and threw their arms about his shoulders, and he struggled for a while with a woman who embraced him and bit him ferociously on the neck. It was the woman they had passed on the road.

He found the Satyr, and the Satyr, solemnly awed, walked at his heels through the jubilants. "There is the Captain," the girl said.

The Captain was quite drunk and standing in the doorway of the hearse-car. "Evander, my boy," he said, "you have been gone so long—we had all begun to be extremely concerned. Come here and try this delicious brandy. You look so troubled, my boy! Surely you don't object to our little celebration . . . ."

"Ah, true!" said the chaplain. "For poor Ghiobbe."

"Yes, my boy," said the Captain.

"The war is over, Tenente," said the Satyr.

Evander found his words coming thick and blurred. "Get these people out of here," he ordered the Satyr, who continued to stare dumbly at him.

But their emotions having been by now well primed, the jubilants began to protest and to weep violently.

"We have relatives among these people," the *soldati* wailed.

"We were hungry, sir."

"Poor Ghiobbe," intoned the chaplain.

"Ask the boy, *Capitano*, if he does not care for a drink," said an imperious voice, and the woman who had bitten Evander was back—the sad-faced gothic woman, and she took Evander by the arm and began to plead with him, nipping tentatively at his neck and ears. "I am Ghiobbe's sister," she whispered. "Drink to my brother who is dead."

He shoved the woman away, and then she began to curse him, hissing through her teeth. The Captain roared with his mincing, childish laughter. "Oh, Evander! That was extremely funny!"

The tears, the sobs, there was a frenzy of weeping. As quickly as Evander managed to clear one car and load it with the staggering, wailing soldiers and had moved on to the next, the first car was invaded by the women, weeping in the finest operatic tradition, turning their dissolving faces to him like lumps of marzipan, pleading for a reversal of his order. His legs shook in a chill of anger.

He at last succeeded in propping up the Captain between the two cars, and the old man stood there swaying and tittering, making a great show of fending off the insistent women. "The war is over, my boy, and we had a little celebration. It's only right . . . . out of respect for the dead. I don't like the way you're acting . . . ."

"What the Captain says is true," said the Satyr.

"The war is over!" the women shouted.

Finally the whistle shrieked and the train moved along the band of villagers, now silent, pressing together about the dying fires. Evander saw their eyes following the cars, unblinking, lifted blankly, suddenly becalmed like water in an old well.

"Ah, my boy, I hope you aren't angry," said the Captain.

"I confess I found it a most refreshing entertainment. We have all gone through a very grievous experience . . . ."

"Poor Ghiobbe," said the chaplain.

His anger had subsided, but Evander could find no words to answer the Captain. As the train passed the last group of villagers he saw the gothic woman standing alone, her eyes glittering in her bony face, and he saw also, unmistakably, that she wore the Captain's trousers beneath her greasy skirts. She looked very fierce there in the cold moonlight—Ghiobbe's sister—and then she began to run along the embankment. She ran beside Evander's car, lifting her skirts, making obscene gestures with her hands; and as the train gathered speed she halted and dropped her body in a grotesque little bow, spreading her skirts in the manner of an actress before a curtain, her long face slit with a harpy's smile. Evander shuddered and in the gloom of the car he saw the faces of his companions lifted blankly and expectantly; he slid the door shut and their faces were canceled, and the train rolled across the floor of the valley, like a great harried snake seeking darkness.

Warren Chapman

Where Teetee Wood Lies Cold and Dead

"Powell!"
No response.
"Powell!"
A boy in the second row left of the Assembly Hall popped
up. He was round-shouldered, small for a fourteen-year-old, and
appeared even smaller than he was because he stood hunched
over the boy in front of him as if he were reading over the boy's
shoulder. His skin was dark, his hair brown and fine, long, curl-
ing a little over the tips of his flat ears, brushing his eyebrows,
and accentuating the numb expression of his dark eyes and the
sagging set of his mouth. The Prefect on the platform looked
down at the drooping figure of the boy. He sighed, an exaggerated gesture of hopelessness.
"Stand up straight, Powell."
The boys in the Assembly Hall snickered. Powell pulled
himself erect, though his head still inclined forward. His eyes
were on the shiny oiled hair of the boy in front of him.
"Get a broom and report back to your job," the Prefect said.
Powell edged along the second row into the aisle and walked
the length of the Assembly Hall toward the door, with a long-
striding, staggering gait. Snickers and smiles met him and pursued him like waves mingling with a backwash.
(The School character. More entertaining than a movie.
Leave it to Powell, he's good for a howell.)
When he got outside and met the evening sunshine and heard
the first tentative song of the crickets secure in the shadow of the

river bank, he began to relax. His stride shortened as he passed
along the sidewalk beside the Main Building, dragging his hand
gently over the rough red wall, unconsciously counting the
crevices between the bricks. His face abandoned the sullen expression of the Assembly Hall and became almost cheerful. He
entered a plain doorway in the side of the building and made his
way to Classroom C. The door was open. In the classroom the
Inspector waited. He was sitting languidly in a first-row chair,
his long legs stretched in front of him, his fingers beating the arm
of the seat.

(The Sixth-Former Son of God sitting in his judgment chair.)

The sullenness returned to Powell's face.

"I'll sweep it again," he said, before the other could say anything. "Just sting me an hour and I'll do it after dinner."

"You'll do it right now," said the Inspector. "And you'd
better hurry up or you'll be late for Chapel."

Powell went to the rear of the room and retrieved his broom
from its hiding place among the bare pipes of the plumbing. He
began poking it between the seats.

"You know you're not supposed to keep your broom on the
job."

"I'll take it back to the dorm."

"It only takes about ten minutes twice a day to clean up this
room. There's hardly any mess at all in the morning. Hell,
Powell, I don't want to sting you an hour *every* time I inspect your
job."

(Black grains of sandy dirt, the droppings of my friends at
Chapin School.)

"How many hours of detention have you got against you,
Powell?"

"I don't know. Fifty. Sixty."

(Curl your saint's lips in a whistle of surprise.)

"Do you think I ought to give you some more? Look at this
room. Did you wash the blackboards?"

The Inspector got out of his seat and picked an eraser from
the floor and placed it on the tray under the chalky gray slate.

(Shrug. What can I say? Yes, yes, sting me some more
hours. I love to spend my afternoons in working off your punish-
ments, in raking leaves and washing dirty windows.)

"What's the matter with you, Powell? I've been at Chapin

five years and I've never seen *anyone* collect the penalties the way
you do. I know it's not so easy to push a broom, especially if
you haven't done much work before. But, hell, kid, you're just
beating your brains out. Why don't you wise up? It's for your
own good."

Powell swept a miniature storm of dirt from one row and began on the next.

(What does he expect me to say to him? It's for my own
good. It's always for my own good. He sounds just like Father.
I'm sending you to Chapin, Thomas, it's for your own good.)

From the sidewalk that ran along the outside of the building
came the rush of sound, the shuffle of feet on cement, the murmur
of disembodied voices and distant words without contexts.

"Come on, Powell," the Inspector said. "Assembly's over.
Let's get to Chapel."

Powell swept the dirt into a little mound near the door.

"Come on, Powell. You can do the blackboards after dinner."

Powell returned the broom to its hiding place in the corner.

"I'll put it away later," he explained.

He saw the bouncing figures of boys through the mosaic
sunshine outside the windows.

"Hey, Powell! How many hours you got now? Hey, Powell!
Have you worked it up to a hundred yet?" The boys laughed,
the unconcerned, thoughtless laughter that knows it is immune
to its own jokes.

(Leave it to Powell.)

He took his position in Chapel among the other members of
the Third Form and knelt on the cool flagstones. The sun was
still high, but it filtered darkly through the red, blue, and green
of the narrow stained-glass windows with their jigsaw, leaded
patterns, their pictured saints enshrined above Latin comments.
The gold and red altar with its tortured Christ nailed to a wooden
cross gleamed in the flames of six candles and sparkled in the
rays of six incandescent floodlights installed in the ceiling of the
chancel. Slowly and softly the organ played "To a Water Lily."
The Prefects and the Sacristan sat isolated in the choir.

(Here they come out of the sacristy. Quincy is serving tonight with the Old Man in his white robes two paces behind.

They laughed at me when I had to serve. Look at Powell in his red cassock and white surplice. You'd think he was descended from heaven to see him kneeling there in front of the altar. They laughed at me when I snuffed the candles because I teetered one of them and they thought it was going to fall over. They don't sting you for mistakes you make in Chapel. The House of God. The Old Man changed his white robes today. I wonder what the laundry charges for washing a monk's robe.' Do it for charity, clean the worldly stains from the unworldly cloth. I wonder what he says to himself when he kneels there. I wonder whether he ever feels ashamed. They're getting up, we can sing now. I don't mind it when we sing. The voices soar like a glider.)

The headmaster, in the white robes of his Episcopal monkhood, got up and genuflected before the altar. Quincy imitated him carefully, and the two servants of God made their way to their positions beside the Prefects in the choir. The organ awoke and raised its voice in melody.

> Dear Lo-rd and Father of mankind,
> Forgive our foolish ways . . .

(Ham, Shem, and Japhet. Adams One is reading the lesson tonight. He stung me two hours once for sweeping dirt under the master's desk. He'll start reading in a loud voice and end up in a whisper. I wonder how it feels to get up there and read aloud in front of the whole school. St-st-st-stutter. They'd laugh at Powell. They take the readers in alphabetical order, Abbott, Adams, Anderson, Barstow, I'm glad my name is Powell, when I'm a Sixth Former I won't have to read three times in one year. Now he's through. What would happen if he tripped over his cassock and fell and got a nosebleed in Chapel? Would they send him down to the infirmary or I wonder whether the Old Man could cure him with a prayer? Our Father which art in heaven, hallowed be Thy name. Thy kingdom come, Thy will be done at Chapin as it is in heaven. Give us this day our daily detention and forgive us our sixty hours. I wonder why they call a prayer a *Collect*, what do they collect in a Collect? The Old Man is praying for Teetee Wood. They banged his coffin against the pews when they carried him up the aisle because he was so fat and heavy. I skipped his class that Friday when he had a cold and three days later he was dead, leave it to Powell.

Last class he ever taught and I had to skip it and then he died. I asked the undertaker whether he was stiff and the undertaker moved his arms for me, I guess they relax when they get that stuff in them instead of blood. He was the second person to be buried in the new graveyard behind the Chapel. God's Half Acre, the Old Man keeps talking about God's Half Acre, I think he wants to get it filled up. I wonder whether they would bury me there, they'd probably make me work out my sixty hours of detention first. God the Father, God the Son, and God the Holy Ghost make His face to shine upon you. Now Quincy has to put out the candles. I hope he knocks one over, I hope he knocks it clear off the altar and spills wax all over the carpet.)

Powell buttoned his coat under his chin and pushed his way up the path toward the home of Timothy Tobias Wood. The first winter fall of snow had melted and become slush and then had frozen in the afternoon. His shoes scraped over the ashes strewn on the path for the sake of safety, but he slipped and fell, stinging his hands on the sharp slag. As he brushed the snow from his coat he could hear the shouts of the Sixth Formers flooding the hockey rink half a mile away, their voices shrill with the excitement of what promised to be the first real freeze of the season. The Chapel, sprawled on the hillside a little below Teetee's house, was lit faintly by a light burning in the sacristy. It looked cold and ill at ease in the snow.

(The Old Man's probably in there drinking up the wine, counting the cassocks to make sure I didn't steal one. God the Father, God the Son, and God the Old Man. He loves the Chapel because it's so English, it's like one at Eton or Cambridge or something, with the bell tower and those bells that split the heavens on Sunday morning. I wonder whether God listens to that racket way up in the sky, I'll bet he can see the sound come flying up at him. It's the only thing we do that the Catholics don't, we make more noise than they do, and everything else is just like being a Catholic. The Old Man wanted me to go to Confession. It's good for the soul. I'm sending you to Chapin School, Thomas, it's for your own good. For God's sake, watch what you do there. I had to show my bankbook to Father Reynolds before he'd let you in.)

Mrs. Wood answered his ring. She was old and rather round and looked a little like Teetee, the way wives come to look like their husbands after they have been married for a long time. He asked for Mr. Wood, then quickly hung his head and scraped the ashes from his shoes on the fiber mat in the doorway. He did it nervously, as if he did not expect to go in. Mrs. Wood looked at him hesitantly, still blocking the doorway. Before she could make up her mind whether to invite him in, Teetee's voice came from the block of light that marked the living room.

"Close the door, Nellie. Are you trying to murder me?" The voice was thick and the question was punctuated by a retching cough.

"It's someone to see you, Timothy," she apologized.

"Well, close the door. Leave him on the inside or leave him on the outside, but close the door."

Mrs. Wood pulled him in and slammed the door loudly. "It's one of the boys," she said. Teetee's answer was lost in a paroxysm of coughing. Mrs. Wood made no move to show Powell the living room.

"Mr. Wood has a terrible cold," she said. "Couldn't you see him some other time?"

"Shut up, Nellie!" Teetee shouted. "Come in, whoever you are. Bring him in, Nellie."

Reluctantly she led him into the illumination of the living room. Powell raised his head quickly and saw the gross figure of Teetee embedded in an overstuffed chair. His face was red against the antimacassar. He was wearing an old smoking jacket over a shirt that was mottled with perspiration, and he looked a little drunk. Powell hastily dropped his head and scraped the sole of his shoe on his ankle. Before he could speak, Teetee said, "Well, if it isn't Powell, the school scandal." He lurched out of the chair with his hand extended. There was the sound of tinkling glass, and a dark stain spread over the carpet beside Teetee's chair. Mrs. Wood coughed nervously. Teetee stopped and looked down at the spilled remains of his drink, then he looked at Powell and grinned foolishly.

"Cough medicine," he said, and laughed. "Cough medicine, Powell. When you've been at Chapin School as long as I have, you need a lot of cough medicine."

Mrs. Wood cleared her throat. Powell turned toward the door, but Teetee grabbed his hand and began to shake it. "Sit down, Powell," he said, pulling up a spindly chair beside his overstuffed one. "And get me another drink, Nellie. The bottle's on the floor."

Mrs. Wood said, "Timothy . . ."

"Stop looking so shocked, Nellie. This boy's name is Powell. Nobody's name is Powell ever went around snitching." He deflated into the big chair and began fumbling with the upset glass, dropping the spilled ice cubes into it with a faint tinkle. Powell sat down on the other chair and looked at Teetee and then at Mrs. Wood, and then at his shoes.

Mrs. Wood said, "I think Mr. Powell had better come back tomorrow, dear. And you'd better go to bed with that cold."

Teetee said, "Listen to the suggestive tones, Powell. The voice of authority concealed in the dulcet suggestion." He shook his glass. "Dulcet. Sweet, soft. Latin, *dulcis*. This is *dulcis* domestic bliss, Powell. They don't teach it here. Between the Old Man and the Old Lady I became what I became. You see before you the hulking remains of the man who dedicated his life to the American schoolboy, God bless the son of a bitch. Foundered off the cape of *Sic itur ad astra*, winter, 1936." He paused. "School motto," he added reflectively.

Mrs. Wood said, "Mr. Powell, your Latin teacher is drunk. I believe your Sixth Formers have an expression for it. They call it 'stinking'."

"*Amo, amas, amat*," Teetee said.

Mrs. Wood went on without looking at her husband, "Nevertheless, you'll be doing us a favor if you don't talk about this."

"I won't tell," Powell mumbled.

"It might injure Mr. Wood's reputation with Father Reynolds."

"It might. It just might," Teetee said.

Powell got up and muttered, "I'd better go." He turned to Mrs. Wood and said passionately, "You can trust me, Mrs. Wood. Please trust me." Then, as if he had revealed some ugly stain on his soul, he hung his head and fell into his customary slouch.

Teetee suddenly shouted, "For God's sake, Nellie, stop badgering the poor boy. And stop badgering me, too, and get me a glass with some ice in it." He turned to Powell and continued, "If I've said anything unbefitting the pink ears of a Chapin boy, I apologize."

"But you haven't, sir," Powell exclaimed. "You haven't said anything. I like to hear you talk. I could listen to you talk all night." He stood awkwardly in the center of the room, plucking at the Latin grammar in his pocket. He could hear Mrs. Wood's footsteps jogging down the hall, exclamation points of disgust. Teetee rested in his chair, breathing heavily. When he spoke, his voice was quite normal.

"What did you want to see me about, Powell?"

"My Latin, sir."

"Yes. Your Latin. I missed you in class today. I missed your strange and exhilarating interpretation of this noble tongue. You're Powell Three, aren't you?"

"No, sir. I'm just Powell. There aren't any other Powells."

"I guess that was fifteen years ago. There were three Powells. Powell One, Powell Two, Powell Three. I suppose they were your brothers and you are the dying gasp of the reproductive cycle."

"No, sir. I haven't any brothers."

"So much the better for them. They can't come to Chapin School. It's the custom to send the whole family to Chapin. I think they even send the girls. Another five years and I'll be teaching the children of the children I taught before. For the partisans of Mr. Chips this might seem like an endearing attribute for me to have. But don't you believe it, Powell. Don't you believe it. I'm the whore of wisdom and the pander of education. Once I tried to teach these whelps, but you don't teach at Chapin. You anticipate the College Board Examinations. Oh, you don't know how clever I've become at outguessing the College Boards. You don't know how many maternal egos I have satisfied by passing their idiot children on to college. My gall is divided into three parts. What are you doing here at Chapin, Powell?"

"I guess my father sent me."

"We're brothers, you poor boy. We're caught at the opposite ends of the same system. We're particles of fear—mama's fear that she won't do right by her children."

"My mother is dead, sir."

"Not as long as Chapin lives. Drink a toast to Chapin."

"No thank you, sir."

"Drink a toast to Chapin, God damn it, or I'll flunk you for the next four years. Five years," he corrected himself. His hand swooped down beside the chair and came up with a half-filled amber bottle. He splashed some of its contents into his glass and handed the bottle to Powell.

"We must be sanitary," he said, coughing. "Take the bottle and drink, damn you, drink."

Powell took the bottle quickly and put it to his lips. It burned his throat and a volatile spray flashed up in his nose and set it afire. He choked, but took a second swallow and then another smaller one.

"To Father Reynolds, the savior of mama's writhing conscience," Teetee said. He put down his glass. "Have you ever played, Powell?"

"Played?"

"Yes, played. Not played at football and baseball and all the games that mold American manhood—good phrase, mold American manhood—mold it to the desiccated little prune it is. I mean played with toy wagons and electric trains and sticks and tree-climbing, by yourself." He waved an et cetera with his glass.

Powell's face became animated. "I have some model planes, sir."

"Fine. Get the hell out of Chapin and play with your model planes. If your name ever comes up at a faculty meeting I'll vote for your expulsion. It's the least I can do." He stared at Powell fiercely. "Now get out. Don't worry about your Latin. You don't enjoy it anyway. Just get out."

Powell looked at him, his eyes gleaming with excitement. Then he turned and ran toward the door. As he grabbed at the knob, he heard Teetee lurching after him, crying, "Wait! Wait a minute!" Teetee came up to him, his hands groping in his trousers pocket beneath the smoking jacket. He pressed a tiny object in Powell's hand.

"Take this," he ordered. "My conditions of surrender."

Powell opened the door and ran out into the wind. When he

reached the light illuminating the road, he examined the object which Teetee had given him.

It was a Sen-Sen tablet.

It was on a Friday night that Powell visited Teetee Wood. On Monday morning, before the School was awake, the tenor bell in the Chapel tower began tolling. A little later, the change ringers began a set of doubles with one side of the clappers muffled to give an echo effect. Father Reynolds announced at breakfast that Teetee Wood had died at four-thirty in the morning, having succumbed to pneumonia. Powell went up to his room after the morning assembly and lay on his bed until the Second Prefect found him. The Prefect stung him two hours and sent him back to his classes.

Because it was Thursday night, the Student Council was meeting. Powell was sitting with the Third Form near the front of the Study Hall. His algebra textbook was lying open on the desk, a sheet of blue-lined paper beside it, an automatic pencil diagonally across the paper. He was hunched over the book, staring at it intensely. But the work paper was blank and the point of the pencil was broken. He heard two boys whispering behind him, and quickly picked up the pencil as if he were going to write.

(They're whispering. Factor $2a^2$ minus $5ab$ minus $3b^2$. I've got to do these tonight. There must be a way to do them. Mr. Hooker said I'm bright. He said I just didn't seem to have the gift for mathematics; a times b equals ab, a factor's just like that only bigger. They've stopped whispering. Lord, what will Hooker say, couldn't you do it, Powell, or didn't you do it? Lord, there's the Sergeant at Arms behind the swinging doors. He doesn't want me this time. He knows where I sit, he wouldn't stop and look for me. Don't look up, pretend you don't know he's there. He'll walk up behind me while everyone tries not to look and tap me on the shoulder and lead me off to hell like a devil with a captive soul. It's not so bad, though. They can't hurt me.)

"Powell, report with me up to the Council."

The Study Hall was quiet as he put his book away and

clipped his pencil in his pocket. With his long, erratic strides, he followed the Sergeant through the swinging doors and out into the warm spring air. His guide held open the door of the head-master's study so that Powell could precede him into the room. A brilliant hot sun of light from a gooseneck lamp on the head-master's desk shone full in his face. There was no other light in the room, and he could not make his eyes penetrate beyond that dazzling glare. He felt the Sergeant brush past him and heard a chair creak in receiving the Sergeant's body.

"Stand under the light, Powell."

(It's the Senior Prefect. They've done this to me before. They can't scare me. It's like initiation into a fraternity, Alpha Beta Zombie; a times b equals ab.)

He moved nearer the desk and squinted to avoid the fury of the light. His body sagged as if it had been hung up by the nape of the neck.

"Stand up straight, Powell. It's not often that anyone comes up here three times in one year. Usually once is enough." The Prefect's voice filled the room as if it issued from a loudspeaker. "Either the boy straightens out or we're through with him. Chapin has been pretty good to you, Powell. The School has given you every chance. We've cut down your detention twice. But it doesn't seem to make any difference. You seem to get stung hours faster than you can work them off. We've talked it over tonight and we've asked the headmaster what he thinks about it. He has something to tell you. But before he does, I—we are going to tell you some of the things which have been reported to us about you in the last week."

Paper rustled.

(The Old Man's here. It doesn't make any difference now. God, God, what will Father say. He'll send me to military academy, how bad o' me. Bad, bad, bad.)

"You were late to assembly twice. You skipped a study period and a class, you missed your job entirely three times, and the rest of the time it wouldn't stand inspection. You failed to report to Mr. Cromwell for detention once, and when you did report you loafed on the jobs assigned to you and did them so sloppily that Mr. Cromwell had to go find you and make you do them over again. Your marks have got worse every quarter . . ."

(The catalogue of my sins. Didn't I do anything right? I

sang in Chapel; I amused the School. They laughed at me when
I sat down at the detention board, they didn't know I could get
sixty hours. Teetee Wood liked me, but he's dead. He stood up
for me once. God, the Old Man's talking. He was crouching
there in the dark, hark, hark, the Old Man.)

The voice of the headmaster leaped up from the darkness
as if it, too, came from a loudspeaker. It filled the room and
beat at him from all sides. It lisped and whined, alternately
boasting and commiserating with itself. Then it became physical, took on weight, filled Powell's ears, and slowly forced his
head toward the floor.

". . . When a boy enters Chapin, he and the School make
a bargain. You haven't lived up to your bargain, Powell . . .
I made this school twenty-six years ago out of an old farmhouse,
with eleven boys who had a lot of spirit. I made it, Powell, I made
it myself with my own hands . . . You aren't a Chapin boy,
Powell, and you never could be, because you haven't got the plain
ordinary guts . . . I've written your father a letter . . ."

(Dear Lord and Father of Chapin School, forgive our foolish ways. All right, I'm bad, I'm bad, we'll take a vote, we'll
vote by rote, I'm bad.)

"Finish the school year, then don't come back."

Powell's roommate said, "Jeez, that's tough."

On Sunday morning while the bells in the bell tower were
exulting to God, Powell went to the laundry in the basement of
the Main Building and got some Bon Ami in brick form, some
rags, and a shallow pan of water. He then reported to the Dining
Hall and was assigned the task of cleaning two large windows in
order to decrease by two his sixty hours of detention.

(The bells, the God damn bells, they'll shake God loose from
his heaven and split his eardrums. What God needs is a little
peace and quiet around here so he can meditate on the Old Man.
1 2 3 4 5 6 7, 2 1 3 5 4 7 6, 2 3 1 4 5 6 7. Change ringing. It's
English, so it must be good. Good enough for Chapin and the Old
Man. It's not bad when they muffle them on one side, it sounds
like an echo, 1 2 3 4 5 loud, 1 2 3 4 5 soft. They only muffle
them when someone dies and on Good Friday. God's Half Acre
with Teetee Wood and that boy who gave us the bells stuck in it

for ever and ever, amen. 3 4 2 6 1 7 5. Grandsire Triplets. The bell tower will fall some day, nothing could stand that racket. Rest in peace under the bell tower with the bells spitting and sparking in your ears eight days a week and the organ playing "To a Water Lily" while the Old Man prays for some corpses to fill up his graveyard. The singing is nice, though. They ought to jazz it up, though I guess they can't play the organ very fast with all those keys and stops and pedals, it must take the grace of God to get two melodious notes out of the thing in succession.

> Je-sus Christ,
> The Ho-ly Ghost,
> Of first-team angels
> Quite a host.
> God, God, rah, rah, rah.

They laughed at me when I almost knocked over the candle and they laughed at me when they saw my sixty hours of detention. Why don't they just hang me in the bell tower and be done with it, tie me to the clappers like the girl in that poem, "Curfew Shall Not Ring Tonight." That's Powell up there in the tenor bell, you can hear him tolling Teetee Wood. They stung him more hours detention than he had hours life, leave it to Powell, the School criminal. You aren't a Chapin boy, Powell, because you haven't got the plain, ordinary guts. I've written your father a letter. I hate his guts, my fine Bon Ami Old Man father and confessor with his dirty white immaculate robes, I hate his bowel said Thomas Powell with his damned old self-righteous school with the Prefects dancing on his fingertips and Jesus beaming at him through the colored glass. We're caught in the system, it's your mother's conscience. Fine, go play with your model airplanes, Teetee said, but Teetee Wood lies cold and dead.)

He finished the windows, leaving smears of Bon Ami and lint clinging to the corners of the panes. The boy next to him looked over, smiled contemptuously, and shrugged. Powell returned the rags and the pan to the laundry, then made his way to the cloister that connected the bell tower to the Chapel. The Grandsire Triplets soared over his head. He bent down and removed a loose stone from the foundation of the cloister, revealing the narrow space between the floor of the cloister and the rough ground. Behind the stone, sheltered from the winter snows and the spring rains, were three model airplanes. Their tissue-paper fabric was loose and wrinkled and their wings were a little warped, and they were dancing from the vibration of the bells. He selected the model of the Stimson Cub. He looked around to make sure that no one was watching. He suddenly heard voices in the cloister right above him, and crouched down next to the foundation with his head almost on the ground. He could feel the sound of the bells. The voices vanished in the tumult. He looked over the edge of the cloister floor and saw Father Reynolds and another man disappear into the bell tower. He replaced the loose stone and ran into the woods which came almost to Teetee Wood's house, carrying the Stimson Cub with him. He walked through the lush green forest, nursing the plane carefully through the young second growth that invaded the path from both sides. The sound of the bells became fainter, as if the noise could not penetrate the blanket of birch and ash and maple.

The trail led to a clearing that overlooked the valley. It was on a slope that flowed down gently to the green and yellow floor, then leaped up again suddenly to meet the hills on the other side. The valley extended about five miles, but to Powell it looked like a mattress, a crib, perhaps; and he could rest his head at the northern end and his feet at the southern, and the forests on either side would cradle his body and keep him from rolling off.

He began winding the propeller of the plane with a quick motion of his hand. He adjusted the rudder and pointed the nose toward a clump of trees on the floor of the valley. He released the propeller and shoved the plane gently forward. It wavered for a moment, then suddenly began to climb in a large circle. He watched it, his head turning to follow the course of the plane. It soared upward until the rubber motor gave out, then began gliding down in uneven sweeps. He waited until it almost touched the ground, then ran down the hill to retrieve it. He caught the plane in his arms and carried it back up the hill and launched it again.

Behind him, the Grandsire Triplets ceased abruptly. He knew the boys tugging at the ropes would be going in to change for dinner.

Laughing and shouting, he ran down the hill to catch the plane.

Sue Davidson

The City of the Angels

When, three years after the war ended, Mrs. Springer's
health became poor, the family decided to move to California. It
was not altogether the state of the mother's health that decided
them, for the doctor had not said that continued exposure to Wisconsin winters would be absolutely fatal to her. It was, rather,
that Mrs. Springer's poor health coincided with an almost simul-
taneous desire on the part of her children for a change of
residence.

There was actually, each of them felt, nothing to hold them
any longer in this small town that was their birthplace and home.
Mrs. Springer owned the house, but that could easily be sold.
Mr. Springer, at his death, had left very little else but the house
—no business interests for John to look after, no profession for
him to step into after he got out of the Army. The older sister,
Hannah, secretary at a feed company, had been bored with her
position and her pay check for some time. And Constance, who
left high school at seventeen to marry a soldier, and was divorced
eight months later, had the least possibility of a future in Green
Lake. It had become difficult in recent years to get a good job
without a high-school diploma; and Constance could not bring
herself to return to Green Lake High, where all the teachers knew
about her. Hannah said it embarrassed her just to walk down the
street since Constance's divorce. Twenty-nine now, and unmar-
ried, Hannah had not much patience with the younger sister.

As for Mrs. Springer herself, anything that John and the girls wanted was all right with her. She did not take her illness too seriously; she believed, rather, that the strange aches in her arms and legs and back emanated from the ache in her heart for the discontent of her children since the war was over. Mrs. Springer was not sorry the war was over; she had been, throughout, acutely conscious of death and destruction in other parts of the world and had prayed for peace to come. But in spite of this, she recognized that the war years had been happy ones for her children. There was, for all of them, a pervasive note of expectancy in the days of those years, a feeling as of a curtain rising. At any moment the drama of all their dreams might be achieved. The end of the war, though stirring, would not end the drama; the acts would go on and on, each one a greater fulfillment. Mrs. Springer felt for John, Hannah, and Constance a deep sadness, watching the anticipatory brightness dimming little by little from their eyes as the town settled back into its prewar insularity. If moving West meant that the children would regain their affectionate attitude toward one another; if it meant that they would all laugh and chatter together as in the days gone by; if it meant that they would once more carry within them a vision of lives beautiful and triumphant, then Mrs. Springer would be satisfied.

They had not, at first, any definite idea of where they should go, except that it must be a city. It was the doctor's suggestion that the dry climate in a place like Tucson, Arizona, might be good for Mrs. Springer that led eventually to the final decision to move to Los Angeles. As long as they were going West, John and the girls thought they might as well go all the way to the Coast, where there were greater opportunities for young people.

A week after their arrival they bought, through an agent, a duplex belonging to a family that had moved back to New York. Mrs. Springer, marveling at the unobstructed view of fig trees through the arched picture window, and warmly aware of the length of time it had been since Hannah had made a cutting remark to Constance, said to the agent, "Why in the world did they give it up?"

"Oh," the agent said, "I don't know. They were New Yorkers. So go argue with a New Yorker. I guess they missed being holed up in the snow nine months out of the year, or their relatives back East, or something."

Mrs. Springer was born and raised in the house her grand-father built in Green Lake; after her marriage, she moved into the house her husband built. The sensation, therefore, of living in a place that had been lived in by strangers was odd, ghostly; and she found herself speculating often upon the Levines, the former owners. Of course, the Levines were not the only people who had lived here; the building was fifteen years old, and the Levines had occupied it for only two years. But Mrs. Springer did not know the names of the preceding families; besides, the fact that the Levines had moved to California from another state, like the Springers, made Mrs. Springer feel a certain kinship with them.

Neither of the apartments was occupied when the Springers moved in. They found tenants for the smaller half of the duplex and took the larger half for themselves. Mrs. Springer imagined that the Levines had done the same thing.

Although the apartment had not been decorated for seven years, Mrs. Springer attributed to the Levines all the distinguishing marks of personality and incident left upon its walls, its floors, its surrounding plot of land. A corner of the kitchen had been scratched with red crayon. Someone had tried to erase it, but the name "Bud" still showed quite plainly. There were other evidences of the Levines' little son—a cracked celluloid airplane on a closet shelf, a wastebasket, forgotten or discarded, upon which was stenciled an illustration of Old Mother Hubbard gazing desperately at her hungry dog. There was another child too, an older one, a girl. The stacks of *Seventeen* and *Mademoiselle* in the garage bore witness to this. Mr. Levine was a man who was fond of employing his skill in carpentry about the home. There were two handmade birdhouses on poles in the side yard, and extra shelves built into the kitchen pantry. The poor fellow had trouble with his feet, and to ease their swelling often used a hot footbath of the Epsom salts Mrs. Springer discovered in the bathroom medicine chest.

The only member of the Levine family who did not, during the first month in the duplex, come through clearly to Mrs. Springer was Mrs. Levine. Mrs. Springer had nothing to go on, for Mrs. Levine had vanished without a trace. But the very fact itself that no possessions of Mrs. Levine remained behind with the inanimate mementos of the rest of the family contributed to an attitude toward Mrs. Levine, if it failed to supply an image. The abandoned articles seemed, without so much as a hairpin or a garter to keep them company, somehow motherless. So that whenever Mrs. Springer's efforts to summon up Mrs. Levine concluded in the emptiness with which they began, Mrs. Springer was overtaken by a feeling of vague antipathy, the restrained contempt of the indomitable toward a deserter. Mrs. Levine, she was convinced, had, in some undefinable sense, deserted Mr. Levine, little Bud, and her teen-aged daughter.

Constance, who helped Mrs. Springer get the apartment into livable order, collected the Levines' discarded possessions and burned them along with the general debris of housecleaning. Mrs. Springer thought they might keep the Mother Hubbard wastebasket, but Constance said, "Nonsense."

The Springers had arrived in Los Angeles in the middle of the public school term, which meant that Constance must put off her registration for three months. It was scarcely worth the trouble to look for a job for such a short period; so Constance went to the movies or to the beach, or puttered about the apartment, painting her nails, setting her hair. John was more fortunate. He had, to Mrs. Springer's delight, determined to take advantage of the GI Bill, and succeeded in getting in at U.S.C. in time for the spring quarter. He was majoring in journalism.

Although John received compensation for Mrs. Springer as a dependent, and they had the rent from their tenants, and Constance's generous alimony checks, Hannah felt she must take a job immediately. She went to work as a secretary again, this time in an insurance office; but she had no intentions of staying there. She enrolled in a free adult education course entitled "Poise, Personality, and Psychology." There were no men in this class, but for the time being Hannah did not mind that. She felt that the course would prove infinitely valuable. By the time she should have finished it, she was certain of being able to break into one of the big movie agencies as a receptionist. There she would meet the sort of people she wanted to meet, people with something more to offer than those who were her daily fare at the insurance office.

Mrs. Springer did not want Hannah's habitual uneasiness over money matters to spread to John, who needed perfect peace of mind in order to concentrate upon his studies. She was, there-

fore, scrupulously frugal with the house money; and although
her illness made it impossible for her to hold a job, she earned a
little through addressing envelopes at home for a mail-order firm.
Moreover, she avoided getting started with doctor bills in Los
Angeles by neglecting to contact a new doctor. She renewed her
prescription, writing to the druggist at Green Lake for it; and
tried to spend as much time in the sunshine as she could snatch
from her housework.

Behind the house was a small patio where, for a while, Mrs.
Springer sunned herself. The first time she saw the patio,
Mrs. Springer recalled an article she had read in a magazine a few
years back. "Californians," the article had stated, "do most of
their living out-of-doors. This is especially true in and around
lovely, sun-kissed Los Angeles, justly named 'The City of the
Angels,' where life is lived almost exclusively on the patio."

Looking over the useless, cobwebbed furniture of the patio
now, and at the weeds springing through the cracks in its tiles,
one could almost hear the first family that owned the house ex-
claiming, "We'll simply *live* on that patio!" In the first flush of
enthusiasm, when some attempt to "simply live" out there was
still being carried on, it had been furnished with a white tin
doughnut of a table, through whose middle an umbrella was
thrust, camp chairs to gather round the table, and an uncomfortable deck chair. But slowly, the exigencies of life must have
crept in upon the family. Inside the house there were bills to
worry about, babies to tend, pots to scrub; the people in the house,
as though the patio were in Africa, had greater and greater difficulty in reaching it. At last they sold the house, patio, patio furniture and all. Other families moving in always intended to do
something about the patio; but, held off perhaps by its initial
air of unconquerable desolation, they moved out again without
disturbing it. The weeds grew up; the furniture absorbed the
rain; the insects came to build. Now the table was a disk of rusted
lace flecked with a few clinging dots of white paint. All that
remained of the umbrella was its pole. The camp chairs, a
twisted heap of splintered sticks and rotten canvas, lay beneath
the fragmentary shadow of the table. The frame of the deck chair
stood yet, but its cushions had been removed, in all likelihood
to be put to some more practical use.

But the worst feature of the patio, and the one that was responsible for its ultimate effect, was the fishpond. At first Mrs. Springer neglected its importance, since it was not in the center of the patio, but off to one side. Then, gradually, she realized how, without moving to look into it, she was aware of its waters; and how, consistently, her eyes were drawn to gaze upon its mutilated statuette.

In the course of the years the upper portion of the statuette had cracked and fallen away into the pond; and one could now only reconstruct what it must once have been by means of the remaining lower portion. There was a pedestal supporting a giant turtle from whose neck extended not a head, but an iron rod like an outthrust tongue. A chubby leg, broken off at the thigh, knelt on the turtle's back; and at the turtle's side was a matching dimpled foot braceleted in rusted coils of chicken mesh. As though this foot had stayed healthy, greedily absorbing all nourishment, while its leg wasted away, it was serviced above the ankle only by another thin, upstanding rod.

The pond itself, choked with dead leaves, dead insects, figs dropped from the trees, bits of rag, resembled a dish of stale green vegetable soup. Unaccountably (perhaps the Levines had owned them) monstrous carrot-colored fish still swam in the murky water, bumping hungrily in a circle about the statuette. All was enclosed with a strong rail fence, leaning slightly inward, as though tenderly to guard the putrefaction there.

Because, if she sat unoccupied upon the patio, the fishpond and its tenants had this power to intrude so forcibly upon her, Mrs. Springer began to make a habit of carrying a book out there. She would place a cushion at one end of the deck-chair frame, and, with her back turned to the fishpond, attempt to concentrate upon her novel or biography or history. But no genre and no style and no amount of Mrs. Springer's will power could overcome the pull of the wreck at the edge of the patio; and sooner or later she would confess to herself that her mind was not following the printed page, but, instead, the flaccid movements of the goldfish in their gluttonous, incessant search for food. She felt that if they could crawl as well as swim, they would swarm up to devour the headless turtle and the amputated child.

At last she gave up altogether her attempt to use the patio for its intended purpose, and took her cushion and her book to the front lawn, which, because of the number of trees, was damper and not so sunny. Inwardly, she reproached Mr. Levine for buying the goldfish. Perhaps little Bud was interested in animals; but could he not have bought a dog, a cat, or even some nice white chickens? She did not blame Mr. Levine for allowing the broken statuette to stand; because she knew now that the statuette alone would have been innocuous. It was the goldfish that lent to the statuette whatever qualities of terror it possessed. Mrs. Levine was an enigma still, but this much was certain: spending as much time at home as she did, Mrs. Levine must have found out the goldfish, too, and begged for their removal.

In the end, after giving the matter more careful consideration, she decided that it could not have been Mr. Levine, or any of the Levines, who had put those fish into the pond. The fish had simply been there already; and the Levines, like Mrs. Springer herself, had not been able to think of any satisfactory way of getting rid of them.

II

John had been troubled for some time by doubts concerning the suitability of journalism as a career for himself. Now, toward the end of the spring quarter, he was absolutely certain that it had been a poor choice, and that his childhood ambition to become a doctor should no longer be ignored. There was, of course, nothing that could be done immediately about the change in plans; but it was a load off his mind to have settled the question of what courses to take during the summer session.

The temporary gloom that John's mental struggle had draped over the household was lifted, and Mrs. Springer thought, "Everything good happens at once." For not only was John's future secure, but Hannah had at last met a man who seemed to be seriously interested in her.

In the weeks just preceding these two gratifying events, Mrs. Springer had sometimes thought that she would actually lose her mind, not only because of the anxiety she shared with her children, but because of the intense physical pain it seemed to provoke. She had been especially upset one night when John, staring wretchedly at the snack she had brought to his desk, said, "It was a mistake to come here. I wish you could have managed to stick it out in Green Lake. The field's not so crowded there, and I could have gotten on the newspaper without even *going* to college."

Mrs. Springer had been swept with an enormous wave of guilt. In view of the responsibility of her health for the move, it seemed an act of willful stubbornness that she felt no better here than she had in Green Lake. The fact that she had not urged the children to leave Green Lake offered no comfort; they had still, she was certain, left primarily because of her. She wanted to tell John that she would not mind a bit returning to Wisconsin; but she was stopped by the realization that return was impossible. Return would be an admission of defeat; and in a town the size of Green Lake, defeat was not a private matter.

Besides, they could not afford to move back, as Hannah often pointed out. Hannah, too, before meeting Bob, was in the habit of discussing the advantages of Green Lake over Los Angeles. For one thing, living was so much higher in Los Angeles. With Hannah's money being poured constantly into family expenses, she said, she could not even save enough to get an outfit that might create the necessary impression at the movie agencies. She had applied at a couple of them on her day off, with no success. Her "Poise, Personality, and Psychology" teacher had warned Hannah in advance that she would get nowhere without the expensive-looking clothes proper to the movie industry.

They had all, then, been under a strain, with the possible exclusion of Constance. It was to be expected that Constance, so young, so pretty, and with no responsibilities, should escape any deep agitation. Except for a period following upon her divorce, when Green Lake censure interfered, Constance had always had plenty of beaux; and she continued to have them in Los Angeles. Between dates, she helped Mrs. Springer around the house, although this did not work out too smoothly. Constance's brief domestic experience had given her very definite, and undeniably excellent, notions of how a household should be run; and she was not able to hide her frequent irritation at Mrs. Springer's failure to grasp the better ways of doing things. Yet Mrs. Springer could

not very well turn over the household duties to Constance altogether, as this would interfere with Constance's freedom to come
and go as she pleased, a freedom Mrs. Springer felt she deserved
after her long hibernation in Green Lake.

For the most part, however, Constance was really good-
natured; and because she had always been popular herself, generous enough to forget Hannah's past sharpness and to be as
thrilled as Hannah and Mrs. Springer about Hannah's beau. It
was, as a matter of fact, Constance's idea that they should invite
Bob to dinner. They had not, before the dinner party, ever seen
Bob; for it was more convenient for Hannah to meet him downtown after work. Constance said that she would also invite Rickey
Loring, a man she'd been going out with quite a bit; and they
could have a sort of party. The air of festivity was contagious;
John's confidence in his decision about a profession became even
brighter; and Mrs. Springer was happier than she had dared,
recently, to dream would ever be possible. She had feared that
the last vestige of hope for her family, like the stone of the
broken statuette, was crumbling away, just as it had crumbled
for the Levines.

It was perhaps due to the greater sensitivity developed by
unhappiness that during the period of discouragement Mrs.
Springer's understanding of the Levines progressed at such a
rapid rate. To begin with, her own bodily pain brought to mind
the discomfort Mr. Levine suffered with his feet; and she came
to the conclusion that he had been in the infantry in Europe, where
he had contracted trench foot. This gave to his ailment a justifica-
tion her ailment did not possess; and thinking of his pain, her
own pain often faded. She was struck, also, with a fact that
should have been obvious from the first, that the Levines must
be Jewish. Simultaneously with this realization, the name of the
Levine's daughter came to her: it was Deborrah, Debby for short,
the same as the name of the Jewish girl who had been in Mrs.
Springer's fifth-grade class. The tears sprang to Mrs. Springer's
eyes the first time it occurred to her that Debby's classmates in
Los Angeles might have taunted her with the same ugly words
that the Green Lake children sometimes flung at the other Debby.
Perhaps even little Bud had been affected, had sensed the ancient
hostility in the air and vibrated to it with inward terror, giving

no outward sign, digging on wordlessly in the soil with a battered tin spoon.

But when better times came, Mrs. Springer firmly pushed the Levines from her mind. She knew that she should have been thinking less of them and more of John, Constance, and Hannah. Simply because her children had been, for a while, a trifle short-tempered with her, a trifle critical of her, was no excuse for such divided sympathy. Now that they were happy again, they would offer her a share of their happiness; and it was ungrateful of her to concern herself with the affairs of the Levines, rather than with those of her own family.

. . . Except, of course, that when she thought of the Levines, she persisted in a nebulous sense of Mrs. Levine's desertion of them. But this was probably a delusion; and, in any case, surely there was nothing she could do about it, even if the delusion happened to be accurate. She did not so much as know the Levines' New York address.

The dinner party was so gay, such a success, that Mrs. Springer told the girls, seriously, she thought John should write it up to send to the *Green Lake Times*. It was held on a Saturday, and the whole family participated in the preparations. Constance cooked the dinner; Mrs. Springer cleaned the house and filled it with flowers from the garden; even John helped, polishing the silverware and the glasses. Hannah lent a hand here and there; they wanted her share to be lightest, so that she would have adequate time to set her hair, fix her nails, and rest for an hour after her bath, with her eyes covered by cotton pads soaked in witch hazel.

Both young men arrived with flowers for Mrs. Springer, which had to be put in Mason jars, since all the vases were occupied by the roses from the Springers' garden. Bob's bouquet was of jonquils and blue cornflowers; and he said to Mrs. Springer, "I didn't expect your eyes to be bluer than the flowers." Her face crimsoned at his words, and in the midst of her delight, she was ashamed of her confusion. She was not accustomed to compliments; the children, like their father, were so reserved.

Constance, whose warmth toward strangers could never be counted upon, put herself out to be friendly and amusing. In spite of being delayed in the kitchen until twenty minutes before the guests arrived, she looked as fresh and lovely as always. Hannah, her cheeks flushed with excitement, appeared nearly as young as Constance. At dinner, it came out by chance that Bob was a jazz fan. Constance was a jazz fan also, and the two of them had a long and lively debate over the respective merits of two "hot trumpet" men. No one else at the table understood what they were talking about; but they all enjoyed listening. Bob and Rickey stayed on until midnight; and when they left, Bob said to Mrs. Springer, "I hope I'm going to see you often." This was practically a declaration of his intentions, as Mrs. Springer said afterward to Hannah. Hannah laughed, and blushed. She was so grateful to Mrs. Springer and Constance for the lovely impression they had created that she hugged both of them before she went to bed. Constance's physical delicacy caused her fatigue at the smallest effort; and she was tired out by this time. She shrugged away and said acidly, "O.K., you'll get your man. You don't have to kill me over it." And Hannah, generally so touchy, that night merely laughed and gave Constance another hug.

The dinner party launched the Springers into a summer that was cool and fair and full of promise. There was about those early summer days that same note of expectancy that had sung through all the day-by-day events of the war. John returned each evening from his classes fired with enthusiasm for science, filled with awesome relief that he had seen the error of last quarter's immature ambitions. He spoke with contempt of "the lords of the press," and told Mrs. Springer that only in the sciences could one escape from the petty, obscuring considerations of personality, into the indifferent objectivity of Truth.

The girls were closer to one another than they had been since childhood, and it was no wonder, for they had now so many interests in common. Hannah consulted Constance on questions of what to wear for various dates with Bob, and the two compared notes on their respective evening entertainments. Sometimes they double-dated. Constance had a different boy friend nearly every night; and because the child seemed to be having such a good time, Mrs. Springer could not bring herself to argue with her when she decided to put off her high-school registration until fall.

Since Constance knew a great many people who played the

horses, Hannah asked her advice on how to rid Bob of his obsession for the sport. Hannah had no particular moral objections to horse racing; but she did not relish the possibility of marrying a man who might gamble away his pay check and her own. Her discussions with Bob on this subject had so far netted no results. Although Bob had not definitely asked her to marry him, Hannah said that for his own sake she had pleaded with him that he put aside some savings for his future. Hannah thought that only a man from an extremely improvident family could have developed such careless habits, and she frankly told Bob as much.

The girls talked these things over mostly on Sunday mornings, dawdling over the third cup of breakfast coffee. There was usually no time for chatting after evening meals, because they both rushed away to get dressed; and John went to his room to study, or took a girl to a movie. The girls spoke quite freely in Mrs. Springer's presence; and this was so rewarding for her and so interesting that frequently she omitted going to church altogether. But she did not omit saying private devotions, day and night, so thankful was she for the contentment of her children. Of secondary importance, but duly recognized, was her thankfulness for the improvement in her health. The dampness of the coastal climate had receded with the summer; and Mrs. Springer felt certain that the doctor had been wrong in recommending Tucson where, she understood, the summers were hot and uncomfortable.

Toward the end of July, when the weather in Los Angeles was also growing warm, Hannah suggested that they might have another dinner party. Hannah thought it would be good for Bob, who had been rather dispirited of late, to get the atmosphere of a family gathering. Constance was apathetic to the idea; but John said he would like it, for he wanted to invite a girl from the humanities class he'd been auditing. After a little prodding, Constance agreed to ask one of her young men—not Rickey, who bored her, but the stocky young car salesman who was her current favorite. Mrs. Springer suspected that Constance might be in love with him; she was even quieter than usual of late, and her face often wore an expression of brooding sadness that was otherwise inexplicable.

John said that it was too warm to eat inside, that it would be much more pleasant to have dinner on the patio, by candlelight. He said he would clean up the patio himself, and move the table and chairs out there. However, he was kept so busy between his studies and his girl Amy, that he had not, by the evening of the party, had a chance to clean up the patio; and he was fretful as Mrs. Springer set the table in the dining room. Mrs. Springer tried to soothe him, assuring him that he would see, it would be a lovely party in spite of the heat.

But it was apparent almost from the start of the evening that it was not going to be a lovely party at all, no matter what efforts Mrs. Springer might make. For one thing, Hannah had insisted upon cooking the dinner this time because, as she said, she wanted Bob to know she could "do something more than pound a type-writer." The preparations rushed her in her toilette, so that she was exasperated and perspired, and did not look her best. The meal was unpalatable; but to make matters worse, Hannah called attention several times to the fact that she had cooked it, as though she expected to be congratulated on her achievement. Besides this handicap, Bob and Constance, who had provided much of the hilarity at the other party, on this evening did not exchange more than a few words. As a matter of fact, they scarcely looked at one another; and Mrs. Springer wondered if there had been a dis-agreement of some sort on one of the double-dates. Mrs. Springer tried to get them together by bringing up the subject of jazz; but all that resulted were some remarks from Constance's beau about Spike Jones, followed by a short monologue on the 1950 Chevrolet.

John and Amy, admittedly, talked a great deal; but their talk was not of a kind that the others could enter into, or enjoy listening to. They leaned eagerly toward one another across the table, pouring out a torrent of language that centered about such exotic terms as "existentialism," "the metaphysical school," "the romantic revival," "neoclassicism," "the cult of satanism." Hannah tried to speak above their voices, interrupting herself to glare at them furiously; but John and Amy were oblivious to everything. They left shortly after dinner to attend a lecture on one of the "isms" that had been under fire at the table. Al-though everyone had been annoyed by the sound of their voices, their departure left behind them a series of dreary silences that were worse; and the party broke up before ten o'clock.

Hannah got into the habit of saying, in the weeks that followed, that it was this horrible party that first alienated Bob. She was particularly bitter with Mrs. Springer because, although her mother had not precisely suggested the party, it was her never ending admiration of "family gatherings" and her descriptions of those she had known "when she was a girl" that had instigated Hannah to it. Mrs. Springer was positive she had not mentioned these parties of her youth since Hannah was fourteen years old, but she was so sorry for Hannah that she hadn't the heart to contradict her. As the weather grew hotter, and Bob's proposal did not materialize by the date in August she had expected it, Hannah grew increasingly irritable. It was not only Bob's failure to propose that was depressing, but she did not see him as regularly as heretofore. The heat affected his health; he was often too ill to leave his room, and he refused Hannah's offers to come over and take care of him on the ground that this would be compromising to her. When he went out of town on business, he no longer sent her the amusing post cards that had marked their earlier separations. Hannah said, moreover, she didn't believe he was out of town every time he said he was; but she did not dare to check up on him, for fear her suspicions would be confirmed.

But if Hannah's personal affairs were going badly, at least John's were not. John seemed to have found the girl of his dreams; and to all appearances, Amy was as fond of him as he was of her. They were constantly together; when studies prevented their seeing one another, they had long and earnest telephone conversations about the future of Soviet literature and the decline of the American theater. And it was partly through Amy's perceptive analysis of him, and her tender encouragement, that John had at last isolated the only endeavor worthy of his life's energies: the study of "belles-lettres." In a world, John said, that was hellbent on sacrificing everything to the worship of science and the exaltation of mechanical progress, it was his duty to help to do what could be done to preserve the little remaining veneration for works of the human spirit and imagination. Doctors of the body, John said, would continue to arise in numbers; but doctors of the soul, they were growing even more rare.

Mrs. Springer was distracted from her joy in John's happiness by her concern over Hannah's misery. She knew that this was wrong of her, ungrateful. It should be enough that one of the three children was happy. Constance, of course, never complained; but Mrs. Springer was anxious about her, too. Constance was far more active than a girl of such delicate health should be; Mrs. Springer had been unsuccessful in her efforts to make Constance get enough rest since her divorce, when Constance considered all parental authority was ended. Now Constance was exhausting herself more than ever before with endless social engagements, returning from dates sometimes as late as four in the morning. The strain was beginning to tell; Constance looked positively ill. She was thin as a wraith; her dark eyes were ringed, enormous in her wasted face, the lids purple with fatigue.

Constance's appearance frightened Mrs. Springer, as did the nervousness which had come to characterize all the girl's movements. Sometimes Constance's hand shook so that she could not hold a cigarette. As these signs grew daily more pronounced, Mrs. Springer could no longer pretend to herself that they sprang from mere overexertion. Something was eating away at Constance inside, some trouble.

And, because Mrs. Springer was convinced now that Constance's physical decline sprang from some deep and painful source, the hardest thing of all to bear was her silence. If only Constance would allow Mrs. Springer to help her! Perhaps there was no way her mother could solve Constance's problems, but at least she might comfort her. Mrs. Springer knew, possibly she knew this better than any other single fact of human experience, the anguish of having no one to confide in, no one to turn to for sympathy. She longed to offer Constance her sympathy, her love, but Constance's remoteness, not only now, but over the years, forbade it.

With Hannah, it was different. Hannah was very frank in pouring into her mother's ears all her anger, suspicion, frustration. Yet Mrs. Springer did not believe that she was of any more service to Hannah than she was to Constance; because Hannah gained no calm or relief from talking to her mother, but only became more enraged and embittered. If Mrs. Springer dared to offer Hannah a word of encouragement or affection on these occasions, Hannah would laugh in her face, her eyes blazing with what appeared very like hatred, and say, "I don't want your advice. What in the world would you know about it? Haven't you done me enough damage already?"

She would leave Mrs. Springer frantic in her renewed efforts to tear from her brain the secret of what fearful damage she must once have done Hannah. But the multitude of her past mistakes was so overwhelming that she could not distinguish from among them the particular, most pernicious mistake, in order to make amends for it.

As Hannah became more articulate, Constance grew more mute; and, further, Constance absented herself from the house for whole days, without so much as saying good-bye or leaving word where she might be reached. At last Mrs. Springer resolved that, since Constance would not speak to her, she must speak to Constance. Surely it could do no harm. If Constance should refuse to respond, still, neither of them should have lost anything.

It had been so long since Mrs. Springer and Constance had exchanged any words of a personal nature that Mrs. Springer required a little time to gather the courage to break through that wall of reserve not of her building. She planned the whole thing very carefully. Almost the only time she would be able to get Constance alone was early in the morning, when she returned from one of her dates. That was really all to the good, since darkness would cover the embarrassment they should both be feeling. In the days before the encounter, Mrs. Springer began to think that she should have planned this long ago. Probably Constance was only waiting for her mother to make the first sign; she might be shy, or ashamed, or uncertain of her mother's full readiness to accept without censure whatever burden Constance let fall from her lips.

Mrs. Springer had no difficulty in staying awake until Constance got home; she seldom rested well under any circumstances until her children were safely within doors. When she heard the murmur of voices on the front porch, she rose from her bed and made her way to the living room. There was a tiny blue night light burning in the wall; Mrs. Springer sat down on the sofa beneath it and waited until Constance had closed the door behind her. "Constance?" she said.

Constance was not startled, as Mrs. Springer had feared she might be. Her voice was calm, almost as though she had long been expecting her mother's voice to come to her through the darkness. "Yes?" Constance said.

"Constance," Mrs. Springer began firmly, using the words
she had rehearsed, "I feel that you are troubled, and I wish I
could help you. Dearest Constance, please help me by telling me
what I can do to help you."

Constance moved over to the sofa, just as Mrs. Springer had
dreamed she might. Mrs. Springer could see her face clearly in
the blue light. Constance could see Mrs. Springer, too; her dark
eyes looked straight down into Mrs. Springer's own. The eyes of
Constance were as flat and passionless as the eyes of the goldfish
in the pond.

"I tell you what you can do," Constance said. "You can mind
your own God-damned business."

Constance turned away out of the light and left the room; but
Mrs. Springer did not follow her. Mrs. Springer remained upright on the sofa until the sun rose. Then she went into her bedroom to get dressed for the day.

Constance slept late that morning and went out immediately
after dressing; Mrs. Springer did not see her again until five
o'clock. She caught only a glimpse of her then, as Constance had
a dinner date. In the days that followed, Constance's brief time
at home was spent chiefly in bed, or in the shower, so that it was
not necessary for Mrs. Springer to meet her eyes.

It was just about this time—perhaps the very same week,
she was not sure—that Mrs. Springer first realized that little Bud
was ill. The pains in Mrs. Springer's arms and legs and back
were so aggravated recently that she did not get much sleep.
Lying in bed at night, with her eyes open, she pondered over little
Bud. He had marked the house in other places besides the
kitchen; she found proofs of his activity in the torn wallpaper
around the bathtub, in the pencil marks dug into the telephone
shelf, in the pine knots carefully pushed through in the linen
closet door. Since Bud was not a destructive child by nature,
there had to be another explanation for his misbehavior. Mrs.
Springer had not far to go in arriving at the explanation: Bud's
confinement in the house had tried him beyond all patience a five-
year-old could maintain. Yet Mrs. Springer was so familiar with
Mr. Levine's kindness that she knew Bud's confinement could be
for no other reason than Bud's own good. Bud was a sickly child,

and the dampness of the climate made it essential that he be restricted often to the house.

Bud's illness was a respiratory one; he had great difficulty in breathing at night. Sometimes the constriction in his chest and throat and nose was so intense that his breathing could be heard all over the house. Mrs. Springer knew just how it sounded.

About two weeks after she had spoken to Constance, Mrs. Springer suddenly awakened in the middle of the night from an unexpected nap. She raised herself on her elbow, listening. The breathing was louder than she had ever heard it before, and it came from the rear part of the house.

Mrs. Springer knew that she could no longer lie in bed and allow the child to suffer that way. She would find some way to ease his pain. She would rub some Vick's Vapo-rub on his chest, make him swallow an aspirin, give him a cup of hot tea with honey and lemon in it. She put on her slippers and her robe and hurried from the room. The child was beginning to cry now.

"I'm coming, darling," Mrs. Springer whispered, "I'm coming this minute."

Now she bent over his bed. His hair was matted with feathers from the pillow, and his nose was running; yet even in his disarray, his beauty made her catch her breath.

"Bud, darling," Mrs. Springer said, "don't worry, Bud. I'm here!"

The sound of her own voice reached Mrs. Springer's ears. Her hands went to her mouth in horror. She rose trembling from her knees and tried to focus her eyes upon the scene about her.

Moonlight flooded the empty patio.

III

Now the pain was unflagging, rising to unprecedented peaks, dropping back to its former level for an hour or two, so that the next ascent could have a fresh effectiveness. The excesses of Mrs. Springer's affliction forced her to lose all caution: she told Hannah she must see a doctor. Hannah said, well, she would ask if anyone at the insurance office could recommend a physician who was reasonable in his fees.

"I want," Mrs. Springer said, "the Levines' doctor. I know I can trust him."

"Who on earth are the Levines?"

"This is their house."

"Oh, the Levines. Well, I'm sure I don't know who the Levines' doctor was, or even if they had one. What an absurd idea," Hannah said.

"They had one," Mrs. Springer said; and although she knew she should not do it, she hunted through the old papers and telephone books that had never been removed from the garage for a hint of who the Levines' doctor might be.

She wanted to get in touch with the Levines' doctor, not only for her own sake, but because she thought it was time he turned Bud over to a good specialist. The family doctor had done all he could for Bud, and Bud was no closer to recovery. Mrs. Springer did not know where the money for Bud's specialist was going to come from, any more than she knew where Hannah would find the money for her mother's medical needs. Mr. Levine could not seem to hold any of the jobs that paid well; and with John's government checks no longer coming in, the Springers were not any better off than the Levines.

Sometimes it was very confusing to Mrs. Springer that so many separate events should be going on at one time under one roof. No sooner had she turned, it seemed, from contemplation of a problem of Bud's, or Debby's, than she was perplexed by a problem of John's, or Hannah's.

At other times Mrs. Springer recognized her confusion as an error in time. The particular misfortunes of the Levines that were absorbing her now had actually happened a year ago, before they moved back to New York. It was only the startling clarity of Mrs. Springer's perceptions of those misfortunes that gave to them the vitality of present events. Indeed, so graphic was the struggle of the Levines that Mrs. Springer was not altogether certain that her error about time wasn't the other way around, and that it would turn out after all that the struggles of John and Hannah were what was past.

Past or present, John Springer quit attending U.S.C. His zeal for "belles-lettres" withered away when Amy, a girl he had sincerely believed in as the epitome of high culture, became involved with some man who owned a lot of cattle in Texas. John said that it was good riddance, and he hoped she'd settle down in a huge, vulgar mansion to raise a gang of bourgeois brats whose only ambition would be to own the biggest television screen in the country.

With the disappearance of Amy and "belles-lettres," nothing that could be called a new inspiration came to replace the discarded ones. John dropped out of school in order "to think things over," but his thoughts sparked no impulse to action. Most of his time was spent on the patio, where he sat unoccupied in the sunshine, motionless as the broken furniture. His eyes died in his face, like dead eyes Mrs. Springer had seen once before, she could not remember where. Mrs. Springer shuddered at the sight of them, and did not dare either to question or to comfort John. When Hannah nagged him about going to work, he laughed and said, "Yes, what more would you have me do for the sake of this nest of singing birds? Pick citrus fruit? Teach the rhumba to fat ladies at Arthur Murray's? Car-hop in epaulettes at a Dolores'?"

Mr. Levine, on the other hand, wanted to work but was let out of one position after another. Mr. Levine knew the reason. The migration of such large numbers of Jews to Los Angeles since the war was causing recurrent waves of vigorous anti-Semitism. Even employers who had no prejudices were forced, because of public censure, into discriminatory practices. Mr. Levine knew of businessmen, themselves Jews, who would not hire a Semitic-looking person.

Debby found the same attitude widespread at her high school. Among her fellow students in the graduating class there was continual muttering that the reason it was so hard to get into U.C.L.A. and U.S.C. was because of all the Jewish students who were pushing in. They had a better chance, it was said, because they were "greasy grinds" who, unable to compete in athletics, spent all their time studying. This made Debby self-conscious at the same time that she burned at the untruthfulness of the charge. For Debby herself studied a great deal; but this very characteristic had made her as fully misunderstood and unpopular with the Jewish students as with the non-Jews.

It was probably Debby's resentment, and the considerations for her future and little Bud's, that brought on the decision to move back to New York. Mrs. Springer heard very distinctly

the argument Debby made that finally drove Mr. Levine to prepare for the move.

"I'm tired of being a scapegoat," Debby protested to her
father. "I'm sick to death of it and sick to death of this place.
Please, let's go back to New York, Dad."

"But, Debby," her father said, "what's the use? There's anti-
Semitism in New York, too. You know that as well as I do."

"Yes," Debby said, "I know that. But at least it happens in
a familiar environment. At least the ugliness comes in an environment where no one's led to expect anything else. At least it comes
undisguised, not coated over with this hideous pretense of sunshine and health, orange juice and swimming-pools-for-all."

"No, darling," Mr. Levine said, "it's only an illusion you
have that New York is better than Los Angeles, because you're
not *in* New York." But his face was set in lines of weariness; and
Mrs. Springer could see that he was weakening, that he, too, was
almost believing that New York City, where he'd had a good,
steady income, was better than Los Angeles. She longed to hear
him say something that would convince Debby that the Levines
must stay right where they were, in this house.

"No, no," she wanted to say to Debby, "don't run away, please
don't. What about me? Have you forgotten about me?"

But she could not speak to Debby that day; for just as she
opened her mouth to whisper, "Debby," that odd girl who roomed
with Hannah passed through the hall. Mrs. Springer avoided
looking at the girl, but she knew the girl looked at her and read
the whisper on her lips, for she heard the creature give a short,
contemptuous laugh.

She did not forgive the girl that laughter, for it destroyed
her very last opportunity to speak to Debby. It was shortly after
this conversation between Debby and her father that Mrs.
Springer knew the Levines were gone. A peculiar silence settled
over the house, in spite of the fact that John, and Hannah, and
Hannah's roommate continued to pass through the rooms, play
the radio, run water into the tub. The silence was more real than
the sounds. Mrs. Springer listened with all her might, but no
longer could she hear Bud's breathing in the night, nor the whirr
of Mr. Levine's lawn mower, nor Debby's hesitating voice as she
read aloud, *"Pendant le demi-siècle..."* There was no doubt of
it: they were gone.

And although the departure of the Levines was foreknown; although she had, in fact, lived through it many times already— whether in imagination, or in recollection, or in actual experience, was of no account—this time there was a difference. This time there was no sense of expectation in the silence, but a sense, instead, of final things accomplished.

"This time," Mrs. Springer thought, "they will not come back."

At this, the pain of her loss filled her so completely that it left no room for the consciousness of physical pain. Or, Mrs. Springer thought, the physical pain, being the weaker, had been absorbed into the pain of her loss, so that there was no longer any distinction between the two.

Because the pain drew so much of her attention to what was going on inside her, Mrs. Springer was sometimes able to forget her fear of what was going on about her. Nevertheless, the other occupants of the house, when they passed by her, had begun to inspire in her an unmistakable feeling of dread. They did not speak to her, or make any attempt to molest her, but Mrs. Springer thought: "They are biding their time."

She became adept at a trick of blurring her vision so that she could not see them clearly. Every once in a while a detail broke through: Hannah's roommate, although she continued to look ill, was much fatter; Hannah herself was thinner; John had grown a beard.

Most of all, she wished to concentrate upon her inner silence. The silence grieved her, but it was precious because it was all she had left of the Levines. She lived in continual apprehension that some tumult of shattering proportions might force her from the silence of the Levines into the events of the world about her.

Perhaps it was her fear of just such a tumult, and her failure to make any preparations for it, that brought it on. For a number of days, maybe a week, Mrs. Springer's ears had been delightfully numb, when one night the quarrel between Hannah and Hannah's roommate began.

It was early, and Mrs. Springer was lying fully dressed on her bed when the angry voices broke through her abstraction. She tried to reseal her ears, but she could not; and so, while she listened, she gripped the mattress to prevent herself from leaving her bed. It was bad enough to hear them, but it would be worse should she be drawn into the same room with them.

"You streetwalker!" Hannah cried. "You common street-walker! Sneaking around with him behind my back like the cat you are!"

The roommate's voice was lower, weighted with the same contempt that was always in her laugh. "There's no reason I shouldn't see him as much as I like," she said. "After all, it's his child."

"You planned it," Hannah said. "You planned the whole thing to take him away from me!"

"Take him away from you?" the roommate said. "That's a good one! Nobody had to take him away from you. You never had him." She laughed her chilling laugh. "You never had anybody, Hannah, and you never will."

"I ought to kill you," Hannah said. "I'd like to kill you."

Mrs. Springer leaped from the bed and ran down the hall. Blinded by light, she leaned against the living-room door. Then her sight cleared, and she saw that it was Hannah who was seated, her head in her hands, while the roommate stood over her. The roommate's paper-pale face was set in a ghastly smile. She turned upon Mrs. Springer her dark, dead eyes; and Mrs. Springer, unable in her panic to avoid their gaze, knew for that moment whose eyes they were. She began to cry.

Hannah raised her head. "Oh, it's you, is it?" She stared at Mrs. Springer, and her face darkened with hatred. "Yes," she said, "cry! You ought to cry. You encouraged her. You taught her those sneaky tricks, with your pampering." She rose unsteadily from the sofa. "Cry! I wish you'd cry yourself into your grave! I wish—"

But Mrs. Springer heard no more, for she had turned and fled back along the hall to her room. She locked the door and shoved a chair against it. Trembling, she waited for them to come for her.

There were no footsteps in the hall; the voices went on in the living room. Mrs. Springer tried to hear what they were saying over the loud pounding in her ears. Perhaps they were planning to come in through the window. She ran over to the window, pulled it down, and locked it. Then she returned to the door to listen.

They had apparently decided to let her alone for the time being, for they returned to their quarrel. Mrs. Springer heard Hannah say, triumphantly, "Didn't work, did it, Constance? He won't marry you either, will he?" and the girl's reply: "I should have known anyone who'd have anything to do with you would be a bastard all the way through."

After a while, John's voice joined the others. He shouted at them that he was going to call the police. The roommate laughed her contemptuous laugh. ". . . picture of manhood!" she said.

". . . perfect companion," John's voice came back. ". . . hot young whore . . . dried-up, sex-starved hag!"

There was a choking sound; then Hannah spoke, but in a voice so lowered with viciousness that it came through to Mrs. Springer only as a long hiss.

But John heard what she said; and his responding fury seemed to rock the house on its foundations. "Yes!" John thundered. "Yes, God damn it, and I hope you're all satisfied, you bitches! Whose bloody fault is it? Who thought it was such a God-damned good idea? Who dragged me out here to ruin my life? Who forced me to give up everything for this dead end!"

Now the three voices mingled violently. There were broken cries, and curses, and once, briefly, the sound of hysterical sobbing. Then a voice, Mrs. Springer could no longer tell whose, screamed shrilly:

"She's the one! With her fake sickness! For the sake of a cracked old woman! She's the one!"

SHE'S THE ONE! SHE'S THE ONE! SHE'S THE ONE!

They were coming for her.

They were coming for her; but Mrs. Springer had no time to think about that now. Up to this moment, all her faculties had been strained to the point of their coming; but now their coming had lost its power to terrify. Now she could not heed their coming because, as she stood there, a sound far more significant than the roar of their voices or the thud of their feet came to freeze her heart to its core.

For over the roar of their voices and over the thud of their feet she had heard, quite distinctly, the most terrifying sound in the world. Over the roar of their voices and thud of their feet she heard, unmistakably clear, the ear-splitting splash that came from the patio.

There was not a moment to lose. Mrs. Springer jerked open the top drawer of her dresser and pulled out the purse in which she kept her cash. She grabbed her coat and hat from the closet and ran to the window. Unlocking it, she slipped through and dropped to the ground.

She did not look at the pond as she sped past it and down the driveway. She knew without looking that the goldfish were clustered about their long-awaited prey, their flesh swelling, swelling. She knew, without staying to look, that when it was gone, they would at last turn to devour one another.

At the corner of Melrose and La Cienega she hailed a taxi. It was a long drive; and on the way she had a chance to straighten her hair, to put on her coat and hat. She was already quite calm when she paid the driver at the entrance to the station.

There was no difficulty in obtaining a coach ticket for the midnight train. She found the correct window immediately, and the ticket seller understood just what she wanted. Since she had an hour before the train pulled out, she washed up and then bought a few things she needed at the station drugstore.

The train was fairly crowded, but a pleasant-looking woman moved a package to make room for her. The woman said her name was Mrs. Hanson, and that she was going to New York City. "Are you going to New York, too?" she asked.

"Oh, yes. I've been away far too long as it is, but there were some affairs I had to take care of in Los Angeles." As she spoke, she realized that she could not remember exactly what these affairs had been; but it did not seem to matter very much.

The porter turned out the lights in the car, and people began to push back the reclining chairs. They spoke in lower tones. Mrs. Hanson was very friendly, and an excellent conversationalist. She talked energetically about her impressions of Los Angeles, about her family in New York, about the probability of the train arriving on schedule.

At last Mrs. Hanson said she thought they'd better get some rest while they could, and she plumped up the pillow she had rented from the porter. "By the way," Mrs. Hanson said, "as long as we're going to be together for a while, I just might want to know what to call you. You haven't told me your name."

Mrs. Hanson's companion smiled her apology. "Oh, I'm terribly sorry," she said. "How rude of me! It's Levine—Mrs. Levine."

Then she settled her head against the towel-covered back of the chair; and in no time at all, she was asleep.

Susan Kuehn

The Searchers

There was no trace of Danny. He had been lost six hours by
then. Lights swung in the darkness as our search party found
the way back along the trail we had cut in entering the woods.
Mud, caked by water, made my feet so heavy that it was hard to
lift them each time. All around, there was the green smell of
water, of sweat and damp wool clothes, and always the scent of
the wet, decaying earth. We came on the clearing of my father's
farm suddenly to see it filled with people and alive with moving
lights.

When my sister June hurried toward us, her hair was mussed
up, and the wet night air made it spring up around her face.
"What did you find?" she shouted.

I had to tell her there was no sign of her son. June was eight
years old when I was born, but now I felt like the oldest. "We'll
find him," I said. "Don't worry." But it was like talking to a
stone.

She nodded, and some life came back into her face when she
clutched at my arm. "You're not going to give up? You can't
leave him alone in the woods at night."

"There must be fifty people out there now. They told us to
turn back and get some rest."

"Graden, I'm sorry. I guess I'm half out of my mind," she
said. She looked around the crowded yard. "Where's Kendall?"
she asked, hunting for her husband. "I don't see him anywhere."

"He wouldn't turn back. He's still out there."

I looked at the dirt-smeared faces of the other men in the half-brightness of flashlights and lanterns and saw that most of them had long red scratches on their foreheads and cheeks. I felt my own face and took my hand away when I touched a gummy line at the jaw. A dot of caked blood lay in my palm. Everywhere in the woods, the branches had reached out to hold us back. Sometimes they held like rope around the waist, and we had to push hard to free ourselves, but there always would be the little, soft-looking ones that were the worst after all, because they clawed at our faces and clothes. Danny's little light sweater would be chewed to pieces by those thorny green branches alone.

Women who lived near enough to make it had come, bringing food and coffee that we swallowed standing up that night, because the ground was cold, and there wasn't anywhere else to sit. A truck moved into the yard, carrying army cots, and we learned we were supposed to sleep there.

But I couldn't sleep for blaming myself. Danny might have been here now if I hadn't broken my promise to him. When June and her family drove up from Chicago, I had helped Danny build a little house in our back yard. It was going to be a copy of our place, front porch and all, and when he started working on it, Danny forgot all about his toy-model car collection. "You promised me you'd help with the house," he had said that morning. But I had to be a big shot because it was Saturday noon, and drive into Byron City in Kendall Jackson's blue Buick Riviera for everyone to see. I had bought Danny a can of brown paint at the hardware store, to make up for leaving him behind. I felt it still in my pocket when I rolled over on the cot.

I opened my eyes to see June moving around the yard with the other women, pouring coffee and saying nothing. Inside the house, her little girl began to cry, and June hurried in, coming back to stand in the doorway with Marcia in her arms.

"What are they here for?" the little girl asked. She stared at us. "When's Danny going to come to bed?"

"Never mind." June's voice was flat. She looked like Dad then, with the bones sticking up through her skin, and her lipstick gone.

"It's not fair for him to stay up later than me." But Marcia didn't complain when June took her back inside.

June had been shouting for Danny when Kendall Jackson and I drove back from Byron City. Dad had been watching him when he disappeared, but Danny had gone so quickly that there was no way of telling which direction to follow. Help had come fast. All afternoon a string of cars drove up the bumpy dirt road that led off the highway. Nap Stoner came with Sherman Blatnik, his deputy. Sherman had brought his two bloodhounds with him —queer, ugly dogs with big muscles and sagging faces. I suppose it was the first time Sherman Blatnik had seen June in all the time she had been gone, but all he did was ask for something of Danny's so he could give the scent to the bloodhounds. She brought out his pajamas. They were blue, with little figures of Mickey Mouse on them. The druggist, Everett Handler, and the Cranstons had come over right away, and in the middle of the afternoon, forest rangers and game wardens began to turn up. Just before it got dark, National Guardsmen came. As each group started out, Nap Stoner or Sherman had given a pistol to the leader. When Danny was found, there would be four shots.

I could hear Dad's voice again as I lay on the cot. "This picture was taken in April, when Danny was in his school play," he said. "He's got real light curly hair. You'll be able to see it against the trees." His one good hand couldn't hold the picture still. "I told him to find me a little piece of wood for his house. I thought he was just going around the yard," he said, and you could tell by the way he said it that he had gone through the story so many times that the words didn't have any certain meaning for him any longer. "I just turned my head not more than fifty, sixty seconds."

I could hear Marcia sobbing inside the house. "Was she outside with them when it happened?" Nap Stoner asked.

"She's too young to understand. She never says the same thing twice," June answered. I watched her high heels sink into the earth beneath the sparse grass. "She thinks it's some kind of game."

"I just turned my head not more than fifty, sixty seconds," Dad said. He sat in one spot, not moving except when he turned to peer into the black edge of woods. And he was listening. I could tell that. Then he stood up and wandered off to the left.

"Where are you going?" Nap Stoner asked.

"Over to those spruce trees. I think he must have gone into the woods there."

"We've looked there," Nap told him. "The hounds didn't even get a scent."

"I was sure it was over there," Dad said, walking back to his seat. I noticed then that it was a stuffed parlor chair he had brought out from the house and set on the ground. I could remember when Mother picked out the red slip-cover material, and it looked crazy to see that chair sitting there on the grass.

I watched Everett Handler lie down on the cot next to mine. He was an ugly, good-natured man with scant, light eyebrows and lashes around his pale blue eyes, which gave the appearance of being all white. Before June had left for Chicago, she used to take me in town with her and buy me a Coke at Everett's drugstore while she leafed through the movie magazines. That was one thing you could say about Everett, that he never complained when you looked through magazines you didn't buy. After June finished paging through the pictures of the stars, she would hold her chin up and throw her hair back over her shoulders. She combed her hair a lot those days.

What was it like for her, I wondered. When June married her boss in the Chicago insurance company, Dad and I hadn't gone. Instead, we used the train tickets and clothes money to buy a silver tray. Dad asked her to visit us, and once it looked as if they were coming, but at the last minute they couldn't make it after all. We didn't really believe they would come this time either until we actually saw them drive into the yard. Kendall Jackson had a little, trim mustache that reminded me of a movie star, but I couldn't remember just who. And although June didn't go into town and say hello to people she knew, she seemed glad to be back.

But there was one thing she didn't mention, and finally Dad spoke about it. "You didn't ask about Sherman Blatnik," he had said that morning in the kitchen.

She held a wet glass out in front of her. "How is he?" she said.

"He used to drop in and ask about you before you got married," Dad told her. "He's got a good farm and some hunting dogs."

I had watched her move back and forth from the cupboards.

I liked the striped skirt and the high-heeled pumps she wore. "I'm glad he's doing well," she had said.

I lay on the cot, watching the sky and wishing I could fall asleep instead of thinking. When I saw the lights coming out of the trees, I thought maybe I had slept and turned the stars upside down in my mind so that they were on the earth instead of where they were supposed to be. But they were only more flashlights.

It was funny, I thought, how everything had happened at once. Dad got crippled in the tractor accident, and June went to Chicago. That morning, Danny had asked Dad why he couldn't move his arm. June had told him not to ask such things, and it surprised me to see her face get so red.

When someone touched me, and said it was time to start out again, it was early morning. During the night, tents had been pitched across our property, and big food tables had been set up close to the house, where men now stood in a line waiting their turns. Nap Stoner was talking to some groups of men, new arrivals who had driven in that morning, and getting them ready to start into the swamp. Some of them I knew, but most of them I didn't.

"I've never seen so many men together like this except once," Mr. Cranston said when we were waiting in the coffee line. "It was a posse for a killer."

We started out again. The balsam and cedars were far enough apart at the edge so you wouldn't think they were dangerous, but the woods were a tangle farther in. The ground was springy and wet all the time, no matter how little rain we had, and a storm two years before had knocked brush and trees down over holes so you could fall twenty feet if you slipped into one of them. Sometimes, if a dog got lost and didn't return, people believed that this place was where it went. I had gone in there once, daring myself, but the thick tangle of trees made me turn back. I had cut in only far enough to say I had been inside. Even though it was bright outside, the trees were dark and wild-looking. Shaggy and massed together, there was a coldness about them. You could smell them, the oldness and the stale, molding pull in the nostrils.

Nowhere, even at our place, had there been a footstep of Danny's to follow, and we didn't see any now except for our own, looking like blurred scars in the muddy earth as we moved along. Although it was warm for October, it was moist inside the woods, and I put on the jacket I had tied around my waist. The land sloped downward toward a cedar bog. Danny had been wearing green overalls with a jersey of the same color, but everything here was green—dark, pale, medium green. I hunted for a glimpse of his blond hair, and once I thought I saw it and shouted, but it turned out to be a clump of yellow leaves. A hole in my boot sole began to leak water until my right sock was wet through. I couldn't remember what kind of shoes Danny had worn.

All morning the woods were full of sound. Our group had Everett Handler, Joe Cranston, and his father in it. I didn't know the others by name. The men kept on shouting, but they stopped when they were too out of breath to keep on moving and call for Danny at the same time. I saw that Everett was getting winded already from so much walking. Finally, Mr. Cranston called back to us to rest for a minute. Although he was pretty far ahead, I could hear him talking to Everett.

"It's funny it would come down to her depending on us," he said.

"That must be almost ten years ago," Everett told him.

"That doesn't change it any," said Mr. Cranston.

We started out again. As I watched birds skim out of the trees and flutter against the leaves, I envied them because it would be so easy to fly and not fight through the wet, uneven ground as we had to do. A bee would buzz around my head, or a mosquito would sing in my ear so that it was a relief when it finally stung me and died with my slap. But the sound that I heard all the time was the noise of my own breathing. I kept wishing that I could put one foot down after the other and be sure I was stepping on something safe and level and certain. It was funny how, in a clearing, a spot a hundred yards away could look so comfortable, but it was just as full of briers as the rest of the land when we reached it. It was all a web of twigs that cut against our faces.

I left my jacket hanging on a tree, because it was too heavy and caught too many thorns. Since it was red, I knew I could find it again. The ground broke away when I moved down a steep hill toward the creek in front of me. The grade was so sudden that my shoulder nearly touched the earth, and the wet, black dirt crumbled under my boots to roll into the ravine below.

Then my feet, that had been so sure before, couldn't keep up with the speed I was traveling, and I found myself rolling too, but never as fast as the crumbling earth that slid and ran down the hill before me. I fell all the way, and my mouth was full of dirt when I stopped. More stones broke loose under my feet. With a wrench inside me, I heard them drop and roll against the rocky edge of a hole I might have stepped into myself. When I looked down into the hole, I didn't find what I was looking for and yet afraid to see. He wasn't there.

It was easier to climb down a hill than to go back up again. I couldn't find anything to cling to. Small plants growing on the hillside pulled loose in my fingers as I grasped them. I walked in the creek, because there were fewer branches there to slap against my face and catch on my clothes. Finally, I found myself standing in water that reached only an inch below the top of my boots. I tried to climb the steep slope of brown earth, but it broke apart underneath my feet and sent me back again to the water with a splash. I stood in the creek again, watching the water drip into the pool at my feet. There was no way of knowing how long I stood there, too tired to move right away and wondering how soon the water would rise above my boots. The sky was nearly hidden by the trees, and I had no watch. I didn't feel as if I had a bit of strength left. Sometime later, I saw a root embedded in the ground, the only thing I hadn't noticed before, and I held it in my right hand and put my left behind me for leverage. The root held, then moved out of the ground. I held it with both hands for the last try, but it pulled loose and dangled from my fingers.

When I got my breath back, I clutched the ground, clawing it while I crawled up the hill. It worked. But when I went to get my jacket, it was gone. I wondered who could have taken it, because I had the right tree sure enough. Didn't I? I couldn't remember, and I knew I, too, was lost.

Terror came sudden and swift when I saw I had closed myself in with branches. Where was the opening? How had I come into this place at all? When I tried to part the thorny branches, they caught at my sweater and pants like barbed wire so I couldn't move. They made holes in the cloth and worked their way past the material into my skin. As I clawed, searching for an opening, a branch snapped against my eyeball. For a long time, I was afraid to open my eye for fear it would fall out.

The smell of molding ground was heavy around me. I looked down to see a fresh footprint in the wetness, but I realized almost right away that it was my own. I had made it only a few minutes before.

"Danny!" I yelled. I knew now how scared he must be, how tired and wet and scratched. "Danny!" Far off, I could hear the shouts of the men. What if Danny, too, tried to shout at us and was caught somewhere in a hole so he couldn't move? I moved, to hear the marshy ground suck against my foot. It wasn't safe to stay there. I yelled out for Danny once more and heard something come through the twigs and dry branches. They crackled like fire as they broke. It was Everett Handler, panting as he cut away the branches to free me. He had found my jacket. It had been only a couple of yards away all that time, and the men, too, were closer than I had thought. It took us only about fifteen minutes to get back to them. Because there was no place to sit down, they half leaned against the birch trees surrounding us. The birches weren't strong enough to hold our weight, but the other trees had too many needles to be comfortable. A few of the men were smoking.

"Do you remember the time the little girl got lost over near Pear River, and they found her just as good as new?" asked Everett. He wiped his steaming face against his sweater sleeve.

A few of the men remembered.

We came out of the woods for the second time on Sunday afternoon, to meet the faces of Dad and June. Their eyes were dark, made small by lack of sleep. Marcia knew what it was all about by then.

"Danny!" she called as she ran over to the edge of the woods. "Come back and finish your house." June had to run after Marcia and catch her in her arms to keep the little girl away from the trees.

"Danny, why don't you answer?" she shouted, trying to get away from June. "Mother, can't you make him *talk* to me?"

But most of the time, Marcia stayed close to the house and didn't complain when one of the other women watched over her to give June a rest. Jackson spent nearly all his time in the woods. When his group came in, he would join another, eating whatever food he could find to carry.

The damp night air was no good for Dad, but he wouldn't go

inside. That night I found him standing in the yard, looking at a mound of stones and wood.

"Danny's house," he said. "He never got to finish it. Do you suppose he tried to build something out there?"

"It's going to be all right," I told him, and thought of the water holes inside that were deeper than a man is tall. "We're going to find him."

"I shouldn't have asked her to come back at all," Dad said.

Word came on Monday night that one of Sherman Blatnik's hounds had struck a fresh trail on the ground above the cedar bog. When Nap Stoner's party came back with the news, June stepped forward as if she couldn't quite believe it. Nothing would stop her from going out herself as we all started back toward the woods.

"Why don't you stay here?" Kendall asked her. "If we get a track, I'll let you know."

"I've been here too long. I've imagined myself out there so many times that I might as well be," she answered, and there was no way for him to keep her back. She moved ahead as fast as anyone, although her feet kept slipping, and her breath came in jerks.

"You're tired already," he said.

"No," she said sharply. "Leave me alone."

"I've done all I could," he said. "I've looked until it doesn't seem possible he's in there at all. He had his toys. Why did he go looking for a piece of wood?"

"He was building that house. Maybe he liked it because I used to live there. Isn't that a reason?"

"But he had his toys. I don't understand it."

"You shouldn't keep asking that," she said. "Maybe he'll tell us himself. Maybe they'll have found him when we get there."

"Don't," he told her, and the word was like a shout. "Don't even hope until we *know*."

"You don't think we'll find him, do you?" she asked.

"We can't be sure until," and he stopped for a second, "until we get there and find out."

I walked behind them, swinging my flashlight off toward the trees. Everything seemed much stiller than it was by day. Kendall lit a cigarette, and the smoke curled up as if it were climbing the beam of light. I turned the flashlight on the ground. It was funny to see my own feet come out of the dark, as if they weren't part of me any longer.

There were bonfires in the swamp, and you could see them shining through the trees. They were beacons for Danny and places where the men could warm themselves and dry their clothing. Guides and trappers were crisscrossing the ground when we got there. I heard Sherman Blatnik's voice before I saw him.

"The dog's lame, but we've got to hold to the scent while it's warm," he was saying. Then, in the swinging gleam of a flashlight, I had a glimpse of his cap and his dark face, made darker by a growth of whiskers. I watched June rush toward him, while Kendall walked over to Nap Stoner. Looking at her and Sherman Blatnik, I wondered if things might have been different if he could have done as much for her ten years ago as he was doing now.

"What have you found out?" she asked.

"Nothing yet," and his voice was soft. I watched him take June over to the nearest bonfire to wait while the search went on. Then he came back to the dogs, and I could see her, huddling her hands into her sleeves as she stood with her back to the fire.

Each minute could bring Danny or another sign of him, but the minutes went by empty until Sherman Blatnik's dog went completely lame. Someone was sent back for fresh hounds, because Sherman refused to give up until another dog came to pick up the scent. But it was no use The first hound simply couldn't go on, and when they came back with another, the trail had been lost.

I think that was when June gave up hope. She left the fire and didn't look at anyone. She didn't seem to feel even Kendall's arm holding her to keep her from stumbling. Once I saw her pull her arm away from his. It was a long, terribly quiet walk back. All through the woods, it smelled like decay.

When they told Dad that the scent had faded, he was quiet, and I was afraid he was going to collapse. He gripped the stuffed arms of his parlor chair, just staring into those trees. I noticed he was trying to say something to June, but he couldn't seem to get started.

"I tell you it's my fault," he said finally.

"Don't blame yourself," June said in a strained voice.

"I've got to tell you," he said. "I dozed off for a minute in the yard. That must be when he wandered off."

Something flickered up on her face to fade out there. "Asleep?"

"I was happy, I guess," he said, as if he were apologizing. "It was nice out, and I was thinking that you were home again. And Danny was out there playing next to me. I just dropped off."

June's face was all closed up so you couldn't see anything in it. "I understand," she said.

More men kept on coming every hour. An airplane flew over the next day to help guide search parties through the densest part of the woods, although we probably didn't cover more than six square miles altogether. The mosquitoes got worse every time we went in. I thought of Danny's thin jersey almost all the time, but the idea of what must be going through his mind was something I didn't want to think about.

A photographer who had driven up from Minneapolis edged around, taking pictures. He got Dad to stand at the place in the yard where he had first missed Danny. Then he had June pose for him, and somebody brought Marcia out to be in the picture. At the entrance to the woods, the men's feet had worn a heavy band of boot prints into the grass Dad and I had planted. The prints were ground into the earth, and they looked more like huge toothmarks than anything else.

All day long in the woods, the sky had the same color. It appeared in scraps between patches of interlaced branches above our heads, always gray, although the gray had a glow behind it at noon. The brightness behind the sky went away as it got later. It was flat gray just before it turned dark. Old leaves of red and yellow had fallen into the mud where they seemed to be melting into the ground as if they had been chewed. That night was bad, worse than usual, because a mist crept into the trees. And we were so tired by then that it didn't seem worth it to stand in line for food any more, and time passed steadily without any sharp moments. They were all alike.

I was asleep when I heard the pistol shots. When I was on my feet, I heard them again, and the people rushing toward the woods made me certain that it had been no dream. But instead of

four, they came two at a time. It was Jackson who got excited
this time.

"Did you hear it?" he shouted at June, although she was
beside him.

"Yes," she said. "I heard the shots." But her voice didn't
lift to his.

Somewhere near the house, I heard the women start a hymn
that was sung at the Lutheran church in Byron City. Men left
their cots to dash off into the swamp. I felt a long shudder of
relief run through me like a chill.

Jackson was gone when I looked again for him. As I ran
toward the balsam trees at the swamp opening, the shouts had
died down, and there was only the women's singing and another
sound, the heavy breath of Everett Handler beside me.

"I wonder why it was only two shots," he said.

"They add up to four," I told him. "That's the signal."

"But they weren't together."

We moved faster than we ever had, along a trail that had
been cleared out by four days of men passing through. Before
we had gone half a mile, lights came toward us, and I saw Mr.
Cranston and Sherman Blatnik carrying Nap Stoner.

"Nap fired those shots," Mr. Cranston said. "Fell in a bog
and maybe broke his leg."

"Go and tell her," Sherman told me. "It was no signal."

Danny would not be found. The hounds followed scents, then
lost them again as they trailed off into nothing. It was like looking for something lost inside the house that was there a minute
ago, and finally searching places where you knew it couldn't be.
They brought in the dogs to rest. Their flews hung down so far
it was a wonder their collars didn't choke them. By Wednesday,
all the hounds were lame and couldn't keep on. The National
Guards started to leave, and when their leader said that Danny
couldn't still be alive, he said just what most had been thinking.
Nap Stoner had sprained his ankle when he fell. Sherman Blatnik took his place and said he would keep on going. The Guard
members went away because they had done their best while there
was the most hope, and people from the resorts began to drift off,
too. Once the feeling started to grow, there was no holding it

back. As each group slipped away, Dad tried to make them see that Danny was big and strong for his age and dressed in warm enough clothes to keep him alive. Finally, the Byron City group started leaving on Friday, not long after we heard Nap Stoner had pneumonia. They remembered searches for other children who were never found.

Sherman Blatnik told June the men would give up the search by nightfall if they weren't any luckier than they had been up to then. There hadn't been a sign—no discarded jersey or lost shoe fallen in the trailless woods. Although I expected June to, she didn't speak but looked at Sherman and nodded. It was Dad, instead, who tried to argue with the men.

"Give it one more day, why don't you?"

"There's no use," Joe Cranston's father said.

"He just wandered off in a minute. He couldn't have gone so far that you could miss him," Dad said. "I just looked away for a couple of seconds."

Dad didn't say any more after that. He just looked from one face to another, searching for something he never seemed to find, because he finally turned away and walked into the house. I'll never forget how strange that red parlor chair looked then, standing alone on the bumpy ground. As he went in, I thought the sky grew darker, dim somehow. When he was gone, Jackson tried to keep the men going.

"We can't stop now," he said. "We'll never know what happened to him if we do. I've got money." It was the first time he mentioned what we all took for granted.

"It wouldn't do any good," Everett Handler said when it seemed that no one at all would answer. "How can you spread any amount of money among so many men?"

"It can be done," Jackson said, but June stopped him.

"No," she said, "they don't ask for pay." Then she looked straight at us, and in spite of the men's talking about her going away from Byron City as she did, they couldn't say she wasn't strong. "It has to be stopped sometime. You can leave now. It won't help to stay for nightfall." I looked at her and expected her to scream out, and I finally wished she would let go, but her face was tight.

Most of them turned for home then. "I've got to get back,"

Everett said in his gentle voice. "My wife can't handle the drug-store alone." His big face was splotchy, and I suppose the week had been harder on him than he ever let on. Four men stayed. Besides myself, there were Jackson, the newspaper photographer, and Sherman Blatnik.

I never thought of stopping. I was afraid to, because then I'd imagine how different things would have been if I hadn't gone into town in that fancy Buick. And I thought I could make it up to him with a little can of brown paint. The others had their reasons clear enough. One had to finish up his job, and the other wanted to show that he wasn't holding what had happened almost ten years ago against anyone. And there was Jackson, who would keep on going as long as he could. But I wonder if the men who weren't with us any longer hadn't been the best of the group. They had stayed all that time, although few of them had ever seen Danny, and though some blamed June for leaving their town.

The sky, drab all day, seemed to draw into itself as we walked toward the woods for the last time. Suddenly something damp was cold against my face, and it was snowing. Hopelessly, we stood and watched the loose, filmy mass come down, sparse at first and then quickening until it spun at us with frantic force. It hung to the shoulders of our coats and began to cover the ground.

"That means it's freezing," Jackson said in a dead voice. "We might as well give up."

Although it was midafternoon, the sky turned dark. As I watched Sherman Blatnik and the photographer drive off, the snow slanted down against the road. Nobody was in the yard any more; not even the chair was left. Jackson went in, and I watched the lights turn on inside our house. He and Dad sat across the room from each other. I saw June touch Dad's shoulder, and she tried to smile. I went in then, and at the doorway, I took off my cap and shook it to get off the snow. Some of the flakes had melted already, and I watched one cling to the damp wool, stretch out, and hang there before it fell to the floor. That was what losing hope looked like.

Constance Crawford

The Boats

Everyone had to come to Walt Pener's boathouse eventually since it was the only place on the lake which sold gasoline
for the speedboats and repaired them when they leaked, sputtered, or would not go fast enough. The boathouse leaned back
against the steep sandstone cliff, and docks were strung along the
shore, flapping and creaking as the wind pushed the water under
and between the metal barrels which floated them. The docks
and the yard were usually in a state of workmanlike confusion,
and on week ends the slips by the gasoline pumps were so crowded
that there were always several people circling their boats slowly,
offshore, waiting their turn. The men in loud shirts and boys
with backs the color of their mahogany speedboats were always
bustling in and out, discussing horsepower and varnishes and
racing technique with the big husky Swedes Walt Pener hired
as mechanics and dock boys. The few sailboat owners who came
to have sails mended or rudders repaired were quiet and a little
out of place.

Everybody seemed to know everybody else at the boathouse,
and Joan Halderman liked to come here, especially lately, and
watch, pretending that she, also, knew everybody and they knew
her. Now she sat on a pile of boards, facing away from the blind-
ing late-afternoon glare of the water. The sun was warm on her
back, browning it still deeper, but the wind off the lake was rising,
rustling the row of poplars, rushing in the pines on top of the cliff.
Her shadow lay before her on the asphalt of the yard, and she

watched the wind pick up long strands of her hair and wave them out from her head—like flames.

Wondering if her hair had grown to reach her waist yet, she bent her head back and her hair fell down, soft and thick and tickling. By twisting her arm behind her, Joan could feel that the longest hairs came all the way to her waist. But she jerked her head up quickly when she remembered that Ed might be watching and think she was foolish and a sissy. Ed was a friend of hers who worked with boats better than anyone, better, even, than Walt Pener himself. Ed had beautiful lumpy, strong arms and Joan wondered if he ever noticed how long and wavy her hair was and how well she could judge boats herself.

Then, with a shiver of anticipation, Joan saw that the thing she had been waiting for was going to begin, and she forgot about her hair. The gray work boat had reached the dock, towing a big speedboat that was listing badly. It belonged to Mr. DeYoung, Joan knew, who was a Yacht Club officer. This afternoon the boat had been found loose, banging against the rocks in a windy, deserted bay on the north shore. Now one man floated the boat onto the carriage, which was on a steep track leading down under the water. Ed started the mechanical winch, and the carriage was drawn up the track into the yard. The boat was glossy and dripping, and water spouted from the cracked bottom. Above the water line was a great splintered hole. Joan stood up to see better as Ed started to work, taking out the ruined plank. He was deft and strong.

"What happened this time, Ed?" she asked, and he glanced at her, squinting against the sun.

"You here again, kid? Look out now." He wrenched a piece of wood free and Joan could peer through the wound into the boat's very insides. "Found her banging on the rocks somewhere. Fifth time this *week* a boat's been turned loose. People better start buying locks. Yes, sir." His voice trailed off, and he was absorbed in his work.

"Yeah," said Joan, sitting down again. "They've all been nice boats, too, you notice?" She waited for an answer and then continued. "This has a hundred and seventy-five horse Fireball, doesn't it?"

"Yeah," he said. "Say, girls aren't supposed to know about

engines." But he said it slowly, still working, as though he weren't even thinking about her.

"But *I* do," Joan said.

"H'm. How old are you?"

"Thirteen. Well, really nearly fourteen," she said, knowing he would believe her, for she looked much older than twelve and a half.

But he only said, "H'm."

Ed swooped the plane again and again along a plank, and the shavings curled up and dropped off as though his swinging movements had made them grow, by magic, out of the metal tool. His arms were strong and brown, with yellow hair on them. Joan imagined him wrapped in a red and gold cloth, stalking through a green jungle, cutting the creepers and twining things from his path with a long knife. "When I was little," she said, "about eight, my father and I sailed a boat around in the South Seas. That's where I learned it all. About boats." She was going to go on, but Ed straightened and looked up the road which led down from the top of the cliff.

A yellow Cadillac stopped in the yard, and a man in bright Hawaiian-print trunks and shirt got out and came over to Ed. The man took the cigar from between his teeth and puffed the air out of his red-veined cheeks with a hiss of exasperation as he saw the hole in the side of the boat. He grunted. "They'll jew me plenty again this time. Huh, Ed?"

"At least it didn't get to the motor, Mr. DeYoung," said Ed.

"Your boss'd say that's a damn shame." The man laughed, belching a cloud of smoke into the air. Joan sat on the pile of boards and listened only halfway to their voices. She studied Mr. DeYoung's feet in their leather sandals, and then his knobby, hairy knees. His shirt was open, hanging on each side of his round stomach. The smell of his cigar called up from somewhere, far back, the remembrance of her father, who had once scooped her up from the floor and set her on the table, which was wet from a glass someone had spilled. Everyone had laughed, and the smell of the cigars had hung all through the room. Joan hadn't thought of her father for a long time—maybe for the whole summer—and she wondered a little what he was doing, if perhaps he *could* be hunting big game or horse racing as she sometimes told the people who asked.

"Son of a bitch," muttered Mr. DeYoung, running his hand over the chrome strip on the hull. Joan began to listen, knowing he was thinking of the person who had turned his boat loose to drift. She watched with pleasure as he winced, noticing another deep scratch on the side. He groaned again. "The cops are going to get that guy, believe me."

"I guess people will have to begin buying locks," said Ed quietly, and Joan hid her smile behind her hand. She hoped Mr. DeYoung would scream and threaten the culprit with death, but he only muttered, "Son of a bitch," and "Who the devil . . . ?" a few times more, slapped Ed on the shoulder, and drove away. The tires of the Cadillac skidded on the gravel as he turned onto the main road at the top.

Joan watched Ed for a while longer. She hugged her knees and kept her feet up off the cold asphalt, listening to the roar of the wind. She dreamed of speed—flying, running, riding on a wild black horse, the biggest and wildest horse.

"Time to quit," said Ed, putting his tools in a box. "So long, kid."

The wind had begun to cut through the sun's warmth on Joan's back, and she was glad to get up. "So long, Ed." Though the boards were splintery, she skipped down the docks, because Ed was her friend and it had been an exciting afternoon. She decided to walk along the beach instead of taking the regular trail that ran through the pines and was smooth and civilized for the city people. The sand was cold, but, to show herself that she was tough, she ran where the water was ankle-deep. The golden spray shot up all around, and the drops, when they struck her, stung like hailstones. At the point, the wind always drove the foaming water onto the sand in miniature breakers which, if she watched long enough, would turn into real ones, salty and roaring. The rocks here, now turning bluer and colder as the sun sank, were jumbled down the beach and out into the water. Joan always thought it was as though a giant had sat once on top of the sandstone cliff and let gravel trickle idly through his fingers.

Since the sun was still up, Joan knew it must not even be six-thirty, and her mother and Steve would be having just their first highballs. It was too early to go home, for if she did, she would get there before dinner and they would think that she had nothing to keep her busy. In the next inlet, the public beach would be

empty now. Joan decided to go around and sit on the diving board
for a while and watch the seaweed which always twirled around
the string of floats used to keep the dude swimmers in the shallow
water.

Back in the bay, the water, sheltered by the point, became quiet
suddenly, smeared with green reflections from the opposite shore.
Joan lay on her stomach and dangled her arms over the sides of
the diving board, feeling her hands grow heavy. She hung her
head over the end, looking back at the beach, making herself
believe that the sky and the sand had changed places and that the
trees here were rooted by their slender tops. Then three boys
came onto the sand, intruding into that strange world, destroying
the illusion that it was the earth, and not she, that had turned
upside down. Joan sat up quickly, and, hugging her knees, stared
past the boys with cool, gray eyes to show her unconcern. They
sounded like little children, giggling loudly. They, who could not
possibly have understood, had interfered with her. The breeze
lifted her hair softly, and she felt solitude around her like a cloak.
But when the boys began skipping rocks over the water, she
watched in spite of herself.

One of them they called Mort, and he had red hair which
jerked in front of his eyes whenever he drew his long, freckled arm
back to throw. Once the smallest boy took such a running windup
that he splashed into the water, soaking his tennis shoes. They all
laughed loudly, the other two patting the little one on his back.
Joan no longer was protected by her isolation, but felt shut out
of their gaiety. She let her legs down over the side of the diving
board and swung them rapidly, gazing up at the pines bordering
the beach, but the boys did not even glance at her. They had seen
a frog squatting on a rock which jutted out of the water, some
distance from shore. The frog stared arrogantly from bulging,
half-closed eyes.

"O.K., ol' frog," the boys said, but even when the stones
started splashing into the water around him, the frog sat motionless, disdainful. The boys became more earnest, gathering hand-
fuls of rocks, taking careful aim, but always missing their target.
They can't do it, Joan thought, they can't do it. She leaned back
and contemplated the opposite shore. Out of the corners of her
eyes she could see the boys were getting exasperated, and their

throws became wilder and wilder. Two of them finally gave up, and only the red-haired boy kept on.

Joan got up slowly, dropped onto the sand, and chose her rock. A round one with enough roughness to give a good grip, she made sure. Scuffing her feet a little, she walked down the beach to get a better aim. She noticed with pride how quiet and steady her heart beat against her ribs. She was the heroine who, with only a whip and a chair, approaches the ferocious tiger. She took aim, and the boys turned to watch her. She missed the frog, but her stone struck the bigger rock just at the water line with a hard *splut* sound which Joan remembered clearly afterward. The frog leapt upward with a little squawk, flopped into the water belly first, and disappeared.

Placing her feet deliberately, looking straight ahead, Joan walked away up the beach, as a heroine should, curbing her urge to run and laugh, until she was on the trail, hidden in the pines. Then she ran as hard as she could, and as gracefully, beautifully. Horrid, stupid boys. But she hoped she would see them again and they would ask her who she was. Her legs obeyed her especially well tonight, gathering up, loosening out, taking the ground with great strides, great—powerful—strides. It was what they said about race horses.

In front of the Yacht Club dock the trail tipped downhill and threaded between the boulders. Joan disdained the people who took the easy way, and she could run straight over the pile of rocks without slackening speed. Little rock, big rock, one with moss; black one, cracked one, jump across—the words always chanted themselves through her head, and tonight they had to go faster than ever to keep up with her feet. Her hair flew and jerked and swished over her back. The rocks blurred by under her and she landed lightly on the pine needles on the other side, breathing hard with excitement.

Here the houses began, and Joan could see their lights blinking on, up the hill. The wild part of the trail was past, and so she walked slowly, as quiet as an Indian, through the darkening columns of the tree trunks. She was a scout, and if any of the white men, in their hillside forts, should look out, searching, they would glimpse a shadow, only for an instant, and would hear no sound.

Before climbing the hill to her own house, Joan stopped and looked past the docks, out over the open water, where the bats were darting to and fro in the half-light. She heard the rising rush of the wind far away in the trees on the opposite shore, and even here, on the sheltered side, the water was slapping against the creaking docks. She decided that later tonight she would walk clear around to Forster's, where the hills were low and the wind swept down across the bay.

Climbing the hill toward the houses, Joan realized how cold her feet were and how hungry she had become, but she did not hurry. In this neighborhood only the lake-front houses had great terraces and wide windows, and the farther Joan got from these, the smaller the houses were. Now there were dinner smells in the air, and people were sitting inside, in the flat yellow electric light of their dining rooms. Mrs. Ketcham, a blue bandanna around her head, greeted Joan from her kitchen window. Finally deciding to answer, Joan said, "Hello," and walked on. Jim Cannon, who had one of the fastest boats on the lake, was in his yard, hurriedly putting varnish on a water ski. He had never given Joan a ride in his boat, and she was glad he did not notice her now.

Then she saw the lights of her own house. She disliked their cabin, for that was what it was, a cabin, with blue trim and a steep little roof. There was only one real bedroom downstairs for her mother and Steve, and Joan had to use the slant-walled, half-finished room upstairs. Her windows were not wide casements opening out over the water but dormer windows looking at the steep side of the hill and at the main road just above, where, on week ends, the drunks squealed their tires going around the mountain curves.

When Joan opened the front door, her mother was stretched out on the bamboo chaise longue, and Joan could see that she was not in a good mood, even though the glass in her hand was nearly empty.

"*Well*, the wanderer returneth," her mother called to Steve, whom Joan could see through the open kitchen door. He was stirring something in a pan on the stove and had a dish towel tied around his waist. He turned and glanced at Joan. "Here, set the table, will you Joan? This damn gravy won't thicken."

Joan was annoyed; she *had* come back too soon. As she got

the spoons out of the drawer in the kitchen, she noticed that Steve's mustache looked ragged and his blond hair fell over his sweaty forehead. When Steve had first come to live with them, and they had moved to the mountains, Joan had thought he was very handsome, with his smooth blond hair, jutting eyebrows, and shoulders like the men in magazines. But lately, since he went around in his shirt sleeves most of the time, his shoulders were narrower than Joan had thought. "Don't forget the milk," he said.

"Do we *always* have to . . . "

"*You* should have milk—yes, always."

Joan opened the icebox door and slammed it back against the sink. Steve was always treating her like a child. Still, she got the milk bottle out and brought it to the table in the living room, where they ate. She and Steve did have lots of fun, sometimes. Joan stood by the table and looked at her mother. "Are you sick again?" Joan asked.

"Exhausted," said her mother. "So sweet old Steve is fixing dinner. Have you ever thought, Joan, where you and I would be without Steve?"

"Cut it out, Marcia," said Steve quietly, carrying dishes to the table.

Joan had noticed that ever since her mother had left the rest home last winter she was always tired, although she got more beautiful all the time. Joan wondered if she would ever be so beautiful that a man would work for her the way Steve did for her mother. Even so, she didn't like having Steve with a towel around his waist. "Why don't we get a maid?" Joan asked, after a long silence. "The Bergen kids are always talking about their maid."

Her mother smiled, showing her even, white teeth. "Why, what a little snob you're getting to be!" Her smile faded. "Well, I'd like one, too, but where would we put her? And Steve thinks we should conserve my money." Steve turned and went into the kitchen. Joan's mother got up and came to the table. She had on the dress that Joan liked the best of all. It was bright blue and startling against her white skin and the dark, perfect waves of her hair. Joan had hated her own long, light, tangled hair until one day when Steve and her mother had been laughing and having fun together, and in a loud, jolly voice Steve had called Joan

"the gray-eyed, golden-haired goddess, Athena." Joan wondered
where he had got the name Athena, but she liked it and thought
of changing her name when she grew up. Athena Halderman.
Ever since then, studying her face in the mirror, she had seen new
things, and she knew that 'she was beautiful, almost like her
mother.

Steve brought in the dish of stew and they sat down. Joan
poured herself a glass of milk, hoping Steve would notice how she
scowled. When her mother started to eat, Joan noticed a bandage
around the tip of her index finger. It looked strange beside the
other long, scarlet fingernails.

"Another one broke?" said Joan regretfully.

"Don't remind me," said her mother, putting her hand out of
sight. "I'm so mad I could scream. I did it on the damn garbage
can." Joan knew her mother had been letting her fingernails
grow ever since she had been sick. They made her long, blue-
veined hands even more graceful, and sometimes when she let her
hands droop over the arms of her chair, Joan thought the nails
looked like the polished claws of a tiger or a lion. Joan wanted
to tell her mother how sorry she was about the broken one, but
they were talking of something else and she knew they would not
listen to her.

Joan played with her food, eating only when she thought Steve
would not see. Wishing they would pay attention to her, she
puckered her forehead, trying to draw her eyebrows up in the
middle as her mother did when she was disturbed. Sometimes
Joan even put on special clothes or combed her hair differently
to make them notice, but Steve had never called her gray-eyed
Athena again.

Then Joan remembered how the frog had jumped off the rock
this afternoon, frightened by her miraculous throw. Those stupid
boys must have stared and gaped and wondered who she was as
she walked coolly away, not giving them even so much as a glance.
She wondered if Steve and her mother would realize how magnificent it had been if she told them about it. But they were talking
about people Joan had never heard of, and Steve only looked
at her once and said, "Joan, stop fooling around and eat."

All right, she would eat and they could go to hell. She would
keep all her secrets—and she had plenty. Joan began stuffing

the food into her mouth, gulping and chewing as noisily as she could. A piece of cold carrot fell off her spoon and slid down her bare leg. She would not even tell them the biggest, best secret of all. Just thinking about it made her heart beat faster with excitement. She knew other ways than talking to make people notice her, she thought.

Suddenly, in the middle of their incomprehensible talk, Joan's mother turned to her and said, "Maybe *Joan* said something. Has anyone been asking you about your father?"

"No," Joan said, "but those Bergen kids kept talking about how *their* father did this and *their* father did that. So I just told 'em something about *my* father, for a change." Joan remembered with pleasure that they had believed it all, even the part about Alaska. "Where is he anyway?" she asked, half afraid of a disappointing answer.

But her mother only said, "So that's it. I suppose Mrs. Bergen heard this conversation, too?"

Joan watched her mother's eyes, so dark that behind the reflections of light in them you could not even guess how deep they went. She enjoyed having her mother look at her so closely. "I don't know what I said," Joan answered, slowly, to keep her mother's eyes on her.

Her mother gave a breathy, mirthless little laugh. "And I suppose you forgot that my name is Mrs. Walch now, and not Mrs. Halderman."

"I don't know," said Joan again, suddenly not caring.

Her mother stood up, her mouth set in a smile, but Joan saw that where the dimples usually came, there were only dark lines instead. "Well, it makes no difference," her mother said. "I was a fool to think Lake Benton would be any different from any other place. They're *all* full of catty women."

"I don't see why getting into their stupid Yacht Club is anything to be desired," said Steve. "You wouldn't *like* them, even if they did ask you to play bridge. Now let's go somewhere and forget about it."

"All right," she said lightly. "Where shall it be? To the club for drinks and dancing? To the lovely house of some of our many friends for sparkling conversation? To a lively party, overlooking the lake?"

Steve stood up and smiled at her—a little sadly, Joan saw with bewilderment. "Why not the theater," he said, "joining the gay, after-dinner crowds?"

"Perfect!" said Joan's mother. "There's a new thing with John Wayne and Maureen O'Hara, isn't there? The critics *raved* about it." They both laughed together, quietly, leaning against the table.

Joan could not understand; they had a secret and she was left out. Then she remembered the secret *she* had from them, from everybody, and she began to laugh, too. It was hard at first but then came easier until the tears filled her eyes. But somehow, nothing was funny.

Then Joan's mother went into the bedroom to get her coat, and the laughter subsided. Joan was still vaguely troubled. "Want to come to the movie, Joan?" asked Steve. "You've been getting to bed early lately."

"No, I think I'll stay home," said Joan. "I have some things I want to do."

"O.K.," he said. "So long." And they went out.

Joan waited until she heard the car start outside and then ran up the stairs, two at a time, to her bedroom. She did not switch on the light but got the package of matches which she kept hidden under her mattress. She lit the candle which she had stood in a saucer on the old chiffonier. Joan loved the way the glow filled the long mirror, as though from under water. She took off her faded bathing suit, got the green one from the bottom drawer, and put it on. It hugged her tightly, and in the candle light it had a soft, half-sheen. She liked to run in this bathing suit; it seemed to stretch and relax with her, helping her. She shook her hair down, admiring it. Moving close to the mirror, she smoothed her eyebrows and looked for a long time into the gray eyes in the reflection. The candle was a tiny flame in each one. Finally she blew out the candle and went to the window. She knew the branches of the pine tree outside by heart, and could let herself down to the ground even on moonless, cloudy nights. She never went down the stairs, even when Steve and her mother were gone.

The air was cold now, and Joan shivered standing by the corner of the house, trying to decide where to go. Somehow, this

time, it was different. The excitement of the afternoon had left
her. The wind had risen, as she had thought it would, but it only
made her colder; the moon was thin, already close to the jagged
treetops on Wheeler Ridge. Then Joan remembered her resolve
to go clear to Forster's on the big bay, and she started down the
hill, trotting to keep warm. She tried leaping the ferns, and she
noticed that her feet were now so tough that the pine needles only
felt slippery and never pricked her as they used to. By the time
she was on the trail by the shore, she felt much better, and began
watching, as usual, for strange animal eyes and lurking danger.
Thinking how surprised her mother and Steve would be if they
knew, she almost laughed aloud, but then remembered how important it was for her to keep perfectly silent. The familiar excitement returned, tightening her muscles and making her ready, she
felt, to perform miraculous feats of agility and daring if necessary.

But it was farther to the bay than she had thought. The woods
became thicker, and the lights of the houses retreated far back in
the trees. At one place, the trail crossed a wide stretch of sand
where a stream, now dry, ran down from the hills in the spring,
when the snow melted. The sand glimmered faintly around her.
The wind carried the smell of the marshy plants which grew in
the mud where the lake had receded through the rainless summer.
Joan shivered; when she was nearly across the sand and into
the trees again, a loud grating, rasping cry boomed from the
shore where the row of docks floated on the black water. Joan
gasped and stood rigid; the sound came again, like a groaning
voice. And suddenly, from the trees, great, dark creatures rose
into the sky with a rush of air all around, covering the sliver of
moon. Joan cried out and ran, hardly realizing she had done so
until she found herself standing among the tree trunks, her own
scream echoing in her ears. Her heart filled her temples with
pulse beats.

The lights of the Bergens' house showed a little distance up
the hill, yellow and warm. While Joan looked at them, the sound
came again. Then she knew it was only a fat bullfrog sitting
somewhere in his cold, muddy world under the docks. And she
must have frightened the cranes which always sat in the tops of the

pine trees, like marble statues, until suddenly they would leap into the air with a rush of wings. Joan felt ridiculous standing, cold, in the middle of the trail, her knees shaking. Scared by a frog and some dumb cranes, like a city sissy, she thought with disgust. But she looked at the squares of yellow light from the Bergens' house, and longed to be inside with them. She knew that Mrs. Bergen sometimes read to the two girls and that they always had something good to eat in their hands when they came out to play. They were her friends. Joan started up the little path leading to the house.

But the Bergen girls had straight brown hair and tender feet. They bragged about their boat and the Yacht Club and their father. Joan remembered how they smirked at her sometimes, hating her. Often when she came to play, they wouldn't let her in the house and giggled at her from their bedroom window upstairs. Joan remembered, too, that, in some way, Mrs. Bergen had hurt her mother. Somehow she, like Joan, had been left out.

Joan smiled to herself in the dark, thinking how much the Bergens missed, even though they did have a fast boat. They never had adventures; they just sat and giggled. Those girls never knew how dark and thrilling it was at night, because they went inside and turned on all the lights. Joan forgot about going to Forster's, and she went back down the path quietly.

On the main trail, Joan stopped and listened, looking about her; there was nothing, no sound but the wind. She ran through the ferns down to the shore, out onto the Bergens' dock. It was littered with pieces of rope, a canoe paddle, a fishing pole, and several canvas chairs, one lying on its side. The Bergen girls never put away their things. Joan stood by the slip where the speedboat was tied—loosely tied, Joan saw, so that it banged against the dock when a gust of wind caught it. The canvas cover was thrown over the top of the boat and not fastened. She smoothed the cover and tied it down carefully, as if everything had belonged to her. Excitement flooded through her, more intensely than at any of the other times.

Joan unlooped the stern lines and then had to work over the knotted rope at the prow before it would loosen. Gripping the sides of the boat and bracing her feet against the cleats on the

dock, Joan pushed with her full weight. The heavy boat started
to slide out into the open water. When it was just free of the dock,
she gave one last shove and the dark shape drifted out quietly,
away from her. The momentum of her push spent itself, and the
boat hung in a glassy strip of water for a moment, before the
wind caught it. Then the stern swung crosswise to the wind, and
the waves pushed against the mahogany sides. Joan watched
until the boat disappeared in the darkness. Even though she
held her hands over her mouth, she let out a high, thin little cry
of exaltation.

Sarah Fay

The Death of Pierce

Mimi's sister, Maud, was the only one of the three of them
who was not very sick. She was not allowed to see Mimi much
the first few days, and neither of them was allowed to go into
Pierce's room. All week his door was kept closed, and on the
other side of the door it was silent a great deal of the time. And
always their mother's voice with him was very gentle. Yet the two
little girls were not entirely aware of how sick Pierce was; Mimi,
especially, did not dream of his being in danger.

Toward the end of the week, the trained nurse came. By the
time she was expected to arrive, on an afternoon, Mimi was well
enough to sit up in bed and be visited by Maud. Maud had been
with her ever since lunch, and was sitting on the window seat with
Sandy, her stuffed Scotch terrier, when the sound of a car on the
gravel driveway pervaded the waiting house.

"It must be her," said Mimi.

Maud leaned forward to lift the shade and peeked cautiously
out the open window. "It's a green car," she said.

"What *kind* of car?"

"I don't know," Maud admitted.

At once, Mimi climbed out of bed and went feebly to the
window and looked herself. "It's an Oldsmobile," she stated,
and hurried shakily back to bed. She lay among her pillows,
feeling damp and anxious. During the winter, she had spent
weeks learning the names of cars, so that Pierce would not be
the only one who knew.

"You shouldn't have gotten out of bed," Maud said quietly.

And, quite as quietly, Mimi said, "But Pierce will want to know." Mimi was eight, a year older than Pierce and three years younger than Maud.

The little girls heard their mother go downstairs, and then they heard the screen door slam and her high heels crossing the porch. In the still heat of midafternoon, they heard the two women's voices, fluttering and assured, below the open window.

"What does she look like?" asked Mimi.

"She has red hair."

"Let me see." And, without really wanting to this time, Mimi climbed out of bed again and went to the window.

"You shouldn't," said Maud, and furtively they peered around the edge of the shade.

"She has red hair," Mimi agreed in a whisper. "And big teeth. I don't like her. I'm not going to remember her name."

"It's Miss Dunston."

"I don't care—I'm not going to remember it," Mimi said. "Pierce will hate her, too."

By six o'clock, things looked even more as if they would never be the same again. Their mother and father acted more worried and hurried than ever, and paid the girls almost no attention. The young nurse brought Mimi's supper up to her on Maud's tray.

"There we are!" she said, plumping it down on the bed. And before Mimi could speak, she had bounced from the room, as if this whole thing were a vacation. A minute later, Mimi's mother came in, but she didn't say anything and looked about her in an inquiring way, as if she were trying to remember what she had forgotten.

"Mother," began Mimi in a trembling voice, "I don't have my own tray, or my own napkin ring, either."

Her mother said, "Dear, you must try not to complain. We're all very busy with Pierce, and you can be a big help to us by not fussing."

"It's the third day that I've had to eat applesauce," said Mimi faintly.

"My darling, I can't *help* it—"

There was a high, thin call from Pierce's room, and her mother turned and ran out. Mimi listened, and then, with Maud's tray on her lap and her supper untouched, she began to cry. She felt,

wearily, that things would never be right again. It would be days
before she could get up, and before Pierce could, and they could
run around all they wanted to—climb the barn roof, as they'd
planned, and go swimming again in the pond, and look for the
huge snapping turtle at the shallow end, where the bulrushes grew.
It would be days before things would get back to being the same
again, and already summer was nearly over.

The nurse came down the hall from the linen closet; she halted
outside the door and saw Mimi's tears, and then came in briskly.
When she reached out and put a hand on Mimi's warm forehead,
Mimi stopped crying and sat immobile and straight, like a photograph of herself.

"Poor kiddie," said the nurse. "I guess you feel forgotten.
It's the young man of the house who's getting all the attention,
isn't it?"

Resistantly, Mimi said, "He has always gotten it."

"Don't I know!" said the nurse with a wry smile. "Already!
Little Brother sure knows how to throw his weight around in *this*
house! Well, cheer up, honey, it may not always be his world.
You eat your applesauce and dry your tears. What time are you
supposed to be tucked in?"

"Eight o'clock," said Mimi, with a vague feeling of comfort.

"Eight it is. If Little Brother lets me get away, I'll come in
a few minutes before and read you a story. How's that?"

"All right," said Mimi; she spoke with a touch of reserve, as
Pierce might have said it, and she watched Miss Dunston sway
briskly out of the room. For a while she lay listening to the evening birds in the vine that grew about the house, and to crickets
shrilling from the fields in the tall, dry August grass. Finally
she sat up and ate her supper in the dim bedroom and then lay
back again. From her bed, she watched the moon rise big above
the low pine trees bordering the far edge of the daisy meadow; she watched its deep-rose light grow pale, and waited for
Miss Dunston. But Miss Dunston never came, because Pierce
kept her.

Mimi woke late at night to the sound of low voices. She heard
people moving about in other rooms, in that part of the house
where Pierce lay. Uneasily she listened in the dark. Then she
got out of bed and tiptoed across the room and through the sew-

ing room that separated her room from Maud's. Maud was awake, too; she sat up at once, as if she had been expecting her.

"Maud?"

"What?"

"What's the matter?"

"Pierce must be sick again," said Maud.

By the light of the moon that fell through the vine-dark window, Mimi saw Sandy lying beside her sister on the pillow.

"Maud . . . Let me come in here tonight?"

"Do you think you're well now?"

"Yes. I think I am. My head feels all right."

"They'd be furious, though," said Maud.

"Oh, please, Maud! I'm afraid of the dark." If necessary, things like this could be confessed to her sister.

Diplomatic, Maud paused, and then spoke kindly. "I tell you what, Mim. We'll keep our doors to the sewing room open. They'll never know. And I can hear you and you can hear me."

After a minute, Mimi said, "All right."

"Would you like to take Sandy to your bed? I'll let you."

"No. Thank you just the same, though."

"That's all right," Maud said.

Mimi crossed the dark floor back to her own room; in the moonlight its white walls seemed to stand at attention. She moved to the window seat and found Ralph in his toy crib. Ralph was a baby boy, and her favorite doll. She picked him up now and crept into her bed with him and laid him, carefully, next the headboard. Then she leaned out into the dark, tentatively, toward the sewing-room door, and called, low, "Maud!"

Maud's answer came in a comfortingly loud whisper: "What?"

"Nothing," Mimi said, and lay back again. All at once, she loved Maud very much, quite as much as she had ever loved Pierce. In another part of the house, now, more lights went on, and she heard her mother call, "*Steve! Steve!*"

The sounds that followed were confused; down the hall, across the landing of the stairs, skirts rustled, footsteps fell. Mimi reached upward for Ralph. She was glad she would not have to see Miss Dunston in her bathrobe and perhaps with face cream on; she knew she would not recognize her. Beyond Mimi's door and farther down the hall, there was a disjointed whispering. Her father's voice at the upstairs telephone, indistinct but firm, decisive, and familiar, was what finally calmed her and, after a long time, caused her to fall into sleep again, far from Maud.

The next day was the worst day of the summer. Early, Dr. Jones's 1942 Ford turned into the driveway, spitting gravel slowly. Outside, with the dew not yet gone from the grass, the August heat was already breathless, the sky's color faint.

Miss Dunston brought up Mimi's breakfast and told her to eat what she could and to get into her clothes when she had finished.

When Mimi was dressed, their father led both Maud and Mimi out of the house. Everyone, that day, seemed to forget that it was Mimi's first day up and that she shouldn't be hurried. Their father carried two deck chairs across the lawn to the green shade of the maple she and Pierce had spent the first part of summer climbing. Mimi and Maud watched their father unfold and arrange the chairs.

"Be sure to stay out of the sun," he said, and hurried away again. The little girls sat themselves carefully in the big chairs; they watched him cross the lawn and enter the house and catch the screen door before it slammed.

Maud sat quietly with Sandy at her feet. She was knitting a dark-red sweater for Ralph. Ralph lay on his back on the grass, but Mimi felt too listless even to turn and look at him. Before her, across the lawn, the big house with Pierce in it crouched squat and still; its front awnings were down, shading the rooms from sun. The whole, trembling day seemed green to Mimi; the indifferent trees, the lawn, the fields, even the crouched house shimmered greenly. She knew that if she looked at herself in a mirror, she, too, would be green, and she would feel like being sick at her stomach again. She had been sick already that morning, for the first time in a week, and it had frightened her; they had all been so sure she was going to get well. It had happened while she was in the bathroom, washing her face and hands, and she had not told anyone but Maud, because they would only put her back to bed and leave her and return to Pierce. This summer, more than ever, she was afraid of being forgotten, of Pierce's having all the love. Her head ached as she and Maud sat in the shade—ached hotly, as if the sun touched it through the listless leaves. Now she almost wished they would come and take her away from there, and help her upstairs to her cool room. She would feel better in bed.

She and Maud sat in the shade of the maple and did not talk. The sky was pale. Huge, hot clouds appeared over the rim of the wooded hill across the pond but threw no relieving shadows. The two children heard a car come humming up the road and skid as it swerved into the driveway. Nervously, they shifted in their chairs.

"That's another doctor," Maud said.

"How do you know?"

"I heard them."

"He's driving an M.G.," said Mimi in a voice faint with excitement. "It's the second one I've ever seen in my whole life. Maud . . . I don't feel very well."

"Shall I get them?" asked Maud.

"No, don't!"

From where they sat, they could see a man in a dark suit unfold himself from the low black car. They were too far from the house to see him well, but they could see that he was very tall. As he strode across the porch, whose level lines seemed to waver, blurring him into the heat, their father came out of the house to meet him. Then their mother came, too, and they all hurried toward the front door. It was a remote scene, only half real to the little girls, like one of their father's movies, running too fast and badly focussed: three grownups, each one trying to make the others go in first, and, finally, all three of them crowding in at once.

Mimi and Maud sat very still in the green shade. Time did not seem to pass. Near by, the hot day carried no sounds except the occasional long, dry note of a cricket in the tindery grass; but far down across the fields machinery rumbled like distant thunder, where men were haying in the heat.

Then came a sound from the silent house—a high, stretching scream that seemed to split the very day and, in some way, to sever Mimi from herself. Turning green-cold in the heat, she listened to the sound long after it had faded, then brought her stricken eyes to Maud's. Maud had gone green, too, in the still shade of the tree.

"What's happened? What are they doing to him, Maud? Is he going to die?"

"No," whispered Maud. "He's only delirious."

"What's delirious?"

"Out of his head," said Maud shakily, and she picked Sandy up from the grass and put him in her lap, and tears crept from her eyes. At once, Mimi, too, gave in to the same hot relief. Separated from one another in the big deck chairs, they cried without letting themselves go—as they had once seen their mother cry in front of their father, hardly making a sound.

A long time later, when summer had been lost in September, and the corn in the far fields had been cut, and the first rains had come and gone, leaving the pond higher and the brook full, Mimi was allowed to see Pierce for the first time. Pierce was much better now; he was going to get well. Indeed, things were supposed to be so nearly the same again that Miss Dunston, with much whistling, had packed her bags after breakfast and would be leaving in her green Oldsmobile that afternoon. Yet, at the same time, Mimi knew that things were not the same—not quite the way they used to be—inside her. Now that the time had come, after so long, to visit Pierce, she was not even sure she wanted to. She remembered how mean he could be.

He sat among his pillows looking like a querulous little old man; his freckled skin was pale now from his being in bed so long, and fragile-looking; his crew cut had grown out so that his light hair stood up in small points all over his head. Punily, he sat surrounded by the presents people had sent him. Beside him sat his ancient plaster Mickey Mouse, whose ears were missing.

Cautiously, covetously, Mimi fingered a piece of his new Erector set.

"Don't touch it!" Pierce said.

"Why?"

"You might break it."

Miss Dunston came into the room then; they looked up at her in surprise, for she was clad in a blue knit bathing suit. "I'm going for a swim!" she announced. Her full mouth parted in a smile.

Mimi glanced at Pierce, who pressed his lips together and looked out the window and made no response.

"And if you're good kiddies," Miss Dunston said, swinging a rubber bathing cap by its strap, "you may watch me from the window. I can do a nifty swan dive."

She bounced out of the room in a way that reminded Mimi of a day that seemed long ago—Miss Dunston's first day with the family. Pierce and Mimi heard the screen door slam, as it used to slam all day long when they were well and forever doing things together outdoors.

Mimi sat down on the foot of Pierce's bed, near the window, where she could look out.

"Can you see?" she asked.

"I don't want to see," said Pierce. "Don't sit on my bed."

"Why?"

"Because I'm still sick," he said. "Besides, I don't want you to."

Mimi got off the bed and went to the window. After a minute she said, "She did a swan dive."

"So what?" he asked.

"Well, it was pretty," she said desolately. "And I know something you don't know."

"You think I care? What is it?" Adept, he could often trap Mimi into telling him her secrets before she knew it, and with no more than a direct question.

Innocently eager, she said, "The doctor from Children's Hospital had a black M.G. and I saw it."

Behind her, he was silent a minute, then asked keenly, "What year?"

"It—I don't know," she said.

"You don't even know! What good is it to know the makes of cars if you don't know their years? You're dumb," he said with a robust satisfaction. "Get out of the way, so I can see that old witch dive," he added.

She moved from the window and turned to gaze at his pale, freckled face. "Don't call her that," she said. "I like her. Sometimes I like her better than you."

"Stop leaning on the bedpost," he said. "If you're going to lean on my bed, you can get out."

"Oh, shut up!" she cried. "I'm not ever going to come back here again!" And she ran out of his room.

The house was quiet, but it seemed to Mimi quiet in a different way from what it was earlier that summer. Her mother was in the city for the first time in weeks, having her hair done, and Maud had gone with her to buy more yarn. Except for Pierce, Mimi was the only one in the house. Alone, and with nothing to do, she felt aimless. She went downstairs and out the front door and on into the sunlight beyond the porch. In her bare feet, she wandered down the cool grass of the hill and stopped at the edge of the pond; its surface was dark in places, where afternoon breezes played. Miss Dunston, on the lawn, was bending over, drying her glistening body with one of the guest bath towels.

"Did you see me dive?" she asked.

"Yes," said Mimi. "It was pretty."

"I used to go with a lifeguard," explained Miss Dunston. "He taught me how."

She flipped the towel over her shoulder; together, then, she and Mimi sauntered toward the house.

"Are you sorry you're leaving?" Mimi asked her.

"Frankly, no," said Miss Dunston. "Little Brother was not an easy patient. But one of these days it may not be his world."

"When?" asked Mimi.

"Now, that I couldn't say," said Miss Dunston with an air of withdrawal.

"I love Pierce," said Mimi, "but I like you better. Could you write to me, Miss Dunston, if I write to you? I may be a trained nurse, too, someday—if I don't marry and have babies."

Miss Dunston flicked back her loose, gleaming hair. "Oh?" she asked, remote.

And Mimi then said, with low conviction, "Do you know why Pierce hates me? It's because he knows he can't ever have babies and I can."

But Miss Dunston did not hear this. "Heavens!" she said, and her voice fell to a stage whisper as they walked slowly up the hill. "Will you look? He's peeking at us from his window."

But he was hardly peeking. Rather, he dominated the frame of the upstairs window, and his distant gaze, his diminutive maleness, in dim shadow behind the window's wire screen, seemed to concentrate downward upon the two of them—on the arm of the young woman thrown in careless protection about the shoulders of the little girl. He was there, duskily, behind the screen, but then, when Mimi raised her hand instinctively to wave, Pierce, as though her gesture had been a farewell he would not recognize, suddenly disappeared—left the dark, framed square of the window as vacant as if they had only imagined catching that glimpse of him.

John Ferrone

About My Sons

The address was not in old Rome as he had hoped but there at the very edge of the city. Beyond was open country, shot now and then with an umbrella pine. And as he walked along the unpaved street, Gino saw ahead of him a labyrinth of orange tenement houses, almost the color of the dust he scuffed in, anchored in the ground with the casual permanence of Italian pumice and stucco. Unweathered and unlandscaped, the buildings had a new, unwrapped look.

How did Uncle Carlo come to live here, he wondered. It seemed only a short time ago, in the early months of the Mediterranean campaign, that packages of discarded winter clothing were sent to Rome and crisp American dollars were pinned to the tops of letters. Carlo, decided Gino, must have revived quickly from the war. But then wasn't all Italy reviving quickly? Stuffing itself on ECA and tourist dollars and at the same time muttering oaths against the *americani*, the *turisti*, the *pellegrini . . .*

He was not one, he had told himself, as the ship pointed into the Bay of Naples—a tourist or a pilgrim—at least not of the ordinary sort. His was a unique, private matter. He was coming to see the country whose beauties he had heard his parents speak of all his life and whose food and language he had been nourished on. He might say he was not a foreigner. He belonged to Italy, too . . . a dual citizenship in a way.

Walking along now, nearing the end of the street, he recalled that early feeling which made him special, standing there in the

With permission from *The Pacific Spectator*, Vol. V, No. 3, Summer 1951. Copyright 1951 by The Pacific Coast Committee for the Humanities of the American Council of Learned Societies.

group at the prow of the ship as Ischia, Capri, and then Vesuvius came into sight. Naples! where he would receive his first welcome, the welcome for a cousin too long away.

They welcomed him, how they welcomed him! But not as cousin. He was an *americano.* They knew him somehow: by his shoes, by his belt, by the two back pockets in his trousers. He found himself arguing with the owner of a *trattoria* in Naples over a deft changing of menus . . . and prices; and in Sorrento found himself escaping a pink-faced nun, who had smiled benevolently, asked *"Italiano o americano?"* and whipped out a wooden box from the folds of her robes before he could answer, crying in English, "Give, give, give to the orphanage!" So it had gone. Robbed, cheated, begged from, solicited. What a welcome!

Seeing the number of the address at last, Gino went through a gateway and across an empty courtyard. Why couldn't Uncle Carlo have lived in the heart of old Rome, in the shuttered room of some medieval *palazzo* where Aunt Tina's cooking sent rich herby smells into the brocaded walls? It would have evoked a little of the dignity Italy had lost for him, made this less a duty detour.

A pale lizard zippered across the orange dirt in front of him and started up one of the walls where it hung in a crescent as though held by the sunlight. Italy was good lizard country, there was such an inexhaustible larder of flies. It's a wonder the little animals didn't grow to be monsters and start devouring *people.* But there were few flies here, for which Gino was thankful, hoping it indicated cleanliness in the apartments around him. Above, every other window gave out on a balcony, from which he imagined the women shouted and gestured to each other like Mussolini from the Palazzo Venezia, draped their cold-water laundry in the sun, or escaped the nighttime humidity of their rooms. As though it were the sign of some strange cult, a cluster of fat onions hung from many of the window frames. Gino wondered if Uncle Carlo or Aunt Tina might be watching for him. He was several days late and had not let them know of the change, there had been so many ruins and churches to see. No one watched. A girl in a beltless dress watered a vermilion geranium.

Stepping into a hallway marked *Scala A*, Gino went up a cement stairway. The apartment was on the second floor, iden-

tified by a brass plaque with the family name in a whirling script.
In spite of himself, he smiled.

The woman who answered the door was tiny and agile, with
a warm brown face unstill as a rabbit's. She peered at Gino for
a second, put her hand to her mouth, then fled down the hallway
calling, "CARLO, CARLO, HE IS HERE. Come in, come in,"
she said, running back and motioning to Gino with a great fluttering of her arms. "We thought surely you would arrive Monday. CARLO!"

Turning in a confused circle, she ran ahead of Gino into the
kitchen, pulled out all the chairs from the table so he might choose
any one of them, whisked the flatiron from the flannel on the
table, folded up the flannel after it, and returned the iron to a
low gas flame. It all happened in a few seconds, Tina shrieking
with laughter the whole time, as though she believed it was good
to have much movement and noise when people are new to each
other. She subsided in a swooping intake of air.

"Sit here," she said, "here . . . here . . . wherever you like."

But Gino was looking at a squat, doughy man sitting with a
fixed smile like an ivory idol. A great balloon of flesh puffed over
his trousers, and he wore an undershirt of knitted wool, exposing
his shoulders, which sprouted long white hairs. And there was a
look of age about him that came from a kind of ivoried yellow-
ness. His nails were yellow, the two teeth showing in his smile
were yellow, his eyes around the iris were yellow, and even his
mustache and thinning hair had a hint of yellow in them.

"Here," said Carlo, pulling a chair close to him, "by me."

When Gino came near, Carlo excused himself for not standing, took Gino's hand with an eager grasp, and pulled him close
to kiss him on both cheeks, grazing his face with an abrasive
growth of beard.

"Luigi's son," he said. His voice was abrasive, too. "How
long we have waited—eh, Tina?"

Nodding and cackling with delight, her hands clasped, Tina
stood apart as though Gino were behind glass.

"You, you!" she said. "Monday I fixed *cotoletta*. Tuesday,
involtino. And Wednesday . . . what was it Wednesday . . ."

"But never mind," said Carlo. "He will stay with us for a
while now."

"I must go back this afternoon," said Gino, prepared to add that he had bus reservations to Florence. Actually he would go to see the tumbled marble of the Roman Forum.

"This afternoon!" Carlo scoffed. "Think how we must talk and eat and drink. This afternoon! No, I do not like it, not at all. Tina, the wine."

She responded as though he had pushed a button on her, and her scurrying made Carlo seem even older, less ambulatory. How wise Italian men were, Gino decided, who married women ten years younger than themselves. Tina brought three glasses and a bottle of white wine to the table.

"*Orvieto,*" said Carlo. "It is good."

For the first time, Tina became aware of her husband's attire. "Look at him," she said, pointing with an empty glass. "Not even a shirt to cover his body. All dressed for company!"

"Run along," said Carlo. "Gino does not care, and besides I am not at the opera house."

"He is home all the time," Tina confided to Gino. "He does not even go to see his sons and their wives."

"Why?" asked Carlo, knotting his fingers at her, "when they come to see me? And one hundred kilos is too much weight for an old man to carry very far."

Gino had come to Italy with a meager knowledge of his uncle's life. The letters had always been few and since the war, fewer. But he had thought Uncle Carlo worked in a bakery or a restaurant.

"You do not go to work?" he asked.

"Work!" said Tina, teasing. "His only work is getting his body out of bed and back again." She imitated him snoring. "All the time," she said.

"Wait!" said Carlo. Then he turned to Gino to give his story, the truth. "In the morning I have my *caffè espresso* and bread. I read the paper—no, two papers. I have my *pranzo, then* I go to sleep. And what is wrong with that? I have nearly seventy years. One day," he said, "in the *panatteria,* I felt very ill— here, in the head. It was my blood, my heart . . . something. I took off my apron, dusted the flour from my hands, and crept out. I never went back. See? This hand does not move very well. My two sons said, 'You have worked long enough; we will take care of you.' They are good boys. You will meet them. My brother, does he work?"

"Yes," said Gino.

"But you will take care of him soon?"

Gino nodded. What good did it do to tell Carlo the best thing an old man can do to prolong his life is to remain active?

"That is fine," said Carlo. "You must take care of the old people. Without them . . . what would you be?" His upturned hands sustained the question. "But tell me more about my brother. He is happy?"

"Yes."

"And well?"

"Not too well. He has too much blood."

"Ah yes, like me."

"The doctor says he must drink only one glass of wine a day."

"And you say he is happy?" Carlo chuckled. "I remember when he could drink five liters of wine. By himself. Yes, five. He was young then and full of life like you. Tina, Gino has something of Luigi in him—about the mouth."

"Yes," Tina agreed, "his smile is like him, and his nose, too—straight and strong."

Carlo raised his glass. "Let us drink to your father."

They drank: Carlo and Tina, to a young man full of life who consumed five liters of wine at one sitting; Gino, to a quiet white-haired man who nursed one glass through his evening meal.

"You see?" said Carlo, draining his glass. "If I went to the doctor of your father, he would say, 'No more wine. You are old and will die.' But I know I am old and dying, and why should I want to live longer? Tina, some coffee . . . I have lived much." He reflected on this, as if reviewing the whole of his life, and then he said, "But how do you like Italy?"

"Italy?" Gino repeated. Carlo had an expectant smile. "Italy . . . Italy is fine. Sometimes I feel alone and strange."

"I know," said Carlo, "as it was for me in America. You know I have been there? And sent for your father?"

"Yes."

"Two times I was there, oh, many years ago."

"Yes," said Gino. "During the war when my father had to

worry about you so much, he said you should never have gone back to Italy."

"Who is to say?" said Carlo. "Eh, Tina?"

Tina cackled. In the presence of strangers, it was a safe, ambiguous answer to anything Carlo might ask. She had now put a shiny cylinder on the table, larger than a flashlight, with a hollow in its base for an alcohol wick. Carlo touched a match to the wick, setting up a transparent blue flame; then he pushed a demitasse cup under the slender spout curving from the side of the cylinder.

"Yes," he said. "Who is to say? I came back. And why? Because I could not stay."

No, thought Gino, America is not the place for you if you want to sit home and grow fat, a weight on your sons.

"There was work there," he reminded Carlo.

"Yes."

"Enough food."

"Yes."

"And money."

"And money . . . after. Let me tell you." Carlo could laugh now at the memory of the thing he was about to tell. "Let me tell you about my first job. It was at the dock, loading and unloading ships. You know?"

"*Stevedore*," Gino said in English.

"Yes, that was it. And I knew just two words: '*T'ank you*' and '*sonnamonbitch*.' Imagine yourself in Italy . . . Because I could not ask questions, I could only work. I worked hard, and at last I got my first pay. I was very happy walking along there on the dock, counting my money, looking downward. Then almost at my feet I saw a wallet. As far as the stove from me; but before I could reach it another man—out of the air he seemed to come—stepped in front of me and picked it up. Quick! Like that. You know how much was inside?"

Gino shook his head.

"One hundred dollars. The man could speak a little Italian. He said, 'Come on; we will share it.' He took me behind a shed where there were barrels of potatoes. 'First,' he said, 'I will need change.' I said, 'I have only a few dollars.' 'That will help,' he said. Just when he took my money another man came up, and they started to argue—'waa-waa-waa-waa' in English. I did not know why they argued. And suddenly the second man took the wallet, the money, and ran off. The first man ran after him."

"Of course," said Gino, who was anticipating.

"I ran, too," Carlo continued. "But I could not catch them." He shook his head over the recollection. "I had no one to tell this to. I walked, I walked. Then I saw the two men together talking and laughing. I ran up to them and said, 'Give me back my money.' They pushed me away thus; then they called a policeman. Now, I thought, I will get my money. They talked to him in English, and you know, he chased me off. I was more sad. I said to myself, what place is this where a policeman will not protect you!" He ended his recital as he had begun, with a laugh.

"Yes . . ." said Gino, uneasy with the feeling of an intended accusation in the story. "And then you came back? Because of that?"

"No, no. I stayed one year. I worked on a railroad, in a bakery, in a tailor shop . . . many jobs. Then I came back."

The coffeemaker on the table began to spurt out its black silt, and when one cup was half filled, Carlo pushed the second under the spout. The stream sputtered and ended in a bright, sagging bubble.

"I came back to get Tina," said Carlo, offering one of the cups to Gino.

"Yes," said Tina. She was putting a pot of water on the stove. "I was in America too. I worked *Broadway eh Fourteen Street.*" It was the first English she had spoken in many years, and she shrieked at her courage.

"*Fiff floor,*" Carlo added, following her cue.

"*I make araincoat,*" Tina went on. "*First day I go to man, esk 'How I esk for job?' Him tella me. I go to boss, I say the way the man say, 'Good morning Mr. JeckESS. Give me job, you sonnamonbitch.*"

She laughed wildly at herself.

"*You got the job?*" Gino asked, grinning.

"*What you t'ink? Him say, 'You goin' ahell'.*"

They all found this amusing, but at the same time Gino thought it was unfair of them to remember these episodes out of all they might have remembered.

"But some of the people were nice to you, weren't they?" he asked. "You had good times, too?"

"Sure, sure," said Carlo. "Sometimes many of us from Italy would have a little *festa*. There was happiness, too."

"But still you came back."

"Yes," said Carlo. "And how can I explain it to you? I cannot explain it to myself. I just did not feel right," he said with a churning motion over his belly. "Here inside."

"It is too bad," said Gino, thinking how they might not have been reduced to beggary during the war.

"But look," said Carlo, ending the memories with a slap on Gino's knee. "It was not all for nothing, those early days. You are here, happy and full of health, to reward me. A few meters of railroad I left behind, yes, and a little sweat. But you, you make me feel I have a share in your country. Here, your coffee is getting cold."

Gino took up the thickly sugared liquid and began to sip it like liqueur. With the same slow relish, he considered his answer.

"Sometimes," he said, "I think all Italy believes it has a share."

Carlo had the suspicion of a smile around his eyes.

"And maybe," he replied, "all Italy is right. In the past it has given much. In a way you cannot see." He cocked his head to one side. "Everything, you know, cannot be marked with a big white sign, 'Built by the ECA'."

He said it as easily as he put his cup in its saucer; to keep from making noise. But it jarred Gino.

Before he could answer, Tina, who seemed to be paying little attention, came chattering to show him a handful of stiff, uncooked spaghetti.

"You like this kind?" she asked. "Or do you want *rigatoni* or *tagliatelli*?"

"This is good," said Gino.

"Yes, yes," she agreed. "It is all good. But every little shape tastes different. It is funny. Does your mother fix this for you?"

"Every Thursday."

"Only on Thursday?" Tina clucked her tongue as she dropped the spaghetti into the boiling water, throwing in some salt after it. "See how thin you are! And your poor father . . .

This one—if I did not fix *pasta* every day, he would bellow the roof down upon my head."

Frustrated by the interruption, Gino turned back to Carlo prepared to cancel out any share Italy might have by a revelation of its dishonesty and ingratitude. As though he foresaw this, Carlo asked, "And did you expect to find us in such a fine house?"

"It is nice," Gino managed to say. If American dollars had gone into it, the result was peculiarly Italian: the eternal stone floors, the small sink with it entrail drain exposed, the shuttered window opening to the balcony where a mint plant grew in a rusty can, the pale-green paint everywhere.

"Two years we have been here," said Carlo. "Before that, we lived over there, about two kilometers, near San Lorenzo."

"It could not have been as nice as this," said Gino, thinking to be flattering.

"It was not," said Carlo. "Not after the bombing."

"Ah," said Tina, joining in from her place at the stove. "You should see. So much plaster—like smoke—everywhere. My majolica in pieces . . ."

"All our relatives came up from Naples, Capua, Benevento," said Carlo. "They thought Rome would never be bombed. Twenty-three of us living in our four little rooms."

"They brought lice," said Tina.

"But they were no safer here," said Carlo. "Two hours it lasted . . . in the noon sunlight. It was August. Poof! poof! poof! and San Lorenzo looks like the Roman Forum—but not so beautiful."

"The Allies did it, didn't they?" said Gino to rob Carlo of the chance for a pleasant accusation later.

"The Allies, the Germans . . ." Carlo replied. "It is all the same when you are being bombed."

"Yes, it was the Allies," Gino repeated. "I remember the newspaper accounts. Protestants, Catholics, everyone protested."

"Because of damage to the Basilica."

"Yes . . . But the damage was slight, the newspapers said, and the railroad yards . . . they had to be bombed."

"Of course," said Carlo.

"It is surprising that no more damage was done. But the pilots and their crews were trained and trained until they knew every stone around San Lorenzo. It was called a classic example of pin-point bombing."

"Ah," said Carlo, "you cannot speak of pin points and bombs in one breath. But so, we forget. Soon there will be new buildings. Maybe they are there already. Italy is used to buildings over ruins. A church over a temple, houses over a market place. You never know what is under you, but because it is under you, you are higher, you see what I mean?"

Gino had an idea he was talking about roots. "Yes," he said, "I see. But you *are* more comfortable here, aren't you? Than you were in the other house?"

"Yes," said Carlo. "This does not smell from the *vespasiano* below our windows. It is clean, new. And it does not shake uh-uh-uh, thus, from the trains. But one gets tired of broken stone and plaster, you know? I believe all Italy is tired." He sighed as though to dramatize this. "Yes, she is very tired, and she needs someone to take care of her."

"The United States, perhaps?" asked Gino.

"Who else can do it?"

"Who else would do it?" Gino faced Carlo squarely. If only Tina did not interrupt. "Do you know," he said, "how your country welcomes Americans? I could tell you some things . . . Always we are like a rich uncle from Siena, giving *marzapane* to his nieces and nephews and being hated for everything except his *marzapane*. Yes, the people who have their hands out to catch our money one moment would send us to hell the next. I do not understand it. Why, why should we do it? We ought to stop. Let these people do without us for a while. Then they might show some gratitude. Why should we give and give and give where there is nothing but scorn?"

Carlo settled back in his chair as though he had decided to concede Gino his point and folded his hands placidly over his stomach.

"And how," he asked, "can these people accept as you wish them to where again, in the giving, there is no love?"

"Here," said Tina, "look! The spaghetti is almost done. Are you hungry, Gino?"

"I want to tell you something," Carlo said, ignoring her. "Something about my sons." He leaned toward Gino. "My sons . . . they are young; they are strong; they make enough lire to feed all of us. But they are not yet wise. You cannot hurry wisdom any more than you can hurry good wine, good cheese. Now they take care of me. Did I ask them to do it? No. They did it out of love, and from remembrance of all I did for them while they were still young. And what do you think I would do if they did it out of jealousy for one another, or resentfully, or so they could say to their neighbors, 'See how good we are!' What do you think I would do?" His eyes narrowed. "I would spit on their money and send them from my house. Yes, and I would crawl down to the *panatteria* dragging my old man's stomach on the ground, and put on my apron again before I would take another lira from them."

There was a silence; Carlo held his pose, and then his face relaxed. Slapping Gino on the knee once more as though all had been forgotten, he chuckled and said, "Luigi's son." Tina was saying, "See, Carlo, see!" quite impatiently. "I think it is ready!"

She had dipped her fork into the kettle and come up with one steaming strand of spaghetti, which she brought to Carlo, holding her free hand underneath to keep it from dripping. Carlo took the strand between his fingers, dangled it above his mouth, sucked it between his two yellow teeth, and began to chew. As though he was about to render a decision of the greatest importance, Tina stood watching.

"A little too much," he pronounced finally. "But it is done."

Tina, it was clear to Gino, knew as well as Carlo when spaghetti was cooked; and yet she suppressed her own woman's judgment. In everything Carlo had to rule! But it should have been a ludicrous moment, this of the old man chewing noisily. Gino wanted it to be; wanted to see incongruity between patriarch and spaghetti taster; wanted to laugh inwardly. If you made someone ludicrous, you could discount much of what he said. But somehow, Gino discovered, you couldn't make Carlo ludicrous if you tried. It didn't matter how his bristling jaws made noise as he chewed, or how his belly pushed open the top button of his pants, or how his physical being moldered. The mind behind the yellowed eyes, the accumulated richness of his life, overshadowed all. If Gino had found him in that brocaded room in the heart of old Rome he could not have had more dignity.

Carlo was watching him. "Let me see you smile," he said. He pulled Gino's face around by the chin. "I think you have been traveling too much and are tired. We will all feel better after we have eaten. Tina . . ."

Edgar Rosenberg

Our Felix

Our Felix manages to keep out of trouble these days by copying, hour after hour, a portrait of Henri Dunant from a prospectus which the Red Cross woman handed him at the Lausanne station last week. Along with the prospectus, in her kindness undiscriminating, she begged him to accept a bag of figs, the Lausanne papers, and the blessings of God. Whether it was her own God or his Whose benediction she called down on him, she refused to say; and our Felix is so constituted that open questions of this sort are enough to occupy him the rest of the trip. Instead of looking out of the window and saying to himself, "What a beautiful lake!" he cowers in his third-class seat and thinks, "Whose God?" Whose God on which Mount? And thrice engraved, in black and white:

THOU SHALL NOT LEAN OUT OF THE WINDOW

Ne pas se pencher en dehors, rattles the train; *nicht hinauslehnen*; and, most beautiful, most excellent and musical: *é pericoloso sporgersi. Ne pas nicht hinaus é peri . . . ne pas nicht hinaus é peri . . . ne pas . . .* bland, lenitive, and—lo and behold—if he isn't at Vevey already.

"Vevey!" shouts our goodly sir conductor with the Bismarck mustachios; in a tremendously fine bass he yells it from car to car to car. "Vevey!"

So he has come to the end of his journey, a journey so long and so complicated that he hardly remembers how and where it began. Probably it began in the green police car. . . . But isn't it a crazy world, by God, by God! Now that his journey is finished and done with, a terrifying sense of emptiness and longing possesses the boy, as though this final, incontrovertible good-by to all that—good-by, that is, to the dreadfullest part of his life—were more difficult than any departure yet. En route last month he heard a wise man say (and he didn't mean it as a joke either) that the hardest place to leave was a concentration camp; and although our Felix doesn't even have two digits in his age yet and won't for another forty-five and one-third days, he already understands exactly how that concentration-camp man felt. But at the idea of a tenth birthday in forty-five days and no setting for it at all, he fetches another quick sigh, grabs his valise, and then he definitely has to get off the train.

"Well, so long," he mumbles, as though he were stating a general truth, and—plop—he lands in a different world.

His new *maman* must have recognized him by his blue tag the second he jumped on the platform; before he can say "Pooh," this Very Beautiful Lady with lipstick and a show-off hat the shape of an ice-cream cone turned upside down descends on him, bursts into little shrill bird-noises, throws her arms around him with a perfectly implausible display of affection. And, in fits and starts, My Lovely Lady trills—oh, quite beside herself:

"*Mon petit,* little boy—*mon Dieu, comme il est donc. propre*—my my, what a very *clean* young man we are, but listen Philip I'm your new *maman,* Madame Camille Dreyfuss, I'm sure the Red Cross made all the proper—*dis donc,* what a delicious-smelling child, won't Joe, *c'est mon mari,* Monsieur Dreyfuss don't you know, *tous le monde connait* Joe Dreyfuss, your new daddy that is, won't he be the surprised one though; that man swore you would be quite quite unpresentable at first, we even had the teeniest tiff about it last night, oh dear dear oh dear . . ."

What a show-off woman, thinks our Felix, clicks his heels, and says:

"My name isn't Philip, it's Felix, *gnaedige Frau.*" And gropes for where she must have gotten him full of lipstick, and rubs his cheek, furtively, with discretion.

"Felix, of course!" cries the Beautiful Lady who is much too gorgeous to be anybody's mother, "so you are to be our own little Felix from now on!" And then she stands there, plumb in the middle of the station, her adorable little head cocked to one side, her finger

at her lips, looking him over for two minutes as though he were some
old painting, if you please; and she bursts into fifty-five giggles,
perfectly overwhelmed by the idea that he is to be their own little
Felix from now on.

And whisks him off; off they go, visiting literally hundreds of
people who simply must have a look at him before supper, such a
clean young man. . . .

So now he draws and draws and draws. His head, as he works, is
bent low over his drawing; his guileless, unfinished nose all but
touches the paper, casting a shadow over the late Monsieur Dunant's
fine white beard; a few strands of hazel-brown hair have fallen
across his forehead. The tip of his tongue rolls ceaselessly back and
forth between two rows of uneven and slightly yellow teeth, as
though to encourage his fingers to clutch the pencil more firmly, as
though to embolden his moist white hand to guide it up and down
the paper with just a trifle less deliberateness and languor. . . . For
an hour he works without interruption, except to reach out now and
then for his eraser, a softer grade of pencil, or to consult, quite me-
chanically and needlessly, the Dunant original which he has torn
from the Red Cross booklet and taped to the window in front of him.
The window standing slightly ajar and one of the tapes having come
loose, the drawing now swings aimlessly to and fro in the breeze, undecided whether to endure yet a little longer or to tear itself from its
unstable lodgment after all—to be blown about willy-nilly in the
streets below, brushing on its way against your busy citizen, your
silk-hatted dignitary of the Federation and, unheeded and scorned,
to take flight at last over the roofs and steeples of the town, and so to
vanish over Lac Léman. . . .

Our Felix has long ago ceased to pay any attention to the portrait
by the window. For he no longer depends on its guidance. By now
he knows each line, each splotch and shade and mole which the late
Monsieur Dunant claims for his own. And small wonder indeed!
Fact is that our Felix has done practically nothing except copy these
same features ever since his arrival last Thursday; and as though that
weren't enough, he has kept all the drawings in his desk, every
blessed one of them. Not that there are no more interesting things
to draw: the chests and closets in the corridor are crammed with old
magazines and quaintly illustrated romances, giving off a faintly

scented odor of lavender and discreet mortality: exquisite and reassuring is the manner of their dying. . . . And it isn't ambition
either, or stubbornness, or a Perfectionist Complex, which keeps him
at his drawing. ("Our Felix has a Perfectionist Complex," said
Milady between the oxtail soup and the chicken croquettes last night.
She said it apropos of nothing except that, as usual, she and her
husband had run out of conversation.) Felix doesn't care a straw
for perfection nowadays; everybody can see that his fifteenth
Dunant is no better than his first. That young man doesn't have an
ounce of ambition left. Oh, he used to be aspiring enough once upon
a time:

Once upon a time he had been a proud and potent nabob, a
suzerain-person going to battle on a barbed steed that was cleped
Barbarossa or Telramund or Ashur-banipal; he wouldn't know
about their Age, Country of Origin, Parents Dead or Alive, etc., but
their names are fair and he'd cut a fine figure on his bronze horse:

QUINTILIUS FELIX IMPERATOR THE PENULTIMATE.

But he has learned to distrust names: Buchenwald—how beautiful that sounds; Beech Wood, the Forest of Beeches; and as long as
he never saw it with his own eyes, he can still kid himself into re-
creating it in its name's image. Cheers himself up by drumming a
little ditty on the desk with his fingertips:

> In the forest of the beeches,
> Under the crickets and the halfmoon
> They laid down their weary weary heads,
> They laid down their weary weary heads . . .

Bob and nabob, and all these:

A captain in the hussars; an acrobat; a slayer of dragons; a
keeper of Chinamen; a leader of a military band; a starving poet;
a starving fiddler; an Englishman; the first to climb Mount Everest;
somebody going to the gallows to save an impoverished Mexican
felon with that high phrase: "It's nothing, friend, you'd do the same
for me, by God, by God"; and: a builder of bridges; a saviour of
souls; a foundling in pink silk who, they say, is great-great-grand-
son to the Viscount Grey of Fallodon surely; a maker of revolutions;
a maker of films. . . . But the past twelve months, which have
robbed him of his illusory life, have robbed him of his ambitions,
too, once and for all.

"So there!" says Felix and inwardly stamps his foot; "so there!" as though he expected to get even with some unknown quantity by frittering away his time and disclaiming all responsibility for his future. "So there!" as much as to say: I have paid all my debts in advance of incurring them; I have squared my accounts; I don't owe nobody nothing! But because grown-ups (such is their bottomless malice and/or stupidity) still go through the outward motions of holding him to his maturing, his career, his self-making, he has to invent tricky lies these days. And so: whenever one of his dozen new aunts, having discharged the cardinal formulae, as follows:

(1) inspected him through her lorgnette

(2) pinched him in the cheek

(3) grabbed him by the chin and tilted his head

(4) asked him: How old are you, my little man?

(5) assured him that he looks Very Tall for his age

(6) asked him: And how do you like Switzerland?

whenever one of them goes and

(7) (optional)—asks him what he wants to do when he grows up, what do you suppose he tells them?

"I want to be a horse doctor, Ma'am."

Which shuts them up in no time at all, for not one of them has ever seen a horse doctor in her life, and so what can they say except "Now isn't that a grand idea!" or "Ah, a veterinarian." Tush tush. But the Lovely Lady doesn't think it such a very fine idea at all; she makes the nicest little *moue*, throws up her hands in mock terror and cries:

"If our Felix thinks we'd let him get rid of his *nicens* little-boy smell and come home ree-eeking of the stables—uh, pooh, pfui, ugh," and she clamps her fingers over her nose ever so daintily as though he had brought his horse right into the living room with him.

But day in, day out, our Felix continues to copy the drawing by the window (copies it with the same air of preoccupation and languor) because the late Monsieur Dunant's placid phiz, his merry mouse-eyes which smile and smile perpetually as though nothing worth scowling about had ever happened, this face represents, all things considered, the most comforting and cheerful datum our Felix has encountered since he began his trip, his long, complicated trip in the green police car.

And there is really nothing else to do. He has explored his new surroundings as much as he ever wants to explore them and seen whatever his new relations expect him to see. You should listen to them talk their heads off about the "beauties of Nature" and sunsets and things, as though a *sunset* were anything to shout about. And Jesus man what a lake! What a huge affair for a lake that isn't an ocean; but why they should go on about it as though it were something extra-special in the way of a lake is beyond him. Now you take the Koenigsee. . . . The other day his new "father" treated him to a ferry ride all the way to the bastion of Chillon, pronounced Schiong, and a blacker, uglier building Felix has never seen in all his days. And then his new father has to go and show him thirteen (13) medieval torture instruments and grumbles about how outmoded they are, nothing much. . . .

For that matter: why his new parents ever chose to be lawfully wedded husband and wife is more than he will ever understand. Not only is the shopkeeper Dreyfuss a good twenty years older than the Lovely Lady, but he is not at all what you would call a good-looking man: squat, as bald as you can get, with a Hapsburg lip that sticks out inches ahead of him, and big blue baby eyes that don't go at all well with his constant air of spite and abuse. I could draw him easy, thinks Felix with aversion.

But as for Monsieur's lifetime hobby, it is to tell people outstandingly Bad News. "Did you hear about young Passepartout!" says he no sooner than he has slammed the door behind him after office hours. "Heart attack!" And his baby eyes practically pop out at you. "Heart attack!" So naturally the Lovely Lady wants to know whether young Passepartout's heart attack was, God forbid, fatal; and her husband has to admit that, ah no, fatal it was not, but fatal it might have been, and fatal assuredly it would have been to anyone less resistant than young Passepartout. "*Il a trompé le mort*," Monsieur Dreyfuss sourly confesses, as though young Passepartout were the lowest kind of gyp and had personally insulted him by cheating Death out of its due. . . . When he has no bad news to spill, he would just as soon not talk to the Beauty at all, reads the papers at supper, grumbles about Neville Chamberlain, grumbles about Sir Arthur Henderson, about Colonel Beck, about the Czechs, ah those weak-kneed Czechs. Although the Czechs etc. happened at least two years ago, Monsieur still has not forgiven them

and never will; that's Monsieur for you, a memory like an elephant.
Let Hitler only try to get into Switzerland; a fine trouncing he'll get,
that's for sure.

"La la, such a pessimist," tralalah's my Lovely Lady who hasn't
been listening at all. Which it is beneath Monsieur's dignity to challenge, except in a general way. *"L'optimisme,"* says Monsieur
Dreyfuss with shattering unconcern, *"c'est l'idiotisme."* And he
takes out a golden toothpick and taps his cavities as if it were a
divining rod. . . . Apart from his research in Bad News, Monsieur
vigorously tramples over the graveyard of Dead Issues. Everything
is a dead issue with that cynical man, everything. Daladier is a dead
issue, dead as a doornail. Litvinoff is a dead issue. Monsieur Soum-
naire Welles is a dead issue. And when Madame, after a morning
with *Vogue*, inwardly raises her hand to talk about the Duchess of
Windsor and marvels at her taste in clothes and husbands, Monsieur
calls that a dead issue too.

But Felix he treats with the greatest respect, the respect which
your small-town stay-at-homes owe to the tried-and-true Political
Victim that's seen his share of the world. Takes him down to the
store, Monsieur does, makes him sit on a three-legged stool in the
back of the shop, the while he goes about selling his handkerchiefs
and things. But let only Madame So-and-So or Mamzelle What-
Have-You point to our *petit pauvre* over there on his tripod, let her
only ask Monsieur for the reliable report which he and he alone is
qualified to give: and, mum's the word, hush: and Monsieur lowers
his voice to a perfectly ghastly whisper. Psh-psh-pah, ah! tsk-tsk-
tsk, psh-psh-psh, t-tsk! . . . And once or twice he has even gone
to the trouble of taking the customer out into the street where he can
be as explicit and eye-popping as he pleases. "Buchenwald!"

Here it is, only July; the schools won't open for another month
and a half, and in the meantime Felix doesn't know French well
enough to make friends just like that. (His new parents being Alsa-
tian, they suffer each other's silences in German and French both.)
Sometimes, as he watches the boys from his window, he wouldn't
mind joining them in a game of soccer or *balle-au-poing* or ask one
of the older fellows to let him ride his bicycle for five minutes, just
five would be okay. And he always ends up by inwardly shrugging
his shoulders, turns away from the window, begins Dunant Number
15, Dunant Number 16, Dunant Number 17. . . .

Before filling in the background of his drawing (a Red Cross superimposed on the Matterhorn as it fades into a pink mist) Felix takes a little break and gazes out of the window awhile; idly, patiently, with an air of preoccupation and a little languor. . . . Then he might whistle a few of his favorite tunes; he whistles not by pursing his lips, but through his teeth, a trick he picked up from somebody on the road. Konrad was the expert whistler's name, Konrad X. for Xaver Trevorianus, a merry joking lark of a fellow was he, with a heigh and a ho; five (5) languages he spoke, three living plus two dead. On a dirt road south of Namur,

NAMUR: pr.—muehr, Flemish for "name." Belg. province, 3,660 qkm, pop. 324,510, pred. Vallonian; quarries, coalmines. (2) cap. N. at confluence of Sambre and Meuse, junction of 5 RR; pop. 25,354; bishopric; cathedral w. tomb of Don Juan d'Austria; citadel, belfry (XIth Cent., now Palace of Justice.) Signif. cutlery, metallurgy & leather industries.— County N. ceded to Flanders, 1262; to Burgundy, 1421; Hapsburg, 1477. Fr. since 1801; to Nthlds. in 1814; Belg. since 1831——

(Felix had looked it up first thing he got here in their Little Lexicon, L to Zymotic; but the thing was published in 1885, so you couldn't tell)—within sight of the Belfry, Konrad X. popped up; from where? from nowhere, kicking up the dust with his torn mountain boots; and into the dust he vanished at a turning half an hour later, for they were hot on his trail, swore he; and between his coming and his going he taught Felix something useful and solid, taught him how to whistle through his teeth.

"Where you going, Konrad X. Trevorianus? Konrad X. Trevorianus! C'n I go with you please? C'n I go with you, Herr Konrad? Herr Konrad . . ." But the dust and the wind wafted Konrad's answer (if answer he did) out of his hearing; he stayed his beckoning motion, waited, turned, walked on. . . . Imagine him wasting all the time yelling a five-syllable name. Still, it had a fine old pedestal sound. . . .

Felix whistles pretty much the same tunes every day, all of them very dear and good, battle songs all of them, all except one. Just listen to this:

> *Als die Roemer frech geworden*
> *sim se rim sim sim sim sim*
> *Zogen sie nach Deutschlands Norden*
> *sim se rim sim sim sim sim.*

Vorne beim Trompetenschwall
te-ra-ta-ta-ta-ta-ta-ta
Ritt der Generalfeldmarschall
te-ra-ta-ta-ta-ta-ta-ta
Herr Quinctilius Varrus. . . .

Jesus man, what a song! Oh Herr Quinctilius Varrus, oh . . .
Follows Song Number Two, not so tuneful as the first but full of
sadness and yearning, and so he whistles it: slowly, lingeringly:
the beautiful ballad of the two grenadiers who plow through Russia's
icy steppes, and their Emperor, their Emperor imprisoned.

What's wife to me, what's child to me—
Und mein Kaiser, mein Kaiser gefangen,

he whistles for the fourth time and passes on to the next number,
something funny and world-famous; he whistles it, mindful ever of
its renown throughout the Western world: the "So long, old Cheru-
bino" aria from Figaro's "Hochzeit." Now thy days, bim bim bim,
they are numbered. . . . And finally he whistles:

Muss i'denn, muss i'denn
Zum Staedtele hinaus,
Staedtele hinaus
U-und Du, mein Schatz, bleibst hier . . .

He loves that song; that is *his* song, the song of which his father
used to say that it was played on the piers up north whenever one
of the ocean liners, the *Bremen*, say, or the *Europa*, set out on its
transatlantic journey—the song, his mother might add, they would
play for him too, some day, for all of them.

Und Du mein Schatz bleibst hier.

How sad and beautiful that was, how beautiful and sad, with
the ship passing silently out of the harbor and the people on the dock
waving and crying into their handkerchiefs, shouting yet another
farewell, shouting some forgotten word of encouragement to the
homeless departing, and the band growing fainter and lovelier all
the time, and only a stretch of black left on the horizon and then
nothing at all save the water and the sky, the water and the sky. . . .

Standing by the window, whistling his song of the fresh Romans,
sin se rim sim sim sim sim, our Felix suddenly has a wonderful
idea. Here it is:

He decides to write a letter home.

Now it doesn't matter to whom he writes his letter, as long as it goes to somebody in his old town. That alone limits his choice, of course; hardly any of his pals and none of his relatives are left in the town, some having been carried off in trucks at a day's notice, and the rest having been scattered over the four corners of God's green earth, settling in all sorts of unfamiliar places with names of no meaning to anyone who happens not to collect stamps: Curaçao (the Widow Honig went to Curaçao because her quota number to the U.S. of America was 40,512 and they were just getting started on the 28,000's the time she left) ; and Mozambique (the shammoth and the shammoth's wife went to Mozambique, and just in the nick of time, too) ; and the Republic of Haiti; and Río de Oro, the Golden River, the River of Gold. It is not to them that he wants to write.

He might just drop Benno a line. Benno—my God, what a person that was! Benno the Lion of Judah they used to call him, for with his flat nose and thick lips and black curls he looked for all the world like the Emperor Haile Selassie himself that smote the Romans on the Nile: Marshall Graziani knew his cannon's smoke and Vittorio Rex felt his muscle's strength. . . . Not that Felix and Benno had ever been what you would call chummy; if you want to know the Whole Truth, that Lion used to put the fear of God in him with his one hundred pounds naked. "Want to fight!" cries the Lion of Judah, and rolls up his sleeves. "Take off your glasses!" cries the Lion of Judah, and wipes his nose on his wrist. Oh, he could be nice enough when he wanted to be, offered Felix a piece of American bubble gum once when nobody else was around. But let him only catch Felix as One out of Many. Then he'll pick on him sure enough, calls him "Butterfinger Felix" or "Felix the Sissie the Third," as though Felix' father and grandfather had ever been sissies in all their lives instead of fighting for God and their Country like the best of them. Aye, never a week went by without Benno poking him in the ribs, preparatory to Battle; and once he actually gave him a beating just to impress New Student Kuhlatsch who was taller and dirtier than the Lion himself. . . . And then, one fine day, walking with Felix through one of the busiest sections of the city (and only a block away from the Polizeipraesidium at that) the old Lion takes it into his head to roar at the top of his lungs,

Heil Moskau!
Der Hitler is' 'a Drecksau!

and that was the end of their friendship, such as it was.

"For God's sake, filius," said his father, "Keep that incendiary of an Abyssinian out of my father's house, or we'll all end up in the penitentiary for life."

Well, he would not hold the Lion's superior airs against him any longer; he would forgive him the beating, too, and all the other dirty tricks Benno used to play on him. And Benno, he felt certain, would be very glad to get his letter, if only for the Swiss Pro-Juventute postage stamp. He would write to him this very afternoon so that Benno would have the letter before the week end and could show it around. He would just ask his new mother for pen and paper, and get the letter out before the night train left.

It was a very good idea.

II

"Come in," the Lovely Lady cried from within the living room. "Is that our Felix?" she trilled, laughing, tinkling, and she opened the door for him. And bewitching she looked, too, in the merriest pink morning coat you ever did see, with a whole pastoral scene embroidered on it: gilded horses and cows, ornamental chalets, little naked fauns chasing each other along the edge of a brook, dreaming beneath poplars and beech trees and weeping willows.

" 'Scuse me, Madame," Felix began, "could I please have———" and then he noticed that they had a Visitor, and at the sight of this Visitor his mouth fell open with amazement.

Never in his life had Felix seen such an outstandingly well-fed and pampered individual as the gentleman in the tweeds who had made himself at home on the couch. Surely the man suffered from too much glands! His elephantine legs wide apart, his left paw resting on his knee, his right strumming on an exceedingly brilliant watch chain, he held court on the couch with a sense of divinest ownership. He might have been alone in the room: everything else was background, incidental detail, without purpose other than to elucidate him, to direct the spectator's attention to him instanter. His liquid gray eyes, though little more than spindrift in a sea of pink flesh, commanded the scene with an air of regal drowsiness.— This alarming personality now took it into his head to unbutton the single button on his checkered vest, which snapped back to his shoulders so violently that it was difficult to see how anything less

than rope had held it in place to begin with.—And Felix made up his
mind that within the year Monsieur Dreyfuss would have the pleasure of announcing the gentleman's death of apoplexy, in a barber's
chair, while he was getting a shave. . . .

"But of *course* our silly Felix may have it, whatever it is he
wants," the Lovely Lady burst into his mute devotions to the apo-
plectic candidate—he had forgotten all about *her*. "But first," piped
Milady, "first our Felix must say *grueazi* to Monsieur Kisfaludy.
Monsieur Kisfaludy owns the big brewery on Avenue General Du-
four; it pays to be on good terms with him, don't it, Monsieur Kisfaludy?—And this," she introduced him, "is our Felix."

Well, he looks just like a brewer, thought Felix with satisfaction.
And he performed a ceremonious bow to the awe-inspiring personality of Monsieur Kisfaludy. The brewer extended his hairless paw,
slowly and all out of context, for the rest of him remained stiff as the
statue of a Very Fat man.

"Well—well—well," Henri Dunant's compatriot intoned,
"Felix is it? *Felix heisst die Kanaille, ha*! How goes it, Sir Felix?"
He spoke with an effort as vast and majestic as his physical person,
slightly wheezing and puffing after every fourth or fifth syllable.
Agonizing to listen to the man as he created his sentences: syllable
by syllable did he create them.—His sleepy eyes rested on Felix:
benign, lax, noncommittal, negotiating nought but a tremendous
urge to close, if they could only make the effort. And Felix briefly
wondered how Monsieur Kisfaludy saw himself. For obviously he
could never see himself as others saw him. . . .

"Do you know—what the name Felix—means, Sir?" puffed
Monsieur Kisfaludy, pausing to catch up with himself after the word
"know" and again after "Felix." And a dry gurgle which could
bode no good to his barber took effect in the back of his throat.

"No Sir," Felix replied without irony, very curious indeed what
the Very Fat individual might have to say anent his beautiful dead-
language name, even if it took him half an hour to consummate his
explanation.

"Felix," explained the Swiss gentleman, "means The Happy
One. Are you happy, Master Happy One, ha?"

"Yessir," said Felix, careful to avoid the Lovely Lady's per-
manently withdrawn eyes. And he waited for Monsieur Kisfaludy to
start snoring. . . . Instead, the brewer raised his monstrous arm
very very slowly, as though he were lifting it out of a bathtub and

it were still weighted down with water; and he pointed vaguely to
his right:

"Sir Felix: meet Madame Kis—fa— . . ." and whether it
was his exhaustion or his assimilationist complex, he had to let it
go at Kisfa and trailed off into some mumble-jumble do re mi.

Madame Kisfaludy! But there was no Madame! Where—
where! And why should there be a Madame Kisfaludy? Monsieur
Kis looked entirely self-sufficient, sprawling upright on his couch;
he could very well manage without wives. And what sort of wife,
pray, could do justice to such as he? . . . And Felix followed the
slow-motion of his arm in great consternation.

By God: there she sat—a mistake, an afterthought. On a
straight-back chair in the corner, rigid, quiet, self-effacing as be-
hooved her, her hands folded primly in her lap, sat that questionable
figuration, Monsieur K's lesser half. No wonder Felix had managed
to overlook her; a wonder if he hadn't. Beside her liege-lord, Madame looked more like an amoeba than a regular woman. And as
for her features, looking at them microcosmically, they were as
angular as her husband's were round; her nose was long—comparatively long—and pointed, and Felix was pleased to see her
chin describe a very creditable triangle. She wore a black sweater,
adorned only by an oval brooch which depicted, in ivory bas-relief,
a profile as sharp and pointed as her own. But her eyes were soft
and shy; they were also slightly crossed, so that Felix couldn't be
sure whether she was looking straight at him or straight beyond him.
And then she, in turn, held out her hand, a frighteningly ethereal
sort of hand, mere featherweight, and she whispered:

"How do you do?"

"*Enchanté, Madame*," said Felix, bowed from the waist, and
waited for the brewer Kisfa to make some idiotic comment about his
expert French.

"Hah!" wheezed the brewer Kisfaludy, "so we know French
already, Sir Happy One! *Na, épatant*, Sir, *épatant. Na na.* You'll
know French better—than the King of Switzerland—before you
can say—Jack—Jack—Robinson!" At your rate I can wait until
I get blue in the face, thinks our Felix; and while the Lovely Lady
took a bottle of port and three glasses from the cabinet, Felix and
Monsieur Kisfaludy's negligible wife had a little chat.

"How old are you, Felix?" asked she. While she spoke, a nice-
looking blush rose to her cheeks, as though she thought it very

forward on her part to open her mouth in the first place. And she lowered her eyes. But whether she lowered them because she was humble or because she was cross-eyed is her own business.

Felix told her how old he was.

"Quite tall for his age," said the Fat Man in a Very Spoiled and Lordly manner. He might have said: "Kill that man."

"Won't you tell us what you're going to be when you grow up, Felix?"

"I want to be a horse doctor, Ma'am."

"Why, I think that's a splendid idea," she whispered; and Monsieur Kisfalu, admirable and self-possessed person that he was, said:

"Ah, a veterinarian."—In his huge pampered hands, his wine glass looked like a measly thimble, and as though it were a thimble, he emptied it in one gulp. *"Épatant, ah, épatant,"* he announced totally without emotion; and he placed his hand flat on his beer-belly. And he drained a second thimble.

"How do you like Switzerland?" asked his wife.

Felix said Switzerland was a very fine country.

The Beautiful Lady, who had gone out to fetch a tray of pastries from the kitchen, here joined them again and sank down in a corner of Monsieur's dais with a little what-have-you sigh.

"You must be very grateful to your new *maman* and *papa* for letting you come to such a fine home," Madame K. said very very pointedly. And the second she said it, Felix felt like nothing so much as shooting her dead on the spot, or strangling her or spiking her in the Iron Maiden of Nuremberg, by God. Except that naturally Madame Kisfaludy could have fitted very snugly into the Iron Maiden with plenty of room to spare between the tip of her nose and the points of the spikes; that old Iron Maiden was much too big for a real bug like Madame Kisfaludy; so he let it go at shooting.

"Oui Madame," he murmured, for he found it easier to acknowledge such very stupid comments in a foreign language.

"But of course he is grateful," the Lovely Lady cried; and she took his face between her hands and kissed him here, kissed him there, released him with a playful slap on his behind: "our Felix is the happiest gratefulest Felix in the world, the most felixest Felix, as our clever, clever Monsieur Kisfaludy would say, wouldn't you, Monsieur Kisfaludy?"

Monsieur Kisfaludy didn't say whether he would or wouldn't.

"Yes indeed all you happy people," cried the Lovely Lady, "and it took him such a *dreadfully* long time to get here, we'd completely given him up for lost, didn't we, Felix? Now Felix? we did! Tell the truth: we did! And don't you know," she continued, a very dreamy, far-away look creeping into her eyes, "Joseph and I shouldn't have known *what* to do without him."

And here Felix was positive that Monsieur K. and his wife exchanged a *knowing* glance; the wife had to give her whole body a little twist while he needed to move only his pupils.

"*Na so*," went Monsieur Kisfaludy, "better late than never; 'late cometh he but he cometh—the long detour—ha ha—Count Isolan— shall pardon thy delay,'" Monsieur Schillerized with mounting affection and indulgence; and he refilled his glass. Instead of hastening his stroke, the wine brought on nothing more serious than sudden loquacity, bonhommie, good will: the good Seigneur loosened up, expanded, sank a little more deeply into his couch; and then the three of them began to talk in a very musical nonstop French.

La, la, such excitement. Felix made a Big Show of burying himself in a book of which he didn't even understand the title: *The Reflections of a Non-Political Person.* And his respect for Monsieur Dreyfuss with his lethalized issues went up a little, for obviously no very dense individual would ever own such a complicated book. And then, to his astonishment, he saw Madame's maiden name inscribed on the flyleaf. "Camilla Petitmangin." Now what does she want to read a book like that for, Felix wondered in great perplexity, for the nee Petitmangin seemed in the main to read books with titles like *Die Wall Street Moerder, Lady Rowena Trevanion of Tremaine*, and *Die Erste Lady Chatterley*; and she quite raved about the novels of Vicki Baum.

"*Précieuse*," muttered Monsieur Dreyfuss. "*Schund, ça. Quel Kitsch.*" . . . And then Felix noticed that the nonpolitical book was a present for Madame. Beneath her name, he read, in faded ink:

> *Pour ma divine Camille*
> *Eternellement,*
>   Alfredo.
> Lune de Miel
> au Lago Maggiore
> le 14 juin 1930.

Now that's real cute, Felix thought despairingly, real cute that is, for he suddenly recalled (or not so suddenly either) the crazy

precocious books his brother used to read, and his brother dead as
a doornail, or maybe not dead yet either. MISSING, is all.

REGRET TO INFORM YOU THAT YOUR BROTHER
E FREUDENREICH IS MISSING IN ACTION ON
THE EASTERN FRONT STOP DON'T GIVE UP THE
SHIP STOP MAY TURN UP YET STOP KEEP
YOUR CHIN UP STOP SINCERELY RED CROSS.

PURSUANT TO OURS OF ULT. HAPPY TO INFORM
YOU AS NEXT OF KIN THAT YOUR BROTHER
E FREUDENREICH WAS SEEN BY ONE OF OUR FIELD
REPRESENTATIVES EASTNORTHEAST OF NAMUR BELG
STOP LETTER FOLLOWS STOP KEEP YOUR FINGERS
CROSSED STOP SINCERELY RED CROSS.

Dear Feli boy, First of all, I'm alive and well . . . Okay. But
who was Alfredo, who was he, to give a book like this to the divine
Lady, eternally? A tremendously sweet youth, Felix fancied him,
a Trevorianus without a past, with a pistol too, all right, but only to
defend the Lady Trevanion of Tremaine from masked rivals, not
Governments. *Un chic typ*, a genuine giovanni, that Alfredo. Had
most likely bought the book without even glancing at the title because one book was as good to a giovanni like that as another. The
saleslady might have said: Signor Alfredo Sporgersi, this is a very
great book, in fact it was just put on our List of Forbidden Authors,
very dangerous, Signor, *é pericoloso*; and Signor Alfredo, to whom
money and danger were like unto dead issues, had bought it the way
he bought necklaces, rubies, local-color scarfs, and things. Well, it
serves old Dreyfuss right, thought Felix with great pleasure, and he
decided to look up Lune de Miel on the Ticino map first thing after
the Kisfaludys had taken wing again. He was very happy for Madame, very glad she had at least a nice past; what a comedown for
her, though, what a sad sad comedown. . . . Oh Jesus, why did
they have to whisper like that! As if he didn't catch Madame Kisfaludy's foolish furtive glances; as if he couldn't catch on to their
Basic French! *"Les nasee . . . juif . . . le petit pauvre . . ."*
Oh Big Deal. *"Oui, toute la famille . . . tsk tsk tsk . . . comme
dit notre Schillaire . . ."* Big, Big Deal. *"Oui, Madame, son frere
ainé . . . ah, espèce d'animal . . . Itlaire . . . à Bou-kong-wal-
de . . ."*

And suddenly our Felix begins to laugh and cackle and splutter something frightful: he just caught them pronouncing his last name in their idiotic French; they've just done something horrible and grotesque to his lovely last name; and he laughs and laughs and laughs into his book until you're no longer sure whether he is laughing at all. The brewer Kisfa stops quite in the middle of a diphthong, which is a shame; follows a very embarrassing silence; he can feel the Lovely Lady's queer hurt eyes on him: so he cackles something about a funny word he just came across in the nonpolitical text. And lo: a really pree-posterous word leaps up at him from the page, and he unravels it aloud: "aes—aesthe—aestheticistic"; and then they resume their hush-hush business. . . . And finally Monsieur Kisfaludy's nonentity of a wife takes a large silk hankie out of her black leather bag, rubs her comparatively long nose with great fervor and blows it with such a display of noise that Felix is quite startled to hear an explosion like that coming from such a perfect amoeba of a lady.

"Ah, they shall pay for it," puffed Monsieur K., relapsing into German and bringing the conversation back to safe, fundamental topics, "they shall pay for it, every one!" And the Lovely Lady cries:

"I *do* hope they won't have a mind to come marching into Zurich one fine morning; we should be quite at their mercy, you know."

"We have our mountains," the little Madame Kisfaludy whispered with a thrill of pride.

"Ach Madame," the Beautiful Lady cried, angrily pummeling her underdeveloped breasts in self-castigation, "what good are our mountains to us? Who will protect us from their bombs and from their air force? Madame, their ingenuity is incredible. They leveled France in eight weeks, what won't they do to us? And the Italians are absolutely the sneakiest race on earth, 'women, dogs, and Italians,' as the great Stendhal says . . ." Oh, what about your Alfredo, thought Felix, speculating on the inconstancy of her love and the sad laws of permanence. "What can the Swiss fight them with," Madame cried, "cuckoo clocks? Poor Switzerland. . . . They'll kill us, they'll kill us, they'll kill us all!" And her pretty eyes shone with anger and anticipation at the prospect of dying passionately and young.

But Monsieur Kisfaludy has good news for her. Switzerland, the brewer Kisfaludy reported, would never go to war. Never. He gave Madame his word for it . . . The Lovely Lady was glad to hear it.

Ah—but did she know *why* Switzerland would never go to war, Monsieur Kisfaludy asked her very mysteriously. Madame D. absently replied that she did not. And she remembered her duties as hostess.

"Oh I'm sure I don't," she cried, "I'm such a perfect goose when it comes to politics and war things," and she pouted very charmingly indeed. "*You* tell us, Monsieur Kisfaludy; I'm sure you have a very clever reason."

Well yes, he did have an enormously clever reason, the brewer Kisfaludy intimated in his imperturbably lazy way: slightly tilting back his head, his eyes tinier than ever, archly raising his brow, wagging his sausage finger with an air of mischief and conspiracy: "*Ma très chère,*" he began and placed his paw squarely on the Beautiful Lady's knee, "Switzerland will never—go to war—because (and he paused twice as long as usual, paused for melodramatic reasons as well as everything else) because Hitler and Mussolini — made a little pact — a private little — *entente cordiale* — to leave Switzerland—stewing in her own juice—so that—he he—they will have a vacation resort left in Europe — after the war. Hah!" And his shoulders sagged with mute laughter and fatigue.

"Why what a clever remark," mumbled the Lovely Lady absentmindedly, and she shoo'd him off a little and pulled at her skirt . . . But now the tiny Madame Kisfaludy raised her body as straight as ever she could; rapping sharply on the buckle of her leather bag, her voice quivering with the strength of her ideals, she said: "It is in God's hands!" Her disturbing gaze fell on each of them, admonishing and threatening; or perhaps it fell just short of them.

"Excuse me, *ma chère,*" puffed her husband, "it is in the hands of Hitler and Mussolini"; and his eyes closed under the effort of his farsighted rhetoric.

"Why Monsieur Kisfaludy, what a godless blaspheming person you are," cried the Beautiful Lady, throwing up her hands, "for shame, Monsieur Kisfaludy, *fi donc*! It's your gypsy blood, Monsieur Kisfaludy, that's what does it, I'm sure of it, don't contradict me, it is, it is!" . . . This took a while to sink in. And Monsieur K. spread out his palms and gave her to understand that he for one was quite self-sufficient and managed to get along very well without God.

" 'Scuse me, Madame," said Felix, "could I please have some——"

"Now isn't that just like us!" cooed the Lovely Lady, "here we are, talking about such perfectly serious high-minded diplomatic things that we forget all about our silly Felixens; shame on us, Monsieur Kisfaludy!" But what was it our Felix wanted? He wanted something to write a letter with . . . Depend upon the brewer Kisfaludy to make capital out of his letter.

"A letter," humphed Monsieur Kis: "a letter? I'll bet—there's a young lady—at the back of all this. 'A-blushing followeth he her steps,'—as our Schiller says—*na na*," and he winked at everybody in turn, tiresome old fool. And what, might he ask, was the name of the young lady at the back of all this? Marguerite? Hélène? Mademoiselle Maintenon? Ha!

"Benno," said Felix and wondered what Schiller would have to say about *that*.

Schiller said *"touché"* and "ha ha" and "very good, Sir" and *"Benno heisst die Kanaille"* and where did this Benno live?

"Back home," says Felix.

And everybody has a little pause.

"You mean," the Beautiful Lady asked him very softly, stroking his hair, "you mean." And she came to a dead halt and had to give herself another little push. "You mean our Benno is still . . . he didn't go away or . . . Oh dear oh dear," she interrupted herself, faced with the hopelessness of formulating the situation in a phrase. The brewer Kisfaludy, after one long, comparatively penetrant glance at Felix, at his host, at his mate, appeared now definitely to have gone to sleep. And his godly wife kept her eyes on her black leather bag as though she meant to penetrate its essential secrets.

"Well sure, I guess so," Felix replied. "He never went away, I don't think. I don't see how they would have let him; his father was a regular *Devisenschieber*. He smuggled a thousand-mark bill out of the country in a salami and they caught him at it. He got his name in all the papers."

"Why what a clever thing to do," mumbled the Lady distractedly, "a salami, dear me," and she tittered uncontrollably.

"Dangerous!" softly muttered Monsieur Kisfaludy from beyond his dream life. "Quite dangerous."

"And this Benno," the Lovely Lady continued, always stroking him with the same gentleness, monotony, perplexity, "Was he . . . is he then a very good friend of yours?"

"Sure," said Felix.

"Well then, we must certainly write him a long letter," the Beautiful Lady cried, once more bewitching and lively, "we must certainly write our Benno a nice long letter, we musn't disappoint our Benno, now must we, Monsieur Kisfaludy, must we, Madame Kisfaludy?" and she took three or four pieces of stationery from the bureau drawer.

Monsieur Kisfaludy said they certainly mustn't.

III

Towering, bowlegged, a prince of talcum and pomatum, blowing and popping a pink bubble-gum balloon, His Highness Benno Blumenkohl (Bee-Bee to his exclusive camarilla) saunters serenely out of Beierlein's Barbershop, Afric's Odin and Jove every judo-pledged muscle. Nasals: " 'lo, Felix," real royal-like.—"Servus, Benno."

"You going to walk me home?"

" 'kay."

In silence they march. Three o'clock on a Thursday afternoon; pending the evening's whirlwind voice, Nuremberg stays at ease and flagless. Posted at all major intersections, like displaced super-numerary milestones, cheap plaster busts of our late visitor of state, the admiral from Hungary, return the boys' gaze squarely and blindly. The barest, beautifullest geometry distinguishes his Ex-cellency's surfeit-swelled hawk face: his promethean chin might have been hewn to regulations from a black stone in antique years had it not been mass-produced from a common mold the week be-fore last. Felix constructs a theory on Quantity. But Benno, apropos of nothing except the mushrooming admiral and the pressure of their silence, whines suddenly:

"Guess who I just beat up!"

Oh Jesus! Guess who I just beat up! Big deal. A fat lot Felix cares who he just beat up. Who didn't he beat up? Big fat deal.— Felix feigns a defective ear trumpet. Stares across the street, as though all dangers and necessities lay buried in yonder toyshop, amidst the golden whistles and the wooden horses . . . Benno halts, cocks his head provokingly, stamps his foot. "Well, don't you want to know who I beat up!"

And just for that Felix stares some more.

"Hey Fee-lix."

And Felix, with a passing shudder for the quick vulnerability of such as Benno of Judah, turns his back on the whistles and the horses, capitulates: "Who?"

"I beat up Crazy A."

"Crazy A!"

"Crazy A."

Crazy Alberich: the school idiot, your automatic scapegoat; towheaded and spindly-legged; his unlidded violet eyes reflecting a permanent insomniac horror. During the morning break, between the hours of geography—

> What is the German's fatherland?
> Bavarian land? Tyrolean land?
> Or is it Austria's proud estate
> In Victory and Honor great?
> Is't where the busy Switzers dwell—
> That land and people pleased me well!
> *Oh nein! Oh nein! Oh nein!*
> *Das Vaterland muss groesser sein!*

and chains and chains of arithmetic—

$$1+3-2+4-3-1-2+5-3+1+2-3-2=?$$

They play *"Blinde Kuh"*; "come on, Crazy A, let's you and me be the blind cows," and they blindfold him, and their natural laughter, as Crazy A gropes for his moving target within the tight circle which fetters his movements, drowns his mechanic squeaks. He talks in a shrill *castrato* without echo, clearing his throat in imitation of adult sanity, hem, hem, ahem; and when images aspire to his brain where phrases fail, he bends over, his arms hanging limply at his side, like an old zoo-monkey, and he bursts into the craziest damnedest laughter. . . . And then his old pop who is nothing but a chimney sweep himself has to go and pick a two-dollar name like Alberich . . . And so old Benno beat him up. Jesus Christ. And Crazy A—God knows how he even got his vitus-dance fingers to tighten into a fist—groped blindly for an opening and stole a tooth for a tooth. Jesus.

"Yep, I sure beat him up." And Benno takes out a bloodstained handkerchief and unwraps the Tooth. As if having his tooth knocked out by a sixty-five-pound lunatic proved Benno the real old superman . . . Felix eyes the tooth with aversion.

"Well, I guess you know why I beat him up, don't you?"

Felix doesn't.

" 'Cause he called you a dirty jewboy, is why."

"Me!"

"Yep, you. He said Felix the Sissie the Third Freudenreich is a dirty jewboy ahem ahem ahem and he'll go to hell 'cause he's a dirty jewboy, sure enough, that's what Crazy A said. He said you're going to grow horns like a cow, 'cause you're a dirty jewboy. So then he showed me a picture of Moses the Israelite which led us out of Egypt, and sure enough there's old Moses with horns big as a cow. Yessir. So I said, my pal Felix he is no dirty jewboy neither, he's a sissie all right, I can beat him up easy, but nobody's going to call him a dirty jewboy, take it back, Crazy A, or I'll beat you up as sure as my name is Benno the Negus of Addis Ababa. So he said, ahem ahem ahem, you just beat me up, you just try, and I'll just get the police on your pop, ha ha ha ha ha, everybody knows he ain't nothing but a smuggler, and wasn't it the jews which crowned our lord and saviour and redeemer Jesus Christ with thistles and stinkweeds, ha ha ha ha ha, so I beat him up."

Well, he's a fine one to call anybody a dirty anything, thinks Felix, and his own pa a chimney sweep. "Oh," says he to Benno, and, on second thought:

"Well, thank you very much Benno, that was very nice of you." Benno thought it was very nice of him too. And that absolutely exhausted their conversation. But humiliated not so much by the proxy-beating (everybody gets proxy-beatings) as the continual failure of the social graces between them, Felix works up this terrific phony enthusiasm and with a tree-mendously fine show of indignation he turns on Benno: "Well, you sure had to beat him up."

"Why?" says Benno ever so slyly and stupidly—may he drop dead already.

"Well . . ." Felix falters; then, schooled in the flattery of despots, repeats word for word Benno's own *casus belli*:

"You had to beat him up 'cause he called your pal Felix Freuden-reich a dirty jewboy, is why."

"And that's the truth," said Benno. "Have a piece of gum. . . ."

And after all he couldn't possibly have asked Benno, "What's a jewboy, Benno?" because if he had, Benno would have been the first to yell all over school, "Felix asked 'what's a jewboy?' " And by tomorrow afternoon the whole class would have heard about it: the whole class, the whole city, the whole world would yell, "Felix doesn't know what a jewboy is; ha ha ha: Felix the Sissie the Third

doesn't know a jewboy from an unjewboy, Felix don't know what
a jew is, felix jewboy the third don't know a joohooohoooo . . ."
  He flinched.

Breathlessly after supper, Felix reported: "Benno beat up
Crazy A 'cause old Crazy A called me a jewboy behind my back and
I couldn't do anything because my back was turned, I fight my own
battles, what's a jewboy?"
  "Tsk tsk, such language," said his mother.
  She took up a piece of unfinished sweater and began to count
stitches. He watched her face: dedication he saw there and the most
casual and comical of frowns, for it was meant only for the excellence
of her stitches; in larger businesses she stayed serene. Now and then
she scratched her hair with a spare knitting needle, and this idle
gesture invested everything around Felix with a quite unspeakable
joy. Bent over her knits and purls, her lips moved silently; but
from time to time, as if to set the seal on her count, she broke into
fitful speech: "thirty-one, thirty-two, thirty-three . . ." His brother
Emmanuel, a frigid middle-aged person of thirteen winters, read
The Sorrows of Young Werther.
  "Napoleon read this book seven times," he intoned piously, as
though he were pronouncing a Kaddish for the dead young man.
Napoleon had read it seven times, and now he, Emmanuel, read it
for the first time and utterly refused to skip a single page. Felix saw
no reason in the world why Napoleon and Emmanuel should be read-
ing the same book, and from what he knew of Bonaparte he thought
it must be a mighty strange book for the two of them to be reading.
Nor was it illustrated.
  "What's a jewboy?"
  ". . . forty-eight, forty-nine . . ."
  "Oh father, you must read this book."
  "What's a jewboy?"
  "Inscrutable," said his father, "and duplex are the ways of our
penny-a-line memorialists. I refer you——"
  "What's a jewboy?"
  "——to the evening editions. Exhibit A: the *North Bavarian
Observer,* admirable appellant to our few unrepentant gradgrinds,
coldbloodedly attests '*Anschluss Fait Accompli,*' but the *Eight
O'Clock Courier* weeps in red ink '*The Fuehrer Comes Home,*' a
phrase sprinkled with the sweet evergreen perfume of the obituary

sections — '*alle Wohlgerueche Arabiens wuerden diese kleine Hand*—' And sixty million neo-Werthers, filius, weep in responsive beatitude. To whom, I ask you . . ."

"What's a jewboy?"

"To whom, goddamitall, shall we award the apple: to sense or sensibility? Benedict Urban, beg pardon: the *late* Benedict Urban," (senior partner of Urban & Freudenreich, Atts.-at-Law) "was ever on the side of suicidal youth, the cunning magister, and see what it got him?"

OBIIT. MCMXXXV, AET. 40

"What's a jewboy?"

"Filius: methinks it's way past your bedtime. Children, like Hitler, should only be seen and not heard. If you manage to season your admiration for a year, I'll take you to the Olympic movies on Sunday. That's a promise. Off you go. Forward: March!"

But practically in tears now because he worried all afternoon and all evening about the meaning of Alberich's insult, just as he will later worry about the terrible, the obscure, the forbidden incisions on public outhouses, Felix asked syllable for syllable:

"What. Iss. A. Jew. Boy. Pleeese!"

Silence. From their glass cabinet, row upon row in red morocco, untouched, affluent, wise, the compounded statutes of the years gaze down on him, bored and apathetic. And his brother spoke. Lean and red-haired, with careful priestlike gestures, Emmanuel looked up from his book and whispered:

"The Jews are the Chosen People."

The neat, overbearing phrase trickled down the caverns of the boy's mind without echo. Emmanuel's pontifical thesis brought sudden disenchantment. There was no picture in this.

"Who chose 'em?"

"God."

Emmanuel had a way of making even God sound dim. Whatever he touched, he divested of some startling dimension: a friendless, withdrawn adult who made children and adults ill at ease.—His father fidgeted; his mother wound up her silent count.

"What did he choose them for?"

A thin pedagogue's sneer rose to Emmanuel's albino eyes.

"HE didn't choose them for anything. Chosen means the best, the highest."

"So what are they best in! I want to know what they're best in, and you better tell me, by God!"

Emmanuel sighed as if mortally weary of the catechistics. His father interposed: "Go to bed, Felix!"

"What! Are! They! Best! In!"

"Oh father dear father what am I to do with this child? Best means that they're closest to God."

Close to Thee.

"You mean they die sooner'n everybody else?"

Emmanuel raised his eyes heavenward, an early martyr. "Father dear will you please tell this fatiguing child . . ."

Oh now you shut up, you shut up, you shut your . . ."

"Felix."

"Shut up shut up shut up shut up shut up . . ."

"Tsk tsk tsk, children, you should know better than . . ."

"Father I'm not going to stand for this. I want Felix to . . ."

"Felix, apologize!"

"No I won't either apologize I won't I won't I won't . . ." and a dry sob shook his entire body and he burst into tears.

Abashed and scared, Emmanuel said with a show of sullen appeasement: "I didn't mean . . . how should I know . . ."

"He's tired," said Dr. Jur. Freudenreich ironically.

"I'm not either tired," Felix screamed, and it did his heart good to discover how much noise he could make when he only made up his mind about it. And, kneeling on the floor, his head resting on the chair, he sobbed into the fabric: "I just want to know . . . that's all. If they're best . . . how come . . . it's a dirty word. The Crazy . . . A . . . called me a . . . jewboy, so . . . Benno beat him up. I want to know what's . . . a jewboy, is all. That's all. So now you tell me . . . that's all. . . ."

And his mother came and raised him up. "Upsy-daisy"; and she gently forced him into the seat. Addressing her words to the sweater-in-progress, his mother said:

"Mannikins," (thus, to his impotent chagrin she called Emmanuel who was in school called Emma to his face) "Mannikins is right, darling; that's just what it means: God's best and nicest boys. Now you know yourself that Alberich is a very unfortunate boy, he probably picked up the word somewhere without knowing what it means. Don't you remember doing the same thing, sillypie? Don't you remember the time you used to think the Green Minna was a little watersprite, a tiny little elf, instead of a police truck? And how you used to pester your father: is the lady in the circus the Green Minna? Is the tightrope-walker the Green Minna? Is this and this and this the Green Minna? Well, your silly Alberich made the same mistake. And *that*, my little man, is all! is all! is all!"

Yes: he did remember; and he burst out laughing at the unbelievably stupid little boy he used once to be. What splendid progress he had made since then! Was it really one and the same Felix? He doubted it; he distinctly doubted it . . . And, too tired after the evening's pain for further questionings, he went and hid his head in his mother's lap, and he continued his soft laughter against the other Felix . . . A wave of the purest joy flooded him. So it had all been for nothing; all his anguish had been for nothing, for a word ill-used, an identity mistaken. Tomorrow he would find out what rare and brilliant species these Jews were who were the best and the highest, and what would he have to do to join them. Hundreds of questions to be asked tomorrow, thousands of questions. His mother tickled him in the nape of his neck; his mother would answer his questions. Was there a Jew in all of Nuremberg that he could take a peep at him? Did they have one on exhibition in the Tower? Or were all the Jews up in Berlin? Had he ever, unbeknownst to him, seen a Jew? Ah no, that he hadn't; surely he would have known him by some surpassing sign. Perhaps they dwelt in yet more spacious dominions than Berlin. Perhaps they were dead and angels . . . Tomorrow he would ask his mother.

"They are the best aren't they," he mumbled, and: yes yes yes, they were the best, the highest, his parents assured him: the highest and best, Oh: nothing there was he would not do to become one of them: he would pray and work; he would fight and suffer exceedingly. An A in Conduct, an A in Effort. On Barbarossa the White Steed he would ride forth against tyranny and slavery, 'gainst Engelland, 'gainst Afghanistan and Beluchistan and Vatican, against Spain Offices in Morocco; and so his epitaph:

FELIX FREUDENREICH

1930 to 9130

IRON CROSS 1ST CLASS

and

A JEW ALSO

"I fight my own battles."

Quickly he raised his head:

"Is the Fuehrer a Jew?" For surely the Fuehrer was a Jew.

But his mother only said: "Tomorrow." Emmanuel, his passion spent, tittered again and sought his father's eyes. But his father was looking at their stamp collection with treble concentration. Felix idly wondered: how come he's so interested in stamps all of a sudden; and off he traipsed to bed.—

Those were the good days, the golden days.

He thought of them.

IV

Dear Benno!

I hope you are well. I am well. It is very beautiful here.

I have not seen you for two years, time flies. I hope your father and your mother are well, also your brother Ehrhart, also your sister Olga Blumenkohl got married to young Stilling, I don't care if he's a goy or not. I hope they have a baby soon and you will be an uncle. I will not be an uncle unfortunately, that's life. I don't know what happened to my brother. Also my father and mother, if you seen them dear Benno please write me their address right away please and I will be glad to write to them also. How is Lehrer Schimmelpfennig? How is the Stinking Fritz? Did he put some more stink bombs on Lehrer Schimmelpfennig's chair? I hope so. How are Alberich's parents and their motley crew, nine hungry mouths to feed. I do not go to school yet. Because of vacations, also I do not speak French, not much. I met a man he could speak five (5) languages German French and Czech. Also Latin and Greek, a bloody lot of good that'll do him. I seen an old belfry. If you see my brother and my parents, also my grandmother, tell them I am well and nothing much happened after they went except the cook had a baby as per in accordance with previous plans and the painters didn't show up as promised, I held down the fort. I went away also and seen many villages, also farms, also I walked a lot. I been in the Green Minna, that's the truth dear Benno. Honor bright. Also a railroad but no airplane yet. I live in Vevey Switzerland. That land and people pleased me well. The population is 14,000 and much smaller than good old Nuremberg, 70% Protestants, 25% Catholics, 3% Israelites, as well as 2% sundry and nothing, I looked it up. Good old Nuremberg. My new mother is Madame Dreyfuss, it means Frau. Boy is she beautiful and only thirty, she is practically a child. All the women in Vevey put on lipstick, my new father always makes fun of her. He has a golden toothpick and a golden earpick. Boy is he funny. He got mad because the soup got cold, he poured it right back in the bowl. He is a pessimist. The police got my picture dictionary. I stuck a picture of Napoleon Bonaparte on a horse in the picture dictionary, I forgot to take it out. Well, I guess that's all.

Well dear Benno I can do what I like it here and it is very nice. They got a lake. It is called Lac Léman that means Genfer See, it is much bigger than the Starnberger See and the Ammersee, it is 581 qkm, I looked it up. I can see the mts. if I lean out far enough, the highest mt. is called Dent du Midi, dent means tooth and also mountain peak and Midi means south and also twelve o'clock noon, so you see it can mean anything. I lost my kodak. How is your bicycle Carragiola also the dandruff collection for your microscope also the poodle Fifi? We also have a cat, she got no name, they just call her our cat, and no litter either.

After the word "either," Felix, who had been writing like a regular speed demon, inserted two dashes to indicate that he had exhausted this particular line of inquiry, put down his pen, wondered what else might interest Benno. Gazed out of the window for a minute, noticed that a second piece of tape had come loose . . . And suddenly a Very Wonderful thought struck him. Man oh Man, what an idea! He sits up with a jolt, so unexpected and wonderful is his idea. It's just barely possible—well sure, why not! Funny he never even gave it a thought. He certainly would suggest it, he would have to choose his words very carefully, use all his powers of persuasion, and who knows but . . .

Dear Benno old pal [he continued, writing very slowly, pausing after each sentence], why don't you come to Vevey. I shall be glad if you come. You can't stay in Nuremberg. You also are an Israelite and a Jew also. If you come to Vevey it will be better than Haiti or Rio de Oro and a shorter trip you don't have to take a round-trip ticket either. Munich is only 200 km from Switzerland, I looked it up and Munich is just right next to Nuremberg, I came the long way. Via Namur, Belg. You just take the express to Friedrichshafen and the ferry to Rorschach over the Bodensee which is very beautiful and 539 qkm. Or you can take the train to Lindau. Just stay on the train and proceed to Saint Gall via Margareten. There will be a customs inspection at Margareten so just don't buy any salami old sport, well you know what I mean. Switzerland is a very beautiful country, it is the most beautiful country in the world barring none even Lehrer Schimmelpfennig said so. So help me it is. Also I'll tell you something. Your father can have his brewery here, I know a man his name is Kisfaludy, he is a brewer also, he is the competition, he can give your father a Co. or Corp. or Ltd. or G.m.b.H. I could tell him your father was the richest brewer in Nuremberg and a good business man, my regular father said you have to wake up early in the morning to put one over on that old bounder Philip Blumenkohl the cunning magister he'll outlive us all, but please don't tell him dear Benno old buddy or he'll be mad at my regular father. My daddy. Also Switzerland will never go to war and you know why? Benno, I shall tell you why. Because the Fuehrer Adolf Hitler and Mussolini made a pact, a private ontont kordial, that means they will leave Switzerland to stew in its own juice. To have some place to go for a vacation after the war. They haven't got a war here, nothing but manoovers, nothing much. I seen our Fuehrer Adolf Hitler in the newsreels Sunday. Also I seen a flood in Canada. Big deal. The name of the picture was Marie Antoinette. *Very* fancy. An American picture with French titles about this Swedish count who wooed the fair Queen of France, Marie Antoinette. I learned a dirty song on the road. Oh the girls in France, they wear tissue underpants, but don't tell your father. The French Revolution is a dead issue. Well, Benno, I am glad to tell you that our Fuehrer Adolf Hitler looks the same as ever. Our Fuehrer Adolf Hitler held a parade and Benno old sport, guess WHERE! In old Nuremberg, yessir Benno, boy oh boy what a surprise. I seen Nuremberg in the newsreels, I seen the Lorentz Church, I seen Photo Porst the Worlds Largest Camera Supplies, I seen the old Tower, big as life, man oh man, what a surprise. Man, I couldn't believe my eyes. We sat through it twice, I said to Madame Dreyfuss on account of the Canadian flood. Our Fuehrer Adolf Hitler wore his old trenchcoat. Good old Hitler, I guess.

Felix re-read what he had written so far and found it very good and to the point. He made a few corrections, prefixed "very" to just about every adjective and concluded:

That's all. Write me a letter please. It doesn't have to be more than a half a page and you write bigly and I don't care if you get ink and mess all over. I got a birthday in 38 (thirty-eight) days. Please write me a birthday letter. I will be ten years old on August 28th, 1941 A.D. I'm not so dumb anymore, I don't care. I will be very glad if you come soon. Write me when you can come, also your parents, so I can ask Monsieur Kisfaludy aforementioned about your regular father. Also I will pick you up at the station, that is all. Train schedule on request. So long, dear Benno dear old pal, and with the German Salute, Heil Hitler

Eternally your pal,

FELIX ISRAEL FREUDENREICH

(The Happy One).

P.S. Don't feel bad about the beating in front of new student Karl Kuhlatsch, it wasn't much.
P.S. #2. Thank you again for beating up Alberich for me, but maybe you don't remember. How is the old bounder?
P.S. #3. Am enclosing train schedule.

And across the top of the first page:

VISIT BEAUTIFUL SWITZERLAND

LAKES—MOUNTAINS—SKIING

SLEIGHS DRAWN BY LIVE PONIES

AERIAL TRAMWAYS—CHALETS

And with that Felix neatly folded his letter and was about to

address it when it occurred to him that he might just as well send
along one of his seventeen Dunants. Not by way of tempting Benno
God no; the Lion of Judah was the last person in the world to be
swayed by anything so wretched as a drawing; but as a symbol of
something, a covenant. . . .

He took his collection of Dunants from the drawer, examined
each copy, held them up to the light to make sure they were free from
grease stains and, picking out the one he thought the least faulty of
the lot, he stepped up to the window to compare it once more and
for the last time with the original. And at that moment Felix noticed
that a third piece of tape had come loose from the pane, so that the
original Dunant, lopsided and insecure, sustained by the single
tape which remained, kind of skidded to and fro in the wind.

And then something funny struck him, something fishy. It just
flashed across his mind, suggested itself very superficially; and in
it floats again, penetrates a little more deeply, fastens itself a little
more securely—trapped. But the next moment his whole mind is
already filled with his new idea and committed to its inviolability:
and there is nothing now that he can do about it any longer. And
this is his idea: this is the pact which he makes with Benno and
Alfredo Sporgersi and Konrad Trevorianus and himself and all his
days as a kid:

He will count up to one hundred; and if, by the time he reaches
one hundred, the drawing is still hanging in place, well, Benno will
get to Switzerland and everything will be fine and dandy. But if
Henri Dunant should fall before Felix reaches his mark, why
then . . .

So, God help that kid, he begins to count. To make sure he is
not cheating, he glances at the alarm clock every so often; whenever
he gets ahead, he waits for the second hand to catch up with him.
28, 29, 30 he counts . . . *ein-und-dreis-sig; zwei-und-dreis-sig;
drei-und* . . . He can hear his heart beat with suspense and fear;
little tears of sweat collect in his eyes; he doesn't remember whether
the count is 48 or 58; his vision already blurred so that he can no
longer perceive the time, he decides that it must have been 48. . . .
49, 50, he whispers, 51, 52; gets ahead of himself after all; 61, 62
. . . but at the count of 88, a gust of wind, sharper than any hitherto,
sweeps into the room; it rattles against the window panes; cold and
chilling it falls on the boy's cheeks; it grazes his letter, sweeps the
seventeen Dunants from the desk.

Okay.

Okay, thought Felix. I don't care. In thirty-eight days I will be ten.

Off comes the tape.

Well all right, Felix thought. Thirty-eight days is only five and one-half weeks and I've been here one week already. What's a stupid drawing? It's just a drawing. The drawing still stuck to the window. It must be on account of the electric sparks or something, thought Felix. It'll go. When I'm ten I'll have two digits in my age and I won't care about stupid drawings any more. Okay.

For five seconds, no more, the Dunant hovers by the window as though it were really very sorry and all to have to take off, clings to the window in a sort of last embrace, and so it falls.

It falls from the window, to be blown about willy-nilly in the streets, brushing on the way against your busy citizen, your silk-hatted dignitary of the Federation and, unheeded, scorned, to take flight at last over the steeples of the town, to vanish over Lac Leman, sailing into France maybe, across Belgium maybe, retracing his still hopeful dogged steps, oh Namur. . . . The boy shuddered.

And this is after all how his new mother finds him: flung head-long on his bed, his face buried in his pillows, his body shaking with dry sobs. The moment he hears her muffled easy tread outside, he begins to wail and shout and beat his little fists against the bedpost so that she would just *have* to hear him, have to, have to, have to! And then perhaps she would act the way you are supposed to act in front of little children who weep in a just cause. She better come, she better! he screams inwardly; and: in she comes.

Nor asks him any questions. Sits down beside him on his bed, puts her arms around him, strokes his hair. Tilts up his face and bends it toward hers, wipes his tears away with her fingertips. "Oh mommy mommy mommy mommy mommy," he sobs, and once he gets started on the word he can't leave it alone, shrieks it at her fifty times in a row, as though he still believed that it needed only enough noise, intemperance and iteration to make a wish come true. And she continues to run her fingers over his hair, his cheeks, his lips; but a strange look comes into her eyes now: queer, hurt, withdrawn. She allows his head to fall back gently on the pillow, looks away.

Tears fill her eyes. Perhaps, Felix reflects, she doesn't quite understand yet which mommy he means; she can't be expected to know that the Regular has been transferred or is subject to transfer sooner or later: it's my own fault, he thinks, I should have cried myself hoarse a week ago, last month, last Christmas, instead of writing letters to the surely dead. . . . Perhaps she even envies his dead mother the kind of father that came with her; tears, tears, tears, and she whispers:

"Oh little Felix, how sad it all is, how sad . . ."

William S. Schuyler

Back Again

Denning sat between his mother, Felice, and his stepfather, Charles, in the front seat of the station wagon. It was a new car and the seat was as wide as advertised, but Denning's long body was feeling cramped.

Dolf, Denning's small half-brother, tumbled about in the back playing with two of his cars. One of them was an ambulance with a siren that howled out of proportion to its size. The other was a blue plastic coupé with doors that worked and a turtleback that lifted to reveal a white plastic spare tire that could be taken out. Dolf, scarcely four, was adept with the doors and the tire, and made suitable car noises. Dolf loved this blue car, but Denning soon knew that the ambulance with the siren was Dolf's favorite. He raced it along the edges of the seats and windows, and played that the shoulders of the three big people in the front seat were hills.

Denning, with just a little effort, relaxed, loosening his arms and legs and the muscles along his jaw, as he had been taught to do, and when the station wagon moved down the driveway, he was able to dismiss the haven of St. Francis with a nod. He thought even of turning around to the back seat to smile at Dolf and perhaps say something childish and friendly, but in the end he could not, fearing he might not get away with it. Still, he had piled up merits for months for this homecoming, and it was going to work if he thought each move out carefully.

The initial silence among the three of them in the front seat was fitting, he thought. When they got to the county highway, they could talk gaily as if there were no such place as St. Francis and they were really just driving him home from college for a vacation. He could bask in Felice's presence, and tolerate Charles's earthy wisdom. He could thank them for the new gray suit and they could talk about how well it fit even without alterations. They could talk about anything easy like that and everything would go along all right.

The wheels of Dolf's ambulance roared over Denning's shoulders and he felt the vibration of the rusting axles and the tinny siren through his coat and shirt and undershirt. A thrill ran through his scalp, making the hair at his neck stand out, and he wondered if he could ignore Dolf as he had planned. Some alien emotions rose in him, but he put them down.

"Dolf, darling, please sit down," Felice said. She was driving but she reached one of her pretty arms over Denning's head and gently shoved Dolf into the seat, caressing his hair to make him happy. Dolf grunted and subsided for a moment, then started a bell-like noise to go with the siren.

"Dinny-dinny-dinny-din."

The brush of Felice's arm, as she returned it to the wheel, made Denning tingle along his whole left side. The tingling was pleasant, bringing a brief blush to his neck and cheek. He was sensitive to every particle and emanation of Felice, but he would not be concerned or embarrassed by these things; nothing would show through his firm resolve, the excellence of his new calm.

The whee-ing ambulance raced over his shoulder again. "Dinny-dinny-din." The hair at his neck bristled as it had before and he smoothed it slowly with one hand. Dolf would tire of this game in time.

They were climbing the concrete rise of County MM now, but the silence continued. Because of the agreeable proximity of Felice, Denning did not care. Perhaps, he mused, they had decided it was better not to start right off saying shiny things to bring him into the fold; better to let the three of them—four, if you counted Dolf—assimilate each other by a kind of osmosis. That was the sort of reasoning Dr. Vanya used. Fine; Denning liked silence. He had grown fond of it in the long months at St. Francis. He could sit here indefinitely, letting the sweet sensation of Felice permeate him, surround him, and carry him safely along.

He could not quite ignore his right side, which had a very different feeling. Charles touched him there, at the shoulder, elbow, hip, and along the thigh. Casual and relaxed, Charles remained irritatingly unmindful of the familiarity of rubbing against someone who hated him. Denning spent a moment reasoning that he shouldn't use the word "hate" even with Charles—especially with Charles, Charles and Dolf—and then retreated into his reverie.

Charles's shoulder point, Denning noted, was an inch below his. J.T.'s shoulder would have been an inch higher. Denning remembered when he was little, sitting in church: J.T., then Denning, then Felice, together in a handsome row, kneeling, bowing their heads, rising, singing, all together at J.T.'s unspoken command. J.T. had been tall and quietly splendid, and pleased that his wife looked like his son's older sister. Now Denning felt the skin along his right arm shrink. That dreadful muscular presence of Charles! The smell of wool and Dial soap, tobacco and lighter fluid, leather and locker rooms. Ugh. The awful years of locker rooms at school. Towel-snapping, wet sweat sox, and those perforated cylinders of deodorant hanging everywhere.

Denning did not look at Charles—did not have to. He could feel every detail through emotional antennae, and with flagellant pleasure he ticked off the items. Charles is square. He has square, ready hands with freckles. He boxed in school with other square men. One hand is always clubbed around a pipe and the pipe is warm but not hot because men like Charles know how to keep pipes going just right. The other hand is in his coat pocket, rooting for that oilskin tobacco pouch with the stripes and the piece of apple in the tobacco to keep it moist.

"Are they treating you well at St. Francis, Denny?" Charles asked after two miles of County MM.

Denning had preferred the quiet, the inventory of his stepfather. He looked blandly into his lap, hoping they would let the question go. Such a dull question anyway.

"Denning, darling, did you hear?" Felice asked. She made the turn from County MM into the long shaded drive down Chouteau Road.

"They are treating me very well, Felice," Denning said with delicate enunciation. "Each week they give me exactly $125 worth of food, care, picture shows, and consultations." He caressed the last word to convey his revulsion.

Charles's pipe squeaked in the grip of his teeth, but when Denning turned slightly to glance at him, he found the stepfather as relaxed and tolerant as ever.

"Dinny-dinny-din." The ambulance went through Denning's hair and seemed to continue into his brain. He felt the sting of tears coming, but by holding his eyes open very wide, he kept the tears from growing and falling. He asked himself how his mother—Felice—could have borne an animal like Dolf.

Charles, without turning around in the seat, spoke to his son. "Run your cars to the back seat, Dolf boy. Put them in the garage." The garage meant under the seat, Denning guessed, being part of some juvenile make-believe between them. Dolf complied, making happy noises in response to his father's easy command.

J.T. would have said, "We'll have quiet, Denning." The contrast grated.

Denning breathed deeply, as Dr. Vanya had instructed him. "Get out of yourself when things seem difficult. You can do it, you are an intelligent young man." Denning softened the set of his face and forced himself to yawn and look out at the spring green and yellow of the suburban countryside. They were just emerging from the tunnel of maples at the crossing of Robin Road. Straight ahead at the curve Denning could see the entire pattern of the fourteenth hole of Sunset Downs, from the neat square rise of the tee, down the fairway pinched to nothing by trees, to the sloping apron of the green. Charles loved that hole, said it brought out the steadiness of a man. He had told Denning once that he would make a fine golfer with his long supple arms. Denning winced at the memory. How fiercely he had said, "No!" He stared hatefully at the course, picturing Charles, sweating, hammering doggedly at a ball in the sand. Charles's pipe had gone out and for once his preciously even temper had begun to slip. He swore at the ball and slashed, only to drop his pipe into the trap, where he swung at it violently. Denning's eyes narrowed with intense watching.

Felice was watching the road intently. "Denny."

"Yes, Felice."

"You mustn't talk to yourself. Remember?"

"Was I talking, Felice?" Denning knew the back of his neck was pink; but that was one of those things he could control now, his blushing. It would rise no farther. He was glad Felice had pulled him back from that one.

She smiled nicely at him. "Denning dear. It's going to be fun this time." The words were gently spoken, not overly insistent, nor aggresively maternal. Denning looked for a remark suitable to the mood, something to preserve it, being for that moment wonderfully isolated with his pretty mother.

"We are nearly home, aren't we, Felice?" he said in the lowest, tenderest register he could manage. His mother nodded, hope clear in her face.

He gave his attention to the road again and saw that they were well beyond the golf course, passing the sign that announced Hanley Village. Denning was aware of this coy use of the term "village." Hanley Village was not a village at all, but just an area zoned for shops in the vast and valuable unincorporated suburbia known as Hanley.

Denning noted that the Georgian-Colonial shopping center was open for business now; it had just been building when he saw it on that last, hasty trip to St. Francis. He vaguely remembered having been pleased with the new taste in buildings, though he still shared J.T.'s chronic dislike of all commercial intrusion in Hanley.

A second look at the shopping center made him wince. The biggest block of many-paned, white-mullioned windows was slathered across with whitewash figures: "Sugar—10 lbs. 87, Butter—78." In another window an alternating neon sign flickered with mesmeric force: "Rathskeller Beer . . . The Brew for You . . . Rathskeller Beer . . . The Brew for You . . . Rathskeller Beer." Denning shivered.

"Denning." Felice seemed to be trying for the same gentleness as before, without quite attaining it. "Denning, are you cold?" She was looking directly at him, slowing the car.

He was sorry she had noticed his reaction to those silly signs. He shook his head, not trusting himself to speak through the quiver in his throat, holding every muscle tense against another shiver that threatened him. Knowing how very close to home they were— Adams Lane turned off from Chouteau barely a mile ahead—he felt suddenly the full meaning of the coming scene, an expanding stage fright at the very ordinariness of the lines to be spoken, the common moves to make—so easy for others, so hard for him. What should he leave unnoticed, what should he comment on, when should he say, "Hi, Dolf, let me see your toys?" The shiver shook him harder for being suppressed.

Felice, so calm and easy until now, drove with her hands tight on the wheel, staring ahead with unnecessary concentration, making the car move stiffly and too slowly, as if she dared not make it seem that she was hurrying to get there and have it over with, or as if she should stop and rehearse them all.

Charles's pipe smelled bad now, and gurgled as he puffed at it. Dolf pushed his ambulance on small, bored excursions across the seat.

"Charles, please, you talk to Denning," Felice said. The car was moving just fast enough for her to avoid second gear. The pleasant tingling that had been in Denning's left arm turned to pain.

Charles did not speak immediately. He had an infuriating habit —painfully well known to Denning—of holding attention until he was ready to talk, with movements that were unnaturally deliberate. Without looking, Denning could sense the pipe being withdrawn from Charles's mouth, the ash and dottle knocked out through the window, the cleaner produced from an inside pocket and its white, furry length pushed into the pipe stem and then withdrawn, stained with wet brown tars. Charles would bend the cleaner, making a crank of it to ream all the liquid from the pipe.

Denning stretched his legs and set himself for a short, disarming, friendly lecture. Charles's charm was nauseating. Denning was sure that Charles put the clients of his advertising company under a spell with his casual-seeming pipe-and-tweed talk.

Charles turned to Denning. His browned, square face was wise, open, and smiling, punctuated sincerely by his blue eyes. He even smelled friendly to Denning. *Damn him.*

"Denny doesn't want to hear me talk. Do you, Denny?"

"No," Denning answered with equal candor, turning to face his stepfather. He did not like this sort of thing and he would not extend it with stammering and coughing.

"You see, Filly," Charles said, "Denny's aware of the limitations of our visits together. Aren't you, Denny?"

"I am," Denning said. He would not show that the diminutives, "Filly" and "Denny," were like drops of acid on his soul. Actually he was feeling a small surge of victory. He was playing Charles's simple game of man-to-man, and winning.

The impatient driver of the ambulance careened "dinny-din" across the back of Denning's neck once again. The ease of Denning's face set like plaster of Paris.

"Sit down, Dolf," Charles said quietly.

They turned into Adams Lane without comment. Denning held his hands motionless by twining the fingers tightly in his lap. The incidents just past he was putting out of his mind by positive, comscious effort. They had been insignificant, he knew, and he was learning from Vanya how to stand away and look at such things, minimizing them to nothingness with objectivity. It was not difficult to take care of one of them at a time; if only they wouldn't come in floods, he was certain of success.

He felt that all he had to do now was to get safely to J.T.'s house, a mile more or less. He keyed every nerve to this last crucial stretch, smiling grimly inside at his thinking of it as a "làst mile." Charles and Felice were not leading him to the scaffold; they were taking him home. Still, on each side of him he could feel the charged space, as parent and step-parent tensed with him. Only Dolf, in the back, clamored unconcernedly in his private world. Denning wanted to shut them all out for a while and concentrate on the impersonal surface of the dashboard, where his eyes, at least, would not be stimulated to fresh trouble. He did not bother to look at the Frazers' house near the entrance.

It was some comfort to know that when they had turned into Adams Lane they had entered J.T.'s domain, 320 acres of the wood lots and pastures that had been the original Hanley farm, now the heart of the fashionable county. Denning admired the legend of J.T.'s disdain for the soaring value of his property, allowing only two other men to build houses along the lane, selling the land to them for a nominal sum and suavely insisting on approval of the plans before a spadeful of earth was turned.

In the periphery of his vision, Denning sensed that Felice and Charles were looking at him guardedly. They were clearly curious about the center of his attention and disapproving of it. There were little smiles on their lips as if they were keeping their faces flexible to respond to whatever he had to say. They seemed impatient for him to return altogether to Adams Lane and to say something good about it. He did not want to say anything, and he prayed that the twists in the narrow road would demand their care and their eyes. If only he could be in a chair in J.T.'s living room, he thought, everything would be all right. Unaccountably, for a moment, he longed for the safety and order of his room at St. Francis. It was a good room really—comfortable, private, quiet. Frowning, he pushed that longing away and clenched his moist fingers.

The oblique attention of Charles and Felice became intense. Denning felt himself actually prodded, though only the folds of their clothes touched him. All right, he would say something. He would find something absolutely safe to remark about, something permanent, absolute, something completely without intentional meaning. Through the top of his eyes he could see that they were approaching the great tree that J.T. had named the "Lord Oak," the tree that split the lane into two narrow tracks in front of Ely Jantzen's house. There, Denning decided, was something safe. J.T. had loved that house, considering it a proper prelude to the triumph of his own. Denning raised his eyes.

Felice's expectant smile softened. "Ely's forsythia is spectacular this year, Denny. Look at it."

Denning could scarcely see the dazzling shrubs for the sight on the terrace. Three young people, bare-footed and bare-legged, bounced around a badminton net. Two of them were boys, nearly the same age, but of different heights and muscularity. One of them, very brown and with porcelain-white teeth, was exorbitantly strong. In his hand, the frail racket appeared ridiculous. The girl, boyishly built, was distinguished by a narrow bandeau and slightly longer hair. She slashed at the bird and screamed at each volley. Near this tumult, violating the faultless grass like a chromed mole, squatted a car devoid of fenders and hood, its exposed viscera gleaming with shiny metal.

Seeing the station wagon, the girl squealed, whirling away from her game and bounding toward the road. "Hi, Charles! We need another." Denning saw Charles's left ear rise with his smile. Felice was smiling too, and slowing the car. The girl was closing the distance to the car like an eager gazelle.

Denning's look at his mother was sharp with terror. She flushed and put the car in second to pick up speed. To Charles she said: "Wave at Sue, dear, and say, 'Another time,' or something."

Charles's pipe was hard as a poker in his teeth. After a few yards, he said, "Nice kids."

Felice said, "That was Ely's grandniece. Her mother inherited the house from Ely. The biggest boy is Buddy George. I thought you'd like to meet—"

"No," Denning said.

Dolf had his nose plastered against the window. "Hot rod, hot rod, hot rod," he repeated until they were out of sight. Then he grasped a car in each hand and staged a race over his leather and wood landscape.

Denning had his eyes on the dashboard again, wondering if his heart really had come into his throat, when a tortured, hammering whir pulled him up. His ears guided him to a hill on the left. It was the knoll that marked the old margin of J.T.'s property, after he'd sold land to Frazer and Jantzen. It was the highest spot on the place and a favorite terminal on J.T.'s Sunday walks. Sometimes J.T. had let Denning come along to admire the ancient trees and the distant view of their house.

Now a rigid lacework of studs and rafters stood where three white oaks had been, and men in dirty white overalls moved around with hammers and electric saws.

"You remember the Ellis Georges, Denny," Felice said. "They're going to be our neighbors."

Denning's eyes fastened on the dashboard clock. Yes, he remembered the Ellis Georges — and that would be their son back there with the teeth and the muscles. Ellis George was a trial lawyer, a great, blond man with a great, heavy voice. Mrs. George was a tall woman with a woman-golfer's leathery, lined skin. The Ellis Georges had introduced Felice to Charles, but the Ellis Georges had never been guests of J.T.'s.

"Denning, darling, we're home," Felice said. "And please stop mumbling."

"Was I? I'm terribly sorry."

Charles was getting out. Dolf leaped out of the back seat and was saved from a headlong plunge onto the driveway by the reaching hands of his father; or he might have landed safely on all fours like an animal, Denning thought. The two square ones grinned at each other as Charles swung the boy around before putting him down. In Denning's memory there was no instance when J.T. had laid a hand on him, in anger or in love.

"Denning, please," Felice said. "You can take your bag up to your room."

"Where is Brandon?" Denning asked.

Felice's sweet laughter flowed over him. "You're such a wonderful, old-fashioned snob, dear. The taxes took him two years ago. Come, let me look at you." She took her tall son's shoulders in her hands and looked longingly into his face. Denning enjoyed this.

He thought she seemed to want to erase the past half-hour and those thousand dreadful past days with one cleansing contemplation.

Standing there, he was aware of the graceful appearance they must be making together, both of them lithe and fair, and with what J.T. had called the unconscious poise of gentility. The unpleasantness of the ride from St. Francis began to fade, and Denning felt a little giddy trying to match his mother's new buoyancy. He would stay close to her, identify himself with her; the two of them together would rise above everything. After a while, he thought, he could be more like Felice. Her consideration of herself was mature; her beauty was a source of security for herself and pleasure for others.

Since getting out of the car, he had kept himself from looking at the house and grounds, fearful of finding more change, not trusting his reactions; now, with Felice, he wouldn't care. He looked up confidently and found his mother's attention was across the drive, watching Charles, with Dolf clinging to his leg, the two of them so brown and blocky. Felice smiled at them and then at Denning. Denning stiffened at the equality of the gesture.

"Denning," Felice said, "Dolf has been talking about his 'big brudder' all week. You won't disappoint him, will you?" She leaned over and held out her arms to Dolf, who raced into them. The little boy held his face against hers very still, with the solemnity of shared love. "Dolf is easy to like, Denning," Felice went on. "When you're settled here again you can get to know him."

Dolf's capable brown hand reached for Denning's nose. "Dinny-din," he said. Felice retrieved the hand gently. Denning fought the wave of revulsion that threatened him.

The next moments, or minutes—he did not know—were blank and black.

They had moved toward the house when he was conscious that Charles walked alongside him, carrying his suitcase. They were at the front steps. Felice was on his other side, her hand lightly squeezing his arm. Dolf was sturdily trudging up the flaring steps to the green door with the brass knocker. The warm, yellow-brick façade stretched away in each direction.

Denning spoke to the air in front of him, flatly, "One of my blackouts?"

"I wasn't aware of it," Felice said. She sounded convincing.

"Did Vanya say that you were to take me back if I blacked out any more?" Denning stopped them all with his words. Even Dolf seemed to listen; he turned and sat down on the top step; a little brown carpetbagger who had just taken over the plantation, Denning thought. The great, bright April day stood still and hushed. J.T.'s big house waited, undecided whether to accept J.T.'s only son.

Charles reset the pipe in his mouth and turned for the door. "I'm going to have a drink. I'll tell Ida to put on water for tea, Filly." He glanced back at Denning. "Tea or whisky, Denny?" he asked without emphasis.

"I haven't learned about whisky," Denning said, louder than was needed. "What did Vanya say I could have?" He felt a desire to hurt them and himself with rough truth. He wanted to say that he had spent his adolescence, when other boys were learning about whisky and things, at St. Francis. He wanted to discuss harshly what, at this point of the "coming home," was better left alone. He wanted to make Charles and Felice admit that they had conferences with Vanya to discuss his rehabilitation.

"Here is your drink, Denning, see how you like it." Felice stood near him holding a glass. He wondered how long she had been there. His head ached. Several seconds passed before he saw things clearly and realized that they were on the side terrace by the tulips. Yes, they had not dared to change J.T.'s tulips.

Felice bent over him to give him the glass. Suddenly the beating at his temples rocked his head. He was staring at the lightly constrained fullness of her bosom, and could not look away. The revelation was, to him, like complete nakedness.

Felice straightened hastily and moved to her chair, averting her face as she poured tea.

Denning strove to regain composure under a fire of embarrassment for J.T. and a positive jealous loathing for Charles. Though he was not sure he could trust his feet, he rose from the chair and looked out at the tulips. Their precision might be reassuring.

Dolf was running his ambulance down the path between the rows of flowers. "Dinny-din." He never tired of that sound. His small, wobbling bottom in dusty corduroy pants threw the pattern of red and yellow and green out of kilter. Denning ran the back of his hand over his forehead. He heard Felice crying softly behind him in her chair.

"Oh, Charles," she moaned, "he disapproves of *me*." She fled into the house. Denning wanted to tell her that she was mostly wrong, that it was only his head that hurt; but she was gone. He started to turn, but did not, sharply conscious of what Charles would look like.

Charles, too, seemed to have lost some of his calm, his feet making indecisive sounds. Then he was gone, running. "Darling, wait a minute," he called after Felice. "This is only the first day." Denning heard him go up the stairs two at a time.

"Dinny-dinny-dinny-din." Down the path and up the path. Dolf's tireless alarm, the gravelly grating of the wheels, and the rasp of the siren. Little side trips into the earth around the tulips. A cockroach picked up for a passenger on the ambulance. Down the path and up again. The passenger roach, not sick enough, escaped from the ambulance. Dolf reached for him, missed, squealed, reached again, and missed. The wily roach sensed his danger and scurried into the V between two rows of erect green stalks. They were not refuge enough. Dolf said, "I getchoo," and scrambled on all fours into the V. Denning watched dizzily, knowing what would happen, waiting for what this final sacrilege would do to him. The first stalks were resilient, the next and the next and the next snapped under the rushing child. "I getchoo," he squealed.

Denning stood quivering, his head pounding, his nerves wincing as he knew J.T.'s nerves would have winced with each fractured tulip. He gripped the glass in his hand nearly hard enough to break it, un-mindful that its contents splashed in nervous jets on his new suit. It had become a weapon in his hand and he felt that he should go after the boy and beat him with it.

He advanced stiffly down the path, the pressures behind his eyes forcing tears through that blinded him. He stopped to scrub the dampness away with his hand. The action brought clarity to his vision and a moment of clarity to his reason. He turned to look around him, perhaps to see J.T.'s house once more, perhaps to remember J.T., tall, bald, gray-mustached, unsmiling, beckoning him to stand on the terrace with him and look across the acres to the knoll. He wasn't sure.

But there on the knoll was the Ellis Georges' house. The Ellis Georges trespassing on J.T.'s property. "No," he thought, "they are not trespassing; they have bought the land from its new owners, the Charles Kempers." J.T. was dead. "J.T. is dead." He had never really said that before, and he shuddered. It was Charles and Felice and Dolf Kemper now, and the Ellis Georges, and Ely Jantzen's niece. And maybe Denning. He had waited for so many months; he must try.

His eyes were blurred again. He scrubbed at them and stumbled toward Dolf, arms and fingers outstretched clumsily, dropping the glass in the dirt. He had never held a child. What could he say to this artless little animal? "Do you like cockroaches, Dolf?" Could he say that? There was a scream behind him and running feet, and so he hurried to win his objective. He heard Charles's "Damn," and felt Charles's hard body brush him aside. From the ground, amid a dozen prone tulips, he saw Charles lift Dolf tenderly and he saw Felice clasp them both, hanging on them, sobbing. Charles's stout legs were braced and held his burden easily.

In the twilight, the maple tunnel of Chouteau Road flickered gray and blue. The concrete of County MM was an ice chute to St. Francis. Charles pulled air through his empty pipe and frowned. Denning cried.

Jean Byers

Night on Octavia Street

My mother did not minimize any trouble that came to our family. We grew up familiar with such words as "tragedy," "calamity," and "disaster." Her dark imagination and her natural outlook, one of despair, affected all of us, for although even a leaky roof gave me a sense of impending doom, any illness of my father's that lasted more than a day or two made her draw my brother and sister and me near her at his bedside while she whispered, "Oh my God, what will become of us?" Her mournful brown eyes and hopeless voice brought tears from us children, and my father, looking up at such a pitiable tableau, would cry too, protesting earnestly that he was "on the mend."

Her fears seemed to be intensified at night. A light on in the house after we had all gone to bed brought us immediately to our feet, and my heart would beat wildly at the sound of panic in my mother's voice. The light and the voice could mean only that one of us was sick or a telegram had announced a family death or Mama smelled smoke. At the very least, rain was falling and the roof leaked, which would mean trouble and expense. If any of us had to go to the bathroom at night, we used a flashlight so as to cause no alarm, and I was twelve years old before I discovered that this was not standard procedure in all families.

That March when I was twelve I was sent away from home to escape whatever devils were besetting us. My mother had flu, my brother broke his arm, my father had a nervous disorder of the stomach for which he went to a Chinese herb specialist, and my

sister's earnest but inadequate care of the household had to be aug-
mented by a practical nurse whom we could not afford. I would
have stayed to sink with the rest, but when Mama said, "Tragedy
has struck our little family," exile seemed a natural part of it.
Besides, I was the youngest, considered delicate, and I supposed
the best I could do was to efface myself at Aunt Laura's fifty miles
away.

There was no sense of adventure in the trip, although I was
alone and on a train for the first time. I was a waif, and on the
way to San Francisco I could do no more than repeat my mother's
question, "What will become of us?" omitting the "Oh my God"
which I was not allowed to use. I arrived solemn and hopeless
at the high, narrow house on Octavia Street.

I had always associated Aunt Laura and Uncle Swasey and his
sister, Aunt Lissy, with jolly Christmas visits and birthday presents in the mail, but I assumed now that tragedy had so enveloped
my life that everyone would gaze upon me with the same look of
helpless pity I had last seen in my mother's eyes. When Aunt Laura
hugged me fondly and said I'd grown a foot and if I didn't put a
little fat on I'd grow up to be a bean pole like her, she seemed so
much like her Christmas self I thought certainly she couldn't realize why I'd come. She called up the stairs to Uncle Swasey (he
was never called Lewis) and then asked how I liked my first train
ride and didn't I feel grownup taking a taxi all by myself. Her
skirts still rustled when she moved, and she smelled of spice, and
she seemed to be taking my arrival as a jolly occasion. As soon
as round little Uncle Swasey pattered down the stairs, red-faced
and smiling, I was hugged again and told that Aunt Lissy had gone
out to get ice cream for dinner.

When I was sitting high and straight on the edge of the parlor
sofa, I tried to explain the desperation of our circumstances, but
the Swaseys' amiable attention gave me the feeling that twelve-
year-old girls often had family troubles in March; it was to be
taken in the natural course. They had both, it seemed, had the flu
bug at one time or another, they thought Chinese doctors were splendid, just the ticket, and Uncle Swasey remembered that he'd broken
a leg once, as a boy, and been allowed to read novels, ordinarily
forbidden by his father. Had read Scott and Dickens and Steven-
son, and the time had been one of the happiest of his life.

Aunt Lissy came in then, bundled up to the neck in blue wool, her face pink and shining from the wind. She kissed me heartily, said she'd got a quart of chocolate and strawberry mixed, hoped I liked peanut brittle because she'd picked up a pound just fresh, and asked how things were at home. I started my doleful story again, and Aunt Lissy, unwrapping herself, concluded that by April my sister would probably know how to cook. Aunt Laura, on her way to the kitchen with the ice cream, remarked that if Swasey hadn't come into a little money, she might have taken up practical nursing herself, and then I began to cry. The Swaseys put my sudden outburst down to hunger and excitement, I suppose, but actually I was lost. Long faces and nervous hysteria were my scenery and my climate; this change to a calm acceptance of bad luck was too abrupt. Even ice cream and peanut brittle had, at the moment, no effect on my sobs, and I was taken upstairs to bed, given my dinner on a tray, and told, "Good night, sleep tight," by three people showing no signs of alarm.

I lay staring into the darkness, silently repeating my name, my home address, my age and my grade in school. I said 2300 Octavia Street, San Francisco, California, Aunt Laura, Uncle Swasey, Aunt Lissy. Then, as if calling to a receding shore, I said Mama, Papa, Ruth, Jim, and went to sleep.

I awoke with a familiar feeling of terror. It was night, a splinter of light showed under the door, someone was up. Was it merely the bathroom? Had they misplaced their flashlights? I waited. No sound of the toilet flushing. Still, there were no hurried footsteps, no frightened calls, no awful ringing of the phone. I got up and opened the door a crack. The hall was bright and there were faint sounds of movement from downstairs. A broken water pipe, perhaps, or a smouldering carpet or a nervous stomach. I crept out and down the stairs, listening intently until I detected the sound of water running in the kitchen. I waited a moment and then opened the swinging door cautiously. I saw Aunt Laura looking incredibly tall in a purple robe, with her red hair in a thick braid down her back. She was wetting her long index finger in her mouth and testing the iron with quick little pats. The ironing board was up and a roll of damp linen was on the wide end.

She smiled at me. "Did you wake up, dear?" she asked. It was an affectionate question, like "Are you home?" to someone who has just come in from work.

I nodded solemnly, waiting to hear what quiet, unknown terrors came to Octavia Street at night.

"Mustn't go around without robe and slippers on," Aunt Laura said. She unrolled a small, crocheted doily. There was a hiss from the iron and the steam rising and the good smell of the hot cloth. The kitchen clock said a little after two.

"Go around?" I thought. "Go around?" I stared up at Aunt Laura. "What shall I do?" I asked.

"Whatever you'd like, dear," she said pleasantly, "as long as you're quiet. I know Swasey's asleep and I haven't heard Liss up."

I stood there helplessly. We were both wide awake and there was no trouble. There was a placid acceptance of my appearing in the kitchen at that hour, and no inquiry about my business there.

My feet were icy on the blue linoleum and, shivering, I went upstairs for my robe and slippers, lit the lamp on the little oak desk and started a letter to my sister. I said that I had arrived safely, my room had white paper with pink rosebuds, and Aunt Laura got up in the middle of the night to iron. Then I yawned, thought about the warmth of the bed, and left the letter unfinished. When my light was out and I was under the covers again, I heard a door open and close across the hall and quiet steps go down the stairs.

The next time I awoke the bright March sun was lighting my room. I heard the sound of water gurgling in the tub, and Aunt Lissy's German roller was singing from his cage in her room. Uncle Swasey, his face newly shaven and pink as a pork chop, came in to ask what I usually ate for breakfast and if I had slept all right.

"I woke up once," I said, "and went downstairs." I watched carefully for any sign of disapproval on his face.

"Did you find your way around all right in a strange house?" he asked.

"The lights were on," I said, "and Aunt Laura was ironing in the kitchen."

Uncle Swasey nodded as he brought my robe to me. "I'll show you where all the switches are today so's you won't tumble in the dark."

I sat up in bed, wondering how it would feel to be the first one up at night. "Uncle Swasey," I called when he was going out the door.

"Yes, honey?"

"Were you up last night too?"

"For a little while," he said. "Must have been after you went back to bed."

"What did you do?"

He had to stop and think a moment, as if his night activity were long ago in another time that had no connection with life in the morning. "Nothing much. Found a couple of old snapshots of your mother and Laura when they were girls. Thought Grace might like to get them in the mail now while she's under the weather."

When I went down to the dining room, the sun was streaming in through the bay window and Aunt Lissy was watering the ferns in the wicker stand. The parrot croaked, "See here, now. Good morning to you. See here, now. Good morning to you," and cracked sunflower seeds while the rest of us ate hot oatmeal and bacon and toast with currant jelly. There was a thorough reading of *The Chronicle* with the funnies passed to me first, and conversation turned to this rare, sunny day which meant an afternoon excursion to Golden Gate Park. I was still on guard, however, and watched Aunt Lissy. She was very likely the one. What trouble did she have that the other two should be up at night with ironing and photographs, alert, close to the phone, keeping their panicky cries muted? Her round pink face (she was actually Uncle Swasey's twin) made my dark suspicions hard to maintain, and toward the end of breakfast she remarked to Aunt Laura that she had slept like a log all night except for a few minutes when she awoke and got to thinking about whether to send me to school for the month or get a tutor to come to the house. She'd gone back to sleep before she'd made up her mind which was best.

There are many things that I should remember from the March my mother called "the month of the catastrophe." I know there were trips to Golden Gate Park. There was a neighbor girl to play with, and there was a tutor named Miss Brown, who wore black skirts and white blouses always with a crocheted jabot held at the throat by a cameo broach. There were matinees on Saturday afternoons. But what went on at those times, what Miss Brown taught me, what the plays were about, I do not know. I remember the nights when I awoke, the secret nocturnal prowlings when each of us went about a private project without interference or question, quietly busy in a world no longer terror-ridden. If I slept (as I

usually did) all through the night, I felt cheated, and the very
best of times was to wake up and lie for a moment, feeling the house
secretly alive, recognizing the soft night sounds, and then choose
the thing that would have the heightened meaning at this magic
time.

Once I found Uncle Swasey in the kitchen a little after one in
the morning. He wore one of Aunt Laura's blue aprons over his
brown and purple bathrobe and he was mixing things in a bowl.
The recipe book was open to oatmeal cookies, and he studied carefully before measuring each ingredient. He glanced up at me over
his glasses and asked, "You wake up, honey?"

I said, "Yes," and his only remark after that was, "It says you
pre-heat the oven. Guess I better do that now and mix the rest of this
while the oven's getting hot."

I had come down without a definite plan in mind, but Uncle
Swasey inspired me. I climbed onto a chair and got five recipe
books down from the pantry shelf and started one from the beginning, *Utensils You Will Need in Your Kitchen.* I skipped to
the chapter on desserts, but halfway through Apple Duff I got sleepy
and went upstairs to bed. Uncle Swasey stayed on with the cookies. I never knew him to prepare anything for our regular meals;
cooking was a night project. There were the oatmeal cookies and
some cottage cheese as evidence. One night I did nothing but watch
him put the sour milk in a little cotton bag and squeeze it a bit and
then hang it on a faucet so the whey would drip neatly by itself
into the sink. When the cottage cheese was served at dinner, Aunt
Lissy said, "Why this looks just like Mama's," and Uncle Swasey
answered mildly, "Hope it is, Liss. Made it last night."

Aunt Lissy was the only one whose night plans had a kind of
continuity. If she was up at night, she was poring over a stack of
old magazines that were piled, untouched by day, under the fern
stand in the dining room. She studied the advertisements on each
page with a scholarly thoroughness, and her rewards came almost
daily in the mail. It was the age of free samples, and the tiny boxes
of face cream or soap or baking powder that Aunt Lissy sent for at
night combined the satisfaction of a bargain with the delight of a
birthday present. Her goal was not merely the functional sample;
there was an aesthetic quality to her work. I remember her greatest
pleasure, while I was there, was opening a little packet containing

a red impala tail and a few gray duck hackles sent from a sporting goods house for fly-tying.

She did not mind my encroaching on her territory, and for two nights I worked with her (it must have been all of twenty minutes), following the directions in the finest print, printing my name and address carefully in the tiny space provided on coupons which I clipped out neatly with Aunt Lissy's thin shears. I do not recall carrying the business through to the actual mailing, but two thick envelopes came to Octavia Street in my name. One was a packet of swatches from Dazian's, a theatrical costumer in New York, who offered his glittering samples on the pages of *Stage Magazine*; the other was an intricate tangle of odds and ends from Wright's Bias Fold Tape Company: colored tapes, rickrack, seam binding and almost a yard of stiff white eyelet embroidery. I did not sew, but I guarded these strange gifts carefully, and kept them in a green satin candy box provided by Aunt Laura. One night, alone in the dining room, I removed the parrot's black oilcloth cover to show him the bits of tarlatan and spangled gauze. He ruffled his feathers and blinked and said, "See here, now. Good morning to you." It was too loud a remark for night on Octavia Street and I covered his cage quickly, but I understood it to mean he liked seeing my prizes.

At the end of the month, the question of what was to become of us at home seemed to be solved, at least temporarily. My mother was well, Papa's Chinese doctor had been, as Uncle Swasey said, just the ticket, the practical nurse had been paid and dismissed, and my brother was enjoying the last days of his autographed cast. My sister was practising the piano again and had a new piece, very hard, called "Valse Rubato." It was time for the exile to come home.

This time I had a send-off. The three Swaseys and I went to the station in a taxi, and they accompanied me to my coach seat. I had a box of cookies, a package of dried figs, a bag of Queen Anne toffees and two apples for the trip. I had kisses and hugs, and I gave earnest promises to visit again soon. I remember that all the way home I was hoping that the other passengers would notice me, although I was not sure why I wanted so much to be seen.

My mother's arms were around me as I left the last step of the car. Her anxious eyes studied me and she cried a little, clasping

me desperately to her. Actually she had no reason to think I had
been well and happy. The cookies and toffee were having their
effect, and I suppose I was as solemn and pale as when I had left
her. At home I threw up and then went to sleep for a while and
later was rather a heroine to my brother and sister. Well-traveled,
experienced, recovering from a sudden illness and newly arrived,
I could write on my brother's cast in a condescending manner and
listen to the first page of "Valse Rubato" with remote approval.
Everyone had missed me and worried about me; Brownie, the cat,
would not leave my lap, and I went to bed that night exhausted
with happiness.

I do not know what time I awoke, but the house was dark and
silent, and for a second I did not know where I was. Then I thought
of Aunt Lissy studying the magazines near the bay window on
Octavia Street, and the secret magic of night moved into my room.
I started quickly to capture the wakeful moments, knowing they
might not come again for a week of nights, and reached in the dark
for my robe and slippers.

I moved quietly out to the kitchen, my plans unformed as yet,
but trusting the place as the night center for ideas. At the first
sound of the door, Brownie stretched in her basket, peered bright-
eyed and curious, and ran toward me. She rubbed against me,
jumped up to be cradled, and pushed her nose into my hands. The
purring vibrated through her body and her wide green eyes seemed
full of knowledge. Once I had taught her to retrieve a small ball of
newspaper when I threw it, and nothing seemed more natural now
than to try our little game again, to play off this ecstasy of private
reunion in the mad scramble for the ball and the fetch to my feet.
I tore a piece of paper and the purring stopped. Her tail whipped
back and forth, her ears were crisp and high, her eyes followed the
movements of my hand. I threw the ball and she dashed, skidding
on the waxed linoleum, banging into the stove legs, pouncing with
grace and certainty. Then with a deliberate trot she brought the
paper back to my feet and sat beside it, brisk and ready. I laughed
aloud, knowing that this was right, perfect beyond hope for my
first night awake at home, and I decided to change Brownie's name
to Octavia. I said the word aloud and it sounded very beautiful
to me. I threw again and Brownie dashed and we were both intent
and happy with this endless game, and then the door opened. My

mother stood there, her face white, her dark eyes enormous and blinking in the kitchen light.

"Darling," she said tensely. "What is it? What's the matter?" She wore a loose, white gown, and there were no slippers on her feet.

I felt the fear rising in my throat as I said, "I'm playing with Brownie, Mama."

"Oh, my baby," she cried, and knelt on the floor beside my chair. "Tell Mama, dear. Tell me what's the trouble. Are you sick to your stomach again?"

"No, Mama, no," I said wildly. "I just wanted to come out here."

She put a cold hand on my forehead and ran to the door. "Papa," she called, "Papa, hurry! It's the baby. The thermometer's on the top shelf above the towels." She came back to feel my stomach and look at it under my nightgown and she took my feet in her hands, saying, "There, there, dear, you should have called me right away, you shouldn't have waited here all by yourself."

Papa came in carrying the hot water bottle and the thermometer, and he had the familiar look of desperation. My mother's rapid breathing was audible as my father took my temperature and held his big hand on my pulse.

"I'm not sick," I said, but the guilty tone of my own voice was frightening to me. "I just woke up." I looked down at the cat waiting nervously at my feet, and I looked again at the panic in my mother's face. "I don't want to change Brownie's name," I said. "I don't really want to!" But the sense of it was lost in the high-pitched hysteria, and already I was crying.

"Oh my God, she's had a nightmare," Mama breathed. Papa picked me up as if I were four or so and put my head over his shoulder, patting my back and saying, "There, there, dear, it's all right, there's nothing to be afraid of." He walked back and forth, his loose slippers coming down with hard slaps on the linoleum, while my mother dumped milk into a pan and lit the stove. The loud terror of my crying and Papa's desperate pacing brought my brother and sister from their rooms and they looked up at me, silent and frightened, from the doorway.

Night in its true form was back with me, and I tried hard to stop crying so that I could get away from the bright kitchen and safely back to bed. The hot milk and the promise that Brownie could sleep with me made me quiet enough so that my father carried me to my bed, and finally, the house was once more dark and without sound.

Never again did I leave my bed if I happened to wake up at night. I knew now that wakefulness was a terrible thing and the sounds of it were fearful, and I tried to forget the night of my homecoming. Only once, when I was alone with Brownie, I called to her softly, "Octavia!" She did not respond or look at me. I thought this right and wise of her, for the very name made me feel guilty, as if I had been tried by temptation and had secretly sinned.

Edith Cory

The Hero's Children

They strapped the hero's young son into a seat at the rear directly in front of me, presumably so that I could keep an eye on
him during the trip. It took three husky men—the co-pilot and
two ramp boys—to carry him aboard and batten him down: he was
like a very determined octopus. I waited at the doorway, with the
clip board and passenger list in my hands, not knowing whether
this was being played straight or for laughs. But it was straight,
I decided: the boy was punching for keeps. He was only seven.

"I don't *want* a plane ride!"

The co-pilot knelt beside his captive, for Bob Stecher was a
very kind and gentle man, who knew better than to talk down to
the boy.

"You'll like California, Paul," he said. "They have oranges
as big as your head."

"I *will* come back here!" Paul said. "And I'll wait here for my
father————"

"I told you," said Paul's sister, standing to one side, "we're
going to live *forever* in California."

At that point Frances, the sister, took over, and Bob went on
up to the cockpit. She was only a few years older than Paul, but
her face had a breath-taking maturity. I watched her eyes—which
were as green as clover—when she leaned over Paul: the kind of
girl who had the whole bloody universe sized up. From her point
of view the world must have been quite a dump—her father was
dead now, no mother was in evidence (the newspapers were very
vague on this point), and she had a younger brother completely

From *Stanford Short Stories 1955*. Copyright 1955 by the Board of Trustees of the Leland
Stanford Junior University.

in her charge. She wasn't a tough-looking girl, and no smart-aleck—but she was knowing and bright. Both of the kids were bright.

She had on a dark blue wool dress with white furry trimming, a very practical dress, and well chosen, because it helped to hide her skinny chest and her flat, childish hips. She touched her black pageboy hair with the tips of her fingers, before she climbed spindle-legged over Paul to the seat next to the window.

I watched her methodically establish her overnight case at her feet (no, she didn't like the idea of storing it overhead), remove her beret, stick the enormous pin precisely through the sweatband, after which she asked for, and got, a blanket to cover Paul's legs and her own. Immediately Paul kicked the blanket away from him, and now really warming up to a strapped-down method of attack, he hurled his pillow into the aisle. I brushed it off and tossed it into the storage rack—nonchalantly, so that he'd know he would have to do better than *that* to annoy *me*. When Frances was settled—she looked like a girl for whom time schedules meant as much as tacamahac—I went to the door and waved the ramp boys away.

The engines began to turn over; they coughed, and explosively they caught and began to roar. The plane swung awkwardly away from the gate and the crowd, and taxied, like a duck on land, to the end of the long runway, past the landing lights which reflected the summer sun from chrome and glass. It swung again, abruptly, and up forward they raced the engines, until the heavy vibrations would seem to rock us right off the ground.

Stepping gingerly on the shuddering floor, I walked forward to the door of the cockpit, and then rapidly I worked my way back down the aisle, checking safety belts. Frances was bent earnestly over her brother, but he, staring directly ahead, had stuck his fore-fingers into his ears. When she persisted, he began to sing—or rather to chant—in a monotone so loud he could be heard even above the engines. Heads turned toward him. But his big brown eyes, rounded as if in perpetual surprise, never batted a lash. As the plane straightened for the take-off, I shook Paul gently. When I pressed his shoulder more earnestly he stopped. But he stopped more as if of his own intention, with the small, pink ears still plugged and eyes staring forward. I sat down behind him and kept my eyes on the back of his seat during the take-off.

I could tell, from the way the top of his head turned, that he was watching Frances out of the corner of his eye. Satisfied that she was busy looking out the window, he unfingered his ears. Later, after we had leveled off at 18,000 feet and had reached our cruising speed, I got up and offered them some peppermints. Frances accepted one, graciously and articulately, but Paul simply looked at my hand for a long time. Then he jerked his head up to my face, and after a moment he began to chew heartily. A large bubble appeared from between his rounded lips.

"Now stop that!" Frances said, into his ear.

The bubble grew. It began to take on the proportions of a modest balloon.

"Now immediately!" Frances said.

It was too late. The bubble had burst all over his noncommittal little face.

Frances became somewhat pink in the cheeks, but otherwise she didn't let the exhibition disturb her. She merely bundled her overnight case up from the floor and unstrapped Paul, with specific instructions for him to retire to the rear. So he immediately headed forward—but not quickly enough. She lunged and caught him by the belt of his jacket. Now she half-dragged, half-backward-propelled him to the lavatory. As they disappeared behind the drapery of the washroom cubicle, Frances said to me, but obviously more for his benefit, "He used to be a very nice boy and very bright for his age. He doesn't act like *either* any more!"

When they were gone, I walked forward and tried to loan out my armful of magazines. The clouds were thin and rapidly moving, hustled along by a sharp wind. The plane cut like a wedge through them, droning on serenely. The air was crystalline, and the visibility far below to the precise, patchwork fields was knife-edged. I took down several pillows from the storage rack, fluffing them up for travel-weary officers and war-weary GI's and high priority civilians, while the sun reflected away from the bright metal wings into their eyes. As I dropped again into my seat at the rear, tossing the rest of the magazines overhead, I noticed the one mar on the horizon: some thickening cirrus to the south with dark, ominous edges.

Paul tramped behind his sister on the return journey. He looked quite restored in a fresh white shirt and yellow striped tie under his blazer, hair newly brilliantined, and, of course, face scrubbed.

No sooner had he plunked himself down into his seat than he

started to bounce up and down, up and down, up and down—his eyes all the time resting on his sister's face. For a while she kept her eyes on the book in her lap, and I didn't *know* that she saw him, except that it would be humanly impossible to sit next to a jumping bean without realizing the fact. But now she absent-mindedly, as it were, placed a hand on his shoulder. After a few abortive jumps he quit.

"I'm going to tell Father on you!" he said.

"Are you hungry?" she asked.

"And until he comes home I'm going to tell Grandfather!"

She handed him something, and almost simultaneously a cookie flew into the aisle.

"I'll run away!"

"And hurt Grandfather's feelings? You *remember* Grand-father, don't you? See his picture————"

Grandfather, in Ansco color, followed the cookie. I retrieved the articles and handed them back to Frances, while she was say-ing, "I shall have to get the stewardess to scold you in another minute."

I sat down again to my magazine. Soon I noticed that Paul had extracted himself from his safety belt and was standing up in his seat. He draped himself over the back of the seat and stared stead-idly at me, about the length of a good-sized nose away, those really immense brown eyes leveled right at mine. I shifted my own gaze to the rest of the boy's face. I noticed his upper lip, shaped like a half-moon, without the ordinary hills and valleys at the middle, and his nose, which was a bit too small and flat, a baby's nose, still. He kept staring dead pan at me, and I stared back, not willing to be beaten down by a child.

Paul deliberately lowered his eyes to my shoes, and I saw the long lashes brush his cheek. His eyes moved from my dark brown pumps, up my crossed leg, along the brown serge uniform, up the neck, swiftly across my face, and now those lovely, brown, poker eyes rested on the very crest of my cap. I felt trimmed right down to the marrow, but I had absurdly little understanding of this strange little boy. And I turned away to the patchy cirrus outside and the afternoon sun which lay on the wings like molten nickel. As I watched, some dark clouds passed before the sun, bringing an early half-darkness to the inside of the plane.

When I looked back, Paul was standing in the aisle beside me.

He dragged a watch from his pocket—a very solid round watch, which looked like one his grandfather might have carried—with the conventional fob and an *un*conventional chain about nine inches long. He dangled the watch in front of his face, and I suddenly realized that his eyes must be myopic.

"That's some watch," I said.

"My father has a new wrist watch," he said, in his monotone, which was a perfect match for the straight face. "It's the unde-undest—you can't hurt it."

He looked at the face of the watch. "Four o'clock," he intoned. "Why is it getting dark?"

I noticed that the sun was still hidden behind clouds. Reading lights were snapping on.

"I guess the sun is running from us," I said.

He gave me the nauseated look my remark deserved.

"I'm *seven* years old!" he blasted out.

So then I gave him the straight dope. I told him about the storm front that had originated in the north Pacific, and was moving down across the northwestern United States. These clouds, I said, might be the edge of that front. Then, again, they might just be local weather phenomena, caused by the heat of the afternoon.

He looked impressed but he didn't wait for the end.

"Say—read to me, will ya?"

I thought he had in mind something on the order of Black Sambo or Dick Tracy. But from his hip pocket he extracted a carefully folded newspaper clipping. I glanced briefly down the column, which was a recitation of the exploit which had won his father the Congressional Medal of Honor, posthumously awarded. Paul placed a forefinger—the nail bitten down to the quick—over his father's name.

"That's *my* name, isn't it?"

I nodded.

"It's about something my father did, isn't it?"

"Yes, it seems to be," I said.

He looked rather dubiously at me.

"You *can* read, can't you? . . . Read it then. Does it say when he'll be home?"

He was watching my face as if at any moment it might take wing.

"Did somebody already read this to you?" I asked.

"My sister." And, as an afterthought, he said, "She's only in the *sixth* grade."

I said that I imagined his sister read very well, judging from her conversation.

"Her reading stinks!" he said.

I began to read, with the intention of reading only the beginning, which was general and oratorical, and spoke first of deeds rather than death. But Paul interrupted the very first paragraph by plucking the article from my hand. He stalked away in a livid rage. He marched, militarily dignified, past his own seat, farther up to an empty seat next to an elderly gentleman. I saw Paul appraising the man, in his recently acquired rage and dignity, and I wondered if he had found another object for his disaffection. I hoped not. The old gentleman happened to be the highest ranking officer aboard.

Frances turned toward me and said, "He's furious because the article says just what I told him it did."

I said that I thought it was too bad he was taking it so hard. I meant it was too bad that boys of seven have to lose their fathers.

"He's completely irrational," Frances said. "He hates me now simply because *I* had to be the one to tell him. He doesn't think that I———"

Her eyes lowered, and she turned back to her book, snapping the tiny reading light on. The plane was beginning to rock and I found myself grasping the backs of the seats as I walked along the aisle. The plane was tipping sideways, and it was being caught in occasional updrafts and downdrafts that carried it as ocean breakers carry a board. I would take a step and find the floor rising to meet my foot, take another and find my foot dropping way, way down as if I had missed the last step on a stairway. The wind had turned colder, and for a few minutes I did a rushing business in blankets.

I had barely wrapped one of the coarse airline blankets around my own legs and settled back to wait for this change in weather to worsen or dissipate, when the sign FASTEN SAFETY BELTS lighted up over the cockpit door. As I walked along the aisle inspecting belts, big raindrops began to splash against the windows. Visibility was poor and growing less. I extracted Paul from his seat up forward and returned him to the rear. I wrapped a blanket around him, which he disdained, and strapped him into the seat.

The wind buffeted the plane more wildly now and hurled impossible waves of rain against the windows. I caught the bright lick of a lightning flash and counted until the thunder came: two miles off. All the other noise, even the drone of the engines, was cut off during the heavy roll. I felt suspended for a long, very long, second, while the rumbling broke, rolled up in a crescendo, burst, grew less, rumbled and trembled down and away. A brief moment intervened until the next lightning flashed, and it all began again.

Frances' reading lamp was the only one still on. She wasn't reading; she had apparently forgotten the light. I leaned over from the aisle to tell her to turn it off, and as I brushed past Paul I noticed his face. The whole left side of it was twitching. As I watched, he placed his elbow on the arm of his chair and covered the tic with the palm of his hand, turning instinctively away from the funnel of light. Even after the light had snapped off, I could make out the wry look on Paul's face. He refused to acknowledge me as I stood beside him and watched the rain wash over us, the darkness of the storm clouds swallow us, winding us in shadows. When the pilot began to nose the plane up, steadily climbing 2,000 feet to look for a saddlebag, I caught Paul as he leaned over and started to gag. Quickly Frances and I ripped open his safety belt and brought him to the lavatory. He had to go alone into the small toilet cubicle, while we waited in the wash compartment and could hear him retching on the other side of the thin panel. Outside, thunder burst like the sudden explosive arrival of a jet plane overhead, and roared away.

I remarked that the pilot was beginning to lose altitude, and he would try to find an opening at 16,000 feet. But I could see immediately that Frances was one of those people who don't care to talk about the weather, even when it's rather important to their survival. She nodded, vaguely.

"He misses my father very much," she said. "Paul idolized him. He was a highly intelligent man."

I said that I imagined he also had a rather large vocabulary.

"Yes, extremely," she said. "He understood Paul and me very well. He said that I'm a realist and Paul is an idealist. He thought that neither of us was fully equipped to face life." I noticed that Frances had the habit of biting her nails to the quick, also. "But he said that growing up together each of us might lose a little of our extremes. Which seems to me a very sensible thing to say."

I agreed that it seemed highly sensible.

"I suppose that he *loved* Paul more—being a son and all. Paul is a very loving and giving person, if you don't think that the expression is too trite," she said. "Are you married?"

"Stewardesses," I said, "are automatically grounded when they get married."

I could see that she was storing the information away against the future. We listened a moment to Paul; the paroxysms were growing less violent.

"Then you don't have any children," she said. "You've been very kind to Paul and me. My father said that children are an experience no one should miss."

"You're young yet," I said.

She looked at me with those green, owlish eyes and refused to let me joke with her. She was a very serious girl. And she had a habit of pushing her hair back over her shoulder in the manner of a much older girl.

"I wasn't speaking for myself," she said.

"I'm young yet, too," I informed her.

She said, "I imagine you will want a child like Paul————"

I told her, yes, I thought that would be very nice. But so would having a daughter like her be extremely fine.

"That's very nice of you to say."

I assured her that I wouldn't have said it unless I meant it.

"You're very sincere and kind," she said. "It's too bad that my father didn't marry someone like you—not necessarily of his intelligence, of course————"

She faltered then, and her face flushed excessively. I had never imagined her being caught off base that way.

"I didn't mean you weren't intelligent," she said. "I have no way of knowing about you. What I mean————"

I said that, of course, I understood. She seemed now more likable to me because she was vulnerable to embarrassment like anyone else.

"He loved life," she said, biting one of those chewed-up nails. "He said that one should be able to close one's eyes and see life as a bright circus. A colorful, musical circus."

I listened and heard nothing inside the lavatory.

"I *used* to," Frances said.

"Used to what?" I asked.

"I used to see life as a colorful, musical circus. But now I don't. And I'm rather concerned. I see life as a *gray* and rather *un*musical circus. All shades of gray."

I said that she had, indeed, serious *reason* to be concerned. I hoped secretly that she didn't think I was making fun of her, since my conversation sometimes sounded rather flippant in the face of this serious child. But I had decided it was time to look in on Paul.

He was standing next to the small, round window, wiping the steam away and staring through the pouring rivulets into the mystery outside. With his other hand he pressed that heavy old watch against his cheek, which was wet and streaked. The air was foul. I called him, and he was very angry to find that we had been watching him.

"Go away!" he screamed at us.

"Come back to your seat," Frances said.

"Bossy! Bossy! Bossy!" He let out a piercing yell.

"You're frightened," she said. "Come and sit down."

"I'm not! I'm not!" he cried. "I'll tell Father on you!"

"*Tell* him!" Frances said impatiently. "You're so *stubborn*."

When the children were strapped into their seats again, I patrolled the aisle. The rain washed over us. It was as if some great force stood outside directing a hose against the windows, making the glass opaque. The quick flashes of lightning outlined everything inside the plane for the space of a suspended heartbeat. Walking once past Paul's seat I saw that he had his fingers poked into his ears and his mouth was open. The crashes thundered and reverberated in my ears. The rain was hitting with stronger, harsher "pucks" against the window. When I heard it overhead, bouncing off the metal fuselage with a strange, increasing din, I remembered the coldness in the air. The rain had frozen. We were being pounded by hail.

Fearing the worst occurrence of all—icing on the wings—I dropped into an empty seat near the forward end of the cabin. I felt the wind rocking us like a giant hand, and I listened to the thunder sound through the pounding of the hail. When I saw St. Elmo's fire around the right propeller, I stared for a long while at it.

After an interminable length of time, the wind had perceptibly dropped. I hurried back down the aisle and bent over the children, but I could not make them out clearly, because the darkness of night had closed over the darkness of the storm. The rain, no longer frozen, still pounded against the windows. I stood up, waiting to see if we would cut entirely through the storm front at this point.

Soon thunder broke in the far distance, and the rain was beating only in a soft, rhythmical way against the plane. Looking closely outside I could make out openings in the dark clouds and the light of the moon shining somewhere in back of the patchy cirrus. But the clouds were moving rapidly; the wind was still heavy. When we broke through the clouds into a large opening, I saw the first-quarter moon and the light it cast on the wet wings. I saw the warm light discover the inside of the plane.

Both of the children were sleeping soundly. Paul's head rested on Frances' shoulder, and her arm circled him. Her hand, graceful and determined, hung now limply into the aisle where someone might brush it in passing. Lifting it carefully, I placed it inside the arm of Paul's chair. Neither of them stirred. They were safe, for the moment.

Comfortably settled at last in my own seat, I leaned toward the window and looked out into the sky that had miraculously cleared. I could see the millions of flickering lights below, and above, the millions of glinting stars. It was as if we were walking on a thread, in this limbo between heaven and earth—spinning through thousands of brief miles. The lights were distant and unfriendly, I felt. We were flying now over the clustered population of the coast. Walking a tightrope, I thought, in a rather *gray* and *un*musical circus.

Reflected in the window I saw my own eyes. The image blurred, and the face was no longer clearly mine. I began to wonder what the eyes of Frances would see, looking out into the emptiness— those green, owlish eyes sizing up the universe. Or what about those other, poker eyes in a dead-pan little face? I could imagine the two pairs of eyes together at the window, searching the sky and the ground. I could see them too clearly, and I pulled away from the window, though still drawn to the outside, even when I was able to see only the rapidly moving clouds and the flashing lights on the wing. Was it my imagination that the world seemed awfully big— big enough to frighten a realist, to terrify an idealist?

Settling back in my chair, I hunched over and sat down hard on my hands. Partly because they were cold. But mostly to keep from chewing my nails, my nice, long, lacquered nails.

Wesley Ford Davis

The Undertow

Gently she cracked the bedroom door, peeped in, and, closing it as gently, she tiptoed toward the kitchen doorway. And with a finger on her lips in a shushing sign she gestured with her other hand to her little sister. In the kitchen they made their breakfast and talked in low tones.

"Only one head on the pillow," she said, "and one hump under the sheet."

"Whose?" Fid John asked.

" 'Whose?' You know whose. Hers of course."

Their father by now would be halfway to the lighthouse, his long legs swinging along at six miles an hour, maybe singing, "He hammered so hard that he broke his heart. Then he laid down his hammer and he died." Singing above the surf, putting the seagulls to flight.

"I reckon we can have all the mayonnaise sandwiches we can eat," she said. "How many mayonnaise sandwiches can little F. John Jarrad eat on a bright and Sunday morning?"

"Three and two of catsup," Fid John said.

"Your eyes are about two and a half times as big as your stomach. I'll fix you one mayonnaise and one catsup."

She pulled a chair from the table to the sink, standing on it to reach the shelves, and took down the tall-necked catsup bottle and the squat mayonnaise jar. Pausing, she looked at her sister, the dirty chenille bathrobe, the sleep-matted eyes and tangled hair. "You go wash, and comb your hair while I fix this breakfast, and throw that bathrobe into the dirty clothes and don't take it out again." Fid John turned to leave the kitchen but she called, "Wait a minute!" Taking a strand of the tangled yellow hair she placed it to the tip of her tongue.

"So you didn't wash it again last night. Hasn't Daddy told you the salt water will turn the gold in your hair to brass if you don't keep it washed out? Do you want to live out your whole life looking like somebody has just dumped a bowl of sauerkraut on your head?"

"I was too sleepy. Playing on the rope makes me sleepy, especially late at night."

"All right. Don't bother with it now. Just give it ten licks with the brush and wash your bright blue eyes, and push that incredible robe as far down into the dirty clothes as you can reach."

Fid John made a deep bow. "Yes, Your Highness, if you're so highly and smart, what am I supposed to put on instead?"

"Get a dress out of my drawer if you don't have any. That yellow pinafore that's too short on me."

Fid John started for the doorway, but again she stopped her. "Wait a minute."

On tiptoe she crossed the kitchen and the living room and gently cracked the bedroom door. Lit by the sun, her mother's hair spread in blond waves over the pillow and the hump of her shoulder under the sheet. Closing the door she signaled her sister to the bathroom, the finger to her lip in the shushing sign. It would be much better if her mother didn't wake up until her father got back from his walk. His walk to the lighthouse if he followed the beach southward, to the city pier if he went northward. Sometimes he could ease her fears and soothe her nerves.

In the kitchen again she made the sandwiches, three of mayonnaise and two of catsup. She placed the bottle and the jar back on the top shelf so that Fid John couldn't reach them even if she stood on a chair. If she got her hands on it she would drink the catsup like a bottle of Pepsi Cola, and that much catsup was not good for a growing child. Then she looked for the sharp knife to cut the sandwiches. She looked in the utensil drawer, and among the dishes and beer cans and bottles on the drainboard, and on the dining table. The sharp knife and the can opener were always getting lost.

So with a table knife she sawed the sandwiches diagonally to make small corners for Fid John to bite from. She put them into a paper sack along with an almost empty box of Ritz crackers and a couple of oranges. Hearing her little sister coming, bump-bump-

bump, walking on her heels, she flew to the doorway. She frowned mightily and put the shushing finger to her lips. Little Fid rose on her toes and came lightly as a feather.

She looked into the paper sack. "Where're the tangerines? I starve while I'm trying to peel an orange."

"You grasshopper. If you would take just ten seconds to think, you'd know we finished the tangerines yesterday. Don't fret though, I'll peel it for you. My thumbnail is nearly as good as a knife."

Before they left the kitchen she had to test the beer cans. She lined them up first with all the fat, belted, jolly Falstaffs facing her. For a moment she admired his fine boots and hat and broadsword and then shook each can close to her ear. When there was a slosh she took the swallow quickly with a wry face. "Do you know Shakespeare?" she asked.

Fid John nodded. "Anybody knows Shakespeare."

"You know what? Daddy says that Shakespeare liked Falstaff beer so much he named one of his most famous characters after it. Here he is, right on the can. Sir John Falstaff. Old tub of guts himself."

Fid John begged for a swallow but she refused. "You're not old enough, Little F. You wouldn't like it anyway. It tastes awful."

"You're not old enough either, Bobs Allan. And if it tastes so awful, why do you drink it?"

"I'm the oldest one here, aren't I, when Mama's asleep and Daddy dear is gone, and if the cans are not empty they make a great mess in the garbage sack."

Through the house with the paper sack of breakfast they went quietly, but once off the front porch they went skipping, swinging their arms and singing: "Out of the house go we, Down to the ocean sea, To play on the rope, To swing in the brine . . ."

On the narrow boardwalk that bridged the sand dunes, through the palmettos and cactus and century plants, they slowed down. The walk was narrow and old and rickety.

"You go ahead, F. John," she said, "so I can watch you, and don't fall off amongst the cactus and the rattlesnakes. They'll tickle and prickle you and drink your blood."

At the end of the boardwalk they leaped to the sand, soft and wind-ruffled above the normal reach of the tide, and warmed by the bright morning sun. Before them the waves broke and the foam

scudded like small birds running on the hard beach. They watched
the tall waves breaking against the outer bar and the smaller ones
on the near bar, which at the lowest tide was partially exposed. And
overhead the pelican formations in neat wedges went southward
where they would feed at the tip of the island during the morning
and fly back in the afternoon. Fid John ran to the pile of coiled
rope but she called her back sharply.

"Stay away from the rope. We got to eat first. What do you
think I fixed this breakfast for?"

She tore the paper sack down the side and across the bottom,
spread it like a tablecloth and arranged the sandwiches in two lines,
mayonnaise and catsup. Seated facing each other, Indian-fashion,
they bent their heads and said, "God is great, God is good. Let us
thank him for this food. Amen."

"I'll have to eliminate one; I don't know which I want to eat
first," Fid John said. Her finger moving back and forth she counted,
"Eeeny, meeny, miney, moe. Catch a Negro by the toe . . ."

Barbara Allan watched, wondering how long it was going to
take Fid to learn that if there are just two things to count, the one
you start with is always left. But when the counting was finished,
it came out wrong.

"You counted Negro as two words. It's not two words, it's two
syllables."

"I don't care," Fid John said. She picked up the catsup sandwich and bit as largely as she could.

"Now relax and chew thoroughly, twenty-five times to each bite.
Daddy says your stomach depends on your teeth like a general depends on his troops."

For a few minutes there was only the noise of their careful chewing and the gentle surf. The pelicans wedged by above them and
their big shadows swept along the beach. She thrust out her foot
to meet the winging shadows.

"Hey, Fiddee, what if a shadow could slice you like a knife?
People would be busy running and dodging. I guess they would
have to kill all the birds."

"You crazy Bobbins!" Fid John said.

Fid John finished her two sandwiches and said she didn't want
the orange or any of the crackers. She started to pull the long dress
over her head but Barbara Allan stopped her.

"Now don't you get hasty. You know we can't go in the ocean
until our food has had time to settle. Besides, I'm still eating. It

will take me quite a while to eat both the oranges and the Ritz crackers."

"If Mama wakes up before Daddy gets back we won't get to play on the rope."

Barbara Allan turned toward the house—just the upper half of the screened front porch was visible above the dunes and cactus and palmettos. A mocking bird hopped on the ridge of the roof, but there was no other movement.

"Don't worry. She didn't get to sleep until nearly daylight."

"How do you know? Did you stay awake all night?"

She thought of the beer cans, thirteen of them, and the sherry jug in the waste basket. "I just know. It's Sunday morning, ain't it?"

"Tell me a story," Fid John said, "to help the time pass."

"I'll tell you a true story."

"No. True stories don't have fairies and witches and giants in them."

"I don't care. You're getting old enough to take an interest in true stories. I'll tell you the story of that pelican you're sitting on."

Fid John swung her feet around and shifted her seat on the sand.

"What pelican? How could I be sitting on any pelican? You said this was going to be a true story."

"That's what I said and that's what I meant. That's right where Daddy buried it."

Fid John stared at the spot where her seat had made a shallow depression in the sand and the bits of shell and bits of twig and wood.

"Right here?" She placed her finger on the sand. "Can we dig it up?"

"No. Don't even think about it. It's awful bad luck to dig up any buried thing. And don't tell that I told you."

"Where did he get a dead pelican? I've never seen one even light on the beach."

"You know the rifle that's on the wall? Daddy shot the pelican with the rifle."

The shock and disbelief in the smaller one's face made her uneasy. There was always the question of when and how much of the plain truth the little one should be given. Now that she had mentioned the pelican without really meaning to, she would have to tell the story, as when he shot it, he would have buried the bird and not mentioned it, at least not for a long time, if she had not seen it. But she had seen it, and so he had to try to tell her why people do things sometimes that they are sorry for, or even ashamed of. Or not so much why they do such things as that they simply do do such things and that if you are to like or love, or admire and respect, a person it will sooner or later be a love and respect in spite of such things, which if looked at by themselves would cause you not to love and respect but to hate and despise.

"Look here, Fid John," she said, "you know Daddy dear wouldn't want to kill a pelican. Nobody likes birds any more than he does; he's probably down close to the lighthouse right now looking at them through his field glasses. On a clear day he says he can see the man-of-war birds way out over the ocean."

"Why did he want to kill this pelican for?" She stared at the sand as though she were looking at the bird, seeing it close up for the first time. Barbara Allan remembered the bird, and how she had been unable at first to keep her mind on what her father was trying to say, because she could not see how the flying shape that had been so out of reach in the air and diving into the ocean and bobbing in the surf could also be the heavy, clumsy-looking pile of feathers that sprawled unmoving on the beach. But now she had to tell Fid John, not what she had seen and heard, nor even what he had told her, but a way of regarding it that would be possible for someone three years younger than herself.

"He was sitting on the front doorstep up there." She pointed over the palmettos to the little beach house. "He was cleaning the rifle. Can you remember when he used to hunt squirrels nearly every morning at daylight in the oak woods across the river? And Mummy dear hated squirrel and every day she would say, 'I don't see why we have to eat those stinking squirrels just because you think you're Daniel Boone or Buffalo Bill. It's not as though we didn't have money and had to live off the woods.' But he wouldn't say anything. He just cleaned the squirrels and fried them, along with the steak or chops or whatever he had brought from the store."

"Did he shoot the pelican to eat?" Fid John asked.

"No. Of course not. Nobody eats pelicans. If anybody did, do you think they would be flying up and down this beach every day like they do?"

She was silent for a moment. They watched the wedging flight of the pelicans like planes in formation. She rose on her knees and shading her eyes looked southward along the glimmering white beach. Sometimes she could see her father nearly all the way to the lighthouse, but now there was no movement on the beach, only the flights of birds and the rising and falling surf.

"It was a kind of accident. The pelicans kept flying by in pairs. It was their mating season. And they always flew one behind the other, about two or three feet apart. He kept tracking them with the rifle, not aiming to shoot them, just tracking them for practice."

"What does 'tracking' mean?"

"Well, you take aim on something when it's moving and swing the rifle around to keep the sights on the target. You know how he is about things. How he likes to figure things out. He talked about how fast the birds were flying and how far apart they were and his distance from them, and how by aiming at the lead bird the bullet would hit the one tailing. But then he happened to pull the trigger and the pelican fell with its wings turning like an autogyro. So he put the rifle up on the wall so high that even he couldn't reach it without standing on a chair. And he hasn't used it since."

"Let's call it 'The Story of the Unfortunate Pelican,' " Fid John said.

"All right, that's a good name for it," she said. And so it was a good name for the story as she had told it, as she believed he would have wanted her to tell it to the younger one. For Fid was not old enough to understand the fears that made their beautiful mother so nervous, that made her take too much wine and whisky and beer and swear and curse him for a hypocritical John the Baptist and a pretentious nigger-preaching, low-class, logic-chopping demagogic orator, and a stupid, unfeeling materialist who would swallow the opinion of every stupid, satchel-toting medical doctor. That day, while he cleaned the rifle and tracked the pelicans, she stood behind him, holding to the door frame and poking the toe of her house slipper into his back, saying, "Go on and shoot the birds. That's what you want to do. Shoot all of them. Shoot me. That's what they do where you come from. They burn niggers and hang them and cut off their testicles."

And he had tried not to answer. He spoke to her instead: "Barbara Allan, you go play. Go around to your sister's playpen and play with her." So she walked around the corner of the porch and sat down in the warm sand.

What a puzzle it was. Sometimes for as much as two weeks,

their mother was the best, playing and singing with them at the piano, reading and telling stories, cooking their favorite dishes, working with their father, criticizing and revising his stories, and the two of them in the surf as happy and frolicsome as two porpoises.

From around the corner of the house she could hear them, he saying, "Please, please just go away. All I ask is peace." And she, "Peace! You'll not have peace, not now or ever. With your wives you want peace. The minute you Southern sons-of-bitches marry, you start acting like a Baptist preacher around the house. But by God, I'm not a Baptist preacher's wife. Of course when you're with Barbara Blake or Jill Jones or some other fine bitch you don't preach any sermons."

And he: "If you would take just one minute to think, you would remember that it wasn't Barbara Blake or Jill Jones that I drank a fifth of rum with last night and swam naked in the ocean and lay on the beach in the moonlight with last night. And it wasn't anybody but you that I carried up here in my arms and tucked in bed."

"Oh, you poor abused little boy. He had to put his wife to bed."

"Now please, dear. Try to be fair. I had a wonderful time last night, but can't you realize that that sort of thing can't last twenty-four hours a day?"

"All right. Give me some money and the car keys."

Barbara Allan put her face to the corner and looked with one eye. He shook his head and worked the lever of the rifle. He aimed it toward a sand dune, and she, looking in the direction of the pointing rifle, saw the yellow cactus bloom which the bullet would shatter. But the screen door squeaked and turning her head quickly she saw her mother's long leg move out and the toe of her house slipper strike beneath his right shoulder. Jumping up he whirled around. His hands gripped the rifle so hard that his knuckles turned white in the sunlight. And she said, "Go ahead, shoot me. That's what tyrants do. They kill anybody that opposes them."

Barbara Allan saw her father's face grow pale and then dark. She tried to call out to him but she couldn't make a sound, and she saw his mouth open and his lips move but no words came. Then he turned and walked toward the beach. He raised his eyes and Barbara Allan raised hers and watched the pair of pelicans flying southward one behind the other. And at once, with the sharp explosion of the rifle, the pelican, the one in the rear, spun toward the surf.

"I'm thirsting to death," Fid John said. "We forgot to bring any water."

"You grasshopper. The ocean always makes you thirsty, or sleepy, or hungry. I'll go get a bottle of water."

She had to make sure that Fid John did not go into the ocean by herself. She was too little to go in by herself even with the rope in her hands.

"Now," she said, "while I'm gone, you're Snow White." She broke off a segment of the orange. "Take this. This is the poisoned apple. It puts you to sleep until the prince comes along. And I'm the prince." Fid John ate the orange and lay quiet on the sand. And she ran up the boardwalk to the house. In the palmettos a pair of towhees flitted. One of them called "ree" and the other one "jo-ree" as she ran past. The house was quiet. She thought of the Senator. Maybe he had come back. Maybe he would be lying on the front doorstep. She ran around the house and stopped at the corner and closed her eyes. With her eyes closed she could see him plainly, stretched out sleeping on the top step. She felt her way around the corner and opened her eyes slowly. But he wasn't there. He had been gone since Monday, a whole week. She felt the tears in her eyes and wiped them with her hand. Her father had said that you couldn't keep a tomcat from running off once in awhile.

She crossed the front porch and the living room on tiptoe. Before going to the kitchen she approached the bedroom door and opened it gently. The blond hair lay in a sunlit splash across the pillow. She stared at the back of her mother's head. She wondered if you could really wake a person by staring. Then she remembered she didn't want to wake her mother. She closed the door gently and tiptoed to the kitchen and took a water bottle from the icebox. It was ten-thirty by the kitchen clock. Their father should be home in another hour.

She sang as she skipped down the boardwalk, "A handsome prince comes riding, Prancing his tall white horse." Leaping from his horse he fell to his knees and exclaimed, "Ah, such beauty. The world never saw such beauty." He kissed the sleeping Snow White and she fluttered her lids and opened her sky-blue eyes.

"Now, can we play on the rope?" she asked.

"Uh huh, but first drink of this wonderful potion. It will protect you from all harm." She unscrewed the cup and poured her little sister a drink. "Through many a weary bog and fen I rode to fetch this to the lady fair."

They uncoiled the long rope and dragged it over the smooth beach and into the ocean, and above the soughing surf they sang, "We have no ship but we have a rope to ride the ocean sea————"

Against the shoreward tug of the surf they carried the rope and stopped to rest on the first bar. They sang and giggled with the tickling sand that shifted under their feet and the waves that tried to push them down. "This is as far as you can go, Fiddee. You are not allowed to go past the first knot in the rope. And hang on tight and you'll get a good enough ride."

She took the rope near the end, gripping two knots placed close together, and walked southward on the bar parallel to the shore with the rope stretched tight between them. Facing the ocean she walked to the edge of the bar until she felt the tug of the undertow. She shouted, "Get ready, hold tight." Taking a deep breath and gripping the rope, she plunged into the northward-running current that ran between the two sand bars. It was like a roller coaster, only better. The current carried her and the waves spun her. Better than swimming because it was faster. Faster and faster until the force of the current against the shoreward tug of the rope threw her back onto the sand bar, where, laughing and shouting and gasping for breath, they carried the rope back along the bar to make ready for another ride.

Their father had sunk the big post in the beach and fixed the rope to it and had taught them how to use it, and told them, too, not to use it unless he was with them. But they had learned all about the rope and the current, and she had learned long ago that his orders were for their safety and that he probably knew that they did play on the rope by themselves and had decided it was all right though he had not said so. She had discovered more than once that you reach a point when you have to go beyond what anyone has said you can or must do, or not do.

It was fun but tiring. They soon had to lie on the beach to rest, and on the way they found a perfect sand dollar with its unbelievable design like a flower with fine petals. The ocean was full of marvels.

"An animal lived there," she said. "This is what's left when it dies and the ocean washes it out. This pretty flower on the shell is really just a lot of little holes. The holes were its mouths to feed through. A million mouths to feed through."

One of her jobs was to pass on to Fid the information her father had given her. It wasn't always easy. She had not yet been able to make the little one understand that what people called the undertow, the thing that kept people away from this stretch of beach where they lived, was really a river. "It's not an easy thing to believe," her father had told her, "but the ocean is full of rivers just like the land. It's hard to believe what you can't see. If it weren't for the surf rolling over it you could ride a canoe fifteen miles an hour on that little river out there." She would understand, when she was older and could ride at the end of the rope, and feel the tug and the pull like strong invisible arms around her legs.

They rested in the sun, drowsy for awhile, and collected sand dollars and crabs' pincers and periwinkles and conch shells while the sun rose high and the last pelican formation passed southward. The sky grew hot and still. The ocean breeze ceased and the surf grew quiet. The washed-up seaweed dried in the hot sun and smelled sweet and fishy. Several times Barbara Allan stood as tall as she could and shading her eyes searched the beach up and down for a sight of their father. But there was no one on the beach either way. It was a dangerous beach. No swimmers or sun bathers used it. Sometimes someone would fish the surf for whiting or the channel for sea bass. And it wasn't unusual that her father was not in sight. Sometimes he walked back through the dunes looking for rattlesnakes and tortoises to watch their movements and learn their habits.

They had done everything. They had taken two sessions on the rope and had even built a sand-and-shell castle with towers, dungeons, moats, and drawbridge.

But when the sun lay straight south beyond the lighthouse and it hurt her eyes to look in that direction she knew it was high noon or past and there was still no sign of him. And Fid John said, "I want some lunch." And she said, "Daddy's not back and she's not awake."

"We could have some more sandwiches."

She shook her head, "No, we've got to have some real lunch."

She stood up. "All right. I'll go wake her. With such a long sleep, maybe she will be feeling fine. But you wait here."

"I'm tired of the beach and the big ocean sea. It hurts my eyes."

"All right. You lie down here now. That's it. Turn away from the sun and close your eyes. You've just pricked your finger on the enchanted spinning wheel. I'm the prince that will come along in a thousand years to cut my way through the impassable brambles and to climb the sheer walls to kiss you awake."

With a pointed stick she marked out the walls of the castle.

"Now, nobody but the prince can ever enter. You lie still now."

She skipped up the boardwalk, singing, " 'Twas in the merry month of May, And the green buds all were swelling . . ." It would be better if her mother were waked by the singing and other outside noises. Twice she stopped and faced the palmettos and cactus dunes, one way and then the other, calling, "Kitty, kitty, kitty." She listened and listened for the Senator's miaow. But the only sound was the swishing surf. Closing her eyes she tried to remember. Had he been around on Wednesday or Thursday? No. Just before dark on Monday he had asked to be let out. She had opened the screen door and watched him walk like a king into the palmettos. A whole week ago.

She walked across the front yard and along the side of the house calling and listening. "The trouble is," her father had said, "he has to cross the highway to find a lady friend." She wished now that she hadn't named him Senator Pepper. When she named him, her father had laughed and said, "A politician's career is mighty uncertain."

She dropped to her knees to look under the house. Again she called and searched out the corners, and decided to check on the box while she was under the house. The small, heavy, wooden box sat against the foundation blocks in one corner. She twisted the padlock against its hasp to make sure it was locked. Her father had told her to do this every day. When he gave her the key and showed her the box, he said, "If anything ever happens to me, you're to open the box. Of course, we don't expect anything to happen, but people should try to be ready for accidents."

Standing by the bedroom window she called the cat, pitching her voice higher and higher, not really calling or expecting the cat but making the noise to wake her mother. Then she stood silent waiting for squeak of bedspring, the shuffle of house slippers, and her mother's voice. But there was no sound. Turning, she pressed her nose against the window screen. She saw first the fanwise spread of the golden hair, bright still, though not lit now by the sun; then in the big dresser mirror the brilliant blue eyes, wide open beneath the penciled brows. She waited a moment for her mother to speak.

"Mummy, you're playing possum. I see you. I see you in the mirror."

She squinted her eyes and cupped her hands above them to see the mirror more clearly. The bed, the form of her mother's body under the light spread, the pale face and brilliant lipstick and eyes were like a picture. She scratched the screen wire with her fingernails and called, "Mother! Mother, it's way past lunchtime."

She waited but there was no answer, no movement. She felt a strange sickness in her stomach and a trembling in her knees. She turned from the window, walked slowly to the front yard. There was no movement in the sky or among the palmettos and cactus-covered dunes. Only the gentle surf. It was going to be one of the few still hot afternoons when even the ocean breeze failed. The smell of the dried seaweed came faintly from the beach. Gazing out along the twisting ruts that went toward the highway, she opened her mouth to call the Senator. In the stillness her voice was shrill and loud. She called "Kitty" once and then she ran fast along the twisting ruts, her fingers crossed, chanting silently hocus-pocus and all the magic rhymes she knew, praying that the Senator might be past each successive bend in the road.

Remembering suddenly, she stopped still and with a last look as far as she could see along the rutted road she turned back. She had to hurry because Fid John might decide the thousand years' sleep was up. She might even get it into her head to ride the rope alone and she was too young and not nearly strong enough to ride the pull of the undertow.

Around the house and down the boardwalk on tiptoe silently she ran until she could see the spot on the beach. It was all right. Sleeping Beauty hadn't stirred yet. But they had to have some food. She ran back to the house.

Opening the screen door, she quietly crossed the front porch, went through the door into the living room. There was only the faint sound of her feet muffled by the carpet. She remembered the story of the explorers in the pyramid, their footsteps breaking the silence of three thousand years. She started toward the bedroom but her steps grew shorter and slower. Her thoughts grew solid in her throat and made it hard to breathe. What if she should reach down and shake her shoulder and still she————

She turned away quickly, trying to push her mind backward to undo the thought. And whistling through her teeth she hurried into the other bedroom, hers and Fid John's, and pulling out the dresser drawer, she pushed back the slips and frocks and panties and lifting the paper that lined the bottom found the key to the box. She spread the long loop of twine and slipped it over her head. Lifting the crinkled front of her dress she let the key fall between her breasts. For a moment she stared down at her breasts, remembering the day not so long ago when she had said, "I can't swim in just my panties any more." And Fid John said, "Why not?" And she said, "Can't you see, you grasshopper?"

In the kitchen she quickly filled a big paper bag with the opened loaf of bread and the jar of mayonnaise, the bottle of catsup, a bunch of celery, and a quart of milk and the rest of the oranges. They had to eat plenty of raw vegetables and fruit and milk for their teeth and bones and digestion. She rummaged through the drawers and among the litter of dishes and cans, looking for the sharp knife. It looked as if it was lost for good this time. The sack in her arms, she hurried out of the house and down the boardwalk toward bleak sand. She galloped the great white charger as fast as she dared on the treacherous footing. By now the Sleeping Beauty would surely be restless.

Miriam Merritt

No Game for Children

The crushed limestone trail that led to the cabin twisted through
the trees like two narrow lines of whitewash. On the left the ground
ledged downward toward a creek. The soil was thin as shadows,
barely able to conceal the knolls and shelves of lime and sandstone although it supported a dry tangle of evergreen and chap-
arral. On the right the land sloped upward, covered with a seem-
ingly impenetrable brake of cedar. In the thicker soil of the
roadsides, hackberry and live oak and mesquite grew tall to mesh
their branches over the tunnel of the road so that smoky sunlight
filtered through this canopy too diffuse even to bring a sparkle to
the radiator ornament on James Tennison's car. Branches scratched
his car top with a sound like metal scraped on glass that set his
teeth on edge, and he shivered almost for the shady, lonely auster-
ity of the place. It was so exactly like Larry Carter to die leaving
his wife and children nothing but a cold stone cabin and these useless acres of brush-covered land. Larry Carter. Now there was a
real lily of the valley for you.

The car bumped around a curve and he saw the cabin, a brooding two-story house with an overhanging roof that sloped down on
one side to cover a cement-floored screen porch. The native stone
formed a camouflage of pink and gray and brown and dirty white,
as if the walls were made of patchwork quilts. Although it was June,
the sun seemed as remote here in the clearing as in winter, and thin
beards of smoke floating occasionally from the mouth of the chim-

ney added to the illusion. However, he was not cold, only refresh-
ingly cool in short sleeves.

Walking toward the door of the cabin, James noticed a curious
vine crawling up the wall. It was a blackish, spidery, poor excuse
for a vine and it seemed to move, as if it were visibly growing, but
just as he held out a hand to finger the texture, he saw that the thing
was no vine, but a mass of daddy-long-legs sprawling grotesquely
over the stone. A voice from inside the house made him pause once
more. "Why does he have to come?"—that'll be Ted, James thought
—"We were going to play the game today." James took a deep
breath and opened the porch door noisily.

They were all gathered in the living room—Ellen and the three
children. "Well, hello there," he said heartily, standing in the doorway. Only Ellen smiled back. The children, he supposed, expected
him to twirl a black mustache and heartlessly demand the money for
the mortgage. Somehow he had to make them understand that he
knew he couldn't take their father's place and didn't expect to. He
only wanted a kind of superior friendship.

"Jimmy," said Ellen—the only one who ever called him that—
"how nice," stretching out her hand. "And right on time." Of
course. When Ellen asked him to come to the cabin for dinner and
vaguely set the time as "Oh, whenever you like," he pinpointed the
time of arrival. It was his idea to spend the whole day—"Do you
mind if I take advantage of you and grab a whole day in the country?"—and perhaps make some progress toward friendship with
the children.

"What a nice outfit!" Ellen exclaimed.

"The latest thing in country wear, so they tell me," said James.
He was wearing blue denim slacks with shirt to match, blue canvas
shoes with thick rubber soles and a blue denim cap with a bill on it.
Outside in his car, there was a matching blue denim jacket. Ellen
had told him it got fairly cool out here at night. Now she popped
her hand to her mouth as if she'd meant to say something and
changed her mind.

"What's the matter?" James asked.

"Nothing," said Ellen quickly, but, all the same, he was confused and desperately swept the room for a phenomenon worthy of
comment. Nothing. He advanced heavily to a chair. They seemed
to be waiting for him to say something, but all he could do was light
a cigarette. He stirred in the chair uneasily; if wishes were horses,

he thought, avoiding the glistening eyes of the watching children . . .

"You know what?" little Phil asked unexpectedly. "Ted found a snake yesterday."

"It was a copperhead," said Ted. "Not just a snake. You know where I found it? In that chair you're sitting in. *I* almost sat on it."

"Oh," said James. "I . . . ," he started, and Ellen said, "I . . . "

"No, you first," said Ellen.

"Well, I was just going to say I noticed a bunch of daddy-long-legs crawling up the house outside. I thought it was a vine at first." (Ellen was watching him expectantly.) "What I mean is, you ought to spray around here. Use DDT or something. Snakes in the house, insects all over. Couldn't be very healthy, seems to me."

"Who's afraid of daddy-long-legs?" Ted scornfully asked, looking fixedly at seven-year-old Tassy. "I'm not," said Tassy. "Am I, Mother?"

Ellen jumped up. "I'll make coffee," she said, disappearing into the kitchen. James, longing for such an easy escape, got out of his chair to examine himself in the mirror over the fireplace. He took a little black comb out of his pocket and carefully combed his hair. He wished now he had brought the children something, a game or perhaps some books. After a minute he said, "Tassy, what do you kids do out here? Ride horses, go on hikes?"

"We play games," said Tassy vaguely.

"Games. Hmm. Anything special?"

"Just games," said Ted. "My dad knew how to play swell games."

"Oh." James watched Tassy. The little girl had turned her back and seemed to be playing with something. With her head bent, her brown, straight hair brushed close over her cheeks; there was something in the way the head was poised that reminded him of Ellen.

Phil went up to Tassy. "Let me see it awhile," he said.

"No," said Tassy.

"Aw, I just want to look at it."

"What have you got there, Tassy?" asked James. It looked like an egg or at least something egg-shaped.

Hastily, Tassy thrust the object into her pocket and shifted in her chair to face the group. "Nothing," she said.

"I know all about snakes and bugs," Ted offered. "My dad told me."

"That must be very interesting," said James.

"My dad said if you kill a snake the mate will come to the same place looking for it. Do you believe that?"

"Well, I . . . to tell you the truth, I don't know much about snakes, but it sounds logical."

Little Phil marched up to James. "Are you glad my daddy's dead?" he demanded.

James ran his hand around the back of his neck. Where the devil was Ellen? "Why, no, Phil," he managed. "Of course, I'm not glad."

"Don't talk about it," said Tassy. "It's very sad."

"I know how to climb a tree," Phil said.

"Hah," snorted Ted. "That little bitty old cedar tree. I can climb to the top of the tallest tree around here."

They were silent then. Ted beat a steady tattoo on the rungs of his chair, and presently James began to drum his fingers on his chair arm; his nails made neat little clicking sounds. He willed himself to stay seated instead of going to find Ellen. The remains of an early-morning fire smoked lazily in the fireplace, flared into life briefly, then smoldered again when the sliver of wood was consumed. "Seemore and savemore, seemore and savemore," singsonged Phil, balancing on the imaginary tightrope of the hearth line. Idiotic, James thought aimlessly, but persisted until he pegged the singsong for a familiar radio slogan.

Just in time Ellen returned, bearing a tray with steaming cups of coffee. There was also milk in a cup and sugar in a bowl with the handles snubbed off. James leaped with relief to take the tray.

"Mother, I have to talk to you," Ted immediately said. "No, alone." He dragged her off to a corner and began to whisper, gesturing with his head first on one side and then the other, his face screwed up earnestly. Finally, he called to Tassy and Phil and the three children disappeared outside.

"A game they're playing," Ellen said, with a smile and slight shrug of the shoulders. "I'm to go . . . ," she sprawled unladylike in the chair with legs slanted before her like open scissors, ". . . out in a minute and hold the straws. Alone." She made a big circle of her lips on this word. "I'd better go," she said. "Won't be a moment," this from over her shoulder. "There's more coffee in the pot. And, by the way," pausing in the door, "please excuse the place. I sold most of the stuff in town, but a few things I wanted to keep. I haven't fitted them in yet."

Holding his coffee cup absently, James strolled over to the window. The children were gathered around a tree stump, sawed off smooth on a level with Phil's chest, in the yard near the south end of the cabin. Each of the children placed an object on the stump; James couldn't make out what they were through the window glass. He listened abstractedly.

"Listen, Phil," Ted burst out, "I told you about a million times it has to be what you like most in the whole world." Ellen is really very good with children, James thought, watching her.

"But *he* likes it, Ted," said Tassy.

"Well, O.K., but it isn't as good as Dad's key chain or your egg."

He didn't like to hear children squabble, but Ellen just let them settle it themselves. That was good, noninterference.

"Straws," said Ellen, holding up her hand. "Ted . . . now Tassy . . . and Phil."

"But I wanted the short one," protested Phil shrilly. Ted explained something to Phil—James couldn't catch the words—then Phil began to caper, singing, "I got the long straw, I got the long straw." He waggled it under Tassy's nose.

"Ted," said Ellen, "couldn't you . . ." But she didn't finish and James watched her walk slowly back toward the cabin, her head bent, until she disappeared from the window's view. James did not move from the window yet, but stood looking out, wondering if he really wanted three children, bang, just like that. The kids picked up the objects from the tree stump, then Ted said, "We'll go up to the fence, Tassy. O.K.? Come on, Phil. 'Member, Tassy, you have till lunch." James watched Ted round his car, give one fender a resounding thump in passing, and head for a trail which angled into the cedars past where Ellen's battered station wagon was parked. Phil trotted to keep up. Pretty rough on Ellen, James thought, trying to be mother and father both, and pal, too. She was making it harder on herself though, staying out here.

"Jimmy." He turned at Ellen's words. "What are you doing?"

"Hmm, just thinking. You know, you could do a lot with this place if you'd smooth out the road, cut down some of these trees. Let a little light in. It's too damn closed in around here."

"I don't think it's closed in," Ellen said, smiling. "I feel sort of . . . of free. Then, Larry didn't want to touch anything. He liked a place to be natural. You know, the birds, bushes . . . lizards, even. Just the way we found it. People always seem to want to spoil places.

You know. Make everything precise, clipped . . . a tree every twenty paces, only so many birds per square yard."

"And no people?" James smiled slightly, but he wasn't joking.

"Oh, Jimmy, *I am* sorry. When I get to quoting Larry I forget myself. Come on, let's have a good talk. And some more coffee. Mine got cold, I'm afraid."

Banished from the house by Ellen while she fixed lunch, James took a look at his car and traced with one finger the silvery pattern of scratches which now marred the shiny blue paint. Then with a vague intention of wandering down to the creek and maybe skipping a few stones in the water, he followed one of several paths which led from the cabin clearing into the tangle of trees. At the end of one of the paths, he knew, there were stone steps leading down to the water's edge. His skin moistened under his clothes with the mild exertion, and he observed that the sun's heat, if not its direct rays, penetrated the shade effectively. Little rustlings and chirps kept him wary; he stepped gingerly over the spongy path. Finally aware that he had made the wrong choice, he paused at the edge of a little glade to consider the possibility of striking through the woods to hit the creek path without completely retracing his steps. It could not be more than twenty or thirty feet away, he judged.

He was about to cross the glade when he heard a scrambling noise, and heavy breathing, as of some animal. Stooping, and feeling around, without taking his eyes off the spot the noise came from, he let his hand close on a rock. James did not know what to expect, but he meant not to be caught unarmed. Then, breathing relief, he watched Tassy scramble into the glade, having come up evidently from the creek. He started to say hello, but, realizing she was unaware of his presence, he waited a moment. Without quite knowing why he did it, James made himself small in the shadow of the trees at the edge of the glade.

Puffing and red-faced, her hair and clothes tumbled with twigs and leaves, Tassy sat down near one of the cedar trees on the creek side of the glade. She brushed at her bare arms and legs, which James could see were scratched and dirty. Then she took something out of her pocket, the same round thing she had had in the cabin, James guessed. He watched her polish the object on her shorts. She did not seem to be playing with it exactly, but talking to it, examining it. Her voice was only a caressing murmur so that James could not understand the words, but her complete absorption in this private

little world oddly touched him, and he felt almost ashamed at over-
seeing the little girl when she so obviously thought she was alone.
Presently, she began to fumble around the foot of the cedar tree,
and then her hand came up, empty of the plaything. She stood up
and looking furtively around, crossed the glade and disappeared
in the direction of the cabin.

James waited until he could hear no sounds but the bird and
insect noises; a lizard scuffled through the leaves and, on a rock
which caught one bold finger of light like a prizefight ring, paused
and seemed to consider him. Feeling that he was about to discover
the key to some delicate understanding, James went over to the tree
which grew at the rim of a sharp ledge. It had a strangely gnarled
trunk with some of its roots exposed from countless gully washes.
At first, James could see nothing; he ran his hand over the roughness
of the tree trunk as if looking for a hidden spring. Then he examined
the exposed root with his eyes; it looked like a harbor for spiders
or small, dangerous animals. He shook out his handkerchief, placed
it around his hand, and reached under the root. His hand felt
something hard and slippery through the cloth and his fingers re-
coiled; but he ventured to touch it more thoroughly; it felt hard and
smooth as a river-bed rock. He pulled it out and saw that it *was* an
egg, or rather an imitation egg, made of china and hard and polished as alabaster. Disappointed, though he could not say why,
James returned the egg to its hiding place, then folded his handkerchief deliberately and put it back in his pocket. Kids are funny,
he mused; you'd think they would go for big, expensive dolls or
fancy bicycles instead of playing with something as uninspiring
as an egg. Well, anyhow, he could give them things. He wanted to
give them all sorts of presents. Not spoil them, of course, but kids
wanted to be like other kids, have what other kids had. He might
not know much about children, but he knew that much. He wondered
if Larry Carter had known that, but just couldn't do things right,
just couldn't make a go of things.

Faintly, James heard the call. "Jimmee! Lu-unch!" He stood
up, noticing with chagrin that a brown earth stain outlined the
knobby shape of one knee. Frowning, he brushed at it, but only
succeeded in spreading the stain.

James relaxed comfortably in the hammock, his chin slumped
on his chest, and dabbled the fingers of one hand idly in the mulchy,
needly earth. The afternoon sun, fairly started on its downward

swing, caressed him with gentle patterns of light through the over-head branches and leaves. The air was quiet as sleep, so still it lulled him. He caught the end of what Ellen was saying, ". . . to-gether. Larry had a book on concrete mixing or something. It's rough, I suppose, unfinished, but . . ."

"What?" murmured James.

"The cabin. I don't believe you were listening."

"You can't stay out here forever, you know." He shifted abruptly to look at her. The hammock dipped dangerously with his new position.

"I know. I guess I'm the put-things-off type. I keep hoping something will happen."

"Things don't just happen."

"That's not what I mean really. That is . . . well, Larry wanted special things for the kids . . . not things . . . ideas, attitudes . . . they seemed so right with him. I don't know . . . I can't get used to thinking any other way, and yet, I don't really know what to do."

"What ideas, what attitudes?" James asked, puzzled.

"Well, that's it. I'm not sure now what's right for them . . . the kids. Am I being fair to them? Larry had an idea what was wrong with the world was all these people scrambling over one another, trying to get to the top, keeping up with the Joneses, you know . . . grabbing things right and left. Taking more than they need."

"I'm not sure I follow that," said James. "Sure, you can carry it too far, but it seems a natural thing to me for a man to want to succeed, to want the best for his family."

"That's it, don't you see. The question is, what is best? Enough to eat, shelter, not possessions, but what you need . . . then . . . love, if you will, outside yourself."

"Yes," said James, "and where will you draw the line? While you're being so great about this, what's the rest of the world going to be doing? Do you think people are interested in good examples? You'll be left behind . . . What'll your kids say to that?"

Ellen did not answer. The hammock swung idly. There was certainly some truth in what Ellen had said, but you didn't have to join a bread line to prove it. When you had a family you had a responsibility to them. You couldn't pretend the rest of the world didn't exist.

Presently Ellen said, getting up, "I'll fix us something to drink."

"Let me," he offered, half-rising.

"No, no, you stay here and relax." She strolled over to the cabin. His sister had asked: Why do you want a ready-made family? Why? Who could say? The way silky hair brushed across a cheek, a certain thrilling laugh? He remembered the sense of loss he'd felt when Ellen married Larry Carter whom nobody had ever heard of, and the anger at himself because he hadn't realized before that he wanted Ellen. They had been friends too long then, too comfortable as friends to be anything else, he had thought. Did Ellen know now how badly he wanted her? How badly he wanted to change that willingness to be deprived? Why all that talk then? He hadn't said anything, didn't plan to until the fall. He liked to size things up, make sure he knew what he was doing—and then her husband hadn't been dead a year yet.

It occurred to him that Ellen accepted him too easily as just an old friend, someone to talk to about her husband. Or was *she* sizing *him* up? And what if she decided against him before he had even made his move? That wasn't fair. But no, he thought, he had a damn good chance just because of the circumstances, besides any feeling she might have for him. Ellen could marry him, who was prepared to take on another man's children—there couldn't be many such men in Austin and certainly none so well off as he—or she could . . . what? She'd naturally think of the children. Then remembering lunch, he shuddered inwardly. The children knew how he felt, even if Ellen didn't. He might not ever get along with Ted, he thought, though you couldn't blame the kid right now, certainly. Maybe Ted would like to go to military school. Allen Academy perhaps. That way, they wouldn't always be rubbing each other, they could work out some relationship gradually. Tassy, being a girl, was different, and Phil, at five, was too young to be always making comparisons.

The sound of someone approaching broke into his solitude, and thinking it was Ellen, James sat up. But it was only Phil who marched past, lost in a world of his own, talking to himself. He scanned the ground intently and then searched the treetops and sky. It occurred to James that he ought to start making friends with Phil. "Hey, there . . . pardner," he called. "What are you doing?"

"Looking," said Phil scornfully, as if that should be obvious to anyone.

"Looking for what?"

"The treasure."

"Oh." Casting about in his mind for something to interest Phil, he said, trying to sound confidential, "Listen, Phil, I know a secret." He beckoned.

"What?" Interest flickered briefly in Phil's face, but he did not come any nearer.

James got out of the hammock, trying to think of a suitable secret. "Well," he said, approaching Phil. "Here, grab my finger."

Phil, putting his hands behind his back, moved several steps away. "No," he said with finality.

James pondered this. How the hell did you play a game with a five-year-old? "Don't you want to know my secret?"

"No," said Phil. "Me 'n' Ted have to find the treasure. Tassy hid it 'n' we have to find it."

A mental picture of the hidden egg flashed into James's mind. So that's what Tassy was doing! They must be playing a game such as he had once played. What was it called? He dredged his memory. Oh, yes, button, button, who's got the button. "I know," he said, "we're Indians. Here, you follow me." He began to tiptoe forward, bent over like a crooked old man. Behind him, Phil snickered. James turned, his finger to his lips. "Shhh!" he hissed.

Phil giggled. "You look like a possum eating yellow jackets." At this, he whooped gleefully, stiffening his body and then relaxing it.

James straightened up, exasperated and feeling ridiculous. "Now just what does a remark like that mean? If you don't want to know my secret, O.K." He turned his back on Phil, but with his head twisted so he could watch the kid out of the corner of his eye.

Finally Phil said, "I have to look for the treasure. I can't play with you."

"But that's what the secret is about," said James triumphantly.

Phil's face was a mask, but suddenly his eyes gleamed. "O.K.," he said.

James led Phil to the little glade. "Now look around that tree. No, not that one. The one with the roots sticking out." How could they expect a little fellow to have a chance at finding the button —the egg—without a *little* help. James sat down on a near-by stump. Suddenly he began to call out, "You're cold," or "You're getting warm now," the old childhood warnings slipping easily into his mind. Finally, after a good deal of advice from James, Phil found the place under the roots and thrust his hand in to bring out the egg firmly clutched. He gave a little crow of triumph. "The treasure," he breathed tenderly.

James felt a little twinge of jealousy, or betrayal, or something indefinable, as if he had expected Phil to say, "Gee, thanks," or shake hands or something of the sort, but Phil just admired the egg and said nothing.

"That's our secret," said James finally. "Tassy and Ted will think you found the egg by yourself. Don't tell and I won't either."

Phil looked at him, his face a mask again, as if, now having possession of the egg, he denied James's part in its discovery. He turned and ran off toward the cabin, his short legs churning up the mulchy earth. James followed, strolling, feeling rather good that he had made a beginning on his campaign to make friends with Phil. A shared secret was always a bond of friendship.

When he neared the cabin, Phil began to shout, "I found it, I found it," and the legs flew as Tassy and Ted gathered around him. How could just three children make such a noise, James thought indulgently; the very earth trembled under their pounding feet, leaves and dirt skirled over the ground. James beamed on the little group.

"Oh, I wondered where you were," said Ellen, somewhat distractedly. "Listen, Ted, couldn't you stop this now? Finish it tomorrow?"

"I just took a little . . . ," James started, but obviously Ellen wasn't listening to him.

"We have to do it," said Ted, looking at his mother.

"Oh, is there more?" asked James, really interested now.

Ellen looked at him oddly. "Come on," she said, "I left our drinks in the house. The ice'll melt."

"No," said James. "Just a minute." He wanted to savor Phil's triumph, hear him describe how he found the egg; probably he'd tell some fantastic story.

Ted took the egg from Phil, who gave it up protestingly. Tassy watched; it seemed to James that a look of fear flashed in her face. The little group was tense now, and James sensed that something was wrong. They were all so serious, even Ellen. What the devil were they up to?

Ted laid the egg on the stump ceremoniously, then looked about on the ground for something, finally returning with a sizable rock.

"No," screamed Tassy, "wait!" She picked up the egg, and fondled it for a moment. Reluctantly, she placed it on the stump again, arranging its position slightly. Her face stiffened in a sad, stoical expression; there was no air of protest about her, only resignation. James was troubled, watching the strange little ceremony, trying to reconcile the Tassy he had watched by the tree with this stiff, unhappy little figure.

"O.K.," said Ted, handing Phil the rock with the air of a master of ceremonies. "You found it."

"What?" asked Phil stupidly. James felt riveted to the ground.

"Hit it! That's what happens when the treasure gets found. I told you about a million times. You throw it in the water, or you burn it, or you break it up."

"My God, Ellen," snapped James, "are you going to . . ."

Crash! the rock came down on the egg. Tassy screamed, a terrible sound that made James shudder and start forward as if he could stop the action already completed. His face felt stiff with horror; he turned to Ellen.

"I didn't want you to see this," she said.

Phil began to cry as Tassy pushed one finger among the broken pieces of the egg. "It's empty," she whispered sadly. Suddenly Phil ran to his mother. "I didn't do it," he sobbed. "I didn't do it." He pointed blindly. "He did it. He made me find it."

"Who?" asked Ellen, putting her hand on his head.

"Him." Phil straightened to point at James. "He made me find it."

For a moment they all stared at him. Ellen's hand clutched Phil's shoulder. Ted and Tassy beside the stump were still as statues. Phil pressed against his mother and stared at James with wet wide eyes, quiet now except for an occasional sniff to contain his tears. Would they never move again? James wondered. A little breeze developed, made a tiny whirlwind of leaves.

"I thought it was just a game," James burst out. "Just a game like button, button . . . My God, Ellen, that's no game for children!"

Ted shouted, "It's my father's game. You shut up about it!" Then he was crying too.

"You shouldn't have meddled in it," said Ellen. She picked Phil up, held him protectively.

"For God's sake, how was I to know what . . . look, I'll buy her a new egg. Tassy, I'll get you another." He bent over the little girl, put out his hand to draw her to him, but she shrank away from his touch.

"That doesn't help," said Ellen. "You can't fix things by just buying another."

He stared at her, searching for some sign of their old friendship; she was not condemning this silly game, she was condemning him. Where was the Ellen he had always known? Mother and children closed in together, all of them against him now, retreated into the relationship where he could not follow. He looked down at the ground, looked past the hostile group at the cabin; the web of daddy-long-legs still crawled up the wall. "I think you're sick," he said finally. "You don't know what you're doing."

"You'd better leave now, James," said Ellen. She still held Phil; Ted and Tassy on either side of her pressed close.

"Damn it, Ellen," he burst out angrily. "O.K." He strode toward his car, jerked open the door, and quickly gunned the motor into action. The car screeched around, throwing up clouds of gravel. They had no right to blame him for what happened. Ted or Phil could have found the egg without his help. What about that? He watched Ellen and the children through his rear-view mirror, still standing close together, like a picture in an old family album. Then the car bumped around the curve and he could not see them any more.

Dennis Murphy

A Camp in the Meadow

The camp was built on packed sand to ward off the wetness of the valley. It was a small valley, green but not pleasantly green, wet in all the seasons. The water hung in little pockets beneath the ground in the pastures and meadows, and the mosquitoes hovered close to the earth like a fog. If a soldier left the camp and walked through the meadow down to the first French village, he would become hot with the bites of the mosquitoes and sometimes his foot plunged through the puffed green earth into six inches of slime, bringing a quick, shameful hysteria. The soldiers rarely went down into the village. Some days the sky was blue, but the blue days were not felt for themselves. They were pauses, unnatural and tense, until the air was grey again and warm with drizzle, a wet, sick kind of warmth that pervaded the camp and gave the men there a strange comfort.

The camp stood quite alone, four wooden buildings beneath a flopping American flag. Not long after the war a hundred men had lived in the largest building, the central barracks. Now there were never more than forty. The barracks had a smooth, familiar-feeling concrete floor and a coal-burning stove that was kept cherry-red, even in the summer. At the far end was a tin partition that closed off four toilets, and a shower room that was usually dry. There were streaks of orange stain in the bowls of the toilets.

Milo Jones was a cook. He would get up from his cot in the early morning when it was dark save for the cherry glow of the stove, and through the moving shadows, his feet noiseless on the

With permission from *Sequoia*, Vol. I, No. 1, Spring 1956. © 1956 by the Associated Students of Stanford University.

smooth, warm concrete, he would move slowly and naked down the long barracks. The men slept huddled under their blankets. He walked the length of the barracks and then back again, watching the sleepers in their cots, smiling, stroking his white belly and thighs. Sometimes, if it had not rained the night before, he would dress and walk out into the dark morning, past the orderly shack and tool shed, around the little wet lawn that surrounded the flagpole. He looked for men who had been drunk the night before, who might have slept with their empty bottles in the bushes.

At meal times, when the men went through the serving line, they would not look at the cook. They looked past him, or down at their food. He made them feel something terrible that might grow in themselves. They were afraid of him. He was big and powerful, with hands that grasped ten or twelve dinner trays at once, big-boned and thick-necked, and over it all was a surface of soft, white skin that glistened from his work in the kitchen. When he was sweating and moving, his womanish breasts flopped under his soiled T-shirt. "Why don't you look at me there?" His voice was startling. It was a southern voice, deep and strong, almost kind. "You, Ah say, why don't you look at me?" And he would lean across the serving line, staring, the big red-rimmed eyes bulging from beneath his short forehead. A man would look up nervously from his tray. "Ah say now. That's better now." And he would smile.

In his smile there was a touch, a sign, a fearful window into the terror of the man. His upper lip tightened as it spread, and the lower, wet and sensual, relaxed and fattened below his teeth, hanging, protruding, and yet it was not a leer, for there was restraint in the smile, a terrifying restraint, unreasonable, like the pressing pulse in an unburst sore. "You're not scared a' me, are yuh? You're not scared of old Jonesy?"

He spent much of his time in the kitchen, away from the soldiers. After the evening meal he took a damp sponge and rubbed off the two long dinner tables, rubbing slow and deliberate. Then he would sit alone, waiting, watching it get dark outside. He smoked cigarettes in the dark, waiting there with a strange, tight passiveness, the long ashes breaking and falling on the clean table top. After a time he left the kitchen and walked back into the barracks. The men could feel him enter without lifting their eyes. He walked past them to his bunk, as slow and deliberate as he had rubbed the tables, delighting in their aware- ness and the unnatural quiet. "It's quiet here, Ah say. Why is it so quiet here?" The voice came strong in the stillness, and his face moved with excitement, the eyes alive with insight. The men were unsure and nervous, as if they were near a large, unfamiliar animal. They could feel him in their senses. He was as palpable as the warmth of the stove, as real as the long days, or the camp itself.

During the days the men worked in a ten-acre gas depot adja- cent to the camp. They were told that the depot was the reason for the camp. They realized this, yet it had no meaning for them. In the evenings the men sat on the edges of their bunks in the heat of the stove, or bought wine from the Frenchmen and drank it in the meadow. In the smoky quiet of the wooden barracks they shared their only bond and hope, the thought, never spoken, of home and the time when they could leave the camp. It was their one reality, this thought, and they babied and fondled it in their minds, turning it about in the silence, filtering it like medicine into their sick hearts, portioning, rationing, calculating like men abnormally wise, anxious always that it too should grow dim and die and leave them nothing save the emptiness of the long days. They thought about going home. If their time was growing near they squirmed hot and wretched on their cots, getting up suddenly to open and shut their lockers or walk aimlessly down the bar- racks past the tin partition where they would sit absently on the stained toilets, fully dressed, their heads down across their fore- arms. But if their term of duty had months yet to run they would lie on top of their blankets, still and unmoving. Milo Jones watched and waited. Some of the men, the young or still un- learned, would indulge themselves with thoughts of the future or things outside the camp, and sometimes the silence of the bar- racks would be broken by muffled sobs. The others would turn away from the sounds. But Milo Jones would smile and watch the face of the man who cried, his eyes alive and bulging from beneath his short forehead. When the lights were turned off, the cook would get up from his cot and walk out into the meadow past the men who sat in pairs or alone drinking wine in the dark. As he came by, ghostly and white in his cook's pants and T-shirt, they stopped their mumbled conversations and looked away from him, and when he had passed they drank their wine without speaking. Sometimes, in the mornings, he would find them curled in the bushes. He would poke at them with a stick, chuckling anxiously from deep in his throat, poking and probing them, like a child with a slug he has found in the garden.

One day, when the men came in from the gas depot, they saw a young soldier in dress uniform standing on the steps of the orderly room. He stood by the door in his well-fitting uniform, one hand placed neatly along his trouser leg, the other gripping the duffel bag at his side. He was a tall, red-cheeked, clean-looking boy, fresh and straight against the fading afternoon light. As the men approached, tired but curious, he waved and spoke to them in a half-boyish, half-manly voice. "I'll bet you're pretty tired." He said it like a greeting, enthusiastically. The men shuffled up around him, watching him with quiet interest. "That doesn't look like much fun out there," he said eagerly. His cheeks were shiny red, healthy, nearly moist in their brightness, and he looked down at them from the steps with the innocent confidence of youth. The men watched him with interest.

"Are you a new man?" said one of them.

"Yes, I am," and he laughed. "I guess you'll all call me a 'rookie.' " The man who had questioned him squinted his eyes and looked away.

On both sides of the valley the mountains were becoming dark, a cold, flat brown. The sun had moved behind a westerly peak, its reflection blotted by a roll of fog that hung damp and foreboding along the upper ridges. Soon the fog would push on down into the foothills, and farther, covering the mountains and tightening the valley.

"My name is Donald Fletcher," said the young soldier, still smiling. His eyes were bright with anticipation.

The men took Donald Fletcher into the barracks, showing him where to place his locker and his cot. He was the first replacement that had come to the camp in six months. They put him in the center of the barracks near the hot glow of the stove and then watched him from their cots as he took his belongings from the duffel bag and arranged them in the locker.

"Is anybody here from Colorado?" He talked as he un-
packed his clothes and equipment. "I was born in Colorado," and
he looked down the long row of cots expectantly. "You know,
before I was drafted I was never out of the state. I guess that
seems kind of funny to you." He spoke in a loud, pleasant voice,
glancing quickly from one soldier to another, as if some inner
politeness compelled him to include them all in his conversation.
"We live on a farm," he continued, prompting them. "Are any
of you farmers? I mean before the army."

The men were silent on their cots. The boy spoke with an
enthusiasm, an unaffected enthusiasm that had become alien to
them. He was fresh and bright, sparkling with a natural innocence that shocked and strangely embarrassed them. They shifted
uncomfortably on their cots.

Milo Jones saw the boy the night he arrived, as he was coming
through the serving line at dinner, still in his dress uniform.
Donald Fletcher offered his tray to be filled and the cook, as he
looked up and saw him, gripped his serving spoon and stared, the
muscles tightening beneath the white skin of his fat neck. He
stared, not speaking, the serving spoon suspended between them.
And then the cook smiled, the smile spreading over his face,
slowly, growing like a live thing. "Well," he said. The word was
aggressive and frightening in the suddenly quiet room. "Well
now," he said.

In the evenings in the barracks Donald Fletcher would ask
questions, and for a while he forced a change in the routine of
the soldiers' lives. The unhappy quiet of the nights was filled
with his incessant, chattering voice. He asked questions, simply
because he wanted to know the answers. "Now there's one thing
I really want to know. That little town up the road, Lebec, now
I wonder how that got there. I mean, there should be a reason for
a town. It must be a market center or something. Sam, do you
know if there's a factory up there?"

The soldier called Sam shook his head without speaking.

"Well, I bet there's a factory," offered the boy. "Do you
know what the population is? Sam, do you know how many
people live there?"

"No," said Sam.

The boy paused. "Well, I bet it wouldn't be a very good place to take a pass. Oh, I'm not really anxious to get away. I just got here." He laughed. "But I probably will after a while and it's good to know where to go, just in case."

The men sat on their foot lockers with their arms across their knees, staring out at the stove. They were heavy and tired, closed tight into themselves, and the boy's conversation was unreal to them.

"Where's a good place to go on a pass?" he asked one of the soldiers. "A place you can really have fun." The soldier, an older man, hunched his shoulders and looked down at his boots. He appeared to be only half listening, his manner abstract, showing no signs of either recognizing or objecting to the boy's question.

"I bet you know some good places," coaxed Donald Fletcher.

"I don't take passes, kid," said the soldier.

The boy straightened up on his cot. "Oh. Well, that's all right. I mean, some people just like to take it easy. And that's good," he said eagerly, "it's really a good way to be." He was intent upon pleasing the men, soliciting their response with a sincere, almost anxious tone of voice. But their indifference confused him. He could neither understand nor accept it. He seemed compelled, from the day he first waved from the orderly room steps, to establish some contact, a base of feeling between himself and his fellow soldiers.

One night he said that the stove in the barracks reminded him of the stove that was in the kitchen of his home in Colorado. He began to talk rapidly and excitedly about his mother and his Aunt Lisa, about how they looked in the kitchen as they prepared the evening meal. He sat at the foot of his cot and gestured with both arms, describing the actions of the women who were so familiar and real to him, smiling happily as he talked, his eyes brimming with delight.

"Old Mom keeps catching her apron on the oven handle," he said lovingly, "and it pulls the oven door open and makes the cake fall every time." He paused abruptly. "Did you ever see anything like that? Did you ever see that happen?" But the men neither looked at him nor answered and after a moment of silence he laughed, as if it were his duty.

"I guess maybe that doesn't seem very interesting to you, but it's funny the way you remember a lot of little things, just because they're about your family. There's six of us altogether. Six kids, I mean, not counting Dad and Mom. I'm right about in the middle. I've got three older brothers and they've all been in the service and are out now, back working the farm with Dad." He beamed, lost again in his narrative. "You know, when they were in high school each one of them was president of the 4-H Club. They always said they'd whop me if I didn't get to be president too. They were just kidding, of course, but I did get to be president. When I was only in my second year." His head dropped slightly and his face reddened with modesty. "I was president three years running," he added softly.

One of the men stood up from his foot locker, stretched himself, then turned and shuffled down the concrete floor towards the toilets. The boy was suddenly aware that he had been talking only of himself. "I bet all of you have got some good stories to tell," he said quickly, wanting very much to draw them into the warm glow of his own feelings. "I bet real soldiers like you have got some good ones to tell."

But they stared out at the stove, engrossed, hypnotized apparently by the pulsating cherry-red color, a color that moved at the belly of the stove, bloating bright red, then sucking back to a deep maroon, constant and regular, like breathing.

"Why don't you be quiet, kid." The soldier who spoke did not look at the boy. The air in the room was thick, nervous, prickly.

The boy sat upright, his mouth tightening in confusion. "I didn't mean to bother you."

"Why don't you just be quiet, kid." The soldier's voice was soft and sure, speaking for them all. Some of the men looked up at Donald Fletcher, their passing glance a way of seconding the soldier who had spoken. For a moment they watched him, pitied him.

In the gas depot during the day he did his work efficiently, moving with confidence among the gas barrels, hoisting them to the waist while the other men braced them on their knees with a tired cleverness. He tried to do the work for the others, but they shouldered him aside. It was a month before he learned that he couldn't make friends. He worked very hard during the day and at night he would read his letters from home, writing replies that became shorter as the weeks passed. He sat propped up on his cot, forcing the letters out of his stub pencil, trying to make them sound lively, despairing as he saw them become mechanical and uninteresting. His mother had told him once that his mind was like a beehive. Sometimes a man would pass his bunk and ask him idly if he wanted to go into the meadow to drink wine.

"Well," he would say, flushed with good feeling, "that's really nice of you. I don't drink but that's really nice of you to ask."

He would often look up from his letters and see the cook, Milo Jones, staring and smiling at him. There was something about the cook that caused a quick tightening in his chest, a nervousness that he couldn't explain. He sensed something in the man contrary to what he knew and loved. And Milo Jones, seeming almost to read his thoughts, stared and smiled as if to confirm them.

He came to dread the week ends. Then there was not even the work to occupy the time. His mind would wander absently, and if he tried to read, his mind would wander and fasten upon some meaningless object, the steel leg of a cot, the handle of a locker, or the stove. He would realize suddenly that as he'd stared at that thing, his thoughts had drifted and spent themselves in the oppressive, smoke-filled air. He began to think about going away one week end, about taking a pass and spending two or three days in a city, perhaps Paris. He asked several of the men if they would like to go on a trip, but they looked at him curiously, a bit shocked. It was a bad idea, they said without explaining. It was better to stay at the camp.

But the idea was a brightness, a hope. He nurtured it, cupping it in his thoughts like a delicate toy. A trip was all that he needed. It would save him. And the plan so grew and refreshed him that the idea of being "saved" appeared grotesque and ridiculous. He would stop suddenly in his work to stand and smile at the thought of going away. He had been getting tired. He pictured his mother, the white hair and warm plumpness of her, seating herself purposefully on the wicker chair in the kitchen, her eyes

serious but still dancing. What would she say if she could see
him now? Ah, he knew exactly. "Son," and her hands would be
folded neatly on her lap, "Son, you just need a change." She
would look directly at him, the corners of her mouth firm but
somehow laughing. "You just need a change, that's all." And
that was all. He could see it perfectly now.

He sent out inquiries to travel bureaus and haunted the mail
room for the replies. He talked once again in the barracks at
night, chattering enthusiastically about his plans, not thinking or
caring if the men paid him no heed. "No reflection on you people,
understand, but I'm going to take myself a trip. Yes I am."
When the pamphlets from the travel bureaus began to come in,
he taped them neatly inside the door of his locker, musing over
each of them until he was right inside the bright-colored pictures,
actually smelling the air of the Alps or feeling the breeze of the
Mediterranean against his cheek. He decided with much care
that he would go to Lourdes. The pamphlets that came in the mail
about Lourdes appealed to him most. There were scenes of
churches, and there was a spring there, they said, that had healing
water. He was a Baptist himself, but his family had taught him
to be tolerant of others. Besides, it was not for religion that he
wanted to go to Lourdes. The pictures showed a quiet, dignified
hotel in which he would stay, and a park with green benches and
oak trees, serene and peaceful, but friendly at the same time,
almost like the parks he knew at home.

"I've got sixty-five dollars," he said, excited. "Now that gives
me twenty dollars for train fare and twenty-five for room and
board. I don't know what I'll do with the rest. Just anything,"
he said, swinging his legs off the side of the bunk. "I think I'll
buy souvenirs. Now the folks at home would sure like to see
something from Lourdes. Oh, I guess there's a lot of things . . ."

But one of the men looked up from the stove. "Relax, kid;
cut it out," said the man impatiently.

The boy tried to smile and for a moment he didn't speak.
"You fellows are just tired," he said. But he turned away, humiliated.

He left on a Friday and was gone until the following Monday.
As he moved about the gas depot that Monday morning, through
the dust and the greasy cans, he hardly spoke, but his face, bright

and tense, reflected the lingering fulness of his week end. His eyes were luminous. The men looked at him knowingly, and asked about his trip in flat voices, feeling they owed him that at least. "The people," he whispered, still awed, "the people are wonderful. It's just like at home. You walk down the street and they'll smile and tip their hats to you." He shook his head in wonder. "The people are wonderful. It was just like home."

He seemed to be in a state of reverence. For several days he went about as if in a dream. He laughed at nearly everything the others said, and at night he sat on his bunk, writing long letters to his family and friends. But towards the end of the week he became rather sad, wistful. His days of freedom began to slip from his heart, where he had kept them vital and real, into a far corner of his memory. They were picked at and stripped by the oppressiveness of the camp, until finally the days hung like a skeleton in his mind, torturing and frightening him. He could no longer think about that week end with pleasure. It brought only a quick stab of pain and impossible longing. The grey days, moist and warm, seemed suddenly more terrible, empty and without motion, unbearable. He knew he should never have gone. Milo Jones, the cook, had not spoken to him when he'd first returned. But when a week had passed he stopped him in the serving line. The cook reached out with a long aluminum spoon, blocking his path. He leaned across to the boy, bending forward from the waist, his face close and confident. "How was the trip, boy?"

He took to spending the nights like the other men, staring at the stove, his eyes fixed and unseeing, conscious only of the growing pain in his heart. He had never experienced despair. He had rarely been unhappy. And now he was desperate with sadness, so vivid it was like a cutting weight in his breast. He fought it helplessly. The older men wrapped themselves in apathy, using it to shield off their surroundings, but his feelings, young and strong, could hardly be shackled. He sat with his head in his hands, afraid.

Milo Jones watched him constantly. He sat across the barracks, his white arms bare and strong, his face bright with excitement, his grotesque, womanish breasts pointed and dark through the T-shirt. His eyes were locked on the boy, bright, instinctive, penetrating, faintly protective as the eyes of a wild bird on her young. He got up slowly one night, like a man entranced, and crossed the concrete floor to where the boy sat. Donald Fletcher looked up from his despair into the face of the cook. He was seized with fright. The cook reached out and touched his face lightly.

"Get away," screamed the boy. "Get away, get away. It's you I hate!"

The cook stepped back and for a moment his face was blank. He put his hand to his mouth, as if to shape a smile there. And then he laughed, only a chuckle at first, a twisted little challenge from deep in his belly, but it grew louder, building on itself, loud and awful, challenging.

He poured himself frantically into the work at the gas depot. He hoisted and stacked the barrels, seldom speaking now, working feverishly, trying as it were to plunge himself into the heart of the endless hours. If there was a moment's slack in the work he searched quickly for other things to do, clean the mud from his boots, knowing they would be dirty again in minutes, or rearrange an already perfect stack of barrels. The men watched as if he were something separate from them, an actor on a stage, and they could only feel sorry. "Take it easy, fellah," said one of them. "Don't go runnin' around all excited."

"I'm not excited."

"You just look a little peaked is all," said the man.

"I feel fine."

"Well, you just do like us other fellahs. Why d'yuh want to run around all excited?"

"There's nothing wrong with me, goddamit." They weren't used to hearing him talk like that. It shocked them, made them ashamed.

After the supper meal he took long walks through the meadow. He went in to the first French village and beyond, stopping to stare at people along the road, hanging on them from a distance, watching them until they passed from sight. He walked endlessly, long after dark, stumbling along in the meadow, slipping often into pits of slime, struggling up and going on senselessly. He would not return to the barracks until the lights had been turned out, and he would come in quietly, hot and dirty, and lie fully clothed on his bunk, breathing heavily until he was asleep. He seemed deathly afraid of idleness. The walks became longer and more frantic. At times he would actually run through the meadow, not knowing why he was running, his thighs growing rubbery and unresponsive, his face hot with the bites of mosquitoes, walking, stumbling, running over and through the muddy, false-bottomed grass.

One night, as he came back near the barracks, he passed two of the men who sat in the darkness drinking wine. They called to him idly and he stopped and then walked toward them. He stood looking down at them. "May I have some wine?" he asked in a low voice. The men looked at each other and smiled, and handed him a half-full bottle. He held it lightly against the palm of his hand, feeling the smooth glass surface, and then he drank it standing up, in two or three long swallows. The men were sitting propped against the trunk of an oak tree. They chuckled with appreciation as he drank. When he finished he paused, holding the bottle at his lips, then stepped back a pace in the dark. He gripped the bottle carefully, throwing it full force at the tree. Glass splintered and sprayed on the men and into the grass.

"Goddam, you ain't drunk already, kid," said one of them threateningly. They got up together, moving cautiously to either side of him. "You gone crazy, or what?" He stood quietly, not speaking. One of the men reached out and gripped his arm hard. He lashed at the man ferociously with his other fist. Then a hand came from behind and closed over his face. He could feel pressure on his neck, and blows pounding into his stomach. They took him half-unconscious up to the barracks and laid him on his cot. "There wasn't nothing we could do," they explained sheepishly. "The kid acted crazy."

He lay for two days on the cot, recovering from the beating. He didn't speak to anyone, but lay quietly, looking up at the ceiling. On the second day Milo Jones appeared in the doorway. He stood there until the boy saw him. There was no one else in the barracks. The sun came in through the dust-filmed windows, making long, white shadows across the concrete floor. Smoke seeped from a crack in the stovepipe, drifting sickly through the

still, indoor air. The boy grew tense and raised himself slightly
in the bed. Milo Jones walked towards him. He stood at the edge
of the bed and then sat down softly. The boy's mouth was compressed, his lips tight. He raised his hand away from the blanket,
leaving it there, suspended. The room was heavy with the musty
smell of the stove. Milo Jones looked down at him, watching him
carefully, his eyes keen and calculating. He reached out slowly,
placing his hand across the warm forehead. The boy shuddered,
once, his body shaking with one quick spasm. The hand rested
lightly on the forehead, then moved caressingly through the hair
until it cupped the back of the unresisting head. He pulled the
boy up gently, raising the body from the waist like a dead weight,
placing the boy's head against his moist chest, holding it there
quietly. With his head against the cook's chest the boy began
to cry, silently, almost imperceptibly, the shoulders quivering,
trembling slightly. "That's it," said the cook, his voice low and
soothing. "That's it," he cooed. He held the boy firmly in his
arms, feeling the body relax, and he looked up at the ceiling, his
bulging eyes wet and sparkling. "Yes suh," he said. "That's
better now. That's just fine."

Tillie Olsen

Hey Sailor, What Ship?

The grimy light; the congealing smell of cigarettes that had
been smoked long ago and of liquor that had been drunk long
ago; the boasting, cursing, wheedling, cringing voices, and the
greasy feel of the bar as he gropes for his glass.

Hey Sailor, what ship?

His face flaring in the smoky mirror. The veined gnawing.
Wha's it so quiet for? Hey, hit the tunebox. (*Lennie and Helen
and the kids.*) Wha time's it anyway? Gotta . . .

Gotta something. Stand watch? No, din't show last night,
ain't gonna show tonight, gonna sign off. Out loud: Hell with
ship. You got any friends, ship? then hell with your friends.
That right, Deeck? And he turns to Deeck for approval, but
Deeck is gone. Where's Deeck? Givim five bucks and he blows.

All right, says a nameless one, you're loaded. How's about
a buck?

Less one buck. Company. But he too is gone.

And he digs into his pockets to see how much he has left.

Right breast pocket, a crumpled five. Left pants pocket, three,
no, four collapsed one-ers. Left jacket pocket, pawn ticket, Manila; card, "When in Managua it's Marie's for Hospitality";
union book; I.D. stuff; trip card; two ones, one five, accordion-
pleated together. Right pants pocket, jingle money. Seventeen
bucks. And the hands tremble.

Where'd it all go? and he lurches through the past. 150 draw
yesterday. No day before, maybe even day 'fore that. 7 for a

From *Stanford Short Stories 1957*. © 1957 by Tillie Olsen.

bottle when cashed the check, 20 to Blackie, 33 back to Goldballs,
cab to Frisco, 38, 39 for the jacket and the kicks (new jacket, new
kicks, to look good to see Lennie and Helen and the kids), 24
smackers dues and 10-dollar fine. The fine . . .

Hey, to the barkeep, one comin' up. And he swizzles it down,
pronto. 20 and 7 and 33 and 39. 10-dollar fine and 5 to Frenchy
at the hall and drinkin' all night with Johnson, don' know how
much, and on the way to the paymaster . . .

The PAYmaster. Out loud, in angry mimicry, with a slight
scandihoovian accent, to nobody, nobody at all: Whaddaya think
of that? Hafta be able to sign your name or we can't give you
your check. Too stewed to sign your name, he says, no check.

Only seventeen bucks. Hey, to the barkeep, how 'bout advancing me fifty? Hunching over the bar, confidential, so he sees
the bottles glistening in the depths. See? and he ruffles in his
pockets for the voucher, P.F.E., Michael Jackson, thass me, five
hundred and twenty-seven and eleven cents. You don' know me?
Been here all night, all day. Bell knows me. Get Bell. Been
drinkin' here twenty-three years, every time hit Frisco. Ask Bell.

But Bell sold. Forgot, forgot. Took his cushion and moved
to Petaluma. Well hell with you. Got any friends? then hell with
your friends. Go to Pearl's. (*Not Lennie and Helen and the
kids?*) See what's new, or old. Got 'nuf lettuce for *them* babies.
But the idea is visual, not physical. Get a bottle first. And he
waits for the feeling good that should be there, but there is none,
only a sickness lurking.

THE BULKHEAD sign bile green in the rain. Rain and the
street clogged with cars, going home from work cars. Screw 'em
all. He starts across. Screech, screech, screech. Brakes jammed
on for a block back. M. Norbert Jacklebaum makes 'em stop, said
without glee. On to Pearl's. But someone is calling. Whitey,
Whitey, get in here you stumblebum. And it is Lennie, a worn
likeness of Lennie, so changed he gets in all right, but does not
ask questions or answer them. (Are you on ship or on the beach?
How long was the trip? You sick, man, or just stewed? Only
three or four days and you're feeling like this? *No*, no stopping
for a bottle or to buy presents.)

He only sits while the sickness crouches underneath, waiting to spring, and it muddles in his head, *going to see Lennie and Helen and the kids, no presents for 'em, an' don't even feel good. Hey Sailor, what ship?*

II

And so he gets there after all, four days and everything else too late. It is an old peaked house on a hill and he has imaged it and entered it over and over again, in a thousand various places a thousand various times: on watch and over chow, lying on his bunk or breezing with the guys; from sidewalk beds and doorway shelters, flophouses and jails; sitting silent at union meetings or waiting in the places one waits, or listening to the Come to Jesus boys.

The stairs are innumerable and he barely makes it to the top. Helen (Helen? so . . . grayed?), Carol, Allie, surging upon him. A fever of hugging and kissing. 'Sabout time, shrills Carol over and over again. 'Sabout time.

Who is real and who is not? Jeanie, taller than Helen suddenly, just standing there watching. I'm in first grade now, yells Allie, you can fix my dolly crib, it's smashted.

You managed it just right. We've got stew, Whitey, pressure cooker stuff, but your favorite anyway. How long since you've eaten? And Helen looks at him, kisses him again, and begins to cry.

Mother! orders Jeanie, and marches her into the kitchen.

Whassmatter Helen? One look at me, she begins to cry.

She's glad to see you, you S.O.B.

Whassmatter her? She don't look so good.

You don't look so good either, Lennie says grimly. Better sit for a while.

Mommy oughta quit work, volunteers Carol; she's tired. All the time.

Whirl me round like you always do, Whitey, whirl me round, begs Allie.

Where did you go this time, Whitey? asks Carol. Thought you were going to send me stamps for my collection. Why didn't you come Christmas? Can you help me make a puppet stage?

Cut it, kids, not so many questions, orders Lennie, going up the stairs to wash. Whitey's got to take it easy. We'll hear about everything after dinner.

Your shoes are shiny, says Allie. Becky in my class got new shoes too, Mary Janes, but they're fuzzy. And she leans down to pat his shoes.

Forgotten, how big the living room was. (And is he really here?) Carol reads the funnies on the floor, her can up in the air. Allie inspects him gravely. You got a new hurt on your face, Whitey. Sing a song, or say Thou Crown 'n Deep. After dinner can I bounce on you?

Not so many questions, repeats Carol.

Whitey's gonna just sit here. Should go in the kitchen. Help your mommy.

Angry from the kitchen: Well, I don't care. I'm calling Marilyn and tell her not to come; we'll do our homework over there. I'm certainly not going to take a chance and let her come over here.

Shhh, Jeanie, shhh. He beg that, or Helen? The windows are blind with steam, all hidden behind them the city, the bay, the ships. And is it chow time already? He starts up to go, but it seems he lurched and fell, for the sickness springs at last and consumes him. And now Allie is sitting with him. C'mon, sit up and eat, Whitey, Mommy says you have to eat; I'll eat too. Perched beside him, pretty as you please. I'll take a forkful and you take a forkful. You're sloppy, Whitey—for it trickles down his chin. It does not taste; the inside of him burns. She chatters and then the plate is gone and now the city sparkles at him through the windows. Helen and Lennie are sitting there and somebody who looks like somebody he knows.

Chris, reminds Lennie. Don't you remember Chris, the grocery boy when we lived on Aerial Way? We told you he's an M.D. now. Fat and a poppa and smug; aren't you smug, Chris?

I almost shipped with you once, Whitey. Don't you remember?

(Long ago. O yes, O yes, but there was no permit to be had; and even if there had been, by that time I didn't have no drag.) I remember. You still got the itch? That's why you came around, to get fixed up with a trip card?

I came around to look at you. But that was all he was doing, just sitting there and looking.

Whassmatter? Don't like my looks? Get too beautiful since you last saw me? Handsome new nose 'n everything?

Yes, you got too beautiful. Where can I take him Helen?

Can't take me no place. M. Norbert Jacklebaum's fine.

You've got to get up anyhow so I can make up the couch. Go on upstairs with Chris. You're in luck, I even found a clean sheet.

He settles back down on the couch, the lean scarred arms bent under his head for a pillow, the muscles ridged like rope.

He's a lousy doc. Affectionately. Gives me a shot of B-1, sleeping pills, and some bum advice . . . Whaddaya think of that, he remembered me. Thirteen years and he remembers me.

How could he help remembering you with all the hell his father used to raise cause he'd forget his deliveries listening to your lousy stories? You were his he-ro. How do you like the fire, hero?

Your wood, Whitey, says Helen. Still the stuff you chopped three years back. Needs restacking though.

Get right up and do it . . . Whadja call him for?

You scared us. Don't forget, your last trip up here was for five weeks in the Marine Hospital.

We never saw it hit you like this before, says Lennie. After a five-, six-week tear maybe, but you say this was a couple days. You were really out.

Just catching up on my sleep, tha's all.

There is a new picture over the lamp. Bleached hills, a fresh-ploughed field, red horses and a blue-overalled figure.

I got a draw coming. More'n five hundred. How's financial situation round here?

We're eating.

Allie want me to fix something? Or was it Carol? Those kids are sure . . . A year'n a half . . . An effort to talk, for the sleeping pills are already gripping him, and the languid fire, and the rain that has started up again and cannot pierce the windows. How *you* feeling, Helen? She looks more like Helen now.

Keeping my head above water. She would tell him later. She always told him later, when he would be helping in the kitchen

maybe, and suddenly it would come out, how she really was and
what was really happening, sometimes things she wouldn't even
tell Lennie. And this time, the way she looked, the way Lennie
looked . . .

Allie is on the stairs. I had a bad dream, Mommy. Let me
stay down here till Jeanie comes to bed with me, Mommy. By
Whitey.

What was your bad dream, sweetheart?

She lovingly puts her arms around his neck, curls up. I was
losted, she whispers, and instantly is asleep.

He starts as if he has been burned, and quick to reassure her
begins stroking her soft hair. It is destroying, dissolving him
utterly, this helpless warmth against him, this lovely feel of a
child—lost country to him and unattainable.

Sure were a lot of kids begging, he says aloud. I think it's
worse?

Korea? asks Len.

Never got ashore in Korea. Yokohama, Cebu, Manila. (The
begging children and the lost, the thieving children and the children who were sold.) And he strokes, strokes Allie's soft hair as
if the strokes would solidify, dense into a protection.

We lay around Pusan six weeks. Forty-three days on that tub
no bigger'n this house and they wouldn't give us no leave ashore.
Forty-three days. Len, I never had a drop, you believe me, Len?

Felt good most of this trip, Len, just glad to be sailing again,
after Pedro. Always a argument. Somebody says, Christ it's
cold, colder'n a whore's heart, and somebody jumps right in and
says, colder'n a whore's heart, hell, you ever in Kobe and broke
and Kumi didn't give you five yen? And then it starts. Both sides.

Len and Helen like those stories. Tell another. Effort.

You should hear this Stover. Ask him, was you ever in
England? and he claps his hands to his head and says, was I ever
in England, O boy, was I ever in England, those limeys, they beat
you with bottles. Ask him, was you ever in Marseilles and he
claps his hands to his head and says, was I ever in Marseilles,
O boy, was I ever in Marseilles, them frogs, they kick you with
spikes in their shoes. Ask him, was you ever in Shanghai, and
he says, was I ever in Shanghai, was I ever in Shanghai, man they

throw the crockery and the stools at you. Thass everyplace you mention, a different kind of beating.

There was this kid on board, Howie Adams. Gotta bring him up here. Told him 'bout you. Best people in the world, I says, always open house. Best kid. Not like those scenery bums and cherry pickers we got sailing nowadays. Guess what, they made me ship's delegate.

Well why not? asks Helen; you were probably the best man on board.

A tide of peaceful drowsiness washes over the tumult in him; he is almost asleep, though the veined brown hand still tremblingly strokes, strokes Allie's soft pale hair.

Is that Helen? No, it is Jeanie, so much like Helen of years ago, suddenly there under the hall light, looking in at them all, her cheeks glistening from the rain.

Never saw so many peaceful wrecks in my life. Her look is loving. That's what I want to be when I grow up, just a peaceful wreck holding hands with other peaceful wrecks. For Len and Helen are holding hands. We really fixed Mr. Nickerson. Marilyn did my English, I did her algebra, and her brother Tommy wrote for us 'I will not' 500 times; then we just tagged on 'talk in class, talk in class, talk in class.'

She drops her books, kneels down beside Whitey, and using his long ago greeting asks softly, "Hey Sailor, what ship?," then turns to her parents. Study in contrasts, Allie's face and Whitey's, where's my camera? Did you tell Whitey I'm graduating in three weeks, do you think you'll be here then, Whitey, and be . . . all right? I'll give you my diploma and write in your name so you can pretend you got through junior high, too. Allie's sure glad you came.

And without warning, with a touch so light, so faint, it seems to breathe against his cheek she traces a scar. That's a new one, isn't it? Allie noticed. She asked me, does it hurt? Does it?

He stops stroking Allie's hair a moment, starts up again desperately, looks so ill, Helen says sharply: It's late. Better go to bed, Jeanie, there's school tomorrow.

It's late, it's early. Kissing him, Helen, Lennie. Goodnight. Shall I take my stinky little sister upstairs to bed with me whatever she's doing down here, or shall I leave her for one of you strong men to carry?

Leaning from the middle stair, didn't know you were sick, Whitey, thought you were like . . . some of the other times. From the top stair, see you later, alligators.

Most he wants alone now, alone and a drink, perhaps sleep. And they know. We're going to bed now too. Six comes awful early.

So he endures Helen's kiss too, and Len's affectionate poke. And as Len carries Allie up the stairs, the fire leaps up, kindles Len's shadow so that it seems a dozen bent men cradle a child up endless stairs, while the rain traces on the windows, beseechingly, ceaselessly, like seeking fingers of the blind.

Hey Sailor, what ship? Hey Sailor, what ship?

III

In his sleep he speaks often and loudly, sometimes moans, and toward morning begins the trembling. He wakes into an unshared silence he does not recognize, accustomed so to the various voices of the sea, the multipitch of those with whom sleep as well as work and food is shared; the throb of engines, churn of the propeller; or hazed through drink the noises of the street or the thin walls like ears magnifying into lives as senseless as one's own.

Here there is only the whisper of the clock (motor by which this house runs now) and the sounds of oneself.

The trembling will not cease. In the kitchen there is a note: *Bacon and eggs in the icebox and coffee's made. The kids are coming straight home from school to be with you. DON'T go down to the front, Lennie'll take you tomorrow. Love.*
Love.

The row of cans on the cupboard shelves is thin. So things are still bad, he thinks, no money for stocking up. He opens all the doors hopefully, but if there is a bottle, it is hidden. A long time he stares at the floor, goes out into the yard where fallen rain beads the grasses that will be weeds soon enough, comes back, stares at his dampened feet, stares at the floor some more (needs scrubbing, and the woodwork can stand some too; well, maybe after I feel better), but there are no dishes in the sink, it is all cleaner than he expected.

Upstairs, incredibly, the beds are made, no clothes crumpled on the floor. Except in Jeanie's and Allie's room: there, as remembered, the dust feathers in the corners and dolls sprawl with books, records, and underwear. Guess she'll never get it clean. And up rises his old vision, his favorite vision, of how he will return here, laden with groceries, no one in the littered house, and quickly before they come, straighten the upstairs (the grime in the washbasin), clean the downstairs, scrub the kitchen floor, wash the hills of dishes, put potatoes in and light the oven, and when they finally troop in say, calmly, Helen, the house is clean, and there's steak for dinner.

Whether it is this that hurts in his stomach or the burning chill that will not stop, he dresses himself hastily, arguing with the new shoes that glint with a life all their own. On his way out, he stops for a minute to gloss his hand over the bookcase. Damn good paint job, he says out loud, if I say so myself. Still stands up after fourteen years. Real good that red backing Helen liked so much 'cause it shows above the books.

Hey Sailor, what ship?

IV

It is five days before he comes again. A cabbie precedes him up the stairs, loaded with bundles. Right through, right into the kitchen, man, directs Whitey, feeling good, oh quite obviously feeling good. The shoes are spotted now, he wears a torn Melton in place of the new jacket. Groceries, he announces heavily, indicating the packages plopped down. Steak. Whatever you're eating, throw it out.

Didn't I tell you they're a good-looking bunch? triumphantly indicating around the table. 'Cept that Lennie hyena over there. Go on, man, take the whole five smackers.

Don't let him go, I wanta ride in the cab, screams Allie.

To the top of the next hill and back, it's a windy round and round road, yells Carol.

I'll go too, says Jeanie.

Shut up, Lennie explodes, let the man go. Sit down, kids. Sit down, Whitey.

Set another plate, Jeanie, says Helen.

An' bring glasses. Got coke for the kids. We gonna have a drink.

I want a cab ride, Allie insists.

Wait till your mean old bastard father's not lookin'. Then we'll go.

Watch the language, Whitey, there's a gentleman present, says Helen. Finish your plate, Allie.

Thass right. Know who the gen'lmun is? I'm the gen'lmun. The world, says Marx, is divided into two classes . . .

Seafaring gen'lmun and shoreside bastards, choruses Lennie with him.

Why Daddy! says Jeanie.

You're a mean ole bassard father, says Allie.

Thass right, tell him off, urges Whitey. Hell with waitin' for glasses. Down the ol' hatch.

My class is divided by marks, says Carol, giggling helplessly at her own joke, and anyway what about ladies? Where's my drink? Down the hatch.

I got presents, kids. In the kitchen.

Where they'll stay, warns Helen, till after dinner. Just keep sitting.

Course Jeanie over there doesn't care 'bout a present. She's too grown up. Royal highness doesn't even kiss old Whitey, just slams a plate at him.

Fork, knife, spoon too, says Jeanie, acidly; why don't you use them?

Good chow, Helen. But he hardly eats, and as they clear the table, he lays down a tenner.

All right sailor, says Lennie, put your money back.

I'll take it, says Carol, if it's an orphan.

If you get into the front room quick, says Lennie, you won't have to do the dishes.

Who gives a shit about the dishes?

Watch it, says Helen.

Whenja start doin dishes in this house after dinner anyways?

Since we got organized, says Lennie, always get things done when they're supposed to be. Organized the life out of ourselves. Thats' what's the matter with Helen.

Well, when you work, Helen starts to explain.

Lookit Daddy kiss Mommy.

Give me my present and whirl me, Whitey, whirl me, demands Allie.

No whirling. Jus' sat down. How'd it be if I bounce you? Lef' my ol' lady in New Orleans with twenny-four kids and a can of beans.

Guess you think 'cause I'm ten I'm too big to bounce any more, says Carol.

Bounce everybody. Jeanie. Your mom. Even Lennie.

> What is life
> Without a wife (bounce)
> In a home (bounce bounce)
> Without a baby?

Hey, Helen, bring in those presents. Tell Jeanie, don't come in here, don't get a present. Jeanie, play those marimba records. Want marimba. Feel good, sure feel good. Hey Lennie, get your wild ass in here, got things to tell you. Leave the women do the work.

Wild ass, giggles Allie.

Jeanie gets mad when you talk like that, says Carol. Give us our presents and let's have a cab ride and tell us about the time you were torpedoed.

Tell us Crown 'n Deep.

Go tell yourself. I'm gonna have a drink.

Down the hatch, Whitey.

Down the hatch.

Better taper off, says Lennie, coming in. We want to have an evening.

Tell Helen bring the presents. She don't hafta be jealous. I got money for her. Helen likes money.

Upstairs, says Helen, they'll get their presents upstairs. After they're ready for bed. There's school tomorrow.

First we'll get them after dinner and now after we're ready for bed. That's not fair, wails Allie.

I never showed him my album yet, says Carol. He never said Crown 'n Deep.

It isn't fair. We never had our cab ride.

Whitey'll be here tomorrow, says Helen.

Maybe he won't, says Carol bitterly. He's got a room rented, he told me. Six weeks' rent in advance and furnished with eighteen cans of beans and thirty-six cans of sardines. All shored up, says Whitey. Somebody called Deeck stays there too.

Lef' my wile ass in New Orleans, twenty-four kids and a present of beans, chants Allie, bouncing herself up and down on the couch. And it's not *fair*.

Say goodnight to them, Whitey, they'll come down in their nightgowns for a goodnight kiss later.

Go on, kids. Mind your momma, don't be like me. An' here's a dollar for you an' a dollar for you. An' a drink for me.

But Lennie has taken the bottle. Whass matter, doncha like to see me feelin' good? Well screw you, brother, I'm supplied, and he pulls a pint out of his pocket.

Listen Whitey, says Jeanie, I've got some friends coming over and . . . Whitey, please . . . they're not used to your kind of language.

That so? 'Scuse me, your royal highness. Here's ten dollars, your royal highness. Help you forgive?

Please go sit in the kitchen. Please, Daddy, take him in the kitchen with you.

Jeanie, says Lennie, give him back the money.

He gave it to me, it's mine.

Give it back.

All right. Flinging it down, running up the stairs.

Quit it, Whitey, says Lennie.

Quit what?

Throwing your goddam money around. Where do you think you are, down on the front?

'S better down on the front. You're gettin' holier than the dago pope.

I mean it, guy. And tone down that language. Let's have the bottle.

No. Into the pocket. Do *you* good to feel good for a change. You 'n Helen look like you been through the meat grinder.

Silence.

Gently. Tell me about the trip, Whitey.

Good trip. Most of the time. 'Lected me ship's delegate.

You told us.

Tell you 'bout that kid, Howie? Best kid. Got my gear off the ship and lef' it down at the hall for me. Whaddaya think of that?

(O feeling good, come back, come back.)

Jeanie in her hat and coat. Stiffly. Thank you for the earrings, Whitey.

Real crystals. Best . . . Lennie, 'm gonna give her ten dollars. For treat her friends. After all, ain't she my wife?

Whitey, do I have to hear that story again? I was four years old.

Again? (He had told the story so often, as often as anyone would listen, whenever he felt good, and always as he told it, the same shy happiness would wing through him, how when she was four, she had crawled into bed beside him one morning, announcing triumphantly to her mother: I'm married to Whitey now, I don't have to sleep by myself anymore.) Sorry, royal highness, won't mention it. How's watch I gave you, remember?

(Not what he means to say at all. Remember the love I gave you, the worship offered, the toys I mended and made, the questions answered, the care for you, the pride in you?)

I lost the watch, remember? I was too young for such expensive presents. You keep talking about it because that's the only reason you give presents, to buy people to be nice to you and to yak about the presents when you're drunk. Here's your earrings too. I'm going outside to wait for my friends.

Jeanie! It is Helen, back down with the kids. Jeanie, come into the kitchen with me.

Jeanie's gonna get heck, says Carol. Geeeee, down the hatch. Wish I could swallow so long. Is my dresser set solid gold like it looks?

Kiss the dolly you gave me, says Allie. She's your grandchild now. You kiss her too, Daddy. I bet she was the biggest dolly in the store.

Your dolly can't talk. Thass good, honey, that she can't talk.

Here's my album, Whitey. It's got a picture of you. Is that really you Whitey? It don't look like . . .

Don't look, he says to himself, closing his eyes. Don't look. But it is indelible. Under the joyful sun, with proud sea, proud ship as background, the proud young man, glistening hair and eyes, joyful body, face open to life, unlined. Sixteen? Seventeen? Close it up, he says, M. Norbert Jacklebaum never saw the guy. Quit punchin' me.

Nobody's punchin' you Whitey, says Allie. You're feeling your face.

Tracing the scars, the pits and lines, the battered nose; seeking to find.

Your name's Michael Jackson, Whitey, why do you say Jacklebaum? marvels Allie.

Tell Crown 'n Deep, I try to remember it and I never can, Carol says very softly. Neither can Jeanie. Tell Crown 'n Deep, tell how you learnt it. If you feel like. Please.

O yes, he feels like. *When there is November in my soul,* he begins. No, wrong one.

Taking the old proud position. The Valedictory, written the night 'fore he was executed; by José Rizal, national hero of the Philippines. Taught me by Li'l Joe Roco, not much taller'n you, Jeanie, my first shipmate.

I'm Carol, not Jeanie.

Li'l Joe. Never got back home, they were puttin' the hatch covers on and . . . I only tell it when it's special. El Ultimo Adiós. Known as The Valedictory. 1896.

> *Land I adore, farewell . . . .*
> *Our forfeited garden of Eden,*
> *Joyous I yield up for thee my sad life*
> *And were it far brighter,*
> *Young or rose-strewn, still would I give it.*
>
> *Vision I followed from afar,*
> *Desire that spurred on and consumed me,*
> *Beautiful it is to fall,*
> *That the vision may rise to fulfillment.*

Go on Whitey.

Little will matter, my country,
That thou shouldst forget me.
I shall be speech in thy ears, fragrance and color,
Light and shout and loved song . . .

Inaudible.

O crown and deep of my sorrows,
I am leaving all with thee, my friends, my love,
Where I go are no tyrants . . . .

He stands there, swaying. Say goodnight, says Lennie. Whitey'll tell it all some other time. Here, guy, sit down.

And in the kitchen.
You know how he talks. How can you let him? In front of the little kids.
They don't hear the words, they hear what's behind them. There are worse words than swear words, there are words that hurt. When Whitey talks like that, it's everyday words; the men he lives with talk like that, that's all.
Well, not the kind of men I want to know. I don't go over to anybody's house and hear words like that.
Jeanie, who are you kidding? You kids use all those words at school.
That's different, that's being grownup like smoking. And he's so drunk. Why didn't Daddy let me keep the ten dollars? It would mean a lot to me, and it doesn't mean anything to him.
It's his money. He worked for it, it's the only power he has. We don't take Whitey's money.
Oh no. Except when he gives it to you.
When he was staying with us, when they were rocking chair, unemployment checks, it was different. He was sober. It was his share.
He's just a Howard Street wino now—why don't you and Daddy kick him out of the house? He don't belong here.
Of course he belongs here, he's a part of us, like family . . .

Jeanie, this is the only house in the world he can come into and
be around people without having to pay.

Somebody who brings presents and whirls you around and
expects you to jump for his old money.

Remember how good he's been to you. To us. Jeanie, he was
only a year older than you when he started going to sea.

Now you're going to tell me the one about how he saved
Daddy's life in the strike in 1934.

He knows more about people and places than almost anyone
I've ever known. You can learn from him.

When's he like that any more? He's just a Howard Street
wino, that's all.

Jeanie, I care that you should understand. You think Mr.
Norris is a tragedy, you feel sorry for him because he talks so
intelligent and lives in a nice house and has quiet drunks. You've
got to understand.

Just a wino. Even if it's whisky when he's got the money.
Which isn't for long.

To understand.

(In the beginning there had been youth and the joy of raising
hell and that curious inability to take a whore unless he were high
with drink.

(And later there were memories to forget, dreams to be stifled,
hopes to be murdered.)

Know who was the ol' man on the ship? Blackie Karns, Kiss-
ass Karns hisself.

Started right when you did, Whitey.

O yes. (A few had nimbly, limberly clambered up.) Remember in the war he was the only one of us would wear his braid uptown? That one year I made mate? Know how deal with you, he
says. No place for you on the ships any more, he says. My ass-
hole still knows more than all you put together, I says.

What was the beef, Whitey?

Don' remember. Rotten feed for a while. Bring him up a
plate and say, eat it yourself. Nobody gonna do much till we get
better. We got better.

This kid, overtime comin' to him. Didn't even wanta fight
about it. I did it anyway. Got fined by the union for takin' it up.

M. Norbert Jacklebaum fined by the union, 'conduct unbefitting ship's delegate' says the Patrolman, 'not taking it up through proper channels.' (His old fine talent for mimicry jutting through the blurred-together words.)

These kids, these cherry pickers, they don't know how we got what we got. Beginnin' to lose it, too. Think anybody backed me up, Len? Just this Howie and a scenery bum, Goldballs, gonna write a book. Have you in it, Jackson, he says, you're a real salt.

(Understand. The death of the brotherhood. Once, once an injury to one was an injury to all. Once, once they had to live for each other. And whoever came off the ship fat shared, because that was the only way of survival for all of them, the easy sharing, the knowing that when you needed, waiting for a trip card to come up, you'd be staked.

(Now it was a dwindling few, and more and more of them winos, who shipped sometimes or had long ago irrevocably lost their book for nonpayment of dues.)

Hey, came here to feel good. Down the hatch. Hell with you. You got any friends? Hell with your friends.

Helen is back. So you still remember El Ultimo Adiós, Whitey. Remember when we first heard Joe recite it?

I remember.

(Remember too much, too goddam much. For twenty-three years the watery shifting: many faces, many places, many voices.

(But more and more, certain things the same. The gin mills and the cathouses. The calabozas and jails and stockades. More and more New York and Norfolk and New Orleans and Pedro and Frisco and Seattle like the foreign ports: docks, clip joints, hockshops, cathouses, skid rows, the Law and the Wall: only so far shall you go and no further; uptown forbidden, not your language, not your people, not your country.

(Added sometimes now, the hospital.)

What's going to happen with you, Whitey?

What I care? Nobody hasta care what happens to M. Jacklebaum.

How can we help caring, Whitey? You're a chunk of our lives.

Shove it, Lennie. So you're a chunk of my life. So?

(Understand. Once they had been young together.

(To Lennie he remained a tie to adventure and a world in which men had not eaten each other; and the pleasure, when the mind was clear, of chewing over with that tough mind the happenings of the times or the queernesses of people, or laughing over the mimicry.

(To Helen he was the compound of much help given, much support; the ear to hear, the hand that understands how much a scrubbed floor, or a washed dish, or a child taken care of for a while, can mean.

(They had believed in his salvation, once. Get him away from the front where he has to drink for company and for a woman. The torn-out-of-him confession, the drunken end of his eight-months-sober try to make a go for it on the beach—doncha see, I can't go near a whore unless I'm lit?

(If they could know what is like now, so casual, as if it were after 30 years of marriage.

(Later, the times he had left money with them for plans: fix his teeth, buy a car, get into the Ship Painters, go see his family in Chi. But soon enough the demands for the money when the drunken need was on him, so that after a few tries they gave up trying to keep it for him.

(Later still, the first time it became too much and Lennie forbade the house to him unless he were "O.K.; because of the children."

(Now the decaying body, the body that was betraying him. And the memories to forget, the dreams to be stifled, the hopeless hopes to be murdered.)

What's going to happen with you, Whitey? Helen repeats. I never know if you'll be back. If you'll be able to be back.

He tips the bottle to the end. Thirstily he thinks: Deeck and his room where he can yell or sing or pound and Deeck will look on without reproach or pity or anguish.

I'm goin' now. Goodbye.

Wait, Whitey. We'll drive you. Want to know where you're shacked, anyways.

Go own steam. Send you a card.

By Jeanie, silent and shrunken into her coat. He passes no one in the streets. They are inside, each in his slab of house, watching the flickering light of Television. The sullen fog is on his face, but by the time he has walked to the third hill, it has lifted so he can see the city below him, wave after wave, and there, at the crest behind, the tiny house he has left, its eyes unshaded. After awhile they blur with the myriad others that stare at him so blindly.

Then he goes down.

Hey Sailor, what ship?
Hey Marinero, what ship?

For Jack Eggan, Seaman, born 1915
Killed in the retreat across the Ebro, Spain, 1938

David Dow

Ol' Nick's Wife

It was a usual Thursday night. Beth Ellington was alone. It was mid-September, in the height of the final summer heat spell in the San Joaquin Valley. Nick had gone into Turlock to a union meeting. A staunch union man for twenty-seven years, he had risen to the secretaryship of Plumbers and Steamfitters Local 427. In fact, he had been at a union meeting the night his son was born. Some said so staunch was his support of organized labor that he had been at a union meeting the night his son was conceived, too. This joke hardly seemed funny when the similarity between father and son was hitting you in the face all the time. Besides, thought Beth, it had been told too many times to be funny any more.

It was hard to tell what had made Beth and Nick compatible. Perhaps it was their son; or maybe opposites do attract; or maybe love can turn its back to basic differences for thirty years. Anyway, the fact remained that the Ellingtons, Ma and Pa, were different, and you had to look no further than the flesh and bone that God had given them to guess they weren't alike. Nick was more of a grinning grizzly bear than a man. If not the best known man in town, he was easily the biggest, and the strongest, and the hairiest. He was even a little handsome if you appreciated boyish pie faces with banana-shaped smiles all over the pie. Nick quite conceivably could have made a good two and a half Beths; that is, all except for the delicate features that were still a part of her at almost fifty. Beth was pretty, an ageless beauty. Her figure ranked with any Rockwater schoolgirl's, though it was wrapped around only ninety pounds of lady.

With permission from *Sequoia*, Vol. III, No. 2, Winter 1958. © 1958 by the Associated Students of Stanford University.

They didn't think alike either, even though they came from similar backgrounds. Both were the offspring of hand tradesmen. Both had been given few hopes by their families of rising above their environment. However, Beth had developed a mind that was all the encouragement she needed. She discovered her brains early. Her poems and historical sketches had been a weekly feature of the *Rockwater Light* since her early teens. Her thoughts had always been above the plane of living of her smallish home town. Nick's hopes had never been carried beyond Rockwater. Built to labor and sweat, a rise in status meant only sweating for his own business to Nick. He was proud of his hard-working ancestors. They had sweated hard in coming to California. Nick wanted his son in turn to have their "hair and guts."

Nobody could explain Beth's marrying Nick. Maybe it was Beth's way of acknowledging her imprisoned spirit. The funny thing was that they had been in love then, when Nick was eighteen and Beth a year younger, and they still were. And Beth's ambition had never taken her as far away as Bakersfield.

First it was their struggle to get Nick's shop going that kept them together. N. G. Ellington—Star Plumbing and Heating had rewarded its parents by becoming one of the most successful enterprises in town. Then it was Sam, or rather the ten-year effort to get Sam—childbearing didn't come easy for Beth. And during the whole ten years their differences kept them endlessly amused.

The day Sam was born the differences ceased to be amusing. Both parents wanted a giant. Beth would have an intellectual giant and Nick a physical one, or at least a son that could turn a two-inch wrought-iron pipe in a threader at 104° in the shade and swear that the summer heat would never arrive.

When Sam was eight the Watson's Pharmacy set and the Rex Clubbers were satisfied that the issue was settled. He was big enough then to dwarf the serious-faced woman who held his hand while he crossed the street. Nick's kid. That's what they called him. Body, face, hair, and eyes he was Nick's, and "Say, do you remember that time when that little elephant comes walkin' down the street with the old lady, and Eric Sawatski, that Polish guy, tries to take his little red beanie from him, you know, just screwin' around. And the young punk ups and calls Eric a horse-ass bastard, just pretty as a God damn picture. You know, just like his

old man says, without pluralizin' the 'horse.' Now if that ain't
200 per cent Nick then there ain't no wineries in Lodi. Looks like
the good Lord went an' forgot Beth."

One thing kept Sam from being 225 pounds of Nick's kid: he
had Beth's brains. Ol' Nick's wife was smart, and she was the
first to recognize Sam's possibilities. Not that Ol' Nick wasn't
smart, too. He was smart in a different way. He was Rockwater
smart. Beth was world smart. She wanted to draw Sam into her
world—*the* world. Nick wanted a chunk of "man," not a chunk
of "world." The admiration of the people who stumbled along
the cracked sidewalks of Rockwater was a mark of a "man." And
just when the early fall sunshine was bringing out his most manly
self, Nick's kid would leave for college—would leave the man
and join the world. The grease would still be fresh on his hands
from the man's work in Nick's shop and the jokes still on his lips
that he'd heard from a peach crater or a tractor driver, but the
grease could rub off on the pages of Plato and the jokes could be
bumped aside by the words of Dickens and Marx.

It was a lonely battle, Beth's. Sometimes you could look at
that barrel-chested kid and hear him whoop and roar as he
crushed challenger after challenger in arm wrestling matches and
you'd think that the mother's only stake in him was in carrying
and bearing him. And then you'd see another, older barrel-
chested guy step up and lock arms with the kid and finally squeeze
out a victory and see the kid lift his face in a bug-eyed smile and
you'd be sure the kid had been conceived, nurtured, and borne
by the father alone.

Beth had to applaud her victory by herself because she was
the only one who recognized it, and it was often questioned, at
that. How many times, thought Beth, had she walked to this very
porch and looked down Highway 99 and seen Sam standing under
the fly-infested neon lights in the distance laughing with a bunch
of dirty-clothed men and smiled confidently, knowing her son was
not one of them, and then turned around and seen Nick following
her gaze with a confident smile, too.

She sat on the porch now, taking in the highway, her slight
frame very still. She wondered where Sam was, then remembered
quickly that he would be downtown or maybe at Yanette's place.
Those were the two perennial alternatives. She hoped he was at

Yanette's, though her son's girl friend was only the lesser of two
evils in Beth's mind. Yanette was pretty, and certainly no looser
than the rest of the unattached girls around Rockwater. Yanette
was even halfway intelligent, in a shy sort of way. Just the same,
Beth did not like Yanette for her son. Beth would talk to Yanette,
her astute eyes studying the young roundness of the girl's frame
as if looking for the quality that made her worthy of her son.
Yanette would blink and shift her weight before Beth's piercing
gaze as if she were afraid of Beth's inner thoughts. And Beth
would be thinking that Yanette was Rockwater and Beth's son had
possibilities of not being Rockwater.

Beth studied the town's lights in the distance with the blanket
of tired faces and sweaty bodies beneath them. The canneries
were beginning to lay off and some of the transient harvest families were already on the move south to Bakersfield and Taft for
cotton or north to Lodi for late grapes. Beth was restless tonight,
yet she was bored. She didn't think about being bored because
she couldn't remember when she hadn't been bored on Thursday
night. Beth was even a little happy tonight. She thought about
Monday, three days hence, when her prize would again be past
the temptations of the summer and on his way back to school
and re-spiritualizing. Sam had worked as an assistant in Nick's
plumbing shop during the summer. The warm months had
seemed long to Beth, and the laughs and shouts between Nick and
Sam in the yard below had tolled the minutes of every day. Each
day she had been forced to witness the ties between son and husband cinch closer and more binding.

N. G. Ellington—Star Plumbing and Heating had now become Ellington and Wismer's Star Service. The 1937 recession
had shown that people didn't buy pipe when they couldn't afford
the water that ran through it. Erwin Wismer, operator of a successful string of general merchandise stores around nearby Turlock, had come to Nick's rescue. Erwin had grabbed off a sizable
nest egg selling food and clothing at jacked-up prices to the dust
bowl immigrants of the early 30's. He had sold out and bought
into Nick's shop with little know-how in the plumbing and building trades. He had worked earnestly at first, but many times he
had substituted money for muscle. Despite twenty years of working together, the two partners remained surprisingly distant,

though a kind of formal warmth usually prevailed between the two families.

During Erwin's early years in the business, Nick, Erwin, and Erwin's whiskey bottle had formed an unhappy triangle. Erwin's drunken form had been a frequent part of the landscape of Rockwater saloons. Once, only Nick had kept Erwin's craving from bringing him to an early death. He and Nick had gone into a bar, Erwin well on the way. The green of a stack of bills Erwin waved shone gold in the barflies' eyes. Erwin's boisterous shouts and stack of currency had been all the bait that two Mexican transients needed to try to roll him. Nick had stepped between them, running through one of the attackers with the knife he had meant to use on Erwin, breaking the arm of the other. The incident had abruptly widened the spans between Erwin's drinks. It had been a long time since his last bender.

"Tomorrow's his last day for another year," thought Beth, relieved that the suitcases were already on his bed to be filled with the clothes for another university year.

The summer work itself had been nothing new for Sam. It was the relationship between boss and employee, father and son that changed yearly. Sam had been "meeting" his father at work since he had been old enough to thread pipe nipples. A summer in Manteca, forty-two miles south, working as a hod carrier, had been the only one Sam could remember not having been with Nick.

Beth gazed toward the side of the house, toward a clothesline sagging with men's work clothes. Her eyes fixed on an especially big pair of overalls that looked like they were made for a Turkish wrestler. She swept the length of the line, as though entranced by the strings of T-shirts and shorts and dungaree shirts that shone their drabness in the half moonlight. It would seem good just once to see a dress shirt hanging on that line, or at least some clothes dyed something besides tan, or olive drab, or faded blue; clothes that weren't stained and spotted with mastic, pipe-dope, or oil. Then she noticed a few pieces of her own underclothing mixed in along the line, and she smiled at their insignificance next to the men's tent-like clothes. A bystander would think that African giants who like to play with dolls lived in the old dwelling. She noticed a cotton brassière at one end of the line and her mind switched to a round, unshaven face that strained to keep back the grin as it spoke: "I got the best girl after all, God damn it. Five other girls in your family, none of 'em any bigger'n you, and I got the only one with big tits."

Beth had once hated such outbreaks of vulgarity, but she had worked and lived around Nick's shop long enough so that now only the rankest comments made her wince. Sam's swearing, however, was a different matter. Every time she heard him use profanity, she became the sensitive girl of her early married life, and her blood would freeze and her eyes slam shut.

She walked in the house through Sam's room, and she was again thankful to see the oversized clothes covering the bed and the suitcases half-packed with sport shirts and underwear. She wished tomorrow were Monday, except that she would miss seeing Sam. But at least he would be safe then—"Safe from whatever temptation exists along that dirty street or in that yard of rusty pipe, or in the lines of people along the dirty street."

She picked up an open book from the scarred coffee table in the living room and sat down in a straight-backed rocking chair to read. She read a couple of pages and then glanced up, scanning the overladen bookcase ahead of her. The array of book jackets belonged to a collection of contemporary American and European novels. In a small corner of the shelf space was a stack of *Plumbing and Sheet Metal Workers' Journals*. Beth read incessantly, loading down the mailman with contributions from half a dozen book clubs. She had read more since Sam had gone away to school. Reading had relieved her mind from the comparative emptiness of the house and the sounds of labor below.

Then she heard wheels on the gravel driveway, and she wasn't restless any more. Walking downstairs, she glanced at the clock on the hallway wall. Five minutes to ten. "Hmm, early for Nick to be home. The plumbers must have stuck to plumbing tonight." As she got to the bottom of the stairs, Nick met her coming up. His unshaven, bronzed face was unnaturally grim; his green baseball hat, which he always wore, was in his left hand. He seemed not to notice Beth on the stairway until he was almost past her; then he turned to face her squarely, his thick eyebrows knitted in a grotesque frown, his usually dancing eyes narrowed to dark slits. He nodded, started to speak, and then turned once again up the stairs, motioning for her to follow.

He stomped up the stairs, Beth anxiously at his heels. She fol-

lowed him into the kitchen and she knew something had happened
that night, something big and sad. It took a lot to take the smile
off Nick's face. It seemed he was always laughing or smiling or
wisecracking with someone. He stayed young that way.

He drew a glass of water and consumed it in one draught.
He did the same with another glassful and then sat down, motioning for Beth to sit also. He looked into space for a moment, muttering several soft oaths. Only his lips moved, as if he were repeating a ritualized prayer. Then without turning his head, he
spoke. "Them rotten government bastards killed him, Beth!"

Beth's expression froze upon Nick, as she heard him mention
death. She questioned him automatically, though her intuition
hinted at the answer. "Nicolas, what are you talking about?
What happened at the meeting tonight?"

He grasped her arm lightly. His mouth opened; his tongue
hung suspended for a speechless moment, and then the words
came. "Tonight, Erwin, he gets up to speak at the meeting and
he keels over. Everybody chuckles a little, thinkin' he's drunk or
something, Kitten, but . . . but . . . well, God damn it, he
never got up, Kitten. Erwin's dead. I ain't got a partner any
more."

She sat there, shocked. She didn't know what to do, what to
say. She started crying a little. Nick's partner, Erwin Wismer,
had not been close to the family for a man who dirtied his clothes
next to Nick every day. Beth had not liked Erwin. She had always been suspicious of him, claimed he was forever trying to
take advantage of Nick. Erwin had come into the business when
Nick had no money, since no one else in Rockwater had any
either, except for Erwin, that is. Erwin had invested in Nick's
business, acutely aware that San Joaquin building would boom
with the first shots of the sure world war, if he and Nick could
live on recessionary red a few hungry months longer. Now her
husband was telling her that Erwin, Erwin the opportunist, was
gone, and she was crying, mainly for lack of anything to say; and
she was a little sorry though she wasn't sure whether it was because Erwin was dead or because her husband had lost his money-
making partner. She turned to Nick. "Erwin?"

"They carried him out at nine o'clock. They left it to me to
tell his ol' lady. That'll be harder'n hell." He got up and started
walking around the room. "Kitten, this wouldn't have happened

if it weren't for those particular sons a bitches at the new hatchery."

"What did they have to do with it?" She was at his side, sensing instinctively the need to console her husband, who did feel grief.

"Erwin takes twelve bundles of half-inch pipe out there today and gets it all unloaded—they wouldn't even help the poor bastard unload it—and some horse-ass bastard comes out and tells ol' Erwin, 'Take it back, government specifications call for three-eighths-inch on this job.' So Erwin, with his heart condition and all, has to load all those twelve damn bundles on the truck again and drive back and unload 'em and load twelve bundles a three-eighths on. They're heavy, hell, 230 odd pounds they weigh. And then he drives 'em back and he goes and he's unloaded 'em when he gets this terrible spell like he gets sometimes under his heart, and I guess he went about hell-house crazy 'til he'd laid down for about an hour and sweat about a gallon. He told me he felt crappy tonight, but he was goin' to the meeting anyway. An' when he jumps up to talk in the meeting, all hell broke loose and that was the end of ol' Erwin." He paused and looked down, his mouth still open. His arms, which had been gesturing while he spoke, hung limply at his side. "Oh, Kitten, me and Erwin quibbled a lot an' all and we wasn't warm enough, I guess, but I feel sick all over. I don't know what to do."

She forced a smile and touched his shoulder. "Relax, Nickie; think of Ethyl. What will she do when she hears? Thank God they don't have any children to be hurt, too. Nick, it's too bad you have to break the news to her, but I guess it would be wrong for anyone else to. One of God's obligations, I guess. Ethyl had half expected it, I'm sure. Especially after I talked her into taking Erwin to that coronary specialist in Fresno."

"Oh-h-h Christ, think of it. God, Union Hall went mad. A lot of guys felt mighty crappy tonight. I think I feel as bad as any of 'em. I mean, a guy pulls you out of the depression and you just can't help feeling like you owe him something."

Beth, composed now, her tears gone, reached over and ran her fingers through Nick's thick hair. "Erwin helped us a lot, Nick, but remember, you gave Erwin back everything he ever contributed to the business, if not in money, then in spirit."

"Yeh, but I've been stinkin' to Erwin too many times to . . ."

"Such as saving his life?" said Beth, the sarcasm in her tone lifting one dark eyebrow higher than the other.

"Oh, hell. He'd a done the same for me."

"Yes, Nick, but remember it wasn't *he* who walked into Rex's and saved *you* from being beaten to death. It was *he* and his ever-abundant money he had to flash around and his alcoholic breath that got *him* in trouble, and if you hadn't pulled those drunken devils off him, it would have been *his* life, and *his* money, and . . ." Her voice mellowed. The compassion returned to her face. "Don't get me wrong, Nick. I didn't mean to slip off on a tangent, but I just can't let you even start to eat your heart out over a false sense of obligation. Sure, I know you got to like Erwin. You had to, or you never could have worked with him this long. But mourn him because of missing him, not because of what he missed from you."

"But damn it, I can't be that cold about it!"

"Cut it out, Nickie," she said, again ruffling the sandy hair. The voice almost pleaded now. "I'm sorry, too. You should know that. If not for Erwin, then for Ethyl or for you, because you're sad, or, well, for Sam, because I know he'll be more upset than either of us."

He considered his wife's reply, smiling faintly at her, then sitting down. "Don't know how Ethyl's going to take it. For that matter, don't know how I'm going to tell her. Good thing she don't have kids. Though I know that if I kicked off, you'd have support, cuzza our kid. Why he could practically take over my shop right now and run it alone. He just works there summers and already he can make the whole layout for a house, sewer to fixtures."

A warning of things to come? Nick's words awoke abruptly the question that had been resting on her mind since he had announced Erwin's death. Death or no death, life went on. More particularly, Star Service went on. Nick and Erwin had built such a business now that it took two just to direct the jobs and handle the executive end as well. Nick would be needing a partner now. "Nicolas, you wouldn't really let him?"

"Let him what?"

"Nick, you know, the shop."

"Oh, you mean take over the shop? Hell, he couldn't just take the whole thing over just like a big-ass bird without going through his apprenticeship and all first. I suppose he could be an assistant or something."

"Nick, you wouldn't have him toss everything to the wind?"

"He's going to college, ain't he? Now don't get hysterical. The kid ain't doing nothing he don't want to. He's got a mind. In fact, he's got your God damn mind."

"My God damn mind and your God damn common sense," she said, mimicking the inflection in Nick's voice but smiling to cushion the bite of the words. She lowered her voice. "And, oh, yes, the same hair distribution as Rockwater's first soldier of the plumbing wars, too," she cooed, stroking the fuzzy expanse on the back of his neck.

He looked up at her, wanting to counter with words that might sting a little, but noticing the upturned sweep of her lips, was unable to do so. He settled for "God damned woman" and stared sheepishly at the floor.

They sat there in the dim light of the kitchen, gazing for a moment down 99 toward town. Then they talked, quietly, for a while longer. They talked mostly of Sam and his coming year at college, and the conversation was broken many times by long lags of silence. They had lately found it hard to talk to each other for long periods of time. Consequently, they talked little but were happy most of the time. Thirty years had taught them to understand one another. It didn't matter whether or not they happened to sympathize with what the other was saying.

About eleven o'clock there was the sound of tires on gravel again, followed by the report of loud mufflers as the engine was shut off. Nick and Beth remained seated, listened to the noisy scurrying of footsteps on the stairs. Sam ran into the kitchen, his stocky frame looking immense in the white T-shirt and faded denims he wore. He stood 5' 10" and weighed 225 pounds and his feet, clad in scuffed saddle shoes, were surprisingly small. His smile used his whole face and his wavy, uncombed, tawny hair seemed to be part of the huge grin. He thumped Nick in the stomach and grabbed Beth from her chair, picking her up, tossing her into the air, and then easily catching her and setting her down. His breath smelled faintly of alcohol. "Guess who just cleaned Art Whatchamacalum for ten bucks in snooker?" he asked, with mock defiance in his voice. "Ten bucks, Ma. Aren't I a bitching son?"

"Sammy, I told you not to use that word."

"But, Ma, it's a college word. A symbol of secondary sophistication."

"And is that a secondarily sophisticated wine stain on your shirt, too?" inquired Beth, a kittenish smile on her face.

"That's not wine, Ma. That's chalk offa my pool cue."

"Purple chalk these days, little boy? Where were you playing, Drusetti's Vineyards? Don't forget. I used to have to drag my brother away from pool tables when I was a little girl."

"How much littler, Ma?" He laughed and yanked the blouse out of her skirt.

"Out, damned spot!" she exclaimed, feinting to chase after her son. She stopped short, remembering the serious face sitting at her side, and her smile receded into fixed unemotion. She looked at Nick and knew that he would have to repeat his story again.

"How're things goin' tonight, son?" asked Nick.

"Great. What are you old folks doin' up so late?" said Sam, the cherubic smile still on his face.

"Oh, your Ma and I have been talking."

"Good habit."

Nick neglected the remark. He looked into space, his forehead furrowed. "Things happened tonight, Bud."

The big grin remained. "Who died, Pa—Rex? That'll mean free beer for . . ." He stopped short as he took a second, longer look at Nick's knotted face. He sobered quickly as he realized the blind accuracy of his well-intended kidding. "Dad, what happened? I'm sorry. I didn't mean . . ."

Nick relaxed his frown and forced a sad smile on his face. He walked over and laid a hand on the boy's hammy forearm. "Sit down, son."

"Sammy, I won't even try to break this easy, but you remember that big government screw-up Erwin got roped into today?"

Sam nodded, the muscles in the arm Nick held tightening. Nick gripped harder, hesitating to think of the right words.

"Anyway, Sam, I'm afraid it was too much." He paused. "I'm afraid it killed him. He died tonight at the meeting. Heart attack, I guess."

Beth rushed to Sam's side. His head fell into her side, as her narrow hand slipped around his neck. He breathed very hard and gnashed his teeth hard to stifle the moisture that rushed to his eyes. His shoulders sagged beneath Beth's touch. The words came softly but with obvious effort. "Oh Chr-rist!" He paused. "No, I won't believe it!" He looked up at Beth hopefully.

The compassion rippled her face as she ran her hand across his back. Slowly, tenderly, she nodded.

Sam lurched from his chair and barged out of the room. He ran out on the porch and stood in the warmth of the summer evening, wanting to shut his eyes and then open them, to find that his father hadn't really told him the bitter news. He tried it and was disappointed when it didn't work. He felt very cold. It was bad, all just plain bad. Sam had loved Erwin. Sam loved everyone, but, well, Erwin had just always been there. The only days he could remember not seeing Erwin were when he was away at school.

He felt a human touch and he looked down. Beth was at his side, her soft hands encircling a massive forearm.

"It was coming, son. We all knew it had to happen."

"But why Erwin?"

"Why anyone? Try to forget, Sam. We still have you and you have a great long life ahead of you."

Nick came out and laid a hairy paw on his counterpart's shoulder. "It's okay, Bud. We all feel bad."

"Dad, there's guys out there"—he pointed to the town lights —"that would rather die than go to work tomorrow. And what does He do but pick a good man like Erwin . . . I don't know, Dad. There isn't any justice in life."

"You and me ain't big enough to know anything about it, Sammy. It's all planned out before you're born. Only it is gonna be hard telling that to Ethyl."

Beth, sensing her uselessness, turned and walked into the house.

"Doesn't Ethyl know yet?"

"No, we've gotta tell her tonight."

"You want—*me* to come with you when you tell Ethyl?"

"Yeh, Bud, she'll want to know we care. And maybe together we can break it a little easier."

I haven't ever done anything like this, Pa."

"It's time you grew a little older."

"Pa?"

"Yeh."

"What're you going to do about the shop?"

"I don't know, Bud. We'll talk about it later. Let's go." He laid his arm on the boy's neck and the boy bowed his head and they walked back in the flat and toward the stairs. As they reached the landing, Beth appeared at the top of the staircase. She saw them, one giant's arm around a bigger giant's neck as though consoling him so he wouldn't stamp out a valley or a town. She marked the great similarity between the two for the millionth time in her life and heard the door open and then slam shut. She heard gravel scuffed, an engine roar, and then the gravel disheveled momentarily again. Then she heard nothing and she wondered if her son would return.

The trip up Ethyl Wismer's front walkway seemed like a hundred miles. Ethyl looked worried as she let the two in. A slightly stocky woman, she still had a kind of narrow face that, with her ungrayed black hair, gave a rather pretty, well-kept, middle-aged appearance. "Erwin's not home yet, Nick. He left for the meeting around seven and hasn't been . . ." She stopped short, her face confused; then awareness moved in, around, and across it, cementing the eyes at nervous attention. She stopped, fumbling with the bathrobe she had been adjusting around her.

"Ethyl, this is terrible of us, comin' over so late an' all." Nick tried to postpone the speech he had spoken twice already.

"Nick, has Winnie been drinkin' again or something?" she suggested hopefully, plainly lying to her innermost guesses. She moved closer to the pair, looking anxiously from one tense face to the other. Sam nervously shifted his weight from foot to foot.

Nick looked at her and smiled, a pained, sympathetic smile that told his message before his words did. "It's 'or something' this time, Ethyl. Tell me, how did Erwin feel tonight when I picked him up?"

"I don't know. He didn't say much." She answered, the words barely disturbing the anxious set of her lips, her eyes still looking expectantly at the two.

"Ethyl, I'm afraid I gotta tell ya. Well, you'll understand

after seein' that guy in Fresno an' all. Well, Sammy and me come to tell you that Erwin got pretty sick tonight, Ethyl. In fact, he got so sick, I'm afraid he went home with God this time." He started to explain how her husband had died, but her sobbing cries interrupted him.

"No. No-o-o-ho-ho," she threw herself at Nick and his arms went around her. And then she was against Sam's shoulders, the tears pouring down her shaking face, making the flesh show through where the drops struck his thin T-shirt.

"Ethyl, you know it had to happen sooner or later," said Nick.

"I've lost everything . . . everything!" She hugged Sam tightly, the tears still trickling out of eyes squeezed close together. "Oh, why, why Winnie?"

"Ethyl, it's hard, I know . . ."

"Winnie's everything. We never even had any children. Just me and. . . and . . . Winnie." She rubbed an unsteady hand across her moist cheek. "Nick, you don't know how lucky you are."

"I know, Ethyl. We're damn lucky." He smiled faintly at Sam, a smile that held much more than simple gratitude.

They led her to a sofa and sat her down. Nick told her the circumstances of Erwin's death, and she cried some more. Then there was silence and they sat quietly in the darkness, until Ethyl spoke. "How could I know it'd be this way? Why, there's . . . well, all at once there's nothing, and yet, at the same time, there's everything hitting you at once. The shop, this house—Oh, Lord, this house was Erwin—you know, all this awful thing like a big mountain to climb or something."

"Ethyl, forget about the shop," Nick said, gently sliding his arm around her. Sam did not move. He watched Nick intently as he spoke.

"And then there's all that's in this house—all Erwin's. What will I do in this house with . . . with nothing to do for Winnie."

"Ethyl, you can stop worrying about the shop."

"I haven't even been away from Winnie since we were married."

"Ethyl, what you were sayin', you can forget about the shop. I'll take care of it for you." Again Nick repeated.

She turned, suddenly sensing his words. "The shop. Oh, do

what you want. It's Winnie's, not mine. That's just the way it is. This whole town is Winnie."

"Count on us. We'll do Erwin justice. He's done a lot for me, and Sam—all of us." Nick smiled faintly, pleased to see her tears gone. He checked his watch. "It's late now. You better be quiet for a while. Okay?"

She sat without answering for a moment. "Yes, I guess you'd better let me alone now, boys." She rubbed her eyes. "I've got so much to think about, I don't know what to do."

The men rose, Nick patting Ethyl on the knee.

"And, come an' see me all the time, now. You hear, Nick? Sammy?"

Sam looked at her, his lips compressed to keep back the tears that would be unmanly to show. He nodded. "You can count on it, Eth."

She stood up and followed them out of the room. They turned to face her before opening the door, as if wanting to say some last thing that might help. It was Ethyl who spoke instead, her face pale, her eyes motionless. "I've got a lot of gettin' along by myself to get used to."

They left her, very tired after their thankless mission.

They had started to drive home along 99 when Nick pulled the car into a parking space in front of a gaily-lit tavern. A group of men loudly discussed a magazine that a tall, grinning Mexican held up for the rest to see. A flickering red and blue neon sign over the door showed it to be Rex's Rockwater Club. "We need a stiffener, Bud," grunted Nick, his voice sounding weak.

"If you say so, Old Man," said Sam, responding after an extended silence. "I guess it's my turn to buy."

Climbing out of the car, they walked toward the bar. Intermittent bursts of laughter came from the crowd of men, their heads bowed over the magazine. But each paused long enough to say hello to Sam and Nick. Definitely big business, this knowing the big men in town. The two walked into the bar, and soon they had two bottles of beer in front of them. At first they said little; then Nick started talking. "Where'd you go tonight, Bud?"

"Aw, I hit Yan's place for a while, and then she had to baby-sit for her little brat of a brother so I went down to Bill's to play snooker."

"Spend a lot of time with that gal, don't you?"

"Oh, I suppose you gotta do something."

"Don't you ever work out no more, Sam? Every time I see you you're with that skirt." His voice came in irritated spurts.

"Dad, cut it out. You know I don't play football no more. I got a right to have a chick . . ."

He laid his hand on Sam's arm, sensing his false start. "I'm sorry, Bud. I'm just plain beat, I guess. You know I like yer girl? I'm sorry to start off all ass backwards. Okay?"

"You've had a rough one tonight, Pa. Take it easy." They were silent for a moment as each took a swallow of beer.

"You really got hot pants for her, Bud?"

"Well, yeh, I think so, Old Man. Yan's not as smart as most of the chicks at school, but she's a helluva lot better looking than most of 'em, and she sure isn't spoiled either. Oh, I take out some of the girls over at school and I guess they all like me. I get along pretty good with everybody. But somehow I don't feel like I fit. I just don't feel secure with those school chicks. In fact, somehow I feel older than most everybody at school."

"Well, Yanette'll be out of high school next year and then you guys can start planning something if you're still hot after her."

"We plan now, sometimes. She's old for her age, Pa."

"Yeh, she reminds me a lot of your ma when we got married. Only she's bigger. Same tits, though." He smiled, peeking to see if Sam appreciated his humor. "We were about the same ages as you two, only I was a year younger than you. But I had a job going, and I could afford to support an old lady."

Nick bought them another round of beers and they kept right on talking. Their years side by side, both wearing the same clothes, speaking the same thoughts, thinking the same thoughts —these years weighed heavier with each beer they drank. Soon their hearts shone through each alcoholic sentence. "An' ol' Beth worked her fingers to the bone, right during the depression, so her son could go to college. Hell, you hadn't even been born yet. She thought she could hear her son saying just what he wanted to do. Born, hell, you hadn't even been germinated yet." It was Nick doing most of the talking now. The time and the beers flowed on. Finally Sam spoke. "Old Man, not to change the subject, but what're you gonna do about the shop?"

"Oh, hell, kid, I don't know." His voice came in beery gasps.

"I might even give the whole God damned shootin' match to you."
He narrowed his eyes as if listening to a playback of his words.
"You! Hell, what am I sayin'? If I did that, it'd mean that I was
gittin' old and givin' in to my little upstart punk kid that's hardly
dry behind the ears." The teeth stood out prominently in a fixed
grin.

"Oh, hell, Old Man, you're not gettin' old—just weak." He
thumped Nick in the chest as though he were tapping a water-
melon for ripeness.

"Why, you wise little infant, you. Jus' remember, I can still
clean your bony ass in a arm rassle any time of your young life."

"Stand up for yer big words, Old Man," demanded Sam,
plopping an elbow on the counter.

"Punk kid!" snarled Nick, steadying himself so that he could
line his arm up with his son's. The arms clenched and swayed
back and forth like two elephant trunks locking together. Strips
of muscle stood out on them and glistened in the half-light of the
barroom. Nick forced Sam's arm back almost to the counter;
then the son got his second wind, and, with gnashing teeth and a
guttural roar, slammed Nicks' hand back against the woodwork
with a jar that overturned his bottle. The beer poured out, ran
across the bar, and spattered down the front of Nick's pants in a
steady stream. Neither made any attempt to stand the bottle up.
The other patrons, clad in khaki and faded blue, yelled with
pleasure at the demonstration, and the dust rose from their gar-
ments as they slapped each other with glee. The two gladiators
fell against each other, happily exhausted and laughing insanely.

"You little horse-ass think you're pretty good, beatin' yer old
man," Nick laughed, slipping a woolly arm around Sam's neck
and squeezing hard. "It's a God damn cinch you never got your
God damn muscle from no books!"

"Hell, no, I got it from doin' all your work all summer, you
weak ol' fogey." Sam broke the hold and drunkenly whacked
Nick across the back, falling forward and knocking his own bottle
down.

Their heads fell heavily against the counter, lay there serenely
in pools of beer, and then swiveled and stared at each other, the
ale running down their ears and across their cheeks. Faintly they
recognized the victory in each other's watery eyes.

"You think you're strong enough to be my partner, Punk?"

"You think you're strong enough to handle me, Old Fogey?"

The heads slid gently along the counter, the father's lips meeting his son's nose and kissing it softly. The bond, the gambit, was sealed tenderly, as by two lovers at marriage.

"It's time to plan, Bud."

"Okay, Pa."

They forced themselves to sit up and look around. The heavy patronage had begun to desert the dark room in anticipation of another day's work. A blackboard sat in the corner, blank except from fragments of several baseball scores. Nick slid off the stool and motioned for Sam to follow as he walked toward the board. They tried it one way, and then the next, and when they were satisfied they walked over to an old man sitting at the bar. They pointed to the blackboard. The old man wore paint-stained trousers and pulled out a pair of steel-rimmed glasses to see the board.

"We want her like that, Ule," said Sam.

"Any time you're feelin' sober's okay, Ule," said Nick.

The old man looked at them, smiled understandingly, nodded, and pulled out a sheet of paper and a stub of a pencil. Nick threw a half-dollar on the counter and called in a slurred voice, "Beer for the bes' artist inna whole God damned world." The father and son staggered toward the door. They turned before passing through, and leaning against one another like giant stumps, repeated the chalked words on the blackboard:

"Ellington & Son—Star Service."

Beth heard the tires slide wildly on the gravel that night and she knew *her* son was dead. In fact, Beth almost died herself. She lay the night next to the hulking form sleeping alcoholically beside her, and the tenacious spirit was all but drained from her tired body. The umbilical cord had been finally severed after twenty years, and Beth was not surprised to find that it was she who went hungry. The flow of nourishment had been reversed at some time in the past, and from that time on it was the son that had given life to the mother. Now it was cut, before the birth of new life had taken place, and the deprived fetus would finally starve to an early death.

But there still was a quiver of life, and there was food if the organism could only gasp it. More particularly, there was a spirit that felt itself decaying though it knew that it would suffer long agonizing moments before it would be allowed to die peacefully. And it suffered a long time, and though it smelled the odor of death, it heard the fervent pleas of life. Just before the death it struggled, and the light of life shone through. Mother Nature's sword cut through the barriers of darkness with its double edge gleaming, and the people of Rockwater stepped back in amazement to see "Something God Hisself musta let slip under His nose." The life flowed back in nourishing gusts.

If it had taken ten years the first time, it took twenty to happen the second time around. Beth Ellington, "amazing Beth Ellington," was pregnant again at forty-seven years of age. (She'd even fooled them a little more than they realized. She had actually turned forty-eight the night Sam was supposed to have gone back to school.)

In the ensuing months the town yokels would watch Beth proudly walk the streets of Rockwater, her maternity dress stretched to its fullest as she did her shopping, and they'd guess which was the biggest, "the kid or the ma."

The following June, strangely enough on precisely the same warm day that Sam Ellington was married to Yanette Watson, Beth Ellington gave birth to a six-pound baby boy. It was one of two births that day. Ol' Nick's wife had also been born.

Nancy Packer

Night Guard

" 'Man's age-old melancholy, the coming of autumn,' " said
Mr. Fisher, looking around the table at his daughter Charlotte
and her two children. "That's Whitman, I think." He knew he
had the thought, suitable for the evening, but had he quoted the
words just right?

"The roast won't be worth eating if you don't go ahead and
carve, Papa," said Charlotte, sitting at the other end of the table.
She said it offhand, giving information, but it got to him. There
she goes, he thought. What pleasure does she get from always
telling me? She was a large full-fleshed woman going smiling,
he remembered once telling her, through a pale-pink middle age
and always talking on tiptoe. He knew that trick all right. Meant
it was he who picked the quarrels every time. The way good
women got their way. She was a good woman, but he was not to
be bullied by her or anyone.

"Come to think of it, it's not Whitman, it's Bryant," he said.

His grandson Adam clattered his knife and spoon together,
an impatient gesture hidden under cover of accident. Enough for
Mr. Fisher to notice, but not enough to justify noticing. The family took so much of his time these days, just thinking about them,
figuring out their whys and wherefores. They were so close he
couldn't simply accept them as he once had, he had to understand
them and guard against them. Guard against them, wasn't that a
comment though? That was the trouble with retirement, too much
intensive cultivation, you might say.

With permission from the *Kenyon Review*, Vol. XXIII, Winter 1961. © 1961 by Nancy Packer.

Yet it wasn't all bad. In spite of these irritations, he liked the company, and he liked most of what he knew about them. Especially Julia, he thought, turning to look at her. There she was, deciding between Whitman and Bryant, and knowing the difference too. Plenty smart for eighteen. Black-haired and blue-eyed, small and quick, just as he had been. She seemed more his own daughter than Charlotte's and more than Charlotte was or ever had been. And when she teased him, as he knew she was fixing to do, turning her head so that what she said would sort of slide at him, it made him feel as alive as a young man.

"Whitman never was old enough to make a remark like that," she said. "It must have been Bryant." He made a swipe at her with his napkin and laughed and was about to reply in kind when Adam said,

"I'm getting hunger pains, Grandpa. Are we going to eat or aren't we? Man ate before he ever read poetry, you know."

"Yes," said Mr. Fisher, feeling his old quickness working for him, "and he lived in trees and had lice and wore bearskins instead of those smart tweeds you're got on. So what does that prove? And besides," he went on, "I'm getting mighty tired of carving. Night after night. Why, I suppose I've carved 5,000 roasts in my day." Before the words were well out, he regretted saying them, regretted his tiredness that brought them out. He could feel the family moving in on him, grabbing what he said as a sign of surrender.

"It is a bore," said Charlotte, cheerful and indifferent as if they hadn't been tussling over that one for months. "Let's have it done in the kitchen."

"A handsome piece of meat should be seen whole," he said.

"The man should carve," said Julia. "He should stand up and carve."

"I could do it," offered Adam.

"No," said Mr. Fisher in his hardest voice. "I'm the one to do the carving and I'm the one's going to." So that was that. He didn't mean to be rude but they pushed him so. It took all he could do sometimes to refrain from asking Who buys the meat? Who pays the bills? Who supports the household? Charlotte had forgotten her promise, made when she brought her two children home after she was widowed, that he was to take care of her and not the other way around. Let's get it said now once and for all, he had told her, it's my house and I'm in charge. We won't mention it again. And he hadn't in spite of provocation.

He picked up the carving knife and tore at the roast so viciously, the knife whacking instead of slicing, that it divided, fell apart in no time, and he knew, without looking up, that Adam and Charlotte were searching out the small pieces of meat he had slung out on the white tablecloth.

"Adam," he said, passing him a plate, "you left the car unlocked again last night."

"Nobody's going to take the car."

"Take it or not, I want it locked."

"No sense making it too easy," said Julia.

Adam turned to her. "Then you lock it," he said.

Although Mr. Fisher knew the retort was really meant for him, he waited for Julia to answer.

"When I drive it, I do," she said. Airy voice showing the steel within. "It doesn't take too much effort. You just turn the key. Grandpa wants it locked, lock it."

"That's right," said Mr. Fisher, lifting his hand to silence the deeper quarrel that might emerge. "It was long about 2:00 that I woke up. I never sleep through the night anymore." He knew he had said that before, but it had been true before and he refused to be ashamed. Then, remembering back, they were hardly with him, it was just himself alone and the dinner hour had turned to 2:00. "I heard something like somebody tinkering around the car, and I went out to see. I didn't turn on the light, just slipped out to the front porch. I'm certain someone was there. I saw a shadow on the other side of the car." Then he was back at the table, bringing memory's residue of his fear and his pride. He felt himself beginning to smile. "So I just went out to the car and all around it. Whoever it was must have run off. I guess I scared them off. But the car door was unlocked, Adam."

"You went out to the car at 2:00 at night in your nightshirt?" asked Charlotte, looking grieved and scandalized.

"Don't fret, the neighbors didn't see me." He winked at Julia when she laughed at his joke. "Adam, I want you to . . ."

". . . lock the car door," finished Adam. His bland heavy face took on an unaccustomed worry. "All right, I will, Grandpa.

But you shouldn't be on the streets that late by yourself. Somebody might clout you over the head."

"You might catch cold," said Charlotte.

"Between you and the car, let them have the car," said Adam.

"Why, I thought you put a higher value on that car than that," said Mr. Fisher.

"All right then," said Adam, turning red. He began to eat with fury.

Mr. Fisher felt a little ashamed. "Take a joke, son," he said quietly. "You should know when a man's joking. I appreciate your concern. Though it's misguided."

"No," said Charlotte, "it is not misguided. Adam is quite right. You might get hurt out there."

"Hush," said the old man, "I had my gun." He opened a biscuit and breathed in the fragrant steam. He loved biscuits, nice soft pads to melt the butter on.

"What?" asked Charlotte.

"You what?" asked Adam.

Julia looked at him and shook her head in warning, as if to say Now just listen, you shouldn't have told them that. She was quick to know where the talk was headed, and quick to avoid unnecessary commotion. Like him in so many ways. But sometimes she didn't know when commotion was necessary.

"Did you decide between Bryant and Whitman?" she asked.

"Wait," said Charlotte. "You say you had your gun. What gun?"

"It was Bryant all right," he said. He turned to Charlotte. "I keep my .38 under my pillow nights, so I wasn't afraid. So no call for you to be." Yet, perhaps it would have been better not to tell them. Why did they challenge and push him so? to say things better left unsaid?

"Now really, Papa," said Charlotte, moving in fast. "That's extremely dangerous. It's unbelievable. A gun. Now really. I mean. Suppose you did see somebody, what could you do wouldn't make it worse? That's when you'd really be in trouble. That's when it'd really be dangerous. That's when . . . Really."

"If I saw somebody," said Mr. Fisher, "I'd shoot is all I'd do."

"Shoot?'" said Adam in a low shout. "You can't go around

shooting every time you see a shadow or something. Good Lord. Suppose it was a neighbor? Suppose it was me? Good Lord." He thrashed a moment in his chair, looking exasperated, the old man thought, as only a bland usually good-natured person can. His mother's son. Once aroused, a herd of cattle to stop.

"How many times have I shot you so far, Adam?" he asked. "Don't be a fool."

"But your nightmares," said Charlotte, keeping a level reasoning voice. "You're liable to wake up shooting. I didn't even know you had a gun. Much less . . . Under your pillow. Carrying it out to the sidewalk. Now really, Papa."

"Come on now," said Julia. "Every man has a gun."

Her mother shot her a silencing look. "You know how you are, Papa. You have those terrible nightmares. I can hear you way at the other end of the house. And with Adam and Julia coming in so late . . ."

"I am not going to shoot Adam and/or Julia. I am not a complete fool. Yet. So let's have no more of this nonsense," he said, letting the tone of final command come into his voice. That would stop them once and for all. "When I came to this town 61 years ago, every man-jack here carried a pistol in his hip pocket. And times then weren't as bad as now. Not near as bad. Why, I bet not one of you read the evening paper about that murder not two miles from our doorstep. Armed robbery. Killed a filling station man didn't even have a gun."

But they wouldn't be distracted, their thoughts were stuck. They knew he wasn't to be bullied, it was senseless to try, but they registered their protest with silence. He turned to Julia and said, "What do you think? They do so much talking you haven't said a word and after all you're one of the ones going to be shot."

Julia put down her fork and she spoke so quickly he knew she had been planning it all along. " 'Always the loud angry crowd,' " she quoted, " 'very angry and very loud, Law is we.' " She turned to him and looked, he thought, as if she had swallowed a dozen canaries. " 'And always the soft idiot softly, Me.' "

"Don't be rude to your grandfather," said Charlotte.

"You call that poetry?" asked Mr. Fisher.

"I call it Auden," said Julia.

"And I call it words words words. They ought to put some of these young poets back in the oven a while. They need more baking."

"Young? Auden?" said Julia. "Come on, Grandpa, Browning wasn't the last poet in the world."

"Who said he was? Who said he was?" Mr. Fisher rushed to say. "I've never been afraid of the new and you know it. If it's good. Because I don't happen to like your Mr. Auden doesn't mean I'm an old fogey. But the trouble with you," he went on, wanting to sting back a little, "is, you're afraid of what's old and tried and that's a fact. If it's old you just automatically think it's no good, not worth your fooling with. It's got to be brand new for you else you just dismiss it."

"You're old," she said.

"What do you mean by that?" asked Mr. Fisher quietly.

"I don't notice anybody around here able to just dismiss you," she said, laughing, and he felt her laughter like the lifting of night. "You'd just go up and get that gun or something."

"That's right," he said. And he thought of what to say so quickly that he was amazed with himself. "That's my last granddaughter painted on the wall, looking as if she were alive." He was filled with a rare sense of rightness and he smiled at each of them.

He woke sitting straight up in bed, his fingers pressed against the bones of his face. The covers were a turmoil, half on the floor, half twisted around his chest and shoulders and chin. Then it came back to him. Someone was beating him about the face and head. He was a small boy and it was late night and someone was beating him about the face and attempting to smother him with the covers.

He looked around the room, not sure, even awake, that it had been only a nightmare. The thin arms of the clock, a pale misty green in the darkness, registered 11:37. He had been in bed hours, asleep at least two. Why the nightmare? What had awakened him?

He turned his head sideways off the pillow, heard nothing but the soothing murmur of the clock. He lay back and sighed, waiting to relax and calm down. His was a silent insulated room, down the hall, separated by an unused bedroom from where the others slept. And familiar to him, containing his things from years of accumulation, his huge dresser with the peeling mirror, his cracked marble-top table he could reach out and put his hand on, his double bed with its tall headboard of rough soft wood carved into knobs of roses and leaves. What a lot of excuses and subterfuges they found to get him to throw the thing away, the ugly thing. The ugly thing he had had for 50 years or so. He reached above his head and searched out the very center of the headboard, a monster splintering rose he could, and did, put his finger in up to the first knuckle. Himself again, he got out of bed to smooth the covers.

As he pulled the sheet up and took hold of the blanket, he heard the sound. He straightened at once, letting the covers slip from his hands. It came again, a rubbing sound like a shoe sliding over carpet. The house creaked, settled, the boards whimpered.

Someone was downstairs. The thing he had long dreaded and expected and listened for and waited for each night had happened. A stranger was in the house, would enter the rooms in silence and darkness, rob, rape, murder. And there was no one to stop him. No one except himself.

He forced himself to bend down, reach under the pillow and drag out the gun. It was cold in his hand and slippery from the moisture of his palm. But as he wiped the handle with the sheet and released the safety catch, the miracle happened. The surge of strength. The concentration of purpose. All right, he whispered, all right. He slipped his feet into his slippers, buttoned the top button of his nightshirt and opened the door with his left hand. His right hand held the gun.

The hall was almost in darkness, the night light below threw long dim shadows along the stairway. Quietly—there was only the sound of the back of his slippers slapping softly against his heel—he made his way down the stairs.

On the last step he paused and listened. A breathing sound, faint, as if deliberately through the mouth. He was sure it came from the dining room. There might be two, he thought, there might be more than two. I might not see in time, act quick enough. Then what? Now stop that. Stop that.

He forced himself to step off the last step, slide one foot in

front of the other over the carpet. His step was uncertain, each
foot, as he slid it, wavering, resistant, rebelling against his control. And his arms, hands, neck, tongue, lips turned resistant,
moved each by a command of its own struggling against his command to go forward. And then he himself wished to turn back,
to sneak up the steps to his bed and rejoin his sleep.

The gun. In time, before turning, he remembered that. He
held the butt in one hand, the barrel in the other, and pressed the
tip of his little finger in the barrel. What could they have more
potent than the gun? What could they do he could not do first and
better? What were they he was not more? Everything came together and he ceased to tremble. He drew his arm up until the
gun was straight out in front of him, his finger firm on the trigger.
Turning the knob of the dining-room door, throwing out his foot
to kick it open—gun poised, finger ready—he shouted:

"All right, all right, I'll shoot."

It was Julia. The picture was distinct in the light of the
dining-room chandelier he had not noticed (did no light seep
over the door, none under, none around? had he simply failed to
detect that obvious sign of innocence? failed to save himself this
sudden agony by noticing?): Julia, the book propped against the
squat candelabrum; the glass of milk; scattered sheets of paper.
A picture he might, if he had only thought to, have imagined,
almost seen through the heavy door. Julia's head came up at once,
ducked down, her shoulder jerked up, warding off the expected
blow. It hardly looked like Julia, always so gay and clean, now
furtive and frightened.

"Grandpa," she cried, "it's just me."

"I know," he said.

He dropped the gun to his side and tried to conceal it in the
folds of his nightshirt. He felt his face warming and his eyes
clouding, and the sharp picture blurred. He felt, rather than saw,
her startled eyes upon him, seeing the thin absurd sticks of his
legs, his absurd fluttering nightshirt, his loose-skinned old face,
the gun. He knew how she saw. He saw it so himself.

"I thought . . ." he began. What should he say?

Julia looked away, set aside the glass, closed the book, pushed
the candelabrum from her, seemed deliberately to compose herself. She's just a child, he thought. She's still a child.

"You heard something," she said, calm, matter-of-fact, a voice he quickly hated. "But even so, Grandpa, you oughtn't grab that gun and come running. You might have shot me or something. You might have fallen and shot yourself."

"I did not," he said.

"Might," she corrected him. "Suppose I'd maybe just cut off the light or something. Suppose I'd been walking around in the dark. You might have shot me."

"I wouldn't hurt you, you know that."

"Not deliberately," she agreed. "But be reasonable." She smiled and he could feel it coming, the voice on tiptoe. "You've always been the most reasonable man in the world. The soul of reason. Now haven't you? With your nightmares and those bad eyes of yours. And that gun. Suppose it just went off. Accidentally."

The soul of reason. The putting of it like that made it seem not so. Don't talk to me like that, young lady. "I heard something," he said.

"This isn't like you, Grandpa. You've never been afraid before. You've never kept that gun so close. Why, even that summer we spent in the middle of nowhere you kept it in the trunk, not under your pillow. Remember? So now why?"

"Because . . ." he began, but he couldn't explain. Lamely, even knowing it would be the wrong thing to say, he said, "Somebody might hurt you or Adam."

"Let us take care of ourselves," she said. "Adam's six inches taller than you and forty pounds heavier. Let him take care of himself."

"He's just a boy."

"A boy? At twenty-two? You told me that when you were twenty-two . . ."

"Yes." He knew it was useless to go on. For her, for now, he was hopelessly in the wrong. His mind took another tack. Dangling him on my knee, giving him 50 cents for a movie, teaching him to drive the car, sending him to a fine school. For what? For this? And now her. "You think I'm foolish, too," he said. That ought to bring her up.

She said, "Promise me, no more cops and robbers."

Her hand under his elbow, she guided him through the doorway, and snapped off the light in the dining-room. There was only the night light burning and the hall was quiet and hazy. Quickly he drew the gun up, closing Julia's hand in the crook of his elbow.

"Now what?" she asked. "What is it now?"

"Nothing." He dropped his arm to his side.

"It's all right. There's no one in the house. Just us."

Her fingers tapping reassurance on his forearm revived him and he jerked away. So she did think he was incompetent, an old fool, ready for the trash can. He would not stand for that from her, from any of them, and he would tell her so. He felt anger beginning, but it was too strong, he knew, to be authority, too weak to be force. He had learned not to act in such a balance. Yet so often now he felt it. At a better time he would tell her that he would not stand it.

At the landing of the stairs he stopped and drew back the curtains and gazed out over the housetops, vague below him, to the lights of the city. Julia stood at his side, looking as they had so often looked out of that window, enjoying their small view, and it seemed to him that there would be no better moment to bring her back to him, to save her from the conspiracy. He thought for a ripe quotation.

"You say you know everything, Julia," he said, making his voice a teasing challenge. "Tell me where this is from: 'Now fades the glimmering landscape on the sight, And all the world a solemn stillness holds.'" He grinned at her, cocked his head, waited for her to invent a smart sassy answer.

"I don't know," she said. "Where?"

"Oh," said the old man, hurting with disappointment. "I guess you don't know everything after all, I guess you're not as smart as you claim."

"I guess not," she said. "Where's it from?"

But the name was gone and he was confusion again. He glanced out the window, saw that it was mostly only darkness and night and the trees were bare. He let the curtain drop.

"Where's what from?" he asked. Too late, he knew what. "Oh, it's from . . ." But the name wouldn't come. "I don't remember. I forget."

"Everyone forgets," she said.

"I'm an old man, my memory's pretty dim." With that, a turn

he had never taken before, he felt himself grow weak, and he wanted her arm around him. And he hated her, as he hated Adam and Charlotte.

"Let's go on to bed," she said, taking his arm again. Easily, without his noticing for a moment more than a beginning sense of absence, she slipped the gun from his hand and held it away from him. Was it Julia? He would not have believed it, that she would even want to take his gun, never that she would dare. Had she changed so much, and he hadn't even noticed? Yet each plan he had to defend himself and regain the gun—points, quarrels, fights, commands flowed through his mind—turned foolish to him, weak, without dignity, unlike himself. Silent, still planning, he followed her the rest of the way up the stairs and into his room.

"Grandpa, sleep well," she said after she had smoothed the covers and he had obediently gotten into bed. Then, with decision, she said, "It just has to be this way." She leaned toward him, lips formed to kiss, but he shook her off, brought his shoulder up between them and caught the kiss on the tip of his ear.

"Now give it to me, Julia," he said, "and you go right on to bed. You've teased enough." He waited a moment and then went another way. "Every man has got to have a gun. You said so yourself. I don't want to get angry with you, but that's enough. Now."

"I'm sorry," was all she said, moving toward the door.

He realized his mistake. He had been too easy with her, coddled her, encouraged her to impudence. "Give me that gun," he said, barking each word. In total rushing anger he snapped his fingers and slapped his thigh. She had pushed him too far and now she would see. "When it's you gets scared that's different. Is that it? Are you a coward, scared over nothing? Scared at the sight of a gun? When Adam acts like a fool, you think it's funny. But when you act like a fool, you pretend it's because I am a fool, a senile old fool."

"Don't, Grandpa."

"At least Adam's honest about it. By God, give me that gun. If you don't put that gun on that table before I count three . . . Julia, Julia."

She turned off the light. "Good night," she whispered in a voice cracked and shrill with tears. She closed the door after her and at the sound of the tongue of the door clicking into place and in the sudden darkness of the room, his anger fell apart. She was gone and with her she had taken his gun. Kindly. Even in his mounting fear he knew she meant to do kindness. Not mean or angry, she had simply walked out holding his gun. But without it how could he endure? face up? challenge?

He fell back against the pillows, drew his knees close to his chest, his body pressing deep into the mattress. Sudden sweat rolled down his temples and wet the edges of his cheek. He pulled the sides of the pillow up around his ears and pressed tight with his fingers. He heard the creak of the floor, the muffled closing of a door, the strange sounds of night.

Peter Shrubb

The Gift

What you get for nothing is exactly nothing, in Australia as
much as anywhere else, and Bill Fry knew it as well as anyone in
Sydney. That was why, on the autumn Sunday when Frannie, his
wife, asked him if they were going to tell his parents that afternoon that she was happily p-r-e-g-n-a-n-t again—spelling it out
because Clarissa, their daughter, five years old and all ears, was
in the room with them—he quite cheerfully answered, "I don't
see that we have to; I don't see what's in it for us, except pub-
licity." It rolled off his tongue like gospel.

He was sitting on the window seat in the living room, with the
sun on his back. Clarissa faced him from the center of the gray
carpet, where she was having her ponytail tied. She looked
solemn—and vacant, as if her whole mind pointed backward, to
the ponytail. Behind her, Frannie said, "Oh, Bill."

" 'Oh, Bill' nothing," Bill said. "Tell Mum and you tell the
world. It's our own private business. . . . Our child and nobody
else's." Clarissa, touching her hair with her fingertips, walked
away to the door.

Frannie said, "I really don't see the harm in it."

"What Mum doesn't know, she won't miss." But just as he
said it, he imagined how his mother would smile and smile if she
did know. "*At least* two children—everyone should have *at least*
two!" she would say, and his father would make up some joke
about the expense. His mother would say she didn't care what it
was as long as it was healthy.

With permission from *The New Yorker*, Vol. 37, November 18, 1961. © 1961 The New Yorker
Magazine, Inc.

Bill saw clearly how important a vessel he was, to contain so great a gift, and, feeling generous already—admired, beloved, made much of—as he went toward the door after Clarissa, he said, "I'll tell you what; if it comes up in a natural way, I don't mind."

Frannie smiled. "We can't leave it till they can see for themselves, you know."

"Anyone interested enough to look could see it now."

He tickled Clarissa all the way out to the car, and while they were waiting for Frannie to find her bag he chased her around the lawn. She shrieked, he cackled, and when Frannie came out at last she said they sounded like a zoo. "Whose zoo?" Bill tried to say, and got so tangled up in the two words that Clarissa nearly fell over with laughing.

Then off they set in the little blue Vauxhall, and for some minutes no one said anything. Bill drove carefully, and Frannie and Clarissa watched the Sunday-afternoon houses go past. On weekdays these houses were nothing; they were all red brick, with green and brown lawns in front of them, hedges in front of the lawns, and a few gray and brown trees, and people hid inside them for days at a time. But on Sunday afternoons, hey presto! Children flew over the lawns and around the trees, and even adults, like weights the children had dragged out after them, lay slumped here and there in corners, folded over flower beds and hedges, laboring minutely. There was plenty for people in cars to see.

A bulbous stone fence guarded the hedge that hid Mr. Fry's house, but the little Vauxhall found its way through the gate, past the rhododendrons lining the drive, and pulled up in the thin shade of a bottle-bush tree. Against the fence in the small back yard, between the lilac and the frangipani, in the sun but not the wind, Mr. and Mrs. Fry sat reading the Sunday paper. They waved, and from the car Bill and Clarissa waved back. Bill saw his mother laugh and say something that had no chance of reaching them over the loud death rattle of the engine, and all at once he felt so overwhelmed with love for her simpleness, which his secret would soon beatify, that he feared his face might already have given both him and his secret away. "You look like a couple of old porpoises sunning yourselves," he called.

"Porpoise yourself," his mother replied, coming over to open the door for Clarissa.

"Whozoo!" Clarissa hooted, laughing again. "That's what Daddy said!"

"Darling," Mrs. Fry said, lifting her out.

"Porpoises are in fact the gayest and most graceful creatures in the kingdom of the sea," Bill said.

His mother waved her hand in his face. "You," she said. She looked for Frannie and, finding her, smiled.

"It's lovely to have a spot like this out of the wind," Frannie said as she came round the front of the car. She gave Mrs. Fry a quick kiss and then stood back a pace. "I do like your hair."

Bill knew immediately from her voice that she had not told the whole truth, and silently condemned her for it. But his mother's ear was not so experienced, or perhaps was dulled a little by wishfulness, or age. "They have another man. Do you really?" Embarrassed at looking so new, and at showing her pleasure, she held her hands up and minced around like a manne-quin so that they should see her head back, front, and sides.

"Exactly like a porpoise," Bill said, climbing out of the car. His father snorted, and Bill turned to him. "And there's the other one surfacing! Avast!"

Mrs. Fry turned to Frannie again. "What on earth has got into *him*?"

Frannie laughed, and Bill took off his father's green-brimmed canvas hat and put it on his own head. "Keep it under your little bonnet, *I* always say."

"Has he been in the sun, Frannie?"

"Come inside, all of you," said Mr. Fry in his deep voice.

Clarissa led, stretching her legs up the green steps to the back veranda and standing at the top to see if the others could manage them so comfortably. They all did, Frannie smoothing her skirt, Mrs. Fry watching Clarissa, Mr. Fry rubbing his gray stubble of hair, Bill watching his father's strong square back.

In the kitchen dimness it was cooler. Frannie sank into one of the chairs round the big table with a sigh. "Ooh, I get tired in the afternoons these days."

A dead giveaway, it seemed to Bill. He started to smile, but from shyness covered his smile with his hand and made it go.

Mrs. Fry tickled the soft back of Clarissa's neck and said, "One day you'll have to let us take this little bundle off your hands for a week."

One day sooner than you imagine, Bill thought. But he stood there with his hand on his mouth like a monkey and said nothing; after all, no one had said anything to him.

Clarissa pulled out the chair next to her mother's and climbed up on it. Mr. Fry bent over her. "Would you like to stay with Grandma and Grandpa in their house, Clarissa?" Mrs. Fry smiled and folded her arms on her waist. She was not a large woman, and her face was lined and her hair thinning, but to Bill she gave an impression of strength still.

Clarissa rested her chin on the edge of the table and put her hands over her ears. "Mmm," she said softly, a little doubtfully. Bill smiled at her.

"And sleep in the big square bed at night, *all* by yourself?" Mr. Fry went on. "And let Mummy and Daddy have a nice holiday somewhere on the coast or in the mountains for a week, *all* by *them*selves?"

Clarissa put her hands over her eyes and said nothing.

"I think she likes her own little bed at home best," Mr. Fry said, patting her head. And sententiously added, "And so do I."

Clarissa slapped her hands on the table, and her ponytail flew out. "You'd be to big for my bed!"

Everyone laughed but Bill. Clarissa, swinging on her grandfather's arm, smiled at him. Mrs. Fry went over to the stove.

Bill sat down, and Mr. Fry sat opposite him with his hands on the table. To Bill, his broad, deep, flat fingernails—perfectly self-sufficient, eternal—looked like bright, clean stones.

"How's life treating you?" his father asked.

Bill made a face at the tabletop, grunted, looked up, and saw that no one had been watching for his reply. Frannie was listening to his mother, and his father had eyes only for Clarissa, who now stood with one foot on the bottom rung of her mother's chair and one on the bottom rung of her grandfather's. "Don't do that, Clarissa," Bill said quickly. "They're not made to stand on." He remembered how angry his father had always been when things got broken, and for just long enough to be recognized there stood in his mind the possibility that Clarissa might not be a welcome visitor in his father's house.

"On these old chairs it doesn't matter," said his mother from the stove. "You're only young once."

Heartened by this open declaration, Bill looked up at his father again. "I hear Surtex are putting out a par issue one for four," he said.

"Take them," Mr. Fry said quietly.

Without thinking to the end of what he was saying, Bill said, "That'll bring you up to the five-hundred mark, won't it?"

Mr. Fry smiled. "You'll find out about all that when I'm dead."

Frannie said, "It's lovely getting a letter about a par issue. Bill's explained it all to me, and when this one came I opened it and looked up what Surtex were selling for; and, really, we could get rid of the new shares tomorrow for half as much *again* as we're giving!"

"I wouldn't call it giving," Mr. Fry said.

Mrs. Fry came to the table with the teapot. "If I opened his mail, this monster here would bite my head off."

"Oh, it's only if I know it's just business stuff," Frannie said.

"That's all we seem to get."

"How awful!" Frannie exclaimed.

Her voice carried such a charge of life that Bill had for an instant a clear vision of his father's dry days, so unlike his own, and instead of being angry he almost felt sorry for him.

Frannie said, "My day's ruined if there's no mail."

Bill laughed. "That says a great deal for marriage, doesn't it?"

Mr. Fry now had Clarissa on his lap. "This says a lot," he replied, nuzzling her head with his chin. Clarissa wriggled under him and reached for a slice of buttered date loaf.

"Eat the date as well as the butter," Bill said, and could not help smiling at the eye-rolling, insincere nods with which she answered him. Like a conspirator, Clarissa smiled back.

For a minute or two, no one spoke. Bill watched Frannie and thought that one look at her beautifully pure skin and eyes should be all anyone needed, to know she was pregnant. Why his mother failed to remark on it with joy he could not imagine.

His father, giving Clarissa a sip of tea, said, "And how's life treating you, Bill?"

After a second, Bill said, "Not often." His mother attended to him this time, and nodded; but then he saw her glance slide off toward Clarissa and her face absolutely fill with light as she asked, "Not too hot for your little tongue?"

Clarissa shook her head. "Give me some more, Grandpa— more, more, more, more!" She acted, because now they were all watching her, and with play desperation she pressed her hands over Mr. Fry's mouth so that he could not drink anything.

"Poor Grandpa!" Frannie said. "Aren't you going to let him have any of his tea at all?"

Mrs. Fry put her hand over Frannie's wrist and said in a kindly voice, "How are you feeling now, dear?"

Bill began to wonder, but all Frannie said was, "Like a new woman."

Still warmly holding Frannie's hand, his mother went on, "Bill always liked his tea, too. I could always get round Bill, when he was a boy, with a cup of tea. He was like an old lady with his cup of tea."

"Get round him?" Frannie laughed. "When did you have to get round him, for goodness' sake?"

Mrs. Fry threw her hands in the air. "When did I not!"

"What's all this?" Bill asked.

His mother only smiled. "We survived it all," she said, and began telling Frannie about a Mrs. Jukes, who had not.

"Ha! Old Jukey!" Mr. Fry exclaimed in an unkind way, and returned to Clarissa.

Bill tried to listen to his mother, but Mrs. Jukes was nothing to him. Survived all what? Who? He began to feel left out of things, and inside him the secret seemed to have grown smaller; he imagined it now as being the size of the baby itself—too small, probably, to be seen. Suddenly he remembered what it was that they had all survived. It was his being the only child—and more a repository for hope than a child, he had often felt; more a well, from which pride and comfort were regularly to be drawn. He remembered the arguments this very kitchen had been noisy with when he had begun not to provide them.

Clarissa, the last to finish, gulped down the dregs of her grandfather's tea, jumped off his lap, and ran out to find something to do in the back yard. While Mrs. Fry and Frannie started washing up, Bill and his father went through to the living room.

"The record club sent a Mozart piano concerto this month," Mr. Fry said.

Bill said, "Let's hear it, then."

Halfway through the first movement, Mrs. Fry tiptoed in. Bill sat up with a start when he saw her—she came in so softly—and then immediately and with delight guessed she had come to say that she knew. He felt his ears begin to redden and heat. He pressed his hands over them, gave his shoes a wry grin, and waited. But his mother merely stole over to the magazine rack, took up the top *House & Garden*, turned, and began her silent journey back to the door. Bill looked up in complete astonishment. His mother smiled at him and put her finger to her lips. It was the reverse of what he wanted, and angrily he said the reverse of what he would have like to say. "If you think you're interrupting, you're perfectly right!" he snapped. His mother did not answer; on her face came a strained, set look in which he read that she had not even heard what he said, but only the irritation in which he had said it.

The door closed behind her, and for a moment Bill felt utterly locked in. He looked up, and saw the orange curtains that had silently strangled and suffocated light for as long as he could remember. From the curtain his eye fled to the familiar brown-stained picture rail, and followed it over two imitation-bronze plaques, to the Van Gogh above the mantelpiece, to the Toulouse-Lautrec he himself had given them two years before, to the Paul Nash prints neat in a row. He felt sure, today, that the plaques and pictures were there to hide something. Perhaps his father had a safe behind each one, each safe hiding its contents from the other safes. Everything hidden, everything buttressed. A bullet, even if it penetrated the dark front of the house, could never burrow through the stuffing in the back of the settee.

The first side of the record ended, and his father turned it over in silence. Without looking up again, Bill heard the music through.

Frannie and Mrs. Fry were in the back yard when Bill and his father went to join them. Behind the bulk of the house, the lilac and the frangipani were already sinking into an early dusk, and the ladies with them, in the chairs Mr. and Mrs. Fry had filled when the Vauxhall arrived. "We'll have to be getting along pretty soon," Bill announced.

"Oh, no, Daddy!" Clarissa cried. "I want to stay!"

Her exaggerated despair jangled a little in Bill's ear. More to Frannie and his mother than to Clarissa, he said, "It gets cool as soon as the sun starts going down. And if she plays inside, it always ends up with something broken." The words blew from his mouth, and in every one of them he heard his father's voice.

"I'll be good," Clarissa said.

"It isn't so easy," Bill said.

For another few minutes, Bill followed his father round the miniature vegetable garden behind the garage, listening; and then, by the time they came back to the lawn, it really was evening, with smoke in the air and a thin dark veil between earth and the blue zenith. Clarissa, pink-cheeked, stopped jumping when she saw them.

"Is it time, dear?" Frannie asked, pleasantly.

Bill nodded. Mrs. Fry hurried inside to get another *House & Garden* she wanted to lend Frannie, and in three minutes the Vauxhall was backing down the dim driveway. Bill, turning the car in a narrow street, left the waving goodbye to Frannie and Clarissa. "Come back soon!" Clarissa called.

For the first few minutes, no one spoke. Bill was glad, in his black mood, that autumn was a season of the year and early evening a time of day to which silence was sympathetic. On the footpaths, men in cardigans and pipes raked up the leaves of liquidambars and poplars slowly, as if they feared heart attacks. There were lights behind curtains. Soon everyone would be indoors, out of the dark and the cold.

They waited to turn onto the highway. Frannie said, "Your mother didn't actually say anything, but I wouldn't be surprised if she guessed."

Bill felt as if he were in a film and a great inevitable truck had just roared at him out of the dusk. "Why?" he asked quietly.

Frannie tried to see his face, but it was turned to the window. "Oh, just things she said, things she asked me. I think we should ring them up soon."

Bill jerked the car away in first. "Why wouldn't she say anything, if she thinks it?"

"Well, heavens, I don't know, Bill. I didn't think I was supposed to ask her."

"What the hell does she think she's doing, guessing things
and not saying so! Is she the keeper of the keys, or some damn
thing? Why wouldn't she come out and say it?"

"Don't shout at me, Bill," Frannie said, her own voice rising
a little. "She probably didn't say anything because you didn't.
You're being quite unreasonable."

Bill was so angry that he took his eyes from the road. "I suppose the truth is that you as good as told her! I suppose that's it,
is it?"

Frannie turned away abruptly and looked out her window.
No one said a word more. Under the Vauxhall's little shell of a
roof, by the time they reached home, they could hardly even see
one another.

Clarissa hurried over the dark lawn after Frannie, and without having to be asked sat herself at the kitchen table for supper.
She wanted bacon, but Frannie said quietly that there was no time
for bacon. So she settled for a glass of milk, a piece of toast with
peanut butter on it, and a tiny cold lamb chop left over from
lunch. Bill sat in the living room in front of the gas fire, reading
the Sunday paper. Clarissa finished her toast in silence, and then
said to her mother, who was moving around the kitchen, "There's
a boy at school called Billy, and if he's not good I'll come up to
him and say, 'Billy Davis, if you're not a good boy you'll have to
go home this minute, do you hear? This minute!' "

"Just eat up, dear, and not too much talking," Frannie said.

" 'This minute!' " Clarissa went on, staring at a bad boy who
lived in her head, raising her eyebrows at him, waving one finger.
" 'Just exactly at this very very minute! No sooter, no laner!' "
She burst into laughter. "Mummy, do you know what I just said?
I was going to say . . ."

From the living room, Bill shouted, "Clarissa!"

Frannie said, quite calmly, "Just eat up, dear. It's school
tomorrow, and you must have a big long sleep." She turned the
gas down under the potatoes, said, "You be finished by the time
I get back," and went into the living room to the fire. Bill did not
look up as she sat in the other chair, with the comics, and Frannie
did not speak to him.

When she had finished them, she called out, "Are you ready now, Clarissa?" There was no answer. "Clarissa, are you ready for your bath now?" No answer. Frannie waited, and then said, in a voice clear but not loud, "I'm in no mood for games now— are you ready? Tell me." There was still no answer. Bill lowered his paper, and Frannie, seeing him do it, got up quickly and went back to the kitchen. He heard her make a discontented sound and go through the kitchen into the hall that led to the bedrooms, switching on lights there and in the bathroom, softly calling Clarissa's name.

But in another minute or two she came back into the kitchen; she turned on the outside light and stood at the back door, calling. She went down the steps onto the back lawn, and then right around the house. When she reappeared at the back door, she was still alone.

"Haven't you found her yet, for God's sake!" Bill demanded, made more angry still by the sight of her white, frightened face. Without waiting for a reply, he stood up. "I'll find her," he said. Frannie said nothing, leaning on the corner of the sink, her face turned away.

As he crossed the room, however, his mind surrendered itself, like a thin wall falling, to all that could have happened. She might have gone for a walk, and be lost, or kidnapped, or run over; she might be in a place she could not get out of. She might already be dying. With every light in the house on, he swiftly searched each bright, empty room.

Then there was nothing else for it. He switched on the outside light and went down the back steps, as Frannie had done before. His knee gave a sort of twitch, and he felt breathless. Frannie stood at the door, watching him. "I'll go and turn the front light on," she said.

Bill looked up at her and, doing so, saw—cuddled in the corner between the steps and the back terrace, smiling brightly through the branches of a small oleander—Clarissa.

His heart shuddered as the world righted itself again. When he had breath, he said, curtly, "Come out here at once."

"I found a good place, Daddy," Clarissa said; and, holding her chop bone in one hand, she bent down to creep out under the branches.

As soon as she reached the edge of the lawn, Bill hit her on the shoulder. "What do you think you're doing?" he shouted. "Hiding! Playing games! When you were told to hurry up because it was nearly time for bed! What do you think you're doing?" He had knocked the bone out of her hand, and as she bent down to pick it up she burst into tears. He hit her again. She slipped over on the grass. "You're a naughty girl!" he shouted, and with one hand in her armpit he pulled her to her feet. "A very naughty girl!"

In the light, then, he saw her pale shocked face for the first time. He pushed her away from him, up the steps toward Frannie. "Go in with your mother and stay with her," he said.

He followed them inside and stood in the kitchen while Clarissa was led into the bathroom. "I just wanted him to come and find me!" she wailed. He went back to the fire and picked up his paper again.

His pounding heart worked to repair the damage rage and shame had done. He couldn't read; he could hardly even focus clearly. He sat back, closing his eyes against the light. But after a moment the lonely echoing darkness was more than he could bear, and he opened them again. There was peace in neither light nor dark. He heard Frannie come into the room and sit in the other chair, but he did not look at her. She didn't speak.

In a minute he stood and went back through the kitchen into the hall. He thought Clarissa could probably hear him, but to make sure she knew who it was, he coughed at her door as he pushed it open. There was no sound from the bed. He stepped over next to it and sat down on the edge. "Are you still awake, Clarissa?" he whispered.

She didn't answer.

He stroked her hair. With the tip of his finger he slowly and lightly outlined her ear, and slid from the lobe to the corner of her jaw, down to her chin, and to the hollow under her bottom lip. There he let his finger rest a minute. He knew from her breathing that she was still awake. He leaned forward and put his forehead on the pillow next to her. "I'm sorry I was angry, Clarissa," he whispered. There was no sound. "Mummy and I were frightened, little bird. We didn't know *where* you were." Saying it, he was so flooded with love that he began to lose the sense of his own location, of the conjunction of parts of his body. "I know it was just a sort of trick—but you're our only lovely little bird, and if anything happened to you I don't know what we would do." With a quick grateful movement he put his arm around her and squeezed her. "I don't know what we would do," he whispered again.

For a minute he lay there next to her in the darkness, imagining her small roundness, all her miniature perfections. Then he kissed her soft cheek and whispered good night.

He waited at the door of her silent room to gather himself for the journey back. He tried to lift his head as he entered the living room and sat down again, but it made only a passable show, and he didn't feel ready yet to look at Frannie. He shut his eyes.

Clarissa called out, "Can I get up?"

Frannie looked at Bill.

Clarissa called out again, "Can I get up, just for a minute?"

Bill nodded. Frannie went over and switched on the hall light. "Yes, come on—just for a minute. Daddy says you can get up for just a minute."

Clarissa came into the room with her hands behind her back, squinting against the light. "Come over near the fire," Bill said. "You mustn't get cold."

Frannie sat down again and Clarissa stood facing them both. "Hold out your hands," she said. "And shut your eyes."

They did as they were told. Bill smiled as something was pressed into his hand and small fingers closed his fingers down over it.

"Open your eyes," she said.

They opened their eyes. Bill wanted just to look at her, but obediently he looked at what was in his hand. It was a tiny red-and-white plastic charm that had broken from a bracelet a girl at school had given her on her fifth birthday. Frannie had a pencil sharpener.

"What are these for?" Bill asked.

"They're prizes."

Bill looked with wonder at her serene face. "Thank you very much. What are they prizes for?"

"For you and Mummy," Clarissa said. "I'm going to give you prizes often now."

Light came from behind her, fuzzing the edges of her night-gown and her hair, and from above, falling evenly on her even face. And from her face, it seemed to Bill, light fell—as if the charm were a magic one, after all—into his very soul. There was nothing hidden in her.

Bill fixed the little charm onto his key chain straightaway, to Clarissa's delight; and after she was safely tucked back into bed again, all the way driving down to his parents he thought he could see it hanging there in the dim light of the dash, and even hear the new, soft sound it made when it touched the metal. And it ran through his mind that every child is a chance, a new hope, a new possibility for goodness. For everything else, too, of course. But what else matters? Goodness is our treasure.

He knocked on the kitchen door, went in without waiting for their reply, and said to his mother, who was sitting there sewing, with a very surprised look on her face, "I didn't tell you this afternoon that we're going to have another baby. We haven't even told Clarissa yet."

His mother said "Bless you!" and came round and hugged him. His father said that if they were triplets Bill might be able to sell them to a cereal firm for advertising purposes. But he wasn't serious.

Arthur Edelstein

That Time of Year

"I take the towel, I dry the hand, I hang the towel, I open the door, I leave the room, I close the door, I go the kitchen, I take the breakfast . . ."

"Not the breakfast," Ralph interrupted. "Say what, Mr. Gomez."

Tapping nervously at his mustache, Mr. Gomez stiffened abruptly, the small classroom chair creaking with the movement. He glanced furtively at Mrs. Arundel squeezed into the seat beside him, his eyes pleading for rescue. Mrs. Arundel remained impassive.

"Que? *Que* come?" Ralph asked. *"What* do you eat?"

"Ahhh!" Gomez relaxed. "I go the kitchen, I take the salad, I . . ."

"No no. No take the salad."

"No take the salad?" Gomez went wide-eyed with astonishment.

"Egg, Mr. Gomez. Egg. This is breakfast." Ralph carefully lettered the word on the blackboard—E-G-G. He could smell the chalk dust and he was scrawling on a childhood blackboard at P.S. . . . ninety-seven, was it? Sixty-seven? He couldn't remember. Startled again by the new vividness that had crept into his reveries, he dragged his attention back up the years, to Mr. Gomez. *"Huevo,"* he said, pointing at the blackboard. "Egg."

"Ahh! I go the kitchen, I take the egg, I cook the egg, I eat the egg . . ."

From *Stanford Short Stories 1961*. © 1964 by the Board of Trustees of the Leland Stanford Junior University.

The voice stumbled on . . . egg . . . drink . . . door . . . close . . . go . . . and Ralph gazed out the window, not quite listening any longer. The automobiles below were sleek toys, wet and shiny—and he moved them with his eyes to the traffic light on the corner. Those summer nights thick with the sensations of childhood, hot with the flare of promise. Where had they fled? Suppressing the familiar slide into time, he watched the thin rain slant down the valley of Forty-second Street, punching dents into the bright pools that sagged the store-front awnings. Washed pale by the morning light, a dangling neon sign across the street—*Investigations, Strictly Confidential*—sent erratic reflections sparking off the wet pavement. Ralph tried to shake the throb from his skull, but it wouldn't go. He played little games with his vision, moving his head imperceptibly from side to side until some flaw in the window glass caused the office buildings outside to ripple and billow like a theater backdrop. It made him feel strangely potent. Give a man a big enough window, he thought, and he'll shake every secretary in the city off the boss's lap.

The throb was stronger now, like some giant clock beating muffled ticks into his brain. Why not just walk out there and never come back? God, the places he'd worked in! The joints! All these little part-time jobs that fell just short of wresting his full attention—so that he could think of himself as really, after all, a painter. Even after he'd long known that he'd never be more than a competent draftsman, that ahead lay only . . . what? One of the neon letters across the street wouldn't quite stay on. It slickered crazily, as if fighting the rain—off for an instant, leaving a gap like a missing front tooth, then on again, dancing between orange and cloudy gray. If only the rain would let up before two-thirty. He could see himself dashing uptown to the Art Students' League through all that drench.

Gomez had reached his lunch . . . take the pot . . . pour the soup. . . . The phrases had the rising inflection of questions, and it occurred to Ralph that he had probably let them go on too long.

"Good work, Mr. Gomez; *bueno trabajo*," he said, wondering whether that was the way to say it. "Mr. Santos, you take it from lunch. And careful with that soup. Don't spill it."

Mr. Santos, his bald head reflecting the fluorescent ceiling light, stammered into lunch, drinking the soup, clearing the table, washing the pot. In the street, a girl in dungarees held a newspaper over her head while she looked at the prints in the bookstore window. A Degas dancer, a Matisse poster, some Van Gogh clouds —Ralph passed them each morning on his hurried walk from the subway. And his own painting? His own damned painting? Skillful enough to impress the suburban housewives and the black-stockinged girls who came up from their dance classes in Greenwich Village. But so full of dead spots, so empty of sound for any eye that really knew the language at the tip of a brush. His mind stroked revisions on the latest canvas—cautious, deft, . . . flat. Like a memorized speech. He caught himself red-handed at this reverie and raised an eyebrow. Come off that rock, he thought; you are not Prometheus.

Outside, a truck ground to a stop and sounded its horn insistently. Then a clash of gears and it moved on. Mr. Santos was stacking boxes on his job in Macy's storeroom, piling them hurriedly, racing toward supper. Letting the voice toil on, Ralph threw his eyes slightly out of focus and the big letters painted in reverse on the window seemed to jump out and cling to the buildings on the other side of the street. He read them from right to left, FIORE'S PAN-AMERICAN ACADEMY. Then from left to right, Y-M-E-D-A . . . A raindrop glistened at the peak of the "A." Across the street the neon letter flared once and went out completely. Died, thought Ralph.

As soon as the flickering distraction was gone, his headache came swelling back. *Just a jackknife has MacHeath dear, and he keeps it out of sight* . . . Absurdly the words of the song came with it, synchronizing with the throb in his head . . . *just* a jackknife, *just* a jackknife, *just* a jackknife, *just* a . . . It had rained last night too, he remembered. That's why all that bunch had stayed so late at Lois's. Hoping it would let up so they wouldn't have to run the two blocks to the subway, ducking in and out of store-fronts and doorways along Fourteenth Street. That last pair: the glowering bearded kid and . . . what was her name . . . Melody! Who'd shed her wraparound dress and done an *interpretive* dance in red tights. He should have been overjoyed when the two of them left finally. There was a time when he would have sweated them all out, waiting to be alone with Lois. But now he just poured himself another glass of the cheap Burgundy and thought that maybe *he* ought to leave too.

Somewhere beyond layers of cotton a voice traveled uncertainly home . . . went the house, climbed the stair, knocked the door . . . and Lois came out of the kitchen, freeing her brown hair from the ponytail, letting it splash down around her shoulders. Ralph silently appraised her. Breasts a trifle lower, a trifle flatter. But otherwise everything about the same as ever. Kept herself well, this girl. She was wearing her serious look and he feared she'd broach the same old subject.

"Quick game of jump-rope?" Ralph asked, hoping to create a diversion. He settled into the sling chair, feeling the black canvas go taut on its metal frame. "And while we're on jumping . . ." He undressed her with his eyes.

"Me too," she said, pointing to the bottle. "And don't get so smart, baby. Ponytails are practical. . . . Jumping! I don't like the way you use that word. Says something about your attitude."

Ralph shrugged, and poured her a glass of wine, satisfied with his tactic.

"Had a gorgeous beard, didn't he?" she said.

Ralph tried to muster a touch of jealousy; he knew this trick of hers and mourned its loss of power. Pointing to his mouth, he shaped a silent word.

"Don't be vulgar," Lois said. She plopped onto the couch and rested her bare feet carefully among the glasses on the long low table. "Anyways, I like beards."

"Then grow one. And get your feet off the door. It's not polite."

"Coffee table," she said.

"O Altitude! You dissenters are all alike. Always knocking dead our Sears Roebuck realities, always discovering that a door on blocks is a coffee table."

Lois put down her glass. "By the way, Ralph, up yours!"

"Let's get the crockery," he said. "And don't be vulgar. Says something about your attitude."

Ralph pushed through the beaded brass curtain into the narrow kitchen with several glasses and set them down in the sink,

the brass strands still clicking behind him. A wine-soaked cigarette was coming to pieces in one of the glasses and the edge had a
smeared red mouth on it. Kissing sweet, he thought. Lois brushed
past him carrying a huge ashtray and he touched a conciliatory
hand to her cheek.

"If they ever put a ban on Alan Watts, used building blocks,
and prints from the Marboro book shop . . ."

"Oh, for heaven's sake, shut up," she said, sliding by him out
of the kitchen. "Go write an exposé for *Newsweek*. About how
us non-conformists are the biggest conformists really."

Ralph leaned back against the sink. In the next apartment
a phonograph was playing "The Threepenny Opera" . . . *just a
jackknife has MacHeath dear* . . . He reached up and tapped a
spidery mobile hanging from the ceiling, and watched it turn,
stop, unwind. The painting! God, he'd have to get those dead
spots out. But how? Maybe he'd abandon it and start something
simpler. This eased his tension a bit. Somewhere in the building
a toilet was flushed and he could hear the hiss of the pipes in the
wall behind him. From the other room Lois called something,
but he couldn't quite hear her. The wine was beginning to
press in at the edges of his mind and he stood perfectly still, hoping to keep the faint headache from clamping any tighter, trying
to capture the winey elation of the past, when he used to come
rolling up the stairs, a bit high, and knock lightly on Lois's door in
the middle of the night, feeling like some character in a Lawrence
novel. They were going to have it *all* then. The very center of
existence. The life of sinful art and artful sin. The life of pure
substance. With all the little almost-respectable part-time jobs
somewhere out at the edges, a thin but necessary periphery. The
genteel poverty; that too had been important. And he himself had
been Lois's prize possession, her very own not-quite-employed,
not-quite-married artist . . . how perfect! But as the life of pure
substance shed its substance, the periphery had moved perhaps a
little too close to the center.

It's turned out to be a Huxley novel, Ralph thought. The
headache was pushing in, beginning to thump, and he pressed the
heels of his hands against his temples, rubbing them in slow
circles . . . *just* a jackknife, *just* a jackknife, *just*ajackknife,
*just*a . . .

Lois shouted from the other room. "Ralph, are you listening to me?" The pipes stopped hissing and she lowered her voice. "When are you going to give me another painting? To replace my pretentious prints from the Marboro book shop."

"Yeah," Ralph said.

"What do you mean, *yeah*!" She came rattling through the curtain.

"Yeah," he said. "I mean yeah, that's all." He continued rubbing his temples.

"A yes man. A yes man with a temper. It doesn't make sense." She nudged him aside and turned on the faucet, directing a spray of hot water over the dishes. "Incidentally, I'm thinking of taking the legs off tables and using them for doors."

Ralph was silent.

"The tables, that is. *You* can have the legs. For pool cues." She dried several forks and clinked them down into a drawer.

"Thanks for trying," he said softly. "A respectable try. I'm sorry about the temper."

Lois hung up the dish towel and turned to him, her expression very serious. "Respectability. Let's talk about that, Ralph."

"Here it comes," he said. "I knew you'd get around to it."

"I'm not getting any younger."

Ralph looked away.

"Ralph!"

"Not now, Lois. Don't start that now." Grimly. He said it through curtains of wine.

"Then when?" She snapped it out, staring into his face.

Ralph shoved his hands in his pockets and walked to the window. The inside ledge was wet with rain.

"When, Ralph, when?" she said.

The muffled pulse in his head was thudding, thudding trying to beat its way out . . . *justa*jackknife *justa*jackknife-*justa* jackknife*justa* jackknife*justa* jackknife . . . His thoughts were beginning to blur and shatter . . . Ralph wine . . . when? . . . table . . . legs . . . door . . . bed . . . He gripped hard at his mind, pulling it back into place, gathering the pieces into the present moment . . . I go the bed, I put the sheet, I take the blanket . . .

"Good enough, Mr. Santos," Ralph said. "Good enough,"

hoping he was right. Then he turned and wrote vigorously on the blackboard, the chalk squeaking along his nerves. He wrote as though it had been his purpose all along. A little trick he had, to cover his lapses of attention. Over his shoulder he said, "All right, Mr. Amaya, will you read this?" Somewhere in the rain a police whistle trilled faintly. Mr. Amaya slid his short legs back under the seat and fixed his eyes on the blackboard.

"I go," he said.

"Good. Now past tense," Ralph said. "Past time."

The eyes tightened into wrinkles of concentration. Silence. Miss Lopez sat up tall in her chair, looking straight at Ralph, and he knew she wanted to supply the answer. But he kept his eyes from engaging hers, abstracting them slightly and watching the class. Six forlorn Latins, he thought. How did they ever manage those revolutions? He pointed to the words and said, "Yesterday, Mr. Amaya?"

Amaya squirmed. "I gone?"

Miss Lopez giggled and nudged Mrs. Arundel. But the older woman sat heavy and vacant, gazing at nothing. Miss Lopez threw up her hand and flapped it insanely, like some wild thing at the end of a stick.

Ralph ignored her little commotion. "Gone, Mr. Amaya?" he asked.

"WENT!" The word shrilled out, Miss Lopez standing now. "I went," she shrieked again.

Mr. Amaya's forehead sprouted ridges of surprise.

Ralph looked hard at the girl for a long minute, punishing her with his eyes. A pedagogical gimmick he had seen the great man himself use. Ferocious Fiore, he thought. Fantastic Fiore. He played with the name. Fiore, the fickle finger of Forty-second Street. Feeble Fiore. Fuck Fiore.

Miss Lopez retreated down into her seat, nervously crossing her legs, and Ralph caught the glint of nylon. He gazed for a moment at the soft thrust of her breasts and was annoyed at himself for being so obvious about it. What in God's name was she doing here anyway; she spoke better English than Fiore! Shifting his eyes upward, he engaged hers this time. They were dark and inviting in the olive skin. A false promise, he knew. A bid for redemption. And Lois, he realized, was proportioned just about like Lopez. But somehow the silly girl fidgeting before him

seemed more compelling now. And a hundred others he'd see on
the streets. Tokens of failed affection. Remembering that Lois
had invited him to dinner at seven, he glanced at his watch, and
felt immediately foolish when he saw that it wasn't even noon
yet. He turned back to Mr. Amaya with an uncomfortable sense
that he had both won and lost that little contest with Lopez.

"I went?" Amaya asked meekly.

"I went," confirmed Ralph.

God, for some black coffee now. He flipped out a cigarette
and lit it, the match flame jumping back and forth as he puffed.
The tobacco tasted stale.

"And tomorrow?" he asked. He threw a sharp glance at
Lopez to keep her in her place. Mr. Amaya's eyes were wide
now. Trapped and frightened.

"Mrs. Arundel," Ralph said.

Mr. Amaya let his eyes go narrow with relief.

Ralph pointed at the blackboard and said, "This is October,
Mrs. Arundel. October 10, to be exact. Now speak for November."

Mrs. Arundel pouted.

"I . . . will . . . go," Ralph suggested, putting the same
emphasis on each word.

"Will . . . go," she said. The words seemed to come automatically, as if he had spoken them into some machine and was
now replaying them. The mouth moved back into its pout off
the last vowel, the eyes vacant. Through the partition, Ralph
could hear the faint clacking of Mr. Peters' typing class next door,
and it was the bumping of brass beads, the tap of a brush handle,
the innumerable noise of small machinery and brittle insects, and
all the small sounds of his life. He experienced a faint sense of
slippage somewhere within him. As though some tiny wire had
lost its contact.

"Well done, Mrs. Arundel," he said, "but you didn't flench
your kabe very spoothly.

Mrs. Arundel nodded.

"Thus I refute you, Mrs. Arundel," he said.

She nodded again.

Miss Lopez popped up straight in her chair. She tipped her
head to one side and stared quizzically at Ralph.

"Did you know, Lady Arundel, that I am not who I am?" he

said. "That I am you? That when you leave at two o'clock *I* sit down in your place and let *my* mouth drop open? Did you know that, Madame Arundel?"

Mrs. Arundel didn't nod. She wrinkled her brow, trying to seem thoughtful. The rest of the class looked at him blankly. Uncomprehendingly attentive. Even Miss Lopez seemed puzzled.

"Ah, but I'm too clever to let you see me," Ralph continued. He looked around as if to be sure no one was listening. Then he cupped his hand to his mouth in a mock whisper, and said, "I go fourteen . . . no, fifteen blocks away. Clever?" he paused.

Mrs. Arundel's expression was an agony of misunderstanding. Surely she had said something terribly incorrect. The pressure of her humiliation swept across him, and the wire slid into place. What in hell am I doing, he thought. Kicking sand on ninety-pound weaklings. With a nod, he acknowledged Mr. Amaya's raised hand.

"What means *know*?" asked Mr. Amaya.

Ralph considered for a moment. Then, "Miss Lopez, what means *know*?"

"*Conocer*," said Miss Lopez briskly. Her look of indignation turned to amusement and she began to titter, now that he had favored her.

Cheaply bought, thought Ralph. He turned and wrote on the board: *To know = conocer*. They all copied it into their notebooks, except Miss Lopez, who was whispering loudly in Spanish to Mrs. Arundel. Ralph tossed the chalk up and down in his hand, waiting for her to finish.

The sliding canvas door behind him whacked open and he could hear the typewriters go louder, but he didn't turn to see who was in the doorway. He knew without looking. The brown striped suit, double-breasted and a bit too tight. The plump neck, squeezed into a collar a half size too small. He knew that nothing would happen for a minute or two, that Fiore would just wait there making the most of his jolting entrance. He could imagine the little man standing up to his full height, trying to look tall. All very dramatic. He'd stand there, letting his presence sink in. Then step two: the full entrance and tirade—the comic frenzy that Peters liked to parody, in his shrieking falsetto, over lunchtime coffee in the automat.

Ralph said, "All right, let's do a composition in the note-books." His voice was gentle now, compensating for the unfair vulgarity of his recent joke. He regretted its dismal pompousness. And he wanted particularly to dissociate himself from the little man in the doorway. He picked up Mr. Amaya's notebook and held it above him to be sure they undertood what he wanted.

"Who talk?" Fiore stepped into the room. "Who talk the Spanish here, eh?" He glanced for a rebuking instant at Ralph's cigarette, then away. "Aha! School is place for talk the Spanish, eh? You think is so?"

The shuffling for notebooks subsided and the class set sculp-ture-still. Ralph put the notebook back in Mr. Amaya's lap. But Amaya didn't move; his gnarled workman's hands were clasped, as if in supplication. Miss Lopez looked straight at Fiore, wide-eyed, innocent.

"What for you come here? Is for talk? Eh? Is social club, everybody talk talk talk? No is school for the English? Eh? Since when is no school for the English? I ask you? Since when? When is change from school, become social club? Now is the place for talk the Spanish? No necessary learn the English? What is for then? What this place for? Eh?"

Ralph leaned against the partition, looking beyond Fiore into the window. He could see the wetly reflected shoulders lift at each ejaculation, the arms fly up at each rhetorical question, going wavery across the window. Ralph moved his head, caving in the edges of the brown suit, making the stripes ripple like snapped ropes. Then he turned and stepped through the doorway out on to the loft and the murmur of reciting voices filtering through the flimsy fiberboard partitions that divided the place into tiny classrooms.

A lone voice detached itself from the undertone and came floating out to him . . . *this is a desk . . . a desk is* . . . and then it sank back in, leaving him without the answer. For writing? he wondered. For reading? For working? Brown? Wooden? Expensive? He stepped to the teachers' cubicle and dropped into the worn leather armchair. Which had it been? But it never seemed to matter. Any answer would do. A desk is a . . . desk, he decided. He could hear Fiore through the open door of the classroom, his voice a screech now, supplying the answers to his own string of questions. "Nooooo is place for fun," the "O" dragged out like a wail. "Is school, you hear? Is school school school. Is place for work. No *es por hablar*. In you home *hablando*. In teatro hablando*. Hear? *Escúchame! Escúchame!*"

When Ralph heard him sliding into Spanish, he knew it would soon be over. He twisted out his cigarette in the ashtray, lit another, and slumped down into the seat, his legs stretched before him. Then he blew out a stream of smoke and watched it mushroom up into the ceiling. Someone inside the next partition pushed the door ajar and he could hear Peters working his bunch. "It is just impossible to make you understand. Will you *ever* learn that English is an uninflected language!"

Ralph leaned back and let his arms go limp on the arms of the chair. He could feel the I.R.T. rumbling by under the building, the vibration coming up through the floor into his feet. The trembling climbed to his loins. Then it subsided and filtered back out of him, down into the floor. Fiore was saying to the class, ". . . is necessary to . . ." He hesitated, straining for the right word. Outside, the police whistle tickled the air, hanging like a long dash in his sentence. ". . . concentrate," Fiore finished with exultation. The whistle grew more excited, shrilling out sharp little blasts. Noontime traffic swelling the streets. Another whistle farther off picked up the excitement, faintly counterpointing the first, their voices interweaving like soprano crickets, calling and answering, calling and answering.

Hot summer nights. And his grandfather's urgent voice fusing with the far clatter and rasp of a McDonald Avenue trolley car, the distant chirp of a police whistle. Somewhere nearby the hiss of a water truck spraying the dark streets. And the click click of secret crickets in the overgrown lots. The old man stopped rocking whenever he spoke and his words would coming riding up onto the thick night air. *So who listens, Ralphie? When an old man speaks, who listens?* The evening refrain of age on the front porch. Then the dark drone of summer, and the rocker creaking into it, back and forth, back and forth, on the wooden floor of the porch.

And always, off on the horizon, the amber glow of Coney Island brightening the sky like a promise. The barely audible rumble of a roller coaster swooping and twisting and infecting

the hot world with excitement and wild hope. Down the street
a slamming screen door, an idling car. A growl of skates along
the pavement. And the soft pressure of bicycle pedals at Ralph's
toes, the whir of the chain on the sprocket beneath him. And once
a month his father's hands on the wheel of the old De Soto, Ocean
Parkway sliding in under the naked chrome woman on the hood,
Ralph urging the car on with his small body into that jangle and
flare of wild whirling joy beneath the amber glow. Then a swirl
of rides and melting custard and the trip home, the stomach still
pitching through turns and dips and darkness on the stairs of the
front porch; somewhere a door opening and a voice growing
louder . . . I set the clock . . . I wind the clock . . . I go
the bed . . . I make the bed . . . I put the light . . .

Ralph came reluctantly alert, the voice from Peters' room
biting into his reverie. He tried to relax into it again, but that
wouldn't work and he lit another cigarette.

Mrs. Fiore came scurrying out of the office and stationed herself near Ralph, holding a heavy brass bell in one pudgy hand,
staring at an oversized pocket watch in the other. Suddenly she
jammed the watch into a bulging pocket of her smock, pulled out
a little brass hammer and struck the bell sharply—one, two,
three, four, five. The clang of the bell filled the loft.

Always five, Ralph thought, wondering if that had any meaning. He looked at the back of Mrs. Fiore's balding head—a thing
that always surprised him. "Hall of wonders," he muttered. The
door to Peters' room opened and his students came milling out,
two girls chattering rapidly in Spanish as they passed Ralph. But
when they saw Mrs. Fiore waving a finger at them they went
awkwardly silent. "No speak the Spanish," she warned. Then she
turned and shuffled back into her office. When the door closed behind her, one of the girls whispered to her friend, and Ralph
said, "No speak the Spanish." They walked off giggling. Easy to
be a comedian around here, he thought. Just be serious.

Fiore stepped out of the classroom and stood near the doorway, his face contorted by some deep preoccupation. When he
noticed Ralph, he nodded, said "Is all right," and strode into his
office. Ralph would have thought this a reassuring comment on
the situation in his classroom if he hadn't heard it so many times
before: *Hello, Mr. Fiore. Is all right. Good night, Mr. Fiore.*

Is all right. Nice weather we're having. Is all right. Good morn-ing. Is all right. Is all right. Is all right. It seemed to be some sort of twitch, nothing more. Or perhaps a profound therapeutic comment. A stablizing word ritual. What in God's name *is* all right around here, anyway, he wondered. The wire slipped.

When he saw Peters emerge from his room, Ralph got up and walked briskly into the office, closing the door softly behind him. Fiore was settled behind his desk, copying grades from a chaotic heap of compositions into a formidably thick record book. His wife sat with her back to the door, filing papers at a metal table in the opposite corner of the room. No one looked up.

The desk was magnificent. Large, graceful, and expensive-looking. To one side of it was a Danish chair and a walnut end table with a huge mosaic ashtray sitting shiny and unused on the velvety surface. Ah, Ralph thought, what a fine impres-sion these must make on prospective customers. He looked at the big, framed diploma on the far wall, formal and impressive, like a university degree. This is to certify that Augusto Fiore . . . He knew, if one took the trouble to read it, that it said Fiore had worked for the Grace steamship line as a bursar. Try-ing to imagine Mrs. Fiore as one of the Grace sisters, he cleared his throat very deliberately. There was no response.

"Pardon me," he said. "I know this isn't a graceful time, but can I speak to you a few minutes?"

Fiore looked up in surprise, the movement pushing the flesh of his neck over the striped suit collar. He jumped up. "Is all right," he said, motioning to the Danish chair. "Make a seat, make a seat, Mr. Gould."

Ralph sat down.

"Bad day," Fiore said. "Is rain, rain, rain."

Ralph wanted to say, "Is all right." He said, "That's New York for you."

Fiore pushed a tray of cigarettes toward him and Ralph lit one with a table lighter encased in a miniature suit of armor. "Like to talk to you about my situation," he said. "I've been here two years and I think I've been doing my job." The abrupt-ness of his own voice surprised him. "I ought to be making two dollars an hour like some of the others," he continued, annoyed at himself for basing his request on the salary of others. Another ethic broken. Fiore nodded all through the speech, and when it was finished, the little man sat back and pushed out his lower lip as though considering some factor that couldn't possibly be apparent to Ralph.

"Ah, true, true, Mr. Gould. Two years. Much time. Much time." He stopped talking and pushed out the lip again.

Ralph said, "I haven't bothered you much about it before, but it's reached a point where it's downright necessary. Two years ago was different from today. Times change and things become necessary." He had no idea what he meant by all this, but he wanted to avoid silences, with the two of them just sitting there staring at each other. He was afraid that if this happened he'd break into uncontrollable laughter. And if he did, he thought, no one in this place would even notice. Whenever he spoke to Fiore, he had no sense of communication. It was as though he were talking to the striped suit. But sometimes he suspected the suit understood more than one realized.

"Ah, Mr. Gould," Fiore said. "I like to give this. Is true; things change. But is no possible, is no possible."

Ralph thought he might go on saying that eternally and have to be carried off muttering "is no possible" and be replaced by another little man with a long lower lip.

"Why not?" he asked.

When he said this, Mrs. Fiore looked over from her corner of the room, and Ralph suddenly had the notion that he was really dealing with her and not Fiore at all. He looked back at her to show that he hadn't been fooled. But she returned to her work and he knew that he wasn't going to get the raise. Events were atop him again, the inevitable fruit of his sudden impulses. But what the hell; impulse had brought him into the office, impulse would carry him on now that he was there. When he turned back to Fiore, the lip was forward again.

"You are a part-time, Mr. Gould, not all-time," he said. "Is no the same thing. For all-time professors, okay, two dollars. But part-times, no."

Ralph laughed, amused by the title. "Look, you know that part time or full time has nothing to do with it." He looked over to the corner of the room, but the bald head didn't turn. "Do I get it or don't I?" he said.

He was communicating now. Fiore's eyes went dark and firm. But he remained polite. "I am sorry, Mr. Gould. But no is possible. Is small place. When we are . . ."

Ralph stood up. "Okay," he said. "Okay, never mind." At the door he turned. "Please send me my check. And no speak the Spanish." When he closed the door, a great sense of release came on him. He could feel it all through his body and he was sorry about the tone he had taken with Fiore, since he didn't really need the money anyway. And he liked the little madman.

Peters was sitting on the wooden bench next to the coat rack, peeling a hard-boiled egg, his thin legs crossed and a paper napkin spread over his knees. On the bench next to him were a jar of yogurt and a salt shaker. When Ralph walked over and took down his raincoat, Peters said, "Something going on in the office?"

"Want the place to grow, like Berlitz. So they're giving out bonuses to teachers. Didn't they call for you?"

Peters sighed. "Oh, come off it, Gould," he said. "You're growing tiresome. Utterly tiresome."

Ralph buttoned his coat and turned up the collar. "Just tired, Peters, utterly tired." He put his foot up next to the yogurt, close enough to make Peters nervous, and tightened his shoelace. "Saw the Fiore about a raise," he said.

Peters stopped peeling his egg. "Oh?"

"No good. Said I'd have to be satisfied with two bucks, like everyone else on part time." He knew Peters was getting one-fifty.

Peters set the egg down on his napkin and looked into Ralph's face, trying to figure out whether this was banter. He bit his lip.

Ralph tried to put on his most serious face. "Be seeing you," he said, and walked to the door. On the way out he whispered to himself, "I open the door, I close the door, I go down the steps . . ."

Outside it was still raining and he walked along close to the store fronts, watching his reflection accompany him in the shop windows. In the music store window he saw himself marching among trombones and castanets, sliding immaterially through a piano.

"Come on out of there," he said. "You've been paroled."

The rain touched at his face with cold fingers and he felt the guilty joy of truancy. Under the subway kiosk he stopped and watched the cars edge along Sixth Avenue, their wipers flapping back and forth across the windshields. He could see the gap in the neon sign across the street. And the park behind the Fifth Avenue library. The clock over the music store said 1:45.

Refreshed, he slid his hands from his pockets and went down the stairs two at a time, feeling the firm push of the steps against his soles. He wondered if they'd miss him in the 2:30 session at the League. In front of the change booth a woman struggled with a dripping umbrella and he closed it for her. She said she was very much obliged young man and there weren't many gentlemen left these days.

When he inserted his token and went through the turnstile, the shove of the wooden arm against his stomach reminded him of the dinner engagement with Lois, and he had to thrust down a momentary surge of depression. Later on he'd call and tell her he couldn't make it; he hoped she wouldn't feel hurt. The sense of elation was growing and he didn't want to hurt anyone. He allowed himself a brief twinge of regret for all the unpleasant things he'd said to people lately. Even Peters. He wished he had been a little easier on Peters in the past.

From the almost empty train, Ralph stared through the crosshatch of fine wires in the door glass. Beyond his own reflection he watched a Mojud Stocking sign glide by on the tile wall of the station. Someone had penciled a mustache on the Mojud girl and several obscene words were scrawled across her garters. The station disappeared suddenly and he could see himself looking back from the concrete wall that hurtled along past the train. The arched openings in the wall were flipping by and Ralph followed one with his eyes until it was gone. He was enjoying himself tremendously, like a kid on his first train ride. At Twenty-sixth Street the train went through on the center express track and he watched the steel columns rage across the windows, the station platform flashing on and off between them. He tried to count the columns, but they were rushing backwards like time furiously rewinding itself. When he felt the air go cool, he walked to the front window of the train and watched a spray of bright particles burst from the electric coupler sliding along the third rail. The tracks reeled away, up into the darkness, and ahead he could see the glowing spot where the train would emerge and ride above the surface. The spot expanded, coming on big and full, and rushed up and swallowed the car into daylight. Rain pattered against the window and the droplets ran zigzag down the glass, sending streaks of shadow into the car.

Gradually losing his sense of destination, he passed his own stop and grew into that whole organism of motion, while the jouncing car smashed backward into time, sucking up miles of rushing ties and polished rails. The car became a stationary vibrating room, all the paraphernalia of the world walloping around it, winding back into some gigantic reel, like a film running in rapid reverse; and he hardly knew when he had left the train, his feet walking on wet sidewalks and somewhere out at the tips of the nerves his face touching the cold air of the day, the rain no longer falling.

In the streets beyond Surf Avenue the subway rhythm still echoed in the joints of his body, the electricity of the third rail crackling and writhing across the faint shadows of empty buildings and along the closed steel shutters of concessions and booths, sparking life into unseen globes full of bouncing popcorn and into galleries of snapping rifles and sliding files of ducks. Into crocodile men and two-headed cows parading across rows of flaked and fading posters. And into the cluttered filigree of girders and beams with its diving chain of cars and silently screaming girls.

But as the small sounds of the world reasserted themselves— a distant automobile, the slap of the surf, somewhere the cry of a gull—Ralph became increasingly aware of the deep silence that lay like an ocean beneath them, bearing upon its surface a faint gurgle of rainwater slipping along girders and dripping from a hundred crossbeams into the street and into the far voices of memory stirring within him. The silent trestle of the roller coaster stood nearby on countless legs. The big disc of the ferris wheel. The unpeopled boardwalk, and a tall, ribbed tower, empty of parachutes. Huge discarded toys. Surrounded by all this motionless machinery of pleasure looming like monuments of summer, Ralph felt the weight of their shadows everywhere around him patterning the October stillness. By a sheer act of the will he tried to relieve the weight, brush out the stillness.

But when he closed his eyes, the shadows were still within them.

Merrill Joan Gerber

We Know That Your Hearts Are Heavy

Pigeons are crowding the window sill to keep out of the rain. The drizzle has just turned to downpour, and the birds have flown up from Boston Common. They are stepping on each other's toes to find a footing on the two-inch ledge. The victims of missteps do not fall six stories and spatter their blood on the pavement; they merely hang in midair, flutter a hundred wet black feathers, and immediately land back on the ledge, dancing a wild two-step to get dry.

The phone rings, and I spin around. Before I quite realize it is the phone and not my employer coming in the door, I have hidden in my lap certain papers from the top of my desk that are obviously not the work I am supposed to be doing, and have picked up a pencil, which I poise professionally over nothing. I compose myself enough to lift the receiver.

"One moment, please," says the operator, and then I hear my mother's voice coming to me from Miami.

"Mother!" I cry.

"Janet, darling, how are you?"

"Is anything the matter?"

Long-distance calls always frighten me. My family is neither rich nor sophisticated enough to call merely to talk. There is always a reason. The last call from home came because my mother heard that a hurricane was approaching Boston, and she wanted Danny and me to move out of our rickety attic apartment in Cambridge and go to a sturdy hotel until it was over.

From *The New Yorker*, Vol. 39, April 20, 1963. © 1963 by Merrill Joan Gerber. Reprinted with permission from *Stop Here, My Friend*, by Merrill Joan Gerber (Houghton Mifflin Company, Boston, 1965).

Since my mother does not answer me immediately, I say, "Are you and Daddy all right? Is Carol all right?"

"We're fine," she says. "How are you? How's Danny?"

"We're fine," I say. "Is anything new?"

"How's the weather up there in the North Pole? I thought it's supposed to be *spring*, and the low was eighteen yesterday." My mother studies the Boston highs and lows and reports to us in every letter how much better off we'd be in Miami. She cannot understand why the University of Miami would not be just as good a place for Danny to do his graduate work as Harvard.

"We had a hailstorm last night," I add, for no sensible reason.

"And how is your job?"

"It's fine, it's fine."

I wait, and then it comes. "Janet, Daddy is flying to New York this afternoon. Uncle Benny has had a heart attack."

"Oh, no," I say. "Poor Celia."

Celia is my cousin who is four days younger than I am, and who looks like Elizabeth Taylor. She is due to have her baby any day. I say this to my mother.

"She's due *today*," my mother says. "The poor child."

"Is it very serious?"

"He died, darling. Uncle Benny died."

I am silent for a moment, digesting this. My Uncle Benny is my father's elder brother. He looks just like my father (though I in no way resemble Elizabeth Taylor), and he is very rich and lives on Park Avenue in Manhattan. He has always been my favorite uncle, even though most of the relatives do not like him because of all his money. I think he has always loved me because I look so much like him.

"How is Daddy taking it?" I say. Outside, the pigeons are now standing on each other's heads.

While my mother is saying that he is as all right as can be expected, it occurs to me that I will go to New York to see my father, whom I have not seen in a year. I tell my mother that, and she says she doesn't want me to go, and I say I will, and she puts my father on to argue with me, and suddenly I say something frightful. I tell my father that I want to come because I have never been to a funeral and I want to see what one is like.

He is angry, I am sure. I see him thinking, Do you imagine a funeral is a *show*? And I am thinking, in self-defense, It was very unfair of all of you to conceal Grandma's death from me when I was in college and not tell me till after the funeral, so that I still can't believe she is dead because I was not *there*. I have never seen anyone dead, and I am twenty-two, and I think I must not grow one day older till I do.

But my father is too preoccupied to get angry. He simply says there is nothing much to see at a funeral; he is going to fly back to Miami as soon as it is over, and in just two months, in June, he and Mother and Carol will all drive up to Boston to see us, and there's no need for me to go to any funeral, especially if the weather is bad. He does not sound very convincing or stern, though, which is strange, because those are the things my father usually is.

Finally, I say what one of us always says on long-distance calls, "This is costing a fortune," and my mother gets back on the line to tell me to keep warm, and then I remember that my Aunt Beth, Celia's mother, died less than a year ago, and I ask my mother if Uncle Benny might not have died of just being sad.

"On Park Avenue," my mother says, "a heart attack and too many sleeping pills can be the same thing," and the call is over and I am left with all kinds of terrible thoughts.

I lean forward to stare out over the Common, and the papers in my lap slide to the floor. I pick them up and set them back on the desk. They are greeting-card verses. Someone has told me that you can sell greeting-card verse for two dollars a line. If I can sell one eight-line verse a day, I will be able to quit this job, which I hate, and stay at home and not have to go on the hideous subway every day. The money from the verses will help put Danny through graduate school just as surely as the money from this job in the publishing house.

Today I have been doing Bereavements. In the last week, I have written a number of Birthdays, Get Wells, Mother's Days, Wedding Days, Baby Arrivals, and Valentines. Today, a gloomy April day, seemed appropriate for Bereavements. I think of Uncle Benny, and then I read the verse I composed this very morning:

> We know that your hearts are heavy
> And your sorrow is very deep,
> But remember: The Lord loves all his lambs
> Who rest in Eternal Sleep.

Obviously, it is not quite right. It is not, as my title says, "A Comforting Thought During Your Time of Bereavement." But then, I have never been bereaved; it is no wonder I cannot write sincere Bereavement verses.

I decide I am going to New York despite my parents' wishes. And right now I am getting out of this office; I can't stand it here any more. I put my verses into my purse and go down the hall to tell Mr. Cowper that I have to go to New York to a funeral, and I say it so fast and sadly that he perhaps thinks it is my father and not my uncle who has died.

I take the subway to Harvard Square and walk home from there. Danny has the hi-fi on; he is playing the sad songs of Schubert again—the rain has affected him, too—and when I get to the top of the third flight of stairs I knock on our door. He opens it and I say without looking into his eyes, "I have to go to New York to see my father. My Uncle Benny just died, and my father is flying to New York this afternoon."

"What?" says Danny, and to my horror I find myself smiling as I repeat the words.

Danny does not see. He helps me peel off my raincoat, and throws it across the back of a chair. He turns off the phonograph, and then closes the book he has been reading.

"I have to call the bus station and see when a bus leaves," I say, and at the same instant Danny is saying, "It's a bad day for such a long trip, but I think we can make it O.K. if we drive slowly."

I am shocked. It has not occurred to me that Danny will come. I have been imagining this as a private family affair. Danny does not like families, and he will not like mine. None of them are the kind of people we would have for friends, but I feel for them something akin to love, which makes them bearable, while Danny has no reason at all (except that I am his wife) to be tolerant of their crudities and illiteracies. I fear that he will be impatient, then offended, then angry, and finally will insist that I leave with him, which I will not want to do. I shall see this through to the end, even if it means disregarding Danny's wishes.

However, none of this can be explained. Danny is already saying he will have to miss his advanced seminar, but it is more important that I go to New York.

In less than twenty minutes, we are ready. We leave the attic in a mess—the bed unmade, crumbs under the kitchen table. By one o'clock, we are on the Massachusetts Turnpike. At the Connecticut state line, the rain turns into snow, and we now have to go thirty miles an hour instead of forty.

Before I understand that something has happened, Danny has stopped the car suddenly and is pulling out his wallet. In a moment, a highway patrolman is looking in my window.

"Open it!" Danny says, nearly shouting at me.

The patrolman takes Danny's license and reads it. "Are you going to a fire?" he says.

I wait for Danny to say we are going to a funeral. He says nothing. It seems he has changed lanes unsafely. The patrolman talks across me. He is very young; wet snow is clinging to his hat and to the tip of his nose. He is lecturing Danny about reckless driving, and I keep wanting to say, Please don't yell at us—it is snowing so hard, and my Uncle Benny is dead, and my father has to come thirteen hundred miles in an airplane this afternoon to see his dead brother, and my cousin has a baby in her, which is about to be born any minute.

The patrolman is now writing out a ticket, and is asking Danny if he is a student. He talks on and on, and I could kill Danny for not telling him. I want to tell everyone that someone has died whom I love. It is so important—how can anyone give us a *ticket*?

Finally, we are driving again, very slowly. Danny is chastened. His lips are tightly closed, he is trembling slightly, and I do not say anything.

We get into New York at eight-thirty, and, by calling several relatives, we learn the whereabouts of my father. He is at the Lakeview Chapel, where Uncle Benny is laid out. It takes Danny nearly another hour to find the chapel. Though we were both born in Brooklyn, neither of us knows Manhattan. I walk a few feet in front of Danny as we approach the funeral parlor. My heart is beating very fast. In the lobby, which is very much like a hotel lobby, a man at a desk asks us which "party" we are with. "We are with the Goldman party," I say, and Danny and I look at each other.

Danny has met my Uncle Benny once, just after the death of

Aunt Beth. On our honeymoon, we stopped in New York and had
dinner with him. His two children were there—Celia and Fred—
and Celia's husband, Glen, and Fred's wife, Melissa. Melissa was
obviously pregnant, and Celia was also pregnant, though we did
not know it. My Aunt Beth had always had a delicate heart, and
the relatives attributed her death mainly to the fact that Melissa
was a Catholic.

The night we visited, my Uncle Benny spoke very softly and
sadly. He said he was getting along—he was trying to keep busy,
the children came to dinner once a week, he would get used to
being alone in time. After dinner, he took us aside and said,
"Look, children, if you ever need anything—money, *anything*—
you know it's here waiting for you. Just call me collect. Please
remember that. You know you don't have to be bashful with me."
He put one arm around me and one hand on Danny's shoulder.
"You never have to worry as long as I can help you out."

Danny thanked him, and I kissed him, and for a minute he
covered his eyes with his hand. Then Fred came in to show us his
wedding pictures. Fred's wedding had been an immense affair,
at which it was said my Uncle Benny got drunk and cried, and in
nearly every picture was my Aunt Beth—a large woman, with a
lovely straight nose and her hair pulled back in a chignon. None
of Uncle Benny's brothers or sisters had been invited to the wedding. Only his Park Avenue friends had that honor. The youngest
of the three brothers, my Uncle Sol, had said, "Benny didn't want
his poor relatives from Brooklyn there. God will punish him for
such a sin."

The punishment having now been visited upon Uncle Benny,
Danny and I walk across the soft, deep carpet of the lobby to the
elevator, and are taken to the fourth floor. There is a great commotion coming from the end of the hall. We advance, and enter
an anteroom where there is a coat rack. I glance through an open
door into a larger room and get the impression that everyone is
standing there holding a highball. For one instant, I see my father
—tall, beloved, hunched over slightly, his arms crossed over his
chest as though he is cold—talking to some person I do not know.
I look away, pretending I have not seen him, and Danny takes my
coat and hangs it up. I stand there, looking down at my shoes,

and suddenly my father is hugging me, his suit jacket scratching my cheek. I kiss him, and turn my face away, feeling tears rise and then subside. Then I look at him and say, "Oh, Daddy." He hugs me again, and, remembering, releases me and shakes Danny's hand. Danny is already uncomfortable, but there is nothing I can do. I must think about other things right now. I forget about Danny, and later see him sitting alone in a corner at the far end of the room, his chin in his hand, his eyes staring at nothing.

My father, holding me tightly by the hand, does not reprimand me for coming. I understand that he is glad. We weave around groups of standing people; no one, of course, is holding a highball, but that impression is still with me. I see the faces of aunts, uncles, cousins—all of them from the same neighborhood in Brooklyn, all of them together for the first time in probably thirty years. Most of them have not seen me since I was "so high." A few stop us to tell me that, and to marvel at the fact that I am now married. "Where is the husband?" they say, and I point to Danny, in the corner, who looks as though he might be Uncle Benny's son, the way he is sitting so quietly, staring so sadly at the rug. "Imagine!" they say. *"Married!"* Mostly, they are marveling at how old they have grown. An occasion such as this moves them to philosophy. There is talk of dying everywhere. After all, Uncle Benny was only fifty-four—it could happen to anyone.

My Aunt Ida comes over to us. She is a widow. My Uncle Benny has been supporting her and her nine-year-old daughter Charlotte for the past six years. "Janet dear," she says, "what a stunning suit you are wearing!"

I stare at her. Her brother is dead, and she is telling me I am wearing a stunning suit. Suddenly I am struck by a horrible thought—this is *Celia's* suit I am wearing! Over the years, since Celia and I were children, my Aunt Beth used to make up a package of Celia's outgrown clothes every few months and send them to my mother for me. The last package had been sent about a year ago. It contained the suit I am wearing. Fred's clothes went to my Uncle Sol's son Bill. Even though both my father and my Uncle Sol now lived in Miami, my Aunt Beth, I am sure, had continued to think of them as the poor Brooklyn relatives.

In a moment, my Aunt Ida wanders off, and my father leads me firmly down the length of the room. He says softly, "Have you seen Uncle Ben?"

"No," I say. "Where is he?" at the same moment understanding that he is right in this room with us.

My father puts both hands on my shoulders and gently turns me around, and there, in front of me, is the dead man.

What, when I first came into the room, I thought was a display of flowers is not merely that. Sunk deep into hundreds of expensive blooms is a beautiful coffin. The upper half is open; the lower half is closed and covered with roses. In it lies my Uncle Ben in a navy-blue suit. He is wearing a tie. In his pocket is a handkerchief with the initials "B.G." I cannot look at his face. There is a feeling in my body I have never had before, of something stopping or freezing. My father is beside me, but I know that when I look at the face of the dead man I will see the face of my father —it does not matter that *now* it is my Uncle Ben. I look at the face. It is not my father. It is not my uncle. It is the face of someone who is not there. There are my uncle's cheeks, and his nose, which is shaped exactly like my nose, and his lips, but the color of life is gone. The feeling I have is as real as my heartbeat: he has gone out.

But where has he gone? I become hysterical and turn to my father.

My father steadies me, and leads me out into the hall. Near the elevator, where it is quiet, he sets me down on a bench. "Janet," he says.

I cannot control myself; it is more terrible than I can stand. My father's dear flesh, which I am touching, cannot stay forever. My mother cannot stay, Danny cannot stay, my sister Carol cannot stay. *I* cannot stay! It is too much to explain. I am able only to cry against my father's sleeve. Danny, who has come out after us, is holding one of my hands, and I kiss his fingers, and I kiss my father's sleeve, and then I take a deep breath and stand up.

In a few minutes, we all go back to the filled room. People are looking at me. They are probably thinking, Why is *she* so upset? It is not *her* father.

I speak to no one, and find myself, finally, beside Celia. She is in a low chair, dressed in a black maternity dress, her belly swollen so large it does not seem part of her. She is pale, but she is wearing lipstick, and her hair is fashionably combed. I feel as though she is twenty years my elder. In one year's time, she has had two deaths and a conception happen to her. Nothing has ever happened to me. I don't know what to say.

Celia says, "I'm so happy for you. It must be wonderful to see your father."

"Oh, no!" I say, but she is going on.

"It is *so* nice you could see him after so long. I'm glad someone is getting some pleasure from this."

She means to be polite—she is showing her good breeding—but what can she mean? Her finishing school has not taught her that you do not have to offer your father's life in politeness.

I say, "I'm very sorry, Celia," and she smiles at me. She is very beautiful.

Then I leave her and go to the corner in which Danny has been sitting all evening. He and I sit there together, and I watch my father go back to the coffin and stand before it with his head bowed. What is he thinking? What is he remembering? What is he feeling? "Danny," I say, "I can't stand it. I can't *understand* it."

"Sh-h-h," he says, squeezing my hand, and that is all the help he can give me.

Just then, a little gray-haired man comes into the room. He shakes slightly from a palsy, and he makes an announcement. "Will the immediate family of the deceased view the body once again if they wish to, as the coffin must be closed in a half hour and cannot be opened tomorrow before the funeral."

He leaves as quickly as he has come, and my father moves away, to give Celia and Fred the last half hour.

Fred walks toward the coffin and looks into it, and then walks away, squeezing his eyes shut as though he has a pain in his head that he cannot endure. Celia and her husband approach it, holding hands, and stand before it for a long time. Celia's arm is now around her husband's waist, and I see her clench her hand into a fist and bang it against the small of his back in a tiny futile gesture. I am ashamed of my outburst. She is a braver person than I am.

The little palsied man comes back into the room, and Celia and Glen back away from the coffin. She does not see, but from where I am *I* see the little man take a comb out of his breast pocket, lean into the coffin, and comb my Uncle Ben's hair neatly back off his forehead. Then he lowers the top half of the coffin and seals my Uncle Ben inside.

People are getting their coats. There is some difficulty about where Danny and I will spend the night. My father is staying with my Aunt Pearl and Uncle Carl in Brooklyn. My Uncle Sol, who has flown from Miami with my father, and my Aunt Ida, who lives all the way out on Long Beach, are also staying with them. My Aunt Pearl and Uncle Carl say *we* should come home with them, too, but I know they live in a one-bedroom apartment and have no place to sleep so many people. They will manage, they say, but Danny is doubtful. He would rather we stayed at a hotel. I cannot explain to him that we *can't* stay at a hotel—this is not a night one leaves the family. He should not have come along if he cannot do what has to be done.

Fred comes up and says why don't we stay in Uncle Ben's apartment. There are three large bedrooms (he means we do not have to sleep in the bed that Uncle Ben died in); no one is using them.

Danny is willing, but my father wants me with him. He feels what I am feeling. "I haven't seen her in a year," he explains to Fred. "We'll manage somehow."

Danny and my father and I all get into our car, and we follow my Uncle Carl's car back to Brooklyn. Everyone will meet at the synagogue the next morning at eleven.

Seven people are to sleep in an apartment that has only two single beds—Danny and I, my father, my Uncle Sol, my Aunt Ida, and my Aunt Pearl and Uncle Carl. My Aunt Pearl is trying to arrange things. It seems it is a very delicate question, the delicacy lying in the fact that Danny and I are newlyweds. We are to sleep together, and yet we cannot be given a room to ourselves. Do older people think that newlyweds make love even on the eves of funerals? From their whispering and arguing, it seems so. The conclusion is that we will have to take the consequences of this death. So Danny and I are assigned one of the single beds, my Aunt Pearl and Aunt Ida, who are sisters, the other, and a beach chair is set up at the foot of our bed for my Uncle Carl to sleep on. In the living room, my Uncle Sol will sleep on the couch and my father on another beach chair.

Danny is hating this—he will not sleep in a room filled with strangers; he will not be subject to their curious opinions on young love; he will not be the object of ridiculous imaginings—but he says nothing, because he is afraid to upset me further, and I am grateful.

It is bedtime. To be done with it, Danny undresses and is the first in bed. I am next. We both feign immediate sleep. It is frightfully hot. I am wearing a high-necked flannel nightgown, packed because it was so cold in Boston when we left. It must be ninety-five degrees in the apartment. My Aunt Ida crawls into the second twin bed, which is less than a foot from our bed. She sighs. She says, to no one in particular, "Isn't it wonderful how fast the young can fall asleep?" My Uncle Carl, who weighs over two hundred pounds, gingerly lets himself down on the beach chair, which creaks terrifyingly. "Oh, God," he says.

My Aunt Ida's head is toward me, and she is breathing in my face. I am choking. I cannot move, because I am supposed to be asleep. Danny seems actually to be sleeping. It is the only sensible way out of his ridiculous situation.

For a while, there is nothing but creaks and sighs. I imagine my Uncle Sol and my father already asleep in the living room. The conferences about the sleeping arrangements have embarrassed my father, too—we did not even say good night. My Aunt Pearl comes into the dark room and sits down on the edge of the bed in which Aunt Ida is sleeping. Suddenly a flashlight beam illuminates the ceiling.

"For God's sake, Pearl, what are you doing?" says Uncle Carl from his beach chair.

"Sh-h-h," she says. "Setting my hair."

On the ceiling I can see the giant corkscrew of a ringlet.

"Aw, come on," Uncle Carl says. "Go to sleep, Pearl. It's nearly three o'clock."

"Shut up," she whispers. "I'll look enough like a witch already from crying." There is the clink of bobby pins. *"How* could Benny have killed himself?" she says into the dark.

"Who says that?" says Uncle Carl. "The maid found him dead in bed. A heart attack."

"Don't tell me," says Aunt Pearl. "He was living death all the time since Beth died. His heart was broken. He was a broken man."

"With all his millions?"

"Oh, shut up. Money isn't everything."

"You'll wake the children."

"They're not such children. They're married to each other."

I see on the ceiling a giant corkscrew subdued to a circle. The flashlight must be in her lap, shining up through her hair.

"I once told him to drop dead," my Aunt Pearl says. "God forgive me. I was eighteen and I wanted to go to the roller-skating rink at the Greek's. My father was dead already, and Benny was the head of the family. He said I couldn't go—it was a cheap place; he didn't want me picking up boys. I said too bad, I'm going anyway, so he grabbed me and put me over his knee and spanked me. I told him to drop dead. Heaven help me, Carl—he's dead."

"Yeah, thirty years later," says Uncle Carl. "Look, Pearl, go to sleep. Don't make yourself suffer."

"Suffer, suffer," my Aunt Pearl says. "To be alive is to suffer." She is crying now. The beach chair creaks, and Uncle Carl's head looms on the ceiling. Then the flashlight is shut off.

"Carly, Carly," Aunt Pearl is whispering. "We should only go together. God should be good to us. I don't want to be without you—we should go at the same time."

Uncle Carl is whispering and Aunt Pearl is crying, and, finally, gratefully, I fall asleep.

I wake, and the night is not yet over. There is the sound of breathing all around me. From the living room comes the grating sound of someone snoring. Could it be my father? When I lived at home, he did not snore. But that was years ago, before I went away to college. Danny's knee is in my back and I cannot change position without falling out of bed. I hold back the blanket and step onto the floor. I tiptoe into the bathroom, where I wash my stinging eyes with cold water and comb my hair with someone's green comb. I do not know what to do. I cannot return to the narrow, stifling bed, but neither can I leave Danny there alone. What would happen if he should wake and find himself alone in the midst of all my breathing relatives?

But I will only be gone a little while. In the living room, my father is pressed into a narrow beach chair. He is snoring. I stand above him, wanting to kiss him. "Daddy," I whisper, but he does not awaken.

Finally, I put my coat on over my nightgown and go outside. It is windy and cloudy, but there is a faint suggestion of dawn. My Uncle Carl's apartment is only two blocks from the house in which I spent my childhood, and I walk there. Perhaps *it* will tell me something about where the years go.

The house is smaller and meaner and uglier than I ever imagined. The front yard, which had been like a hundred acres to me, is not more than fifteen feet long. I feel cold and foolish; my nightgown is sticking out from under my coat. I go back and crawl into bed with Danny. I am grateful for his warm body, because I am shivering. The next time I wake up, it is morning.

In the living room, they are finally talking about what they have all been thinking of: the will. Uncle Sol says solemnly, "Ida, I hope you have been provided for."

Aunt Ida says, a little shortly, "There is nothing to worry about."

Uncle Ben has been supporting her for six years, and she evi-dently does not wish to discuss it. She sits on the couch between Uncle Sol and my father, and ruffles her short black hair with her fingers. She does not wash her hair more than once a month. She vacuums it. She uses a drapery attachment from her old Electro-lux, believing that it stimulates the brain. Aunt Ida has been very superstitious since the night Uncle George died; he had a convul-sive seizure on the night of a full moon, and Aunt Ida believes he was under a spell. She swears he bared his teeth at her, like a wolf, before he passed out of this life. He was not "lost" to her, though, since she felt his life force pass into her body, and she be-lieves she has the strength to live and raise her child alone because she has two life forces bouncing about within her. For the last few years, she has been a health faddist. In her purse, she carries a dozen pill bottles.

Presently, Uncle Sol says, "We are not worried, Ida—we only hope Ben had the foresight to make a will." The brothers of the Goldman family have always looked with suspicion on wills and insurance policies. They seem like asking for trouble. "A man like Ben," says Uncle Sol, reflecting rather desperately, "a man with such a business mind must have had the foresight." Uncle Sol leans back, a frown on his forehead. It is known that Uncle Ben, in order to avoid certain income taxes, years ago put one of his corporations in Uncle Sol's name. As a return for this favor, Uncle Ben has been paying Uncle Sol's income tax every year, in addition to paying him a token salary of fifty-five dollars a week. Uncle Ben promised Uncle Sol's son, my cousin Bill, a new car on his eighteenth birthday. Bill is now seventeen. Uncle Sol's meagre earnings from his fabric store will never afford Bill a new car. Neither will those earnings support Uncle Sol's family if the store is his only income. Uncle Sol sighs. "Ach," he says, "an ugly business."

"I wonder," says fat Uncle Carl, sitting on the edge of the beach chair my father slept in, "whether there was fancy paper business—accountants and lawyers, things like that."

"Sure there was," says Aunt Pearl. "A man like Ben doesn't keep his money in a piggy bank."

"I was just thinking maybe he arranged with his lawyer or someone that Ida should be taken care of if anything happened."

"There's nothing to worry about," says Aunt Ida.

Aunt Pearl says, "Carl, run out and get something for breakfast. Bagels and lox."

Carl rises. My father goes to him and presses a bill into his hand. "Buy it with this," he says.

"Don't be a big shot," Uncle Carl says, shoving it back. "I got plenty of money."

Uncle Carl has not got plenty of money. Five years ago, he sent Aunt Pearl to her brother to ask for a loan. Uncle Ben loaned them five thousand dollars to start a dry-cleaning store with. The store failed. Uncle Carl now works as a cutter in a dress factory. It is clear that Uncle Carl is wondering if Uncle Ben tore up that IOU, or if accountants will unearth it and force payment from him. He leaves to get the bagels and lox.

"What about you, Abram?" says Uncle Sol.

"*What* about me?" says my father.

"What do you think about a will?"

"I think we shouldn't worry about it. There are other things to think about this morning."

Uncle Sol is silenced. He and my father look down at their laps.

Aunt Pearl goes into the kitchen to prepare for breakfast. In a minute, she calls, "Ida, come help me."

Aunt Ida sighs, gets up from the couch, and goes into the

kitchen. In a few minutes, Uncle Carl comes back with two brown paper bags. He sets them in the kitchen, and puts up two card tables in the living room. Aunt Ida returns from the kitchen, carrying one empty plate. She places it in the center of one of the card tables, and sits back down on the couch between her brothers.

We hear a cry from the kitchen. "Damn her, damn her, damn her!" Aunt Pearl is sobbing.

Carl runs to the kitchen. "Pearl! What's the matter?"

"My God-damned sister," she sobs, coming to lean against the wall of the living room and pointing at Ida. "I ask her to help and she carries in one lousy dish. I'm up all night, and I have to cook for everyone, and my husband sleeps on a beach chair in his own house, and she sits on her fat behind."

"Pearl," my father says, getting up and going to her. "There's no need to fight like this today. Everyone is upset. Try to calm down."

"Oh, shut up!" she screams. "Who do you think you are—big brother Ben, bossing me all over the place?"

"Stop that," my father says. *"Stop that!"*

"Just like old times," Aunt Pearl goes on, wildly. "Ida gets away with everything and I get stuck with the dirty work. Where was Ida when Mama died? Do you know where she was? She was at a *party!* That's where devoted Ida was."

"Pearl, Pearl!" cries Uncle Sol. "What's the *sense?*"

Aunt Ida is still sitting on the couch, twisting her fingers together.

"Don't *you* talk!" Aunt Pearl shouts at him. "Who do you think it was who almost *killed* Mama? You, with that *shiksa* you nearly married!"

"ENOUGH!" My father, now the eldest brother, now the head of the family, gives the sternest order I have ever heard. "THERE WILL BE NO MORE OF THIS."

Everyone is silent.

Finally, Uncle Carl says, "Come on. Let's have breakfast."

Little by little, the air calms; we all settle down at the table. Danny has come in from the bedroom, all dressed and shaven. He looks embarrassed because he has heard the fighting. "Good morning," he says.

Aunt Ida smiles at him. She is in the midst of lining up her dozen pill bottles on the table. She offers pills to each. "Sol? Abram? Carl? Janet?" We shake our heads. She says softly, "Pearl, you?" Another no. Then, hesitantly, "Danny?"

Danny accepts. Aunt Ida beams. Into his palm she pours pills of many colors, shapes, contents. This is for good blood, this is for the circulation, this is for the liver. One is more mysterious— it is for life force. Danny doesn't wince. He swallows them seriously, one by one. Aunt Ida loves him. She smiles at my father—Your daughter has married a fine boy. She smiles at me—You have a fine husband. Everyone feels a little better.

On the table are onion rolls, bagels, rye bread. There is butter and cream cheese. There is whitefish and lox and sour cream and bananas and pickled herring. There is coffee ·and cream and sugar.

Everyone begins to talk about what a good man Ben has always been. It cannot be denied that he has been very generous to all of them. If he did not mingle with them socially, it has to be understood. After all, his friends were a different type; Beth was a different type. But Ben never forgot his family. They were never in need. Ben always believed blood ties were the strongest ties on earth.

Uncle Sol bursts out, "But why should *he* have been the only one to go to college? Why did the rest of us have to work in the clothing factory? Why was *he* the only one who was *barmitz-vahed*? It wasn't fair." He seems close to tears.

Now they are bringing up old grievances. Ben had every-thing; they had nothing. Ben had an education, Ben had a car, Ben had a *chance*. They had no chance. They are all failures.

My father nods. He is agreeing that he is a failure. It is not possible for me to stand in front of all these people and tell him he is not a failure. I love him. He has done everything for me and for Mother and for Carol. He has worked like a dog in fifteen different businesses and sent me through college; he will send Carol through college. He has taught us to think, he has given us strength to cope with pain and fear, he has taught us to be honest and fair.

Aunt Pearl, who has been silent since the fight, now says, "It's ironical. Don't envy. He's dead, this brother of ours who had everything. His Beth is dead, his children are orphans, his grandchildren he will never see. Such good fortune, such luck is that?"

They are silent, considering. Indeed, the tables have been turned. Here they all sit in Brooklyn, eating bagels and lox, while Ben is in a coffin on his way to the synagogue.

"May he rest in peace," my father says. "No more talk now."

They observe that it is late, it is time to get started. The service is being held at eleven. The table is cleared quietly.

My father tells me to wear something warm. It is windy and rainy again, the worst kind of day for putting away in the earth. Again something is stopping, freezing in me.

We drive slowly through Brooklyn, through Prospect Park, through downtown, across the East River into Manhattan. Somewhere, on the busiest parkway, we have a flat tire. We *can't* have one; we are already late. "Don't worry," says Uncle Carl. "They can't go ahead without us. They will wait." He must be thinking, but not saying, that Benny will wait, too.

My father is out of the car, kneeling on the road. His face is red with the strain of taking off the tire. "Danny!" I cry. "Help him!" He is only two years younger than Uncle Benny.

The flat tire is fixed; we go on. We are aware of how risky the world is.

At the synagogue, I feel dizzy and weak from lack of sleep. Downstairs is a ladies' room. My Aunt Pearl is there before me; she is powdering under her eyes. "Janet," she says to me, "life is worse than you know," and she is gone. I stay there and try to quiet my stomach. I am afraid for my father. I have never seen him cry, but I am afraid I will see him cry today.

When I come up the stairs, an attendant stops me and says I am too late—I will have to wait outside.

"Wait outside?" I cry.

"Are you related to the deceased?" he asks.

"I am his niece," I say, and push past him. I am at least as important to this service as the Wall Street cronies who are here. They cannot keep me out. My father is waiting for me.

All the relatives are in a long line at the back of the room. The front three rows of seats are empty; the rest of the temple is filled. This is the Park Avenue congregation. These are all Uncle Benny's rich friends. We walk down the aisle. My father is holding my arm as he did at my wedding. Danny is walking behind us, alone. The line files into the front row. My father takes the last seat, and there is no room for me next to him. I have to sit in the second row, diagonally behind him.

Celia is also in the front row, looking as though she has not slept at all. She is wearing a black hat with a thin veil that covers her eyes.

The rabbi begins to speak. With a shock I see the coffin, not two feet from my father, right under the platform on which the rabbi stands. The top is completely covered with roses. It is so magnificent a box you can almost see the congregation reflected in its polished sides.

The rabbi is saying what a good man Uncle Ben was, that all of us know what an honor it is for a man's remains to be brought under the sacred roof of the *shul*. This good man was president of the Men's Club. No matter how busy he was, he never missed a Friday-night service. He was religious and pious and honorable. Sometimes, on a weekday morning, he would come into the temple alone and sit at the back, staring at the Ark of the Covenant. Ben Goldman was a fine man. Ben Goldman loved all his children.

When he says that, he looks at the front row, where Melissa sits next to Fred, and he repeats, "He loved *all* his children." The Catholic daughter-in-law is included. This is a generous rabbi.

What the rabbi cannot mention—and what perhaps is Uncle Ben's greatest achievement—is that Uncle Ben has just been given a larger writeup in a new book called "Moneymakers" than anyone else in the country has been given. He has been described as the shrewdest chemical man in America in this book. A photograph shows him watching a ticker tape, a far from pious expression on his face.

The rabbi says, "And now this good soul has gone to join his beloved Beth," and I see my father cover his eyes, and I begin to cry. Danny takes my hand, but I gather momentum and am shaking so hard I cannot breathe.

Men come forward and lift the coffin. Very slowly, they walk toward the back of the *shul*, rose petals slipping off the coffin to fall under their feet. My father is the first to follow the coffin out. I drop Danny's arm and run ahead to hold my father's. He averts his face, and from deep in his chest I hear a ripping sound that I know is the sound of a man crying who has not cried in forty years.

Outside, in the wind, he is in control again. There are seven black limousines lined up to take the mourners to the cemetery. My father opens the door of the third limousine. "Get inside. I don't want you to catch cold."

"Where are you going?"

He points to the second car.

"I want to go with you," I say.

"I have to go with the brothers and sisters."

He won't let me argue. I get into the third limousine. In the second are the brothers and sisters, in the first the children of Ben and their mates, and in front of that the hearse, with Uncle Ben under his roses.

Danny leans back uncomfortably in one of the seats that have been pulled up from the floor—the most uncomfortable in the car. There are six strangers with us in the car. The driver is a pockmarked, yellow-skinned, unpleasant-looking man. Beside him are a couple with bored faces. In back of us are two middle-aged women and one very old woman.

The car moves slowly away from the curb. It is daytime, but the headlights of the cars in the procession are on. The yellow-faced driver maneuvers skillfully in the heavy traffic. This is just another working day for him.

One of the middle-aged women leans forward and taps me on the shoulder. "Are you related to Benny?" she asks in a rasping, masculine voice.

"His niece," I say.

"Are you Abie's girl?"

"Yes."

"I thought so. You look like him. I lived next door to your father in Bensonhurst. I was his first girl. My name is Mickey."

I am repelled. My father has as much as betrayed my mother with this vulgar woman.

"I didn't use to talk this way," she explains. "I had part of my voice box removed. Cancer."

The little old lady now taps me on the shoulder. "You want I should show you the pictures of my grandchildren? I'm your father's Aunt Sadie."

So this is Aunt Sadie, the aunt my father dislikes most. I do not know why, exactly, but I do know her husband owned a clothing warehouse and gave my father—then a boy of eleven—the night watchman's job in it. My father used to sit shivering in the dark, hearing rats run across the floor and imagining horrors he can hardly explain. For this he was paid twenty-five cents a night, while the same uncle sent Benny to Hebrew school.

The old lady is showing me snapshots. "This is Ruthie, she had a birthmark big as an apple, the biggest doctor in New York took it off, she's a beauty now, you could never know."

I nod wearily.

"They kicked me out from the family," she says. "Last winter, I was in Miami Beach, I called your father, he should come to see me at my hotel, he never came. Same with Sol. Probably the wives didn't let. I never liked your mother."

"Look," I say, "we're going to a funeral. Maybe we should all be a little quiet."

She sits back, silent.

We are out of the city at last. It can't be much longer. The couple in the front seat light cigarettes. The pockmarked driver then lights a cigarette for himself. We are coming into open country. The old lady taps me again. "Here," she says. She stuffs something folded into my hand. "That boy next to you must be your husband. I know you had a wedding. I was never invited, but I don't hold no grudge. Just because I was never invited is no reason I can't give a present."

It is a five-dollar bill. "Look, Aunt Sadie," I say. "I don't want it. It's not necessary.

"I have nothing against you," she says. "It's your mother who didn't invite me. Buy yourself something."

We are pulling into the cemetery. My heart pounds and I see a blackness before my eyes for an instant.

The wound of my Aunt Beth's grave is not yet healed, and beside it a new one is open. They are sliding the coffin out of the hearse and carrying it toward the grave. A green rug is placed over the hole, a board across the rug, and the coffin upon the board. This is done very quickly, even before all the limousines are empty.

There is a canopy covering both graves. No tombstone marks Beth's grave; it is not yet a year. A chair is brought forward for Celia. She declines it with a shake of her head.

The canopy flaps in the wind, and the rabbi steps under it, carrying a closed black umbrella. The relatives gather in, and once again the gray-haired, palsied undertaker appears, now distributing long-stemmed red roses, one to each person. His expression is as blank as if he were dealing out a deck of cards.

I try to see past Celia's face into her thoughts. What if that were my father, locked in that coffin? What if his face were being put away from me forever? And then I ask myself a question against all knowledge. How do they know the dead are dead? What if, tonight, Uncle Ben opens his eyes and calls to be freed? Is Aunt Beth lying beneath this very earth, listening? Is she thinking, Finally, Ben, you are coming to sleep?

It seems against all things human, to bury someone under the earth who has breathed in light and air from the instant of birth. Why not lay the dead among green trees, in the open woods? Are not the ants and beetles better than the lead-sealed, waterproof, airtight, thousand-dollar mahogany casket?

My heart is spinning in the pain of its own inadequacy. What does it *mean* for Uncle Benny to be dead?

The rabbi is reading the service in Hebrew. I do not understand it. At the end, at a signal of the rabbi's hand, Celia and Fred step forward. Celia steps too far, upon the unsupported part of the green rug, and lunges forward, nearly falling into the grave underneath. She is caught by my father and Fred, who hold her until she can balance herself again. Fred takes her hand, and the brother and sister say the Mourner's Kaddish: *"Yisgadal veyiskadash Sh'may rabbo be'olmo..."* They say it well—they have said it often for their mother. For a moment, I believe in the prayer; I believe there is God, this is His language, He is there, and Uncle Ben is all right. But my disbelief is suspended only until Celia steps back, nearly staggering, her face gray with anguish.

"Throw the rose," says the rabbi. Celia tosses the rose upon the coffin. Fred does the same. We all toss our roses forward, as though we are playing a game of quoits, and it is over. They are hurrying the pregnant girl out of the wind and back into the limousine.

But it is not quite over. The brothers and sisters of Uncle Ben remain behind. The four of them are crying, facing in the world's four directions, away from each other. Privately, each one is accepting the finality of his brother's death. It seems they are ashamed to look at each other, for when they are done with whatever each has had to do in his heart, they still do not draw together.

We pile back in the cars, in the same distribution as before, and we drive away.

There. I have seen a funeral—I have seen it all, and what do I know? I have understood nothing.

It is silent all the way back to Manhattan. The funeral party meets in Uncle Ben's apartment, where his maid, the colored woman who discovered his body, serves us corned-beef sandwiches and potato salad.

It is announced that the family will sit *Shiva* in two places— the brothers and sisters at Aunt Pearl's house, the children at Celia's house. But it is understood that Celia and Fred will not serve out the week of mourning, sitting on boxes on the floor, barefooted, the men unshaven, the women without color, the mirrors covered with sheets. They are of the modern generation; they have obligations; one of them has got to get a child born, the other has to learn the chemical business. Let the old folks sit *Shiva*.

Pleading his wife's tiredness, Celia's husband takes her away. Melissa and Fred leave with them. The strangers go, and the rest of us are left in Uncle Ben's house.

"There was no will," Uncle Sol says. "Fred told me."

So. All the money is to go to the children. No car for Sol's son, no rent for Aunt Ida. And do even *I* feel a little disappointed?

Nothing matters. I am sick of it all. I want to go home with Danny to our rickety attic where we bang our heads on the ceiling every time we get out of bed. I want to go back to my tiny office and watch the pigeons strutting on my window sill, which overlooks the Common. There are things to do—many things to do— and I understand that that is the only answer I shall have to all my questions.

Robert A. Stone

Geraldine

Geraldine had her shoes in her hand when she came into the
White Way. Pale-faced, she leaned on the bar, brushing gravel
from the bottoms of her seamed stocking feet.

"Oh Jesus," the bartender said. "Why don't you get out of
Port Arthur?"

Geraldine looked at him pouting and frightened. She had
a child's face over a hard mountain jaw.

"Oh, Chato," she said. "Woody's comin', I think. What in
hell do I do?"

"You shoulda been long gone," Chato told her. "You and
Woody both."

Then Woody was standing in the doorway with his hands
in his pockets, the lines of his mouth creased outward in a
broad Indian-looking smile. In the half-moment before she had
managed to kick off the one replaced shoe and break for the
ladies' room, Geraldine reflected that Woody's smiles, when
Woody smiled, were sure lacking in whatever it was you liked
to see in a smile. Chato grunted, turning to watch the action in
his blue mirror.

"Hello, Chato," Woody said.

Geraldine was off the stool and across the room with aston-
ishing speed but the tight white skirt was wrong for her hill-
accommodating strides. Woody had her in no time at all, spinning her back against the bar where she braced on her elbows,
her legs bent behind her, watching Woody move back, slide

From *Stanford Short Stories 1964*. © 1964 by the Board of Trustees of the Leland Stanford
Junior University. Excerpted from the novel *Children of Light* by Robert A. Stone (to be
published by Houghton Mifflin Company, New York, 1966) and reprinted here with permission.

his big hands out of sight and stand tilted on his heels, smiling.
Both she and Chato thought Woody was going to shoot her then.

"Where was you thinkin' to go, Geraldine?" Woody said.

Finding herself still alive, Geraldine straightened and managed a toss of the head. "Well, to the ladies' room, Woody, for
Godsakes."

Chato went into what was supposed to be the kitchen to get
out of the way. Woody, coming in, had locked the door behind
him. Geraldine decided that the best thing to do was to keep on
talking and see how that went. "I believe I don't understand
you," she said. She rubbed her arm coyly, discovering that the
muscle had gone numb under Woody's grip. "Snatchin' on
people."

"You little sneakin' shit-bird," Woody said, "you got money
of mine."

"No such."

"Shit you don't. I give you five dollars to buy hamburgers."

"Woody, I don't—" she jumped quickly out of reach as he
moved forward. "Woody, Wood honey— I gotta go to the ladies'
room. That's what I come in here for."

"Leave them shoes on the bar. And the pocketbook, baby.
Then you go on in there and when you come out I believe we'll
have us a lesson about the right way and the wrong way to treat
little Woody." He smiled again.

The damp cement chilled her bare feet. There were no windows you could get out of, and so what if there were. Geraldine
went down on the cold toilet seat, running the hot water tap over
her left hand until it burned. She felt faint and dizzy. She was
probably catching cold, she thought. Raising her eyes she caught
a glimpse of her face in the wall mirror. Pretty blue eyes, she
thought. My pretty blue eyes. "Belle of the Whorehouse, Mary
Jane" someone had written on the scrofulous green wall above the
mirror. She looked from the phrase to her own image. "Ain't that
me now," she said aloud.

Oh, she was feeling dizzy and sleepy, too. Woody was outside—in the pocket of his jeans was a mean little .38 with a
bullet in each chamber—there was also, she remembered, a
small neat notch on the grip. She was suddenly convulsed with
physical terror—the picture of the blue, scarred metal froze

in her mind's eye—she could not change the image. Her body seemed so soft, so rendable and vulnerable before that piece of steel machinery. Gripping her shoulders with trembling hands, she thought of the soft, bloated bodies of small dead animals on the road. Then the faintness settled back on her, she sniffed—a cold, another cold. She ran more hot water over her hands and washed her face and dried it on the dirty public towel.

It might be like being hit. That didn't usually hurt too much. Something to be got over with. It seemed very natural and right that Woody would shoot her when she went back out. She hadn't much idea why or what over—but Woody was the sort that killed you, she thought. "I don't know," she said to the mirror. But there were so many days, so many goddam nights. What a long time ago that road of days and nights began. And there was nothing to look back on since then that didn't make her sort of sick.

If he does it without talking, she thought, if I don't have to listen to him or look at him, then I'll just be dead and that'll be it.

"Oh I'm tired," she said. "If I could just have a drink first, I'd walk out there and spit in his eye."

She unhooked the latch and went out into the blue glow. Live Fast, Love Hard, Die Young—that was the song Faron Young used to sing. She thought of L.J., who was dead. And the little baby who was dead. Live Fast, Love Hard, Die Young. Lights on the road. Rainy thirsty mornings. Big dirty hands. Die Young.

Woody had emptied her purse on the bar. He was looking at a picture of Geraldine with L.J. and L.J. was grinning and Geraldine was, and holding a little three-weeks baby.

She walked over and stood looking down at the floor and Woody was holding her arm and talking slow—making the speech about the gun and how—talking real slow—he was gonna take that little old gun and stick the ever lovin' barrel right smack up against the top of her mouth and when he pulled the trigger her brains were going to smear the ceiling and so forth. It was one of his favorite lyric recitations and Geraldine always found it a little fascinating to hear.

He hadn't finished when she looked up at him, and seeing her face he stopped, the killer smile creasing his mouth and lighting the dark hard hollows under his cheekbones. He looks like a stain, Geraldine thought, like the kind of stain you see on the underside of a crate of rotten fruit.

"Then they ship you home in a box, sugar," Woody concluded.

She pressed her face close to his, with a rapt child's smile, gently, with infinite tenderness.

"Whatever your name is," she said, "whoever you are—Fuck You."

"Woody!" Chato was out screaming. "Woody!" His voice got high like a woman's. "You all crazy!"

"No trouble to it," Woody said after a while, and put the thing back in his pocket.

"I seen luck run hard," Mary was saying. "But luck like yours I never seen nor heard of."

It was late at night, a week after the cops had grabbed Woody. Geraldine, out of the hospital with nowhere much to go, had returned to the place to pack. But it turned out that she really had been catching cold that night—she could hardly do more than lie around in her old room with a box of Kleenex. And, at first, she could not bring herself to go out very much. Mary came up, sometimes, to keep her company.

"I guess I'm lucky I'm alive," Geraldine said. "I guess so."

"Damn right," Mary said. "If you still alive, you know you're winnin'. He was sure a nut, old Woody."

"Yeah, he sure was," Geraldine said. It had been raining for two days now, raining and hot. Sooner or later she would have to pack up and go somewhere.

"What was it he used, honey?"

"Something they open oysters with, I think. I was sure he was goin' to shoot me. I was sure."

"Why don't you go home, baby?" Mary said. "You got folks in West Virginia. Go on home."

"I reckon," Geraldine said.

"You don't want to set around here fightin' the mirror. Your face'll heal up all right. Get drunk once and cry and then go back to West Virginia."

"No work in West Virginia," Geraldine said. "Just barmaid work and I'm through with that, all right. New face, new life."

"Don't talk that crap," Mary said, sighing at the rain.

The next day she got Geraldine a $10 ride on a fruit truck that was going through to New Orleans. The driver was a Mex from Brownsville. He was all right, Mary said.

Only once in the course of the trip did the Mex refer to Geraldine's face, and then it was very directly. It was practically the only thing he said the whole time.

"Where you meet that guy?" he asked her. Mary had filled him in.

"Fort Smith."

"Why you go with him?"

"For the ride," Geraldine said.

"For the ride," he repeated and glanced at her quickly in the windshield mirror.

That night they were past Orange, crossing the oil barrens near the Gulf. The rain had died to scant drops that padded softly on the cab roof and dotted the windshield. Off to the west, the sun had come through and was going down in folds of sad violet cloud —a little patch of blue open sky glowed above it, looking very far off, clean, remote, inviolable. From that edge of sky to the swelling darkness in the east the T-towers throbbed under pentecostal tongues of orange flame; the pumps rose and fell rhythmically in the glare of night lights—hundreds of towers in irregular rows standing like islands in the wet tall grass.

Geraldine huddled against the door, staring in cool dumb wonder at the towers, tracing their outlines on the window with her finger. Sometimes, she thought, you feel like you been blistered so thick that you're tougher than anything they got and then the next minute you feel like you'll die of the daylight if you can't run and hide. Best to be like the old pros that have to get drunk to feel anything. She felt small and cold over the roaring power of the great truck, twice lost in the endless valley of dumb, giant machines.

But I got to come back, she thought. Woody, that was his name, had not had the .38 that night and she was alive. Best probably to go back to West Virginia when she had the money. If she could get a job in New Orleans she might get it together. But then there wasn't anyone much back home. Her mother was dead, and her father had been years in Cleveland without an address anybody knew. An old unknown aunt still lived in Welch, but any other family she had were in Birmingham or Pittsburgh, Cleveland, Chicago. Everybody was leaving—the mines were mostly closed or closing; the men took their full unemployment, sat around drinking and watching television for six months and then packed up.

Geraldine watched the sky, dark now, and the towers, glowing like the lights of a city. Like Birmingham.

She and L.J. had gone to Birmingham after they were married—she was sixteen then, he was around eighteen—they had gone down looking for work. Rotten it had been. The rooming house was rotten, the baby was all the time catching cold, like back there in Port Arthur it seemed always to rain. And L.J., whose family was Hard Shell and temperance, had started in to drink most of the time. He was always out, hanging around—they were always broke.

She had loved him an awful lot, she thought suddenly. He was so sweet, them freckles, God, he could be so happy sometimes, and he could make her laugh and his body was tight and lean, he felt so good and he loved her back. Coming home after a night around, she'd hate him and curse him up and down and he'd look so sick and green, so pale under his damn freckles, she had to laugh anyway. He loved the baby so.

It had come then that she'd been able to leave the baby with his aunt and take her first barmaid's job—and he'd been moody and raised all hell without seeming to know why. The night it happened he came to the place she worked, starting trouble, and they'd thrown him out and she was so mad she didn't go with him. And then he must have gone on drinking because they said after that he'd been in more than a few fights that night—with some mean-looking boys, they said. One of the mean-looking boys had shot him through the heart on the sidewalk of Montgomery Street after bar closing, but they never found out which mean-looking boy it had been. Things like that happened fairly often in Birmingham.

So she stayed on at the bar, seeing little of the baby, which went sickly about a month later and was pale all the time and didn't take much nourishment and had convulsions finally and died. After that, things were a little blurred. She had moved around a lot. That was most of her life, it felt like, the four years since then. It had turned out that there were barmaids and barmaids and if you stayed at it long enough you just naturally made the second category. And sooner or later by some law of circulation you ended up in Texas. You gotta go up or you go down, they said—down always turns out to be Texas and you can figure anywhere else is up.

Don't feel anything, she told herself, stop it, stop feeling it. You don't have to look in the mirror, you can look at the road. Don't look inside—watch that old scenery and sooner or later you get to the end of it. Because there's nothing to hang on to. Try to hang on, you're a fool. And if you're a girl, maybe, and you're looking to hang on, your trouble will just naturally come from men. Like Woody and like the rest of them. There wasn't but one man for her and he wasn't a man but a boy and he was buried dead. And the baby.

Sleep, she thought. There has to be an end of it, some place warm to sleep maybe. If you could feel there was some place at the end of it—like the patch of sky they'd seen back at the oil barrens—why it'd be better then. Some place like in the Wayfaring Stranger song—no pain, no toil, no danger.

Then for no reason she thought of her father's house, when she was a little girl and it was during the war. Things were good she remembered, everyone said there was plenty of work. In the room where she slept there was a picture of President Roosevelt. He was a great man, everyone said he had Put The Country On Its Feet, he cared for the people, they said. Funny thing to think of. But when she had been a little girl in bed, she had thought of President Roosevelt, how kind he looked, how everyone said he cared for the people, how his voice sounded on the radio. The thought of that picture still came to her as a thought of something powerful and kind, an expectation of warmth and guarded peace, her father's house, heaven and rest and God.

But it's a long time comin', she thought, drifting into sleep. It's a long time.

Biographical Sketches

Donald A. Allan is managing editor of *The Reporter* magazine, where he has been since 1961. He took a reporter's job a week after graduating from Stanford in 1946 and has not since written what he claimed to be fiction. He has worked on papers in and around San Francisco; as foreign correspondent for the United Press in Madrid, Paris, and Brussels; as Rome bureau chief for *Newsweek*; as city reporter for the *New York Times*; as editor in chief of the North American Newspaper Alliance, and as senior editor of *Coronet*. "A Stranger's Funeral" is based on his experiences as a prisoner of war and escapee in Germany in 1944–45, so he has "probably never written any fiction" even though he has published in many places including *Mademoiselle, Esquire, Saturday Evening Post,* and even *Gourmet*. He married Alexandra Temple Emmet in 1965. Mr. Allan says that he was "not cut out to be an artist—no discipline and low standards."

Maxwell Arnold was a Stanford freshman in 1936, dropped out, and returned after World War II to graduate in 1948. "The Grapefruit Thinker" was one of two stories he had in *Stanford Short Stories 1948,* when he won a Stanford Humanities Prize; another of his stories appeared in the 1950 volume. He has had stories published in *Harper's* and *The Sewanee Review,* and he was a Fellow at Breadloaf. He has been writing intermittently while working in the hotel business and advertising. In the national election of 1960, he was in charge of writing advertising for the agency handling the Democratic Presidential campaign. For a time he lived in Gloucester, Massachusetts; he now works in San Francisco and lives with his wife and three children in Menlo Park, in the hills back of Stanford.

Richard K. Arnold was a student at the Creative Writing Center in 1946–47. "A Problem in Creation" was published originally in the pioneer issue of *The Pacific Spectator*. After graduating from Stanford in 1948, he worked for three years at a family-owned New England resort hotel. In 1951 he returned to his native California and entered the public relations field in San Francisco. He took a leave of absence from public relations to be advertising copy director of the agency group serving the Democratic National Committee and candidate John F. Kennedy in the 1960 Presidential campaign. Since 1961, he has been a partner and principal in a public relations firm with headquarters in San Francisco. He lives with his wife and son in Portola Valley. At times during his business career, he has managed to contribute fiction and nonfiction to magazines, and he has written the book and lyrics for three musical comedies produced by San Francisco theatrical groups: *Sweet Executive* (1958), *The Khan Game* (1963), and *Back at the Front* (1966).

Eugene Burdick was born in Iowa and went to school in southern California. He graduated from Stanford University in 1941 and almost immediately joined the navy, was married, and received orders to depart for Guadalcanal. After the war he received a Ph.D. degree in political science from Stanford, where he was also a writing student, and later he was on the faculty of the University of California at Berkeley. He is the author of *The Ninth Wave*, *The Blue of Capricorn*, *Sarkhan*, *The 480*, and co-author of *The Ugly American* and *Fail-Safe*. Several of his novels have been made into movies. A volume of his short stories will be published this autumn. Mr. Burdick died in 1965.

Jean Byers was born in San Jose, California. She now lives in Westport, Connecticut, with her husband, Frederic S. Cushing, and their son James. In Westport she has been a free-lance editor, lecturer, and teacher of creative writing. She is currently engaged in writing a novel.

Warren Chapman was born in 1917 in Pueblo, Colorado. He attended preparatory school in the East and was in the class of 1939 at Harvard. After serving in the army, he was a technical engineer in a Chicago steel mill. He took his Bachelor of Arts degree at Stanford in 1950 and his Master of Arts in 1954 with a year on a Stanford Creative Writing Fellowship. From 1953 until 1965 he was a member of the faculty at Monterey Peninsula College, where he taught English and served as president of the Academic Senate and the Faculty Association. He is married and has four children, one of whom received his A.B. degree from Stanford in 1966.

"Where Teetee Wood Lies Cold and Dead" received first prize in the Edith Mirrielees Short Story Contest of 1950.

Edith Cory graduated from Stanford in 1952, with a degree in English. A year later she returned as a graduate student and instructor in freshman composition. She has worked for an airline, a book publisher, and a motion picture studio. Since receiving an M.L.S. degree from the University of California she has been employed as a librarian. She now lives in Burlingame, California, with her husband, Madison Cooper.

Constance Crawford grew up in various parts of southern California. She received a B.A. degree in English from Stanford in 1952 and spent a postgraduate year at the Stanford Writing Center. She has published stories in *The Pacific Spectator* and *Mademoiselle*. "The Boats" was the winner of the *Mademoiselle* College Fiction Contest for 1951, and another of her stories was included in the *Forty Best Stories from Mademoiselle*. She and her husband, George Houle, lived for the next ten years in France, California (Oakland), Colorado, and Minnesota before returning to Stanford, where he is associate professor in the department of music. From 1955 to 1963, during which time their four children were born, she did no writing, but in 1963 she began to write again.

Sue Davidson was born and raised in Texas. She attended the University of Texas and was on the editorial staff of the *Galveston Daily News*. She received an A.M. degree in English at the University of Chicago. In 1949–50 she was a Fellow in Creative Writing at Stanford, and in 1950–51 she held a Saxton Fellowship. She now lives in Seattle, where she has taught English, drama, and social studies and has been a book editor. Her writing has appeared in *The Progressive, The Nation, Commonweal, Frontier, Liberation,* and other periodicals. A pamphlet, "What Do You Mean, Nonviolence?" was recently issued by Fellowship Publications. She is married to a professor of political science, Alex Gottfried, and they have a 12-year-old daughter, who writes poetry, stories, and polemics.

Wesley Ford Davis grew up in rural central Florida, the background for most of his fiction. He received a bachelor's degree from Rollins College, where he had a speech scholarship. His college years were interrupted by five years in the army in World War II, where he served in ranks from private to captain in the infantry and the paratroops. His serious interest in writing began after an unlucky parachute jump, while he lay on his back with time to think. Early in the war he married a poet, Betty Miller, and they had two daughters, and by them three grandchildren. He now has a nine-month-old son by his second wife, Marian Springer Hopkins Davis, who teaches behavioral science at the University of South Florida. His short stories have been published or accepted by *Collier's, Esquire, Discovery, Everybody's, New Mexico Quarterly, Carolina Quarterly, Swank, Escapade, Best American Stories,* and *Toward Reading Comprehension.* A novel, *The Time of the Panther,* was published by Harper & Brothers, reprinted in paperback by Popular Library, and published in translation in Germany. He has taught English and creative writing at the University of Arkansas and is now associate professor of English and creative writing at the University of South Florida. He is at work on a novel to be called "Confessions of an Alligator Hunter."

David Dow was born in Auburn, California, and attended schools in Sacramento. His first published work, at the age of fourteen, was a poem about Ty Cobb, which led to a meeting with the baseball immortal. At Stanford he majored in journalism and played two years as an infielder and catcher on the baseball team. "Ol' Nick's Wife," suggested by three summers in a plumbing supply warehouse, was written for a creative writing course. The late Frank O'Connor, reading it on a visit to the campus, called it "next door to a masterpiece." After graduation, Dow worked as a reporter for *The San Diego Union,* and then entered the navy's aviation officer candidate program. He served as an air intelligence officer aboard the nuclear-powered carrier *Enterprise* in the 1962 blockade of Cuba. Since leaving the navy in 1964, he has been a reporter and feature writer for *The Sacramento Bee* and a newsman for Sacramento television station KOVR. Now twenty-eight, he is married to the former Tamzene Ann Shay, of Morehead, Kentucky.

Arthur Edelstein was a Writing Fellow at Stanford in 1961–62 and was doing graduate work on a doctorate in English. Two of his stories, including "That Time of Year," were published in *Stanford Short Stories.* He is now a lecturer at Hunter College, where he is also adviser to the Writers Workshop. Next year he will be on the staff of Brandeis University, where he will teach American literature. His critical writings include an introduction to *Sister Carrie* (Perennial Classics Edition, Harper & Row, 1965), an article on Angus Wilson in *Contemporary British Novelists,* and one on Edward Lewis Wallant in *Jewish Heritage,* Winter, 1964. His reviews have appeared in *The New Leader, Saturday Review, The National Observer,* and elsewhere. He is co-editor of *Modern and Contemporary: Nine Masters of the Story,* to be published in 1967. He is the East Coast editor of *Per/Se.*

Sarah Fay was born in Boston, Massachusetts, and received her education there and at Sarah Lawrence College, where the poets Horace Gregory and Robert Fitzgerald were two of her instructors. After her year at the Stanford Creative Writing Center she continued to live and work in San Francisco for several years, but she has spent the past decade as an uncomplaining wife and mother in Baltimore, Maryland. Early this year her husband's business took him to a Boston firm, so she finds herself after many years back on native New England soil, "which in the long run just seems to be my kind of soil." The distractions of married life have curtailed her activities as a writer, but with her youngest child about to enter the first grade, she expects to be released sufficiently to return to the business of writing. The story and short novel continue to occupy her interests. She is married to Gordon Baird.

John Ferrone served with the Army Air Force during World War II and then attended Colorado College and Stanford University, where he majored in English. In 1950 he was awarded a Creative Writing Fellowship at Stanford. That summer he visited relatives in Italy, a meeting that sparked the idea for "About My Sons." In 1951, after receiving a master's degree from Stanford, he worked at the Stanford University Press, and in the spring of 1953 he moved to New York. He has been in publishing since that time, first as an editor in the Dell Publishing Company, then as executive editor of the Odyssey Press, trade division. At the present time he is editor of the paperback division at Harcourt, Brace & World.

Merrill Joan Gerber has published stories in *The New Yorker, Mademoiselle, Redbook, The Sewanee Review,* and elsewhere. A collection of her stories, *Stop Here, My Friend,* was published in 1965 by Houghton Mifflin, and in 1966 it was brought out in an English edition. She received a B.A. degree from the University of Florida, and attended graduate school at Brandeis University. In 1962–63 she was a Writing Fellow at Stanford. She now lives in California with her husband and two daughters.

Boris Ilyin came to the Stanford Creative Writing Center in 1946, just after his World War II army service. A novel, *Green Boundary* (Houghton Mifflin, 1949), was written at Stanford while he held a Writing Fellowship. Since then he served in the Department of Defense and later in the Foreign Service. He lives near Washington, D.C., does not write, but hopes someday to begin again.

Susan Kuehn held a Stanford Writing Fellowship while on leave from the *Minneapolis Star and Tribune,* where she was a staff reporter. She is a native of Minneapolis and a graduate of Wellesley College. For the past twelve years, she has lived in Iowa City, where her husband, Willard L. Boyd, is professor of law at the University of Iowa. As the mother of three children (Betsy, nine; Bill, six; Tom, three), she is involved in car-pool driving, Sunday school "helping," and cookie baking, but she tries to devote the equivalent of one day a week to writing. On these "lucky days" she hires a baby sitter and takes her current manuscript and the world's heaviest portable typewriter to a place without a telephone (usually the university library) and works all day. Most recently her stories have appeared in *Redbook*.

Rhoda LeCocq spent a year and a half going around the world and studying philosophy in France and India since receiving her M.A. degree in creative writing at Stanford. She worked in advertising and public relations in San Francisco and Honolulu for seven years, for a national food chain, for an art academy, and for city and county government. She claims that the two high points in her world travel were meeting Carl Gustav Jung in Switzerland and Aurobindo Ghose, contemporary philosopher, in India. In Honolulu she learned to surf and to paddle an outrigger canoe; since returning to California in 1964, she says she has remained ill-adjusted to wearing shoes. After a year of study in existentialism and Indian philosophy at the University of Honolulu and the Asian Studies Academy in San Francisco, she is doing advanced work toward a doctorate in philosophy at the University of California, Santa Barbara. She has completed only one novel and hopes to return to full-time writing someday and write three more "now in her head."

John A. Lynch served with the 88th Infantry Division in Italy after he graduated from the University of Notre Dame in 1943. At Stanford he held a Writing Fellowship for the year 1948–49. For the past fifteen years he has been a technical writer and editor for the Ford Motor Company, Bendix Aviation, and now the Perini Corporation. He has also taught evening classes in creative writing at the South Bend campus of Indiana University and the downtown campus of the University of Chicago. His stories and poems have appeared in the *Atlantic Monthly, Commonweal, The Pacific Spectator, Prairie Schooner, The Antioch Review, New Mexico Quarterly, Northern Review, University of Kansas City Review, Perspective, Voices, Four Quarters, Modern Age, Georgia Review, Chicago Choice, Critic, Views, Golden Goose,* and *University Review*. His stories have been reprinted in *O. Henry Memorial Awards, Best American Short Stories, All Manner of Men, Beginnings, Best Articles and Stories,* and *Das Antlitz des Kriegers,* an anthology of war stories published in Vienna in 1964. He and his wife and seven children live in Framingham, Massachusetts.

Miriam Merritt had her first novel, *By Lions, Eaten Gladly,* published in 1965 by Harcourt, Brace & World, and in Great Britain by Victor Gollancz, Ltd., in 1966. Her short stories have appeared in *Epoch, The Southwest Review, University of Kansas City Review,* and *New Campus Writing.* She was born in Texas and lives in Houston. A graduate of the University of Texas, she attended the Stanford Creative Writing Center on a fellowship in 1952–53.

Dennis Murphy was an undergraduate at Stanford when he wrote "A Camp in the Meadow." He is the author of a novel, *The Sergeant,* which was published in 1958. During the past several years he has been at work on half a dozen movies in Hollywood and London, and he is presently at work on another book. He was born in Salinas, California, in 1933.

Nancy Packer was a Stegner Fellow in Creative Writing in 1959–60 and is now on the teaching staff of the Creative Writing Center at Stanford. Her stories have been published in *The Kenyon Review, Contact, Harper's, The Reporter, Southwest Review, Yale Review, San Francisco Review,* and *Dude.* She lives on the Stanford campus with her two children and her husband, Herbert L. Packer, who is a professor of law. She was born in 1925 and grew up in Birmingham, Alabama.

Tillie Olsen, born in 1913, grew up in Nebraska, and wrote a great deal as a girl. Her formal education ended "almost through high school." A San Franciscan since 1933, she has lived and worked most of her life far from literary and academic worlds. Having to work as well as raise a family (she has four daughters), she did not return to serious writing until the early 1950's. A Stanford Writing Fellowship in 1955–56 enabled her to quit her job as transcriber and have regular blocks of time ("eight months, three days a week . . . during which I became a writing writer"). It was in this period that "Tell Me a Riddle" (*Stanford Short Stories, 1950*) was begun, which, when completed, received the 1961 O. Henry Award as the best American story published that year. A Ford Grant in Literature was awarded Mrs. Olsen in 1959, and appointment to the Radcliffe Institute for Independent Study in 1962–64. *Tell Me a Riddle,* a collection, has been published in England as well as in this country. In addition to the 1961 O. Henry Award volume, her work has been anthologized in *New Campus Writing, No. 2; Fifty Best American*

Stories, 1915–1965; the Foley *Best American Stories,* 1957 and 1961; and the British *Modern American Stories*; and will appear in Katherine Anne Porter's forthcoming *A Collection of Favorites* and Richard Kostelantz's *The Evolving Form, Stories of the Sixties.*

Jean Powell left Stanford in 1949 to work toward a Ph.D. degree at the University of Wisconsin, where she was a teaching assistant in 1949–50 and the recipient of the Beatrice Kaufmann Award in Creative Writing in 1950–51. Subsequently she has lived in six states and two countries, taught at three universities and one private school, written some stories, and done editorial work and book reviewing. She is married to Robert L. Peters, professor of Victorian literature at the University of California, Riverside. They have four children. A fifth child died seven years ago; a volume of poems written to him by his father will be part of the new W. W. Norton poetry series. The family will live in England this coming year.

Clay Putman was born in Oklahoma in 1924. He is the author of a novel, *The Ruined City,* and a forthcoming collection of short stories. He lives with his wife and daughter in San Francisco, where he is a member of the faculty of San Francisco State College.

Edgar Rosenberg left Nuremberg in 1939, when he was thirteen, and came to the United States a year later, via Switzerland and Haiti. After high school in New York and army service in Europe, he attended Cornell (B.A. 1949) and Stanford (Ph.D. 1958). From 1957 to 1965 he taught at Harvard as instructor and Briggs-Copeland Assistant Professor. The author of *From Shylock to Svengali* (Stanford University Press, 1960) and a forthcoming study of the historical novel, he has published fiction and nonfiction in *Epoch, Commentary,* and *Esquire.* A propos of "Our Felix" he writes: "In May 1963, on a sabbatical from Harvard, I drove to Montreux (the Vevey of the story) and dropped in on Madame's shop. It was darker and sloppier than ever. Madame, its solitary custodian, dropped her knitting and leapt up at me in the hope of substantial foreign business. Monsieur was dead; had been dead for years; but his likeness, clipped from a local paper and taped to the wall, humored my invasion with a shockingly wicked and sleepy grin. Madame is still a big lady (she never had half the looks I gave her in the story), but her eyesight and hearing are sadly failing now; I think she is over 70. Business is worse than ever. I took her out for a long, long lunch at a lakeside restaurant down the road from Chillon; she talked constantly, feelingfully, and querulously, as old people will; back in the shop, she picked out a pea-green tie for me to take back to America. I expected all this romantic reprise to be rather depressing, but it wasn't. It was like music, the whole thing."

William S. Schuyler grew up in St. Louis, Missouri, where he was born in 1912. He received a B.A. degree in English at Washington University in St. Louis, an M.A. in creative writing, and an Ed.D. at Stanford University. He has operated a dude ranch in New Mexico, spent three years in the navy, written western stories for the pulp magazines, and been a college teacher and administrator. He is currently assistant to the academic vice-president at San Francisco State College and teaches in the department of English.

Peter Shrubb was born in Australia in 1928. He graduated from the University of Sydney in 1949 and, after a few years in broadcasting in Australia, came to Stanford as his country's first Stanford Writing Scholar in 1956. He published his first story in *Sequoia* in 1958, and since then he has had stories in a number of American, English, and Australian magazines, as well as in anthologies both here and overseas. He left Stanford in 1958 for England, on the way back to Australia, where he has been teaching English—at present in the University of Sydney—since 1960. "The Gift" was written at Stanford and appeared in *The New Yorker* in 1961.

Robert A. Stone was born in Brooklyn in 1937 and attended parochial schools in Manhattan. He joined the navy at seventeen, served three years in the Amphibious Forces, and participated in the 1957 "Deepfreeze" expedition to Antarctica. On release from service he briefly attended New York University and worked for the *New York Daily News*. In 1959 he traveled through the Southwest with his wife, and he spent 1960 on the New Orleans riverfront. He was awarded a Stegner Fellowship in 1962. His first novel, *Children of Light*, received the Houghton Mifflin Fellowship and Prize and will be published shortly.

List of Fellowships

(F) Fiction   (P) Poetry   (D) Drama

1947–48
Dean Cadle (F)
Boris Ilyin (F)
Robert Sellers (F)
Walton Pearce Young (P)
Pershing Olson (D)

1948–49
John A. Lynch (F)
William Abrahams (F)
Milton White (F)
Edgar Bowers (P)
Alexander Greendale (D)
Thomas McEvoy Patterson (D)

1949–50
Susan A. Kuehn (F)
Clay Putman (F)
Sue Davidson (F)
Helen A. Pinkerton (P)
Lee F. Gerlach (P)
Marlow Dawson (D)

1950–51
Sarah Fay (F)
John Ferrone (F)
Warren Chapman (F)
Catherine Davis (P)
Valdemar O. Olaguer (P)
Alfred Wilkinson (D)

1951–52
Leonard Casper (F)
Edgar Rosenberg (F)
Joseph Stockwell (F)

Margaret Lee Peterson (P)
Frank Durkee (D)
Alvin J. Keller (D)

1952–53
Mary L. Dawkins (F)
Miriam Merritt (F)
Bernard Taper (F)
Charles Gullans (P)
Hugo Theimer (P)

1953–54
Wesley Ford Davis (F)
Shirley J. Hentzell (F)
Marvin B. Schiller (F)
Robert B. Childs (P)
Donald A. Hall

1954–55
Hilary Fonger (F)
Richard Kraus (F)
Eugene Ziller (F)
Thomson W. Gunn (P)
Calvin Thomas, Jr. (P)

1955–56
Tillie Olsen (F)
Denise Petty (F)
William Wiegand (F)
Martin Abramson (F)
Ellen de Young Kay (P)

1956–57
Robert Gutwillig (F)
Dan Jacobson (F)

Robin White (F)
Edith Weinberg (F)
John N. Miller (P)
Alan Stephens (P)

1957–58
Edward Abbey (F)
Larry Phillips (F)
Donald Moser (F)
John Waterhouse (F)
Francis Fike (P)
Philip Levine (P)

1958–59
Wendell Berry (F)
Ernest Gaines (F)
Mitchell Strucinski (F)
Peter Everwine (P)
Stephen Browning (P)

1959–60
Robin MacDonald (F)
Joanna Ostrow (F)
Nancy Packer (F)
Seymour Simckes (F)

1960–61
Peter Beagle (F)
James B. Hall (F)
Larry McMurtry (F)
Gurney Norman (F)
Robert Mezey (P)
James Hill (P)

1961–62
Arthur Edelstein (F)

Sue Haffner (F)
Hugh Nissenson (F)
Charlotte Painter (F)

1962–63
Ed McClanahan (F)
Merrill Joan Gerber (F)
Robert Stone (F)
William O. Walker (F)
Henry T. Kirby-Smith (P)
Michael Miller (P)

1963–64
Jacqueline Bruce (F)
James A. Conaway (F)
Morton Grosser (F)
Raymond Oliver (P)
James McMichael (P)

1964–65
Lawrence J. Davis (F)
Stephen Dixon (F)
Tom D. Horn (F)
Tom Mayer (F)
Kenneth Fields (P)
Robert Pinsky (P)

1965–66
Frank Bergon (F)
Thomas Bontley (F)
Zeese Papanikolas (F)
Sylvia Wilkinson (F)
Eugene England (P)
David Ransom (P)